Hegel and the Philosophy of Religion
The Wofford Symposium

Hegel and the Philosophy of Religion

The Wofford Symposium

Edited, and with Introduction by

DARREL E. CHRISTENSEN

*In celebration of the Bi-centennial
of the Birth of Hegel, 1970*

MARTINUS NIJHOFF / THE HAGUE / 1970

PRINTED IN THE NETHERLANDS

TABLE OF CONTENTS

PREFACE

THE WOFFORD SYMPOSIUM: ITS PURPOSE, GENESIS, AND THEME

The purpose of The Wofford Symposium was to stimulate original scholarship on the theme of the meeting, to provide a forum in philosophy of high quality in the area which Wofford College principally serves, and to make available for publication this collection of papers, which it was felt would meet a peculiar need in the contemporary literature of philosophy.

In April, 1967, I attended the annual meeting of the Metaphysical Society of America at Purdue University. Noting the frequency with which Hegel was brought into the discussions at that meeting, I was led on two occasions to inject the question into informal group discussions in the halls, "Isn't it time some sort of symposium on Hegel was held?" On the last occasion Professor Frederick Weiss replied, "Why don't you start it?" I'm not yet certain how serious the remark was intended to be, but after waiting two months, half expecting to hear of a plan under way, it occurred to me that perhaps what was wanting was a concrete proposal.

After discussing with Philip Covington, Dean of Wofford College, the reasons some persons I knew felt such a Symposium might be timely, I wrote to several scholars whom it seemed to me might make a substantial contribution to such a project. I asked two questions: (1) Do you believe that such a symposium would be timely? (2) Were such a Symposium to be sponsored by Wofford College, could you plan to contribute a paper? I received what I took to be enthusiastic affirmative replies to both of these questions from each of the men to whom they were addressed.

With the support and pooled suggestions of this initiating group, the design of this Symposium was sketched out, including the budget, and approved by the Administration of the College and the Committee on Education of the Board of Trustees.

On July 30, 1968, the Division of Higher Education of the Board of Education of the United Methodist Church made available generous financial support. Additional support was received from the Southern Humanities Conference.

By this time The Wofford Symposium on "Hegel and the Philosophy of Religion" had been scheduled to be held on the campus of Wofford College on November 28-30 (Thanksgiving Day weekend), 1968. The meeting was attended by about 200 persons.

It has seemed to me for some time now that one of the areas in which the potential impact of Hegel's thought has been least assimilated is the philosophy of religion. Because I myself had been for some time occupied with the philosophy of religion as well as with Hegel, my thinking turned in this direction as I discussed with others the possibility of holding this symposium. In addition, it seemed to me that recent events in Hegel scholarship in America suggested that the time had come for symposia on Hegel to be focused upon more specialized themes than past meetings had been. I had in mind here the occasions in the early years of this decade which led to an issue of Tulane Studies devoted to Hegel, to *A Hegel Symposium* published by the Department of Germanic Languages at the University of Texas, and to an issue of *The Monist* being devoted to "Hegel Today."

The theme "Hegel and the Philosophy of Religion" was selected. The focus of the meeting was to be threefold. It should aim at the clarification of Hegel's philosophy of religion. It should contribute to the clarification of the place of Hegel's thought within the historical tradition of the philosophy of religion. And it should support our understanding of how the religious dimension of Hegel's thought stands related to subsequent (and contemporary) theology and philosophy and their socio-political concomitants. Religion is here defined broadly enough to include "secular Christianity" and its counterparts in the Marxist tradition.

Why Now?

The enthusiasm with which The Wofford Symposium was greeted by American academia during eighteen months of planning is best evidenced by the distinguished group of scholars assembled for the meeting. Only a small number of persons who were asked to accept a role on the program found it necessary to decline. This, despite the fact that every effort was made to bring together those recognized by their professional colleagues as best qualified to address themselves to the theme and despite the fact that many of these persons spent many months of valuable time in researching and writing a paper. Regrettably, a number of persons who might perhaps have contributed significantly to the program could not be invited to do so. I can only hope that such persons and the reader will be forgiving of what may seem to be obvious omissions and that the building of programs on other themes to be sponsored by the newly organized Hegel Society of America may in some measure compensate and more adequately utilize the considerable human resources being dedicated to philosophical work related to Hegel.

There have been other evidences that the theme of the Wofford Symposium is felt by not a few to be timely. Since agreeing to arrange the program for this meeting, I have learned that plans are afoot for Hegel symposia and congresses to be held at York University, Marquette University, and (under sponsorship of the Internationale Hegel-Gesellschaft) in Paris (1969) and Berlin (1970,) all during the next two years or so.

In view of all this, it seems not inappropriate to point out what I see to be some of the principal reasons that a conference on the theme of the present Symposium should have been held at this particular time in twentieth century. In doing so, I shall inevitably be sharing some of my own reasons for attempting to become informed about Hegel, perhaps the most abstruse of "well-read" philosophers of the Western tradition.

1) Gödel's proof (1930) has certainly proven to be one of the philosophically most significant events of the twentieth century. Almost forty years of reflection on this (the upshot of which is that no system can be both consistent and complete) has culminated in the observation that this proof may be viewed as a particularization of principles of dialectical logic which (at least until recently) received their most systematic exposition in the philosophy of Hegel. Hegel has been dead to American thought during most of this time. These principles now need to be restudied in the light of their newly, or at least more widely understood, significance.

2) The loss, on the part of modern "over-developed" man, of a sense of the dignity of struggle and a consequent loss of a sense of meaning (and even how such a sense might be come by) occasions a re-examination of Hegel. This loss may both be traced to and seen to be reflected in most contemporary philosophy. Without this sense being reclaimed for human nature, it seems to me that even if we can achieve it, modern man cannot survive an economy of abundance. Hegel's attempt to lay the

metaphysical foundations of human struggle may be the most searching one to date. In any case, it is the granddaddy of most of the alternatives. And it is a good thing to meet the parents of your bride.

3) Many philosophers today have a strong commitment to language analysis as the proper method of philosophy. The focus here is not upon the analysis of what we should mean by what we say but upon what we do mean and perhaps upon what we might mean. All philosophers know that Hegel's is a "philosophy of Spirit," but not so many know that he said, "Language is Spirit." Hegel contributed an important chapter to the history of the philosophy of language. Much remains to be done to exhume this important neglected aspect of the work of this seminal thinker (passed over by his contemporaries), and which is bound to have an effect upon modern language philosophy.

4) As was shown at the Prague Congress on Hegel and Marx (August, 1967) and at the International Congress of Philosophy at Vienna in the summer of 1968 the discussion of Hegel has become an important means for increasing communication between the philosophers from Russia and the "satellites" and those on this side of the iron and bamboo curtains. This, on the one hand, because (for all his differences from Marx) Hegel laid the groundwork for modern dialectical philosophy and, on the other, because all parties to such a discussion can participate without one eye on the press box. It is better to think-out rather than to blindly act-out the struggle in which we are caught.

5) During the past several decades, the existentialists have laid bare important previously neglected aspects of contemporary man's self-understanding, and have enhanced it. Hegel furnishes some important clues for working out how these insights are to be reflected in the redefinition of man's rational faculty and his understanding of what is means to be and act rationally.

6) During the past decade or more, an increasing number of philosophers are reaffirming the indispensability of some kind of metaphysics (most often either as a system of presuppositions or as a system of hypotheses, the latter serving a role analogous to that of hypotheses in science.) This is being reflected in a renewed interest in the classical metaphysical systems, of which Hegel's had so frequently been heralded as the last. As a recent positivist (still living) concludes, " 'Metaphysics is non-sense' is nonsense."

I might further extend this list, but perhaps I have already conveyed the impression that this re-examination of how Hegel stands related to the philosophy of religion, like all authentically historical studies, as it turns out, is also a re-examination of the contemporary scene from a philosophical perspective. I had nothing else in mind.

The timeliness of this symposium and further evidence of the renewed interest in Hegel were further evidenced by the election, at a business meeting held on November 29, 1968 (during The Wofford Symposium), of a committee to look to the organization of an American Hegel society. The initial functions of this society were to be the circulation of a newsletter and the planing of another symposium two years hence. As this volume goes to press, two issues of the newsletter, *The Owl of Minerva*, have appeared and plans are well under way for the first meeting of the Hegel Society of America on "Hegel and the Sciences" to be held December 4–6, 1970, at Boston University.

THE ARRANGEMENT OF THE PAPERS

Except for certain omissions, the arrangement of principal papers, commentaries, replies of authors, and discussions in this volume follows the order of the presentations at the meeting.

Setting aside the Introduction, in general the volume opens with papers dealing with the young Hegel and the influences upon the young Hegel, after which it moves to papers which center upon the philosophy of Hegel's mature years. There are exceptions, however; because the first two papers – those by Professors Henrich and Harris – say a good deal about how Kant influenced Hegel and how Hegel reacted to Kant, it seemed proper to follow these by Professor Workmeister's paper "Hegel's *Phenomenology of Mind* as a Development of Kant's Basic Ontology."

The paper which follows, by Professor Greene, centers more directly than do others on themes fundamental to how Hegel stands with respect to existentialism.

The two papers by Professors Smith and Kline which follow these both in a special way relate Hegel's Philosophy of Religion to "secular" thought.

My own paper does not certainly belong in any particular spot, but because it proposes something of a reconception of dialectical method, it seemed to belong late in the program.

I placed the paper by Professor Lauer last because it seemed to me to treat a theme of overarching import both for the understanding of Hegel's philosophy of religion and for contemporary theology and because, of all the papers presented, it may approach as nearly as any to being synoptic in scope.

It may be worth noting that papers four through six in order of presentation deal notably with the social import of Hegel's philosophy.

In the case of each of the nine major sections of the program, the principal paper is presented. This is followed, in the case of each section of the program except one, by two commentaries. Following this, in turn, is a reply by the author of the principal paper. Finally, in cases where there was time for questions and comments from the floor, edited versions of each of these along with the ensuing discussion is included in this volume.

Persons who attended the Symposium will note the omission of Professor Stephen D. Crites', "Christianity as a *Volksreligion:* Hegel vs. Kierkegaard on 'Christendom,' " the commentaries following by Professors Robert L. Perkins and Arthur Lessing, and the commentary by Professor Victor Gourevitch. Professor Crites preferred that his paper, which turned out to be quite lengthy, either be included entire or omitted from the collection. Regretably, it was found that space would not permit its inclusion, and this after it had been anticipated that the case would be otherwise. It is also to be regretted that Professor Gourevitch in early April found that he would be unable to prepare a discussion which he would find satisfactory in time to be included in this volume.

In the Introduction, I have presented an overall image of Hegel's philosophy with particular emphasis upon its religious dimension as well as upon his philosophy of religion as such. Although the account is synoptic in character, it represents an attempt to do justice to the fact that much of the wealth of Hegel's thought lies in his exposition of particular themes. While my discussion of certain of these will omit such a wealth of significant detail as sometimes to seem to caricature Hegel, I can only hope that the reader of Hegel will understand that in an introductory account, complexity must be sacrificed for clarity. I also attempt to give some indications as to what I find in Hegel which may plausibly be appropriated for today. In contrast to most of the papers which follow, this exposition is almost totally without references either to influences upon Hegel or to the development of his thought. Space would not have permitted both this and what I have done.

I had earlier considered writing an introduction which would make more explicit reference to the various sections of the Symposium than I have made here. I had not anticipated, however, that I would be undergoing emergency surgery midway through my work on this volume. A restricted work schedule during a somewhat lengthy convalescence together with my commitment to Wofford College and to the contributors to see it through the press without undue dealy has made it seem most appropriate to place here, and with only moderate revision, an Introduction to Hegel's philosophy of religion prepared in advance of the meeting.

ACKNOWLEDGEMENTS

I wish to express my thanks to Dean Philip Covington and Charles F. Marsh, formerly President of Wofford College, for their respective roles in advancing the plan for the Wofford Symposium. I also wish to thank Paul Hardin, III, President of Wofford College, for his enthusiastic and thoughtful support of the project, financial and otherwise, which had in the main been planned in advance of his coming to Wofford.

To members of the Education Committee of the Board of Trustees of Wofford College I wish to express my thanks for their underwriting of a budget for the Symposium in advance of assurance that a substantial part of the cost would be covered by grants.

My thanks are owing to my former colleague in the Department of Philosophy at Wofford College, Professor Kenneth Warmbrod, who, in addition to another major task, very efficiently took charge of microphones and the recording of the meeting.

My present colleague in the Department, Professor Dwight Joseph Harris, headed the "Wofford-sweater hospitality fleet" during the meeting and has offered several useful suggestions respecting this volume and, even while "settling in" at Wofford has found time to do some of the proofreading. Professor Harris has my thanks for this.

Mrs. Helga Schmettau deserves the special appreciation of Symposium participants for serving as a most thoughtful secretary and gracious hostess during the meeting.

I wish most especially to thank Professor Charles Barrett of the Department of Religion at Wofford College not only for many helpful suggestions, but also for intermittent dialogue during the past four years which has helped me to an assessment of the role of Hegel in the contemporary dialogue within and between theology and the philosophy of religion, and for (sometimes repeated) proofreading of most of the papers in this collection.

In addition, I wish to thank the following members of the community of scholars with professional interests in the theme of the symposium for early support and valuable suggestions respecting possible contributors and the design of the program: Professors Stephen D. Crites, John E. Smith, H. S. Harris, Gustav E. Mueller, and E. L. Fackenheim. A number of other persons, including Professors Philip Merlan, George L. Kline, and Warren E. Steinkraus have been asked for and have given helpful suggestions. Many others might be named in this connection.

I wish to thank persons on the program who co-operated so splendidly with one another and with me in the sometimes tedious process of re-vision following the meeting and thus have helped make this what I hope shall be found to be a readable book. The many cards and letters I received from you after I was suddenly hospitalized during the time I was editing this collection helped awaken me from a delirium which, along with your gentle good will, I suppose I shall never forget. Professor Charles Barrett deserves my special thanks again for being my stand-in during this period.

My thanks goes to Professor Charles E. Scott for special help in the finalizing of the translation of Dieter Henrich's "Über einige historische Voraussetzungen von Hegels System," prepared for this meeting.

My gratitude is extended to the following persons, each of whom chaired a section of the symposium in the order named: Professors Carol R. Bowman (Memphis State University); Daniel J. Cook (Herbert H. Lehman College); Alan B. Brinkley (Davidson College); John C. Cooper (Eastern Kentucky University); Donald Verene (Northern Illinois University); Quentin Lauer, S.J. (Fordham University); Louis Dupré (Georgetown University); Eugene Kamenka (Columbia University); and Frederick G. Weiss (Florida State University.) Several of these men contributed significantly to the discussions, as the reader may later note.

Finally, I wish to thank Dr. H. J. H. Hartgerink, Director of Martinus Nijhoff, for his early interest in the publication of this collection of papers, which interest, along with suggestions respecting the format of the edited collection, provided a stimulus to those of us involved with the program.

ABBREVIATIONS

I. Works by Hegel

ETW   Georg Wilhelm Friedrich Hegel, *Early Theological Writings*, tr. by T. M. Knox from *Hegel's Theologische Jugendschriften*, ed. by Dr. Herman Nohl (Chicago: University of Chicago Press, 1948).

EdpW   Georg Wilhelm Friedrich Hegel, *Enzyklopädie der philosophischen Wissenschaften*, ed. by Johannes Hoffmeister (Hamburg: Meiner, 1949).

GdPdR   Georg Wilhelm Friedrich Hegel, *Grundlinien der Philosophie des Rechts* (Berlin, 1821).

LPR   Georg Wilhelm Friedrich Hegel, *Hegel's Lectures on the Philosophy of Religion*, tr. from the second edition by E. B. Speirs and J. Burdon Sanderson, in three volumes (London: Routledge and Kegan Paul, 1962).

SL   Georg Wilhelm Friedrich Hegel, *Hegel's Science of Logic*, tr. by W. H. Johnston and L. G. Struthers, the greater part being based on the 1923 Meiner edition (London: George Allen & Unwin Ltd., 1929-51).

HtJ   Georg Wilhelm Friedrich Hegel, *Hegel's Theologische Jugendschriften*, ed. by Dr. Herman Nohl (Tübingen: J. C. B. Mohr, 1907).

Phän   Georg Wilhelm Friedrich Hegel, *Phänomenologie des Geistes*, ed. by Johannes Hoffmeister (Hamburg: Meiner, 1952).

Phen   Georg Wilhelm Friedrich Hegel, *The Phenomenology of Mind*, trans., with an Introduction and notes by J. B. Baillie, Second Edition (London: George Allen and Unwin Ltd., 1955).

LPH   Georg Wilhelm Friedrich Hegel, *The Philosophy of History,* Prefaces by Charles Hegel and the translator, J. Sibree, and a new Introduction by C. J. Friedrich (New York: Dover Publications, Inc., 1956).

PR   Georg Wilhelm Friedrich Hegel, *The Philosophy of Right,* tr. by T. M. Knox (Oxford: Oxford University Press, 1942).

VPG   Georg Wilhelm Friedrich Hegel, *Vorlesungen über die Philosophie der Geschichte,* second edition, with a forward by Eduard Gans and Karl Hegel (Stuttgart: Fr. Frommanns Verlag, 1928).

VPR   Georg Wilhelm Friedrich Hegel, *Vorlesungen über die Philosophie der Religion,* ed. by Herman Clockner, with a forward by Philipp Marheineke, in two volumes (Stuttgart: Fr. Frommanns Verlag, 1928).

VPR, Lasson   Georg Wilhelm Friedrich Hegel, *Vorlesungen über die Philosophie der Religion,* edited by Georg Lasson in two volumes (Hamburg: Felix Meiner, reprinted in 1966 from the first edition, 1925-1929).

VPW   Georg Wilhelm Friedrich Hegel, *Vorlesungen über die Philosophie der Weltgeschichte,* I, Die Vernunft in der Geschichte, herausgegeben von Johannes Hoffmeister (Hamburg: Felix Meiner, revised 5th edition, 1955).

VdGdP   Georg Wilhelm Friedrich Hegel, *Vorstellungen der Geschichte der Philosophie,* ed. by Johannes Hoffmeister (Hamburg: Meiner, 1959).

VdGdP Glockner   Georg Wilhelm Friedrich Hegel, *Vorstellungen der Philosophie,* ed. by Herman Glockner (Stuttgart: Fr. Frommanns Verlag, 1959).

WdL   Georg Wilhelm Friedrich Hegel, *Wissenschaft der Logik,* ed. by Georg Lasson (Hamburg: Meiner, 1963).

Wallace   William Wallace, *The Logic of Hegel,* second edition, tr. from *Enzyklopädie der philosophischen Wissenschaftetn* (London: Oxford University Press, 1873-1950).

II. Works by Kant

KOP   Erich Adickes, *Kants Opus Postumum* (Berlin: Verlag von Reuther & Reichard, 1920).

CPracR	Immanuel Kant, *Critique of Practical Reason,* tr. by Lewis White Beck from *Kritik der Praktischen Vernunft,* from *Gesammelte Schriften* (Preussisch Akademie der Wissenschaften, Berlin, 1902-55), Vol. V.
CPR	Immanuel Kant, *Critique of Pure Reason,* tr. by Norman Kemp Smith from *Kritik der reinen Vernunft,* edited by Raymond Schmidt (New York: The Humanities Press, 1929).
GzMdS	Immanuel Kant, *Grundlegung zur Metaphysik der Sitten,* from *Gesammelte Schriften* (Preussisch Akademie der Wissenschaften, Berlin, 1902-55), Vol. IV. For English tr., see H. J. Paton, *The Moral Law.*
KdpV	Immanuel Kant, *Kritik der praktischen Vernunft,* from *Gesammelte Schriften,* containing the first and second editions of Kant's original work in juxtaposition, these being referred to as "A" and "B," respectively.
KdrV	Immanuel Kant, *Kritik der reinen Vernunft,* edited by Raymond Schmidt (Leipzig: Verlag Reclam, 1924).
RiGbV	Immanuel Kant, *Religion innerhalb der Grenzen der blossen Vernunft,* ed. by Karl Vorländer (Hamburg: Meiner, 1961).
RwLR	Immanuel Kant, *Religion Within the Limits of Reason Alone,* trans. with intro. and notes by Theodore M. Greene and Hoyt H. Hudson (Chicago: The Open Court Pub. Co., 1934).
The Moral Law	H. J. Paton (Transl.), *The Moral Law,* tr. from Immanuel Kant, *Grundlegung zur Metaphysik der Sitten,* from *Gesammelte Schriften* (Preussisch Akademie der Wissenschaften, Berlin, 1902-55), Vol. IV.

INTRODUCTION

I shall here provide a general and introductory account of certain of Hegel's most basic concepts with the aim of showing how these provide background and context for his philosophy of religion. Principal among these will be the concept of thought as mediation (*Vermittlung*), the concept of contradiction (*Widerspruch*), the concept of unity, or the monistic principle, and the concept of the concrete universal. I shall be particularly interested in these concepts as they pertain to Hegel's philosophical method. In defining these concepts, I shall inevitably make statements which may be found to require justification which it is impractical to attempt to supply in this chapter. In some of these cases I shall refer the reader to more detailed treatments. Some issues will doubtless be raised in the mind of the thoughtful reader to which the papers which follow will speak more definitively. Following some preliminary definitions, I shall attempt to illustrate the concepts defined.

Mediation, for Hegel, is the process by which a mind effects a change in a given specific content of thought through its own operations with or upon it. (Such a content of thought and the change it undergoes are generally regarded as representative of an "objective' actuality the self-development of which likewise involves mediation. It will aid the exposition, however, if the representative character of thought is disregarded for the time being.) "Change," in this context, is said to have occurred when a given content of thought is apprehended differently than it was before, which difference is not to be accounted for by reason of a loss of consciousness or memory, but by this content being apprehended in a new way, within an enlarged context and with new significance or meaning. A "content of thought" is anything that comes before the mind. This may be in the form of presentations of sense, presentations of the understanding, or of proposings which involve thinking or acting with a goal in view. Hegel having held a theory of innate ideas, however, there is a wider usage of the term "content of thought" that includes implicit and primitive contents of the feeling consciousness ("the natural man"), which are not available to (reflective) consciousness. This content (like all contents of thought) is intimately linked with the notion of a transcending content of thought, which lies as potentiality within both the contents of the unconscious and within thought explicit to consciousness. At this point, however, it will be simpler to disregard these two kinds of contents of thought and to consider only the contents of thought that come before the mind at what Hegel regards as the level of reflective consciousness. This content of consciousness is, to be sure, related to the other two types, but it will be best not to consider this just now.

By "an operation of the mind" nothing other is to be meant than the change that is effected upon a particular content of thought. This must follow from the fact that the contents of thought, in its various forms that follow from change, are for Hegel the sum and substance of a mind which "has" those thoughts.[1] It will be useful, however, in the interest of moving into Hegel's concepts by degrees, to define an operation of the mind in a provisional way as an act to determine the meaning of a particular content of thought. "Meaning" must here be used in an exceedingly broad sense, if we are to adequately represent Hegel's view, to include import, definition, significance, purpose, and completion.[2]

The term "completion," being the more inclusive of these terms, by being regarded as inclusive of import, definition, and significance and purpose, may best suggest what I mean by "meaning," in the above. An operation of the mind then, may be regarded as an act to determine the completion of a content of thought. Such an operation of the mind includes (1) the realization of a want of completeness of a content of thought. This realization is itself a type of advance or completion. It involves the sense of its limited adequacy. The sense of the limited adequacy of a content of thought suggests at least a vague sense of what the limitation is, the understanding of which may lead to an overcoming of that particular limitation. (2) An operation of the mind also includes the striving to overcome this limitation and, by comprehending, it, to include it within the content of thought, now altered as a consequence of this inclusion.

Before considering the formal properties of this operation of the mind in the mediation of thought in greater detail, it shall be well to consider some examples from Hegel's analysis of the way in which minds arrive at thought mediations. In the case of each example, however, I shall introduce first not Hegel's account, but an example of the type of mental operation which his account was intended to explain. I shall introduce three examples in this way, and follow up with some observations about them, before introducing two more quite different from the first three.

Imagine yourself to be a reasonably intelligent Eskimo who, by reason of the customs of his tribe and by reason of isolation from outside influence, has never heard of nor seen a chair. You are without the slightest notion of what a chair is or what its function might be. Suppose, moreover, that after traveling many days over snow you arrive at the cabin of a white trapper. Upon being taken in, you see an object of a certain shape and of a certain material upon which your host places himself, while inviting you with gestures and the utterance (to you at first meaningless), "have a chair," to place yourself on another object of like shape and material. Viewing the object somewhat skeptically, you give in to this strange custom, and "chair" is adopted as the name of the object upon which you place yourself. A chair appears to you now as an object constituted of pieces of wood arranged with a platform near knee height and a spoked back which supports the body in a crouched position.

Upon entering a second room of the cabin, and seeing another member of the friendly trapper's matching set of chairs, you immediately, and without hesitation, identify this object as also being a chair. Some time later, after traveling with your friend to the nearest village, you find yourself seated upon an object with curved bottom and back made of some strange materials called iron and plastic, and again upon a soft thing with extended things on either side upon which you find it convenient to place your arms. You are taught to call each of these objects a chair. Each of these experiences involves you in a certain puzzlement. What you had thought to be a chair – a platform of a certain height, of wood, etc. – has turned out to have been a mistake. These features of the first chairs you saw have turned out to be accidental. A chair does not need to be made of wood; it does not need to have spokes, it does not need to be hard, etc. Awed by this strange and uncertain new world of chairs, you rightly become hesitant about deciding what a thing must be like properly to be called a chair. This hesitancy is reinforced when you later visit a farmer and hear him refer to the three-legged object upon which he sits while milking his cows as a chair. To live in this strange new world in which people sit upon things, however, it is necessary not only to know which particular objects you have known as chairs but to be able to identify objects upon which you have not been supported as chairs, or as not chairs. If for no other reason, this is necessary so that you may avoid offending someone by sitting upon the section of a desk designed to support a typewriter, or upon a dressing table with lowered center section. You deduce that in all of the instances where a thing was introduced to you in one way or another as a chair, that object, by virtue of certain characteristics, seemed designed to support a human body within a certain range of crouching positions, and a certain minimal and maximal distance above the ground or floor. By employing this minimal set of distinguishing characteristics as your standard, you continue to practice identifying chairs, prepared further to modify your definition as you go along. Thus you are prepared to get on fairly comfortably in this still strange new world furnished with chairs.

At your point of greatest confusion and skepticism, as you performed thought operations by which you were able to arrive at a fairly adequate concept of a chair, you were at a loss to sift out of your experiences one single characteristic which seemed certainly essential and not merely accidental to a thing being a chair. You had a notion of chair, but it was for the moment empty, a notion of which you could not determine the real contents. There was too much material to choose from for its filling. Yet you knew it had to have a real content, on which account your mind moved back and forth between the at first empty and abstract notion and the characteristics of particular chairs that needed to be considered as possible distinguishing characteristics of things called chairs. Each step of your search was prompted by the concrete and immediate experience of another chair, and yet you could not grasp the concept of chair from any one of these particular experiences. The thought content provided by the initial confrontation with a chair is a circular movement from an empty abstract concept to a concept possessed of attributes whereby it is ade-quately representative of a particular chair but inadequate to the next. Thereupon the process begins again and repeats itself until the result is the empty abstract notion of a chair with which you began, now filled with concretely perceived qualities which have been sifted and reduced to a minimal set of defining characteristics. You thus come to have a concept of a chair as it presents itself in concretely given sense experience. This "determined" concept, so constituted as to possess an adequate measure of stability in a world in which people habitually, and in many ways, sit. In this repetitious and circular dialectical operation, the mind may determine that qualities of the chair which early in the operation seemed accidental prove to be most essential to the concept of chair. The concrete encounter remains the test of adequacy of any particular con-cept, though the form of the operation is held by Hegel to remain es-sentially the same. Qualities which prove accidental, it may be noted parenthetically, may prove to have an importance in their own right, apart from the operation by which the concept chair is derived or determined.

This back and forth movement of the mind between the abstract and empty notion of a thing – in the above example, a chair – and those characteristics or attributes drawn from immediate experience by which the concept of that thing is to be cumulatively determined, is an instance of what Hegel regarded as the mediation of thought. The reader of Hegel's *Phenomenology* will have no difficulty in recognizing this as an example of the dialectic of the thing and its attributes.[3] There is little to distinguish Hegel's account of this operation of the mind from that of Aristotle and others except (1) a greater emphasis upon the form of the process by which it is accomplished and, perhaps more importantly, (2) his attempt to see the form of this process as one which has something in common with, and as somehow in continuity with many other operations of the mind at many levels. While it is almost universally agreed today that Hegel's attempt to exhibit an identity of form in all of the operations of the mind was neither completed nor altogether successful in so far as it was completed, I know of no one, with the possible exception of Kaufmann, who would argue that Hegel is to be understood apart from his having made the attempt to display such an identity of form to figure prominently in his work.[4] This being the case, it will be well to consider another example of mediation before making further observations.

Suppose that you are nineteen years old, have been recently graduated from high school, and have succeeded in finding employment as an apprentice carpenter. You are very much in need of the work, and the prospect of eventually becoming a skilled tradesman, should you prove able, seems most inviting. You bring to your newly-found job little skill or practical knowledge, but an eagerness to learn. In the first weeks of your employment you participate in tasks that seem to go forward with prodigious rapidity under the direction of a foreman who orders you to chores that would seem simple if you knew how to do them. You naturally concentrate on learning how to do them, since holding your job depends upon this. You can give little attention to what part your work plays in the progress of the job as a whole or the execution of the architect's plans. Your net services are comparatively meager, since you are almost entirely "other-directed."

After some months of doing a widening range of operations repeatedly, however, you gain sufficient skill and understanding to take independent responsibility for tasks that may require a day or longer. Moreover, you are now working with a journeyman carpenter who, because you have shown diligence to learn, occasionally explains as well as shows you how things are done. You enjoy more freedom to improvise and to develop methods that suit your capacities better than those learned by rote. Your assumption of initiative issues in greater efficiency, and you find the work less arduous because you see it directed toward inclusive ends set successively farther from what is to be immediately accomplished. In due time you are able to grasp the concepts of the architect and to operate without the direction of your foreman. You become your own foreman, in a manner of speaking, and are perhaps on the way to directing the work of others.

What at first had seemed to you an uncanny capacity of your foreman to see the part that menial chores assigned to you might play in the objective to be attained, the construction of a building, has now become a part of the structure and content of your own thought process. "Willing obedience" is now joined to the "boss" aspect within your own mind, which proves to have been a latent and undeveloped aspect of consciousness when you hired out as an apprentice, seeking the self-sufficiency and independence of full manhood. Now this ideal has been realized and the foreman's mentality by which you were awed has become an integral part of your own self-consciousness. You are thus freed from commands which had issued from another.

The reader who is familiar with Hegel's *Phenomenology* may recognize this as a simplified version of the dialectic of the bondsman and the freeman located in a plausibly contemporary setting.[5] The completion of thought here exemplified is an assimilation to the self-consciousness of the apprentice of the self-consciousness of the foreman in his relation to the apprentice. The foreman is first apprehended as opposed to and threatening to the apprentice, an obstacle to be overcome. He is then apprehended as a reflection of the mind of the apprentice (an awed person is aware of something, however dimly understood the object of his awe may be), and then as a firmly possessed content of consciousness fully integrated with the content of consciousness belonging to the apprentice as a person whose work is entirely for another and not fulfilling of the end and aim proper to himself.

In this illustration of mediation, the content of consciousness of the apprentice and, later, the content of consciousness of the foreman, are not perhaps as precisely definable as was the case when considering the mediation of thought involved in the Eskimo's arriving at a well founded judgment of what a chair is. This is owing to the complexity of the self-concept of any particular person. If it is kept in mind, however, that what is of concern here is the content of consciousness of the apprentice *in the role of an apprentice,* and that many other aspects of his mind's life may be bracketed off for the purpose of the analysis, except the enlargement of this *"apprentice consciousness"* to include the *"foreman conscious-ness,"* the example will serve to illustrate a mediation which Hegel held to be universal to all minds that reach maturity. Presumably, he held, and I think rightly, that many human beings might be said to exemplify this mediation, not only once, in the course of preparing for the vocation of their choice, but many times, as tasks are approached in ignorance and dependence upon the direction of others and completed with an enlarged degree of freedom and self-directedness and the capacity for purposeful action with respect to the type of task encountered. There is of course much content of the apprentice mind that may not properly be bracketed out of the account. Even as an apprentice, the young man was in pos-session of relatively adequate concepts of *things* like hammer, nail, saw, crowbar, joist, lintel, facia, work, etc. The self-concept of an apprentice *as an apprentice* is far more inclusive than the concept of any particular thing *as a thing,* or even the concepts of all of the particular things *as things* of which he has plausible concepts. It is because the contents of mind of an apprentice *as apprentice* contain the capacity to determine properly the nature of things *as things* that this mediation is set forth by Hegel at a much more advanced stage of the dialectic than the dialectic of the thing and its attributes.

Recall the concepts of chair at which the Eskimo arrived, first the empty abstraction, and finally the concept as concretely determined by qualities which might rank as defining characteristics. Suppose now that the contents of mind of an apprentice *as apprentice* are viewed as a single concept, and that the integrated contents of mind of the foreman are likewise viewed as a single concept. Now these four concepts may be seen to be arranged in a logical order by virtue of a part-whole relationship they bear to one another. The last mentioned concept, moreover, is "highest" not only by virtue of containing the others within it as parts, along with a multitude of concepts similar to each, but also because the arrival at the latter concept is conditional upon the mind's having arrived at concepts of the types of the former. Had the apprentice not determined concepts of concrete things, like hammers, nails, and boards, he could not through tension and struggle have come into the possession of the self-concept of a foreman. Now there are a number of other operations of the mind the analysis of which is set forth between these two in Hegel's

Phenomenology. Some of these are less clearly and decisively developed than the two I have exemplified by the fictional accounts of the Eskimo arriving at the concept of a chair and the apprentice arriving at the self-concept of a foreman. The examination of these two types of operations of the mind, however, will serve to show how Hegel aimed to make the range of inclusiveness of concepts the determining factor in deciding where a given phase of the dialectic should be placed within his hierarchy of the forms of the mind's operations whereby mediations are derived.

As in the case of both illustrations considered, it may be noted that it is the phenomenology of actual thought *in the process of being thought* that Hegel aims to make the object of his inquiry. Because, in the final analysis, his interest is largely centered upon the abstraction of the forms of thought, however, it is sometimes forgotten that form and content are regarded as inextricable in the actual world of concrete events. The dialectical form of any one of these operations of the mind cannot, he held, be determined except by the analysis of the mind in operation determining a particular content of thought or concept (if not necessarily any one particular content of thought or concept.) It is only through the phenomenological analysis of the mind operating upon concepts and effecting mediations that the forms of these operations is derived, or, as he sometimes preferred, logically deduced. Hegel held, in the case of each of these forms, that it is exemplified in the mediation of a certain class of concepts wherever these concepts are mediated. That a need is found for regarding the form and content of thought as distinct is a concession to the need for abstractions in our discourse and not to be regarded as a reflection either of the nature of the actual world or of the thought by which that actual world is properly presented to the mind as object. When we use these concepts as they are to be understood as defined through their dialectical analysis, what we might regard as their correlativity, their being each mutually defined only in terms of their dialectical relationship to the other, is understood, and the language disease of regarding abstractions as something actual, or as adequately representative of something actual, is averted. These terms so regarded are conceived as representative, at best, of aspects (not entities) of an actual world that in its every concrete manifestation is a formed content.[6]

Imagine yourself as a person of more than average intelligence who has adopted house burglary as a means of winning a livelihood. You live on Chicago's south side in an area in which you find an anonymity appropriate to your profession. You live among other members of yours and related professions. At first your community is small and close knit by a sense of common privation and a well-drawn line between insiders and outsiders. It is considered quite proper to steal from outsiders, but unacceptable to rob members of the community. You prosper from your chosen vocation. The community of which you are a part likewise enjoys a relative degree of unostentatious prosperity and growth. As the community becomes larger and more prosperous, the distinction between insider and outsider becomes less clearly drawn. Some members of your profession learn that stealing from members of the community of thieves is quite as profitable and seemingly safer than stealing from the now more closely guarded suburbs. The code of your community prevents calling in the authorities. As the situation worsens, your efforts as a single individual to effect "justice" respecting your property rights prompts you to pay an organized group for protection. The efficient operation of such agencies has in the past required occasional punishment of offenders of the community code by death. Rival protective agencies now become competitive for power. The resultant increase of unsolved cases of homicide attracts the attention of the authorities, however, who move in and establish a semblance of order. In the mass arrests and convictions that follow the end of "protection" (which also had involved protection from police) you become convicted of several previously unsolved cases of burglary. While serving a prison sentence, you reach the conclusion that the life of a burglar is not compatible with your own self-interest because (1) it leads to burglary being committed against you when you have gained enough wealth to be an attractive victim, and (2) because the power of members of society who are aware of this fact (those who have something worth guarding) is inherently greater, since it is a form of reason, than the power of a community of burglars as such. The members of this larger community, or at least many of them, possess the integrated content of thought both of burglars and burglars who have been burglarized. You also now possess these two contents of thought, and with time for their integration, you emerge a reformed man who sees the laws against burglary as a reflection of your own nature, disobedience to which is at once a form of self-annihilation and the denial of your own potentiality. Your consciousness becomes integral with this law, now recognized as a "law of your very members," obedience to which is willed and not merely imposed by an alien legal system. In time you set up a successful business as a locksmith.

Since the reader is now well enough acquainted with the formal properties of Hegel's method of exposition to recognize the distinction between my hypothetical case and Hegel's way of interpreting it, I have blended the two in the above account. Little additional commentary is required to make it apparent that this fictional presentation exemplifies Hegel's account of the mediation of the self-concept and the concept of legal right [7] whereby the individual comes to have a concrete grasp of what is both inwardly and objectively right for him. In the case of any given statute, its justification ultimately is held to hinge upon this derived status. A law that does not reflect the highest consciousness achieved by the citizens of a state cannot ultimately be tolerated. The breaker of a law that does derive this status first sees this law as an alien force which he blindly opposes, then as a reflection of his own content of consciousness as a breaker of that law, and finally as a law of his own being, now enlarged and matured as a result of the mediation.

Hegel places the exposition of the form of this mediation of thought later in the dialectic than the exposition of the bondsman and the freeman. In this way he expresses the judgment that the concrete concept of law is more inclusive than the concrete concept (arrived at through labor and immediate experience) of the man who produces goods and services by acting, not upon the command of another, but from freedom. His rationale for this order is more open to question than in the case of the order in the dialectic of the thing and its qualities and the dialectic of the bondsman and the freeman. That some men achieve what he regards as the freeman's consciousness and fail to achieve the consciousness of right respecting a particular law, or even law in general, or achieve this (in either case) much later, no one would deny. Neither would anyone deny, I think, that some young men get into scrapes with the law and apparently reform before they settle down to the arduous task of being good apprentices. Thus the order of the dialectic would seem to be less clearly defensible and open to exception here, than in the case previously considered.

Nevertheless, if Hegel were to place one higher than the other in the interest of attempting to carry out his architectonic for the dialectic of the forms by which thought is mediated, reason may be seen for his having placed this phase of his exposition later than the dialectic of the bondsman and the freeman. To appreciate this, recall that when you imagined yourself first as an apprentice and then as a foreman, it was not required that you perceive the importance of your task as in relation to any larger objective than the achievement of a degree of personal freedom and independence, and the completion of an architect's design. The inclusiveness of the self-concept of the foreman as such, did not take into account substantially a whole people (first a small community and then a large one) as does the concept of right. It is the will of a people which is opposed when one commits burglary, and the consciousness that this is so, Hegel rightly held, is ideally heightened in the experience. It may of course be argued that a good foreman is also a good citizen who knows that a national poverty problem is to be most successfully fought with work. To this the reply may be made that a foreman does not need this conscience to be a foreman, even though it may help.

Another objection may be raised. It may be held that, because the reformed burglar acted out of self interest, the public will had no real part in the mediation of thought which he achieved. This objection loses its cogency, however, when it is recalled that it was the will of the people which, at least at one crucial point – the point of his arrest – determined where his self-interest lay. Hence it may be concluded that the reasons for placing the concept of concrete right above the concept of the freeman in the dialectic are fairly decisive, given Hegel's interest in a well organized exposition of the phenomenology of thought. If he intended to imply, in so doing, that mediations of thought of these two types always proceed in this order, he would seem to have been mistaken. While I find a want of evidence for drawing a certain conclusion on this important matter, it is difficult to believe that he would have wished to imply this. In view of the type of criticisms that were leveled against him, however, it is strange indeed that he should have remained too aloof to speak decisively to this issue, had he not wished to imply this.[8]

There are a considerable number of developments within the dialectic the order of which Hegel must have determined by considerations similar to those above noted. It is difficult to believe that the order of the exposition of these developments can be accorded the same significance as the order, for example, of the first two developments, examples of which have been considered, whatever may have been Hegel's view of the matter.[9]

The first and third phases of the dialectic which have been selected for consideration thus far display little originality in their basic content. These themes may be found developed in Kant. The second (the bondsman and the freeman) was, so far as I know, original with Hegel. It has, of course, been made well known through the work of Marx and Engels. These expositions being comparatively well known, do not maximally display Hegel's originality. Nevertheless, they serve my present needs well, which is to define certain of Hegel's fundamental concepts. The concepts with which I am principally concerned are those of mediation, contradiction or negation, the notion of unity as it pertains to concepts, and the concrete universal. The understanding of these concepts inevitably involves an understanding of the formal similarities of particular operations of the mind in deriving mediations of thought, along with the relation held to obtain between these operations, and, derivatively, between their forms. It is precisely in these two areas that the distinctiveness of Hegel's phenomenological method of treating these comparatively well known themes stands out. A brief consideration of examples of mediations of two quite different types than those which have been discussed will complete the necessary background for the definition of the above mentioned concepts within the context both of Hegel's view of the formal similarity of operations of the mind and the relation obtaining between these operations.

At the beginning of this chapter, I proposed to consider first certain "contents of thought" that are also contents of consciousness, leaving until later the consideration of the part played by unconscious contents of the mind and transcendent ideas in Hegel's account of the operations of the mind in deriving mediations of thought. This simplification, to which I resorted out of expedience in the interest of achieving clarity of exposition, must now be recognized as such if an adequate understanding of the concepts being considered is to be garnered. The most divergent types of operations of the mind to which these concepts pertain must be taken into account if their definitions are to be adequate.

The creative activity of the mind extends to the soul, "the idea in nature." The soul, for Hegel, may be said to be the container of all thought in embryonic or unmediated form. It is the content of primitive "thought" (not thought in a proper sense) which is a determined content of the unconscious mind through mediation, which is of interest here. This content takes the form of "feeling determinations," which are "the natural man," and the "evil genius in man." [10] Given its way, the devices of the heart of this natural man finds gratification for every selfish and primitive passion of love and hate. This is the content of the mind which effects its way through irrational urges, and which is expressed in dreams and symtoms of mental derangement, which are sometimes the natural means whereby this content is mediated, at least with provisional adequacy, to consciousness. As with Freud, the dream or symptom of mental disease is a formula for representing the content of this unconscious aspect of the mind to consciousness within the context of a content familiar to consciousness.

A classic example is the case of suppressed desire for sexual gratification which is manifest in a dream in which a flirtation between other persons than the subject is presented. Here the subject enjoys the fulfillment of his own desires while remaining a chaste viewer of a fulfillment he cannot permit himself to own as the object of his desire.[11]

At the opposite end of the spectrum of thought mediations lies the concept of spirit. This concept is in like manner for every man undergoing transmutation. Unlike other concepts, however, it is in every instance inclusive of all other concepts. From this concept, at least ideally and in the case of a well integrated mind, all other concepts belonging to the contents of consciousness may be seen to be derived by analysis. This is the concept of Spirit, or God in his plurality of concrete manifestations. It is this class of concepts which pertain to the wholeness of things, with which this study is principally to be concerned. My interest in briefly introducing it here is simply to note that this type of concept, like all others, is for Hegel ultimately derived through mediation. In a particular case, its contents are always in various stages of being determined. Since each mediation contributes toward a more adequate concept of God, each may be seen in a sense to exemplify this mediation. The mediation, however, which involves a contradiction the overcoming of which requires the integrated faculties of the whole person, exemplifies it best. No mediation that is well determined exemplifies it well, I shall later argue, simply because such a mediation is completely determined and is on this account merely a part of a higher concept which is being determined.[12] An example of such a concept must be a retrospective analysis of a "has been" concept of God,[13] however, rather than one which is currently actual and dynamic. (As a reconstruction by reflection of what has come to be, every concept, and hence every concept of God which, relatively speaking, is actual and dynamic, is nevertheless a reflection of what "has been," and is on this account only relatively current.) The following example of this mediation, unlike the examples which I have thus far used, is taken from ancient history or pre-history. In the nature of the case, the reader might find what would seem to be an example with a current setting to be unacceptable and unhelpful, on which account I have resorted to an ancient tradition.

Imagine yourself on Mt. Sinai in the 13th century. B. C.[14] You have before your mind the memory of a people in slavery and a vision of man as he ought to be, free. You find yourself *called* by the God of your fathers, Abraham, Isaac, and Jacob, to go down into Egypt and to effect the deliverance of your people from slavery, and to lead them into a land flowing with milk and honey. You cannot justify the felt necessity to go by referring to the *call* of this old God, however; He was not one who was ever known to issue such a command. You inquire, "If I go, who shall I say has *sent* me." The reply that comes to you is, "I Am hath sent you." [15] The beingness of things has sent you; the ever present contemporaneity of being has sent you. Signs are required. The crucial one is a *promise*. The promise is that the way will be prepared, and if you go you shall worship again on this mountain. You go; you deliver your people out of slavery; and you worship again on this mountain. You fail to see the full accomplishment of this act of deliverance, the settlement of your people in Canaan, only because you commit apostasy toward this newly conceived God by making His acts out to be the work of your own hands: in the face of a scarcity of water in the desert of Zin, you strike a rock to procure water, instead of speaking to the rock as you were bidden.[16]

An analysis cannot but diminish the dramatic impact of this parody on the story of Moses' call on Mount Sinai. Such an analysis must, nevertheless, be made if the story is to illustrate what Hegel understood to be a mediation of the concept of God. At the highest peak of the religious experience of Moses, he faced full-on the most comprehensive disparity in his life. Because of his religious maturity, this was social in scope, involving the good of an entire people, and not merely a personal disparity, a schizophrenia of his own mind [17] or a disparity between a low (apprentice's) income and an expensive (foreman's) tastes. Facing full-on this disparity, which occupied his complete attention, he found himself in the grasp of an anticipation of its resolution through resolute action. This action at this moment was the action of a being other than himself. Later it was to become a joint action of another and himself. When at length it was apprehended as his own act – when Moses became proud – the concept which had been a concept of God was no longer such in a proper sense. As in the case with the concept of the God of his fathers, this concept too was to be contained in another, but not before its mediation had been completed and this completion enjoyed and celebrated as a complete possession of his own mind in the idolatrous self-worship that is pride. Thus idolatry preceded a new encounter with contemporaneity, with the new mediation to be effected in struggle and overcoming. Thus the God of Abraham, Isaac, and Jacob became the God of Moses too, who later was lost and regained. He did not need to be renamed again, however, because His name was now the name of this actual contemporaneity; the name of this type of mediation in the course of being realized; the name not merely of past divine acts in history, but acts yet to be concretely realized.[18]

From the foregoing it may now be understood why a precise definition of mediation adequate to so wide a variety of types must be a short one, the breadth of which may well be taken (I think mistakenly) for a want of precision in the definition. The inadequacy of the definition of mediation with which I began may now be seen, however; it is too short. I began by defining mediation as the process by which a mind effects a change in a given specific content of thought through its own operations with or upon it. This must now be qualified in two directions. It must be noted, on the one hand, that Hegel held that a certain type of mediation (the feeling determinations) occurs entirely below the level of consciousness, and that, in another type of mediation, one pole of the contradictory or opposing elements that has a part in a mediation is below the threshold of consciousness. Below either of these strata of the mind there is the soul, the idea in nature. Problematical as it may seem, then, the phrase, "operation of the mind" must be reconceived to include unconscious operations of the mind and operations which are essentially one with nature below the level at which the soul determines feelings. It must be noted, on the other hand, that, in the case of a concept of God, the mind does not of itself, and especially at first, effect the change. The change is effected in the confrontation with "something" (perhaps an unnamed) Other – an Other who (or which) [19] in the encounter becomes actual, and who is actualized through the encounter.

The definition of mediation may now be refined as follows: *Mediation, for Hegel, is the process by which change is effected in a specific content of thought (a concept) including thought below the level of conscious awareness and thought in which this change is only in the process of being grasped or actualized in the pursuit of promise.* "Change," in the case of unconscious mediations, it may be noted, may not be apprehended. "A content of thought" may not be directly available to the apprehension of the person whose "thought" it is, but may be evidenced only to others in the report of dreams and symptoms of mental derangement,[20] or through phenomenological analysis. If change, in the case of a concept of God, involves an element of transcendence, it is effected only by virtue of the active participation of the subject; though he is not initially the agent of change, change does not occur apart from his own willing determination. More need not be said about "meaning" and "completion" except that the derivation of the meaning or completion of a mediation is a process that may take time, and in the case of many operations of the mind, may be expected to go unnoticed or unanalyzed or both.

I shall now turn to the consideration of Hegel's concept of *"Wider-*

spruch," usually translated "contradiction." In each of the examples of mediation which has been considered, there has been a development or completion of a content of consciousness which Hegel would have regarded as a concept. In each, moreover, there are present "contradictory" elements the essential and true meaning of which is included within a more advanced, inclusive and more mature concept that is derived by the mediation of the two poles of the "contradiction." The discovery of this "contradictory" element, as such, moreover, is also in each case a mediation of thought. At least among the three mediations which were first considered, however, the sense in which the abstract and empty concept of a thing such as a chair is contradictory to the attributes of that thing is peculiar. This peculiarity may serve to call attention to the fact that the term *"Widerspruch"* seems to carry somewhat different shades of meaning in different contexts along with a commonality of meaning in all, or almost all, contexts in which it occurs. Here the mind finds itself confronted by *conflicting* claims regarding what is given in raw sense experience. Certainly these conflicting claims do not constitute a contradiction in any usual sense of that term, but at most, in a weakened sense tantamount to "opposition." The term "opposition" seems a more appropriate translation of *"Widerspruch"* in the case of the other phases of the dialectic which have been considered as well, and particularly in the case of the latter two, involving mediations of unconscious contents of thought and of the concept of God. While the sense of an opposition of forces is stronger in the dialectic of the bondsman and the freeman, and in the dialectic of the individual and statutory law, making the term contradictory seem less inappropriate, the term opposition, even here, is more adequate to the sense of the accounts. Divorced as it is from connotations which it derives from its use in conventional logic, understanding will be aided if the word "opposition" is consistently rendered as the translation of *"Widerspruch,"* rather than "contradiction." [21] Even the use of this term will present problems in some phases of the dialectic, as will be further noted in a later section.[22] Also, it is to be noted that some oppositions must appear to the finite understanding as contradictions.

An opposition may be initially conceived as a tension and want of reconciliation between two contents of consciousness, both of which claim to image or present the actual. This definition, however, is inadequate in two directions. On the one hand, it fails to allow for the type of opposition of which the individual is not aware, and, on the other hand, it fails to take account of Hegel's view that ideally and ultimately, thought and being (or, the actual) are identical. This view, with its attendant problems, figures crucially in Hegel's dialectic of religion. The following definition of opposition (as a translation of *Widerspruch*) will serve better. *An opposition is a tension or want of reconciliation between two contents of consciousness, regarded as concepts, both of which, where they are apprehended as such, may be seen to image, present, or approximately constitute contents which are in some sense mutually exclusive but which are both actual for that consciousness.* If this definition is to be found adequate to Hegel's position, however, it must be stipulated that such opposing concepts must have a sufficient range of universality to be shared with other minds.

Hegel's use of the term *"Negierung"* (negation), so far as I have been able to determine, is equivalent to his use of *"Widerspruch,"* except that it characteristically has a directional connotation generally not present in the latter. This is to say, *"Widerspruch"* frequently connotes mutual negation of opposites, whereas "negation" does not. The basic meaning of "negation," then, is that a concept "A" stands in opposition to a concept or concepts, "B" without stipulation that "B" stands in opposition to "A." [23]

I shall now consider the notion of unity as it pertains to concepts. For Hegel, concepts, like things, may be conceived as related to one another by a part-whole relationship. Each concept is in one sense a whole, and also a part of a more inclusive whole. *Unity in a concept is coherence of the content of discriminations contained within it.* This means that it cannot contain a contradictory content. The concept of a chair, for example, cannot contain the attributes of black and non-black, wooden and non-wooden, etc. That concept of a thing is a unity which contains a compatible and coherent group of attributes which corresponds to the objects it represents. The concept of a man as a producer of goods and services is a unity when the means and the aim or goal of production (in the case of our example of the self-concept of the foreman, the building) are an integrated part of that concept. Such a concept contains the mediated concepts of concrete objects. The self-concept of the person possessed of a sense of right is a unity when statutes are laws he administers to himself rather than rejects. Such a self-concept, Hegel implies by the order in which he places these developments within the dialectic, is one which may be expected to contain the capacity for self direction in the performance of one's work. It may be noted that the burglar, in our example, possessed this capacity, and it may be supposed that he also was in possession of concretely determined concepts of objects, such as the tools of his trade.

Unity in the case of every concept, is a coherence achieved by the inclusion through struggle and education of what was or might be wanting with respect to that particular concept: The concretely determined concept of a chair possesses unity, but unity of a kind; it is not a unity that includes the purpose of a chair within a context of other objects of purpose. Such a unity is achieved in the mediated concept, for example, of an interior decorator *as an interior decorator.* The concept of an interior decorator, by virtue of his function in the total life of a community, may be a part of the concept of the community of which he is a part. The hierarchy of concepts possessed of an increment of unity, or in the course of achieving a unity reflected in actuality, extends to the concept of God, which is also a concept both possessed of ideal unity and in the course of having that ideal concretely realized, realized as actual. As there is a sense in which the determination of the definition of a chair is never completed, so there is a sense in which the concept of God is never completed. As an actual concept, it is never completed. Although there is a distinguishing connotation attached to His name, which has been considered, His acts in history, for which He is celebrated, are not concluded. In the case of the concept of God which came to Moses on Mt. Sinai, the contradiction between free and non-free as pertaining to the state of a people was conceived as ideally and in principle overcome through an act of the divine will, though this act was only becoming actual in history. Unity with respect to a particular concept of God is fulfilled only as a claim and a promise, though the concept of God, per se, is a model of unity and, it may be added, an exemplification of the triumph of the monistic principle in Hegel's philosophy.

It should be noted that the content of consciousness belonging to each of the second moments of the various phases of the dialectic is characteristically not a unified content. The many possible attributes of "chair" for example are a mere aggregate until the "true" attributes are determined, and at this point the mediation belonging to what schematically may be referred to as the third moment has been achieved. Cases vary, however; in the case of statutory law, for example, the plurality of particular laws does tend to reflect a certain (derived) unity. Laws may need to be changed, however, on which account this is no more than a tendency.

The preceding consideration of the concept of opposing aspects of the content of the mind and the concept of unity as it pertains to the issue of thought mediations, along with the five examples of thought mediations which have been set forth, has provided a background for what I hope may be found to be a plausibly clear account, so far as it goes, of Hegel's concept of the concrete universal. *Hegel accords this name to that operation of the mind whereby opposing aspects of the content of consciousness issue in a mediated concept inclusive of the essential truth of both aspects.* This form he finds to be exhibited in common by every operation of the mind in which concepts are *derived,* as opposed to operations by which given and accepted concepts are *arranged* and related in accordance with the forms of propositions and arguments of traditional (abstract) logic. What Hegel calls dialectical logic is thus never to be confused with logic traditionally conceived, since they have different functions. One provides a phenomenological account of operations of the mind that are essentially concrete and ought never to issue in a tautology. The other is concerned with the manipulation of the concepts, and the forms proper to these manipulations in propositions and arguments, which, to be valid, must issue in tautologies.

Each of the examples of the operations of the mind considered, with a qualification which will be noted, may be seen to have resulted in the derivation of a mediated concept of the type which Hegel held to be both concrete and universal. Each is concrete in that it represents or approximates identity with the given in experience, the nature of this given depending upon the "level" of the dialectic to which it belongs. This given, it may be noted, is not simply bare sense experience, as it is sometimes conceived to be. There is no *bare* sense experience. What is given in sense is already a product of the mind's activity upon something, which something, by the time it is apprehended in consciousness, is inseparable from the operations of the mind already performed upon it. Sense experience, however, is only a comparatively abstract and remote presentation of the actual world in which the subject immerses himself. The given of experience at each level at which the mind derives mediations, is the basis for the concept with which the operation begins, the truth of which has been presupposed and unquestioned. Apart from the ensuing mediation, however, this given proves not to possess the genuine concreteness at first claimed for it. "True" concreteness is concreteness that may be grasped by the mind that has grasped the universality of that which is held to be concretely given. It is this grasp which is exhibited, with a qualification to be noted, in each of the five illustrations of mediations of thought which have been considered.

A chair first presented itself to our now familiar Eskimo friend as a kind of thing. The examination of the concept of this thing led to the discovery that the Eskimo really did not know in what the givenness of this thing really consisted, he did not really know what he was seeing. An operation of the mind was required before genuine understanding came to him, and then he possessed a reasonable concept by which to know a chair (any chair) as a chair. His concept had to possess universality before it could adequately represent the concreteness of the first chair he saw, the chair in which his host the trapper sat.

Our ex-burglar, before he became an ex-burglar, knew the law against burglary as a given of experience. His knowledge was a blindness of the mind, however, and not a knowledge of the concretely actual force which Hegel found the laws of a state to be, until he had ceased to regard this law as a blind irrational force and began to have an understanding of its *reason,* i.e., its cause and the nature of its sanction. He came to apprehend the true concreteness of this law, and to find it to be his own law, at the time that he came to comprehend its universality (as concrete) for at least some members of the larger community whose law it was.

For our struggling apprentice carpenter, the given was tasks, performed more or less blindly and at first meaningless except that they seemed to be the basis for attaining a measure of freedom. From the perspective of the self-concept of a foreman able to follow a master plan, however, he was later to concretely experience these same tasks and many others for what they actually were, at the same time that he could see their universal import and necessity where the construction of buildings (of a certain type and in a certain time) is undertaken.

The God-concept which was the given for Moses as he climbed to the high point of his religious experience was largely informed by that of his fathers, Abraham, Isaac, and Jacob. This God was alleged to have acted in certain ways in history (or prehistory). The concreteness of the new encounter with Deity lay in that it constituted a new act in history, at first ideal and then actual, and an act in Moses' own story. That this new concreteness arose simultaneous with a compelling sense of the universality of this God, under a new name, is evidenced by the fact that it is the deliverance of His *people* that is the object of His action, and also by the fact that this God is held to be active in other persons. He is to "prepare the way" for the deliverance of His people from bondage.

The dream in which sexual gratification was enjoyed vicariously is a somewhat special case. That there is a givenness and a concrete immediacy in what comes to us in dreams no one would, I think, question. If this manifestation of what Hegel regarded as a feeling determination should be found to persist, at least until such a time as the young man rationalizes the content of this feeling determination into a decision to marry, then a certain universality with respect to points in time at which this persisting unconscious mediation is manifest would be displayed. Because time is for Hegel a phenomenon belonging only to mediations above the threshhold of consciousness, however, the universality displayed here, pertaining to points of time at which this determination is manifest, must be regarded as an analogous universality only.[24] The content of a single dream as such would not appear to display a universality in any way distinct from that displayed where the same content is held in the waking consciousness. To consider the specific case, to be conscious of an erotic experience of another would necessarily require that the universality of this experience be at least partially grasped. Where there is vicarious participation the concreteness and universality of the experience would be at once grasped. The individual experiences for himself what he recognizes as an experience desired and participated in by others.

In Hegel's account, operations of the mind below the level of consciousness are, due to their primitive character, somewhat atypical. Nevertheless, as in the case with other types of operations of the mind, these too conform to a general pattern. This conformity to general pattern I shall from this point refer to as "authenticity," which is to be distinguished from "truth" where particular phases of the dialectic are being considered.[25]

It needs to be noted before passing on, that in the case of each of the above examples, the concreteness and universality that is exhibited is distinguished by the character of the concepts which are involved in the mediation. The reader who has not perceived the universality exhibited in each of the first four examples considered, may do well to try to think through the operations of the mind exhibited therein.

There is a species of universality which Hegel claimed for all of the *types* of mediations of the mind found worthy of inclusion within his dialectic which has not yet been considered. This is the claim that the form of these operations is innate and universal as actual or potential to all rational minds. These forms, regarded as abstract and taken as a body, moreover, are conceived as God in His transcendent aspect, God as other to the world. The actualization of these forms in the world is thus regarded as an actualization within various contents of experience, i.e., an experience of the type of Moses on Mount Sinai. This is not the place for a complete exposition of this view. It is mentioned here only to exhibit first an outcome of the position that concrete universals included within the exposition of philosophy are universal in rational minds, and, second, the intimacy with which Hegel's doctrine of God is bound up with the concepts which have been considered.

It may be of interest to note that, since all unified and (dialectically) well-defined concepts are held to be the issue of mediations and are regarded by Hegel as concrete and universal, the concept of the concrete universal is itself implied to be the issue of a mediation of the opposed concepts of concreteness and universality. A practical import of this is that this concept is held to be definable only through the recognition of the correlativity of these two concepts, the recognition that one cannot actually be defined except as it stands in relation to the other. That many philosophical concepts are in practice very often treated as correlative concepts is a tribute to Hegel's account of the matter. This treatment is frequently exhibited in the consideration of such concepts as freedom and determinism, quality and quantity, subjectivity and objectivity, form and matter, mind and matter, substance and function, time and space, and many others. While there are parts of his writings that remain somewhat enigmatic to me, it seems clear that Hegel would have rightly regarded this as evidence of the basic soundness of his method of analyzing the operations of the mind by which concepts are derived, and if some of the operations which he analyzed seem to issue in concepts which are in some sense false or useless, the basic method would appear to remain at least approximately representative of operations which minds actually perform in developing concepts. Hegel successively reworked the dialectic in his attempt to apply this method with greater adequacy. Sensitive as he was to what I have called the transmutation of concepts, moreover, he allowed that such reworking should be the continuing task of philosophy.[26]

NOTES

1. There is also the soul that is "the idea in nature." This soul, however, is regarded as potential thought, and is not in a unique sense the substance of the mind.

2. The need to define "meaning" so broadly in this exposition is owing to the widely varied forms of transformation of thought content which Hegel regards as dialectical. This presents one of the major problems for Hegel scholarship, which is taken up in section VII of this volume.

3. *Phän*, pp. 92-7, or *Phen*, pp. 162-7.

4. Whether and to what extent Hegel's interest in displaying such an identity is dominant in each of the various parts of his philosophy is open to some question. This interest is less dominant in Müller's Hegel than it is generally regarded. Gustav Emil Müller, *Hegel: Denkesgeschichte eines Lebendigen* (München: Francke Verlag, 1959), and "The Hegel Legend of 'Thesis-Antithesis-Synthesis,'" *Journal of the History of Ideas*, Vol. XIX, No. 3 (1942), pp. 411-4.

5. *Phän*, "Herrschaft und Knechtschaft," pp. 148-58, or, *Phen*, "Lordship and Bondage," pp. 229-40.

6. *Wallace*, pp. 236f.

7. *Phän*, pp. 283-92, or *Phen*, pp. 390-400.

8. The deduction of the *concept* of Herr Krug's pen by appeal to the dialectic of the thing and its attributes might have gone some way toward clarifying the relation he held to obtain between everyday concepts and what were proposed as the forms of dialectic, had he been less aloof to public polemics with his contemporaries as individuals.

9. These developments to which the order would seem to be of less obvious and crucial significance belong to the upper reaches of the dialectic, for the most part within the dialectic of the Notion. In these, a primary consideration in the determination of order, I believe, is the definitions, dialectically derived, which issue from different possible orders. The order of the dialectic determines which concepts are to be conceived as related to which other concepts by the part-whole relationship. Especially when these developments are kept in mind, Hegel's system takes on the character of a tremendous language game, played not merely with common language, but with the basic concepts of philosophy as well. As Hegel plays this game, some relatively common concepts, such as objectivity, matter, thing, and duty, are defined in such a way as to render them less than common. Such definitions are meant to be prescriptive, and are deliberate plays in the game. Certainly many of the plays in the game are not justified by considerations of definitions alone. The placement of the dialectic of space and time high in the order of the dialectic, for example, must be held to express Hegel's version of the empirical principle, for which he found sufficient justification.

10. *Die Philosophie des Geistes*, III, pp. 206f. Most of the contents of this paragraph are drawn from pp. 204-7. For a more extensive treatment, see my "Hegel's Phenomenological Analysis and Freud's Psychoanalysis," *International Philosophical Quarterly*, Vol. VIII, No. 3 (September, 1968), pp. 356-378 (hereafter, "Hegel-Freud"); and "The Theory of Mental Derangement and the Role and Function of Subjectivity in Hegel," *The Personalist*, Vol. 49, No. 4 (Autumn, 1968), pp. 433-452. For a further development from Hegel's theory of the unconscious, see my "Toward a Phenomenologically-Grounded Theory of the Unconscious for the Scientific Practice of Psychotherapy," *Existential Psychiatry*, Fall, 1970 (to appears).

11. These feeling determinations of the natural man are roughly approximate to Freud's preconceptual cathexis of libido in that in both cases feeling becomes attached to specific modes of activity. In the case of Freud these are specified as sexual in nature, and are typed according to the area of the body, or "erogenous zone," where this feeling attachment is centered. Hegel, consistent with his phenomenological method, does not specify the particular content of these feeling determinations in specific cases, but is content to delineate what he finds to be the form of the mediation. It should be noted that, also consistent with his method, this form may be determined only in the analysis of particular mediations necessarily having a particular content. See, "Hegel-Freud."

12. Darrel E. Christensen, "Some Implications for the Doctrine of God of Hegel's Concept of Thought as Mediation" (a doctoral dissertation completed at the University of Southern California, 1963), Chapter VII, "The Problem of the Relativity of Concepts of God" (Ann Arbor, Michigan, University Microfilms, Inc., 65-9969). This work will hereafter be referred to as *Thought as Mediation*.

13. I have been momentarily unable to locate a passage in which Hegel, in discussing his method, refers to "the folding of the mind back upon itself."

14. Exodus 3.

15. Exodus 3:14. In the account in its present form, which probably dates from the sixth century B. C., it is Eloheim who *calls* and Jahweh who *sends*.

16. Numbers 20:10-13.

17. See, "Hegel-Freud," pp. 373f.

18. An important resource for this justification is Hegel's treatment of the dialectic of Spirit, the third moment within his account of Absolute Religion. *VPR*, Vol. II, pp. 308-56, or *LPR*, Vol. III, pp. 100-51. While there is no direct counterpart to my usage of the term "contemporaneity," the term does seem to capture the sense of his thought.

19. The problem of whether or in what sense God is personal for Hegel is treated in *Thought as Mediation*, pp. 182-6.

20. *Die Philosophy des Geistes*, p. 206.

21. If Hegel's dialectic of the Idea is to be regarded as a logic, it must be noted that "dialectical logic" has little in common with traditional logic and concepts of contradiction appropriate to each must remain quite distinct. See the discussion of A. Schaff, *Dialektyka marksistowska a zasada sprzecznosci*, Mysl Filoz., 4 (1955) by Henryk Skolimowski, in "Analytical-Linguistic Marxism in Poland," *Journal of the History of Ideas*, Vol. XXVI, No. 2 (April-June, 1965), pp. 235-248, especially p. 241.

22. See my treatment of Hegel on the Religion of Utility, this volume, pp. 000-00.

23. For an illustration of this characteristic one directional connotation of the term, see *Enzyklopädie der Philosophischen Wissenschaften im Grundrise, und Andere Schriften aus der Heidelberger Zeit*, mit einem Vorwort von Herman Glockner (Stuttgart: Fr. Frommanns Verlag, 1927), Section 94, on the "false infinity."

24. As McTaggart has carefully noted, the forms of thought per se are not in time, by which I think he must have meant to say that these forms transcend all particular times. That such exemplary mediations as I have considered would be regarded by Hegel as experienced in time, seems clear enough. The practical import of the fact that the mediation of time (history) and space (nature) is inclusive of most other mediations, being near the top of the hierarchy of the forms of thought, is that time is in the course of being mediated throughout the system. Hegel, because he was reflecting pre-evolutionary biological theory, however, did not follow out this implication of his methodology with consistency, but denied time to mediations of thought within nature (mediations below the level of the human understanding). J. Ellis McTaggert, "Time and the Hegelian Dialectic," *Mind,* Vol. II, New Series (1893), pp. 490-504. Also see J. O. Wisdom, "Hegel's Dialectic in Historical Philosophy," *Philosophy*, Vol. 15 (1940), pp. 243-68.

25. This distinction between formal "validity" and truth is not maintained by Hegel with any degree of consistency, since this distinction like all others, must be contained (as least ideally and in principle) in the Truth that is the Notion. For a detailed consideration of this matter, see my treatment of it in Section VII of this volume, pp. 000-00.

26. Darrel E. Christensen, "Nelson and Hegel on the Philosophy of History," *Journal of the History of Ideas*, Vol. XVIII, No. 1 (September, 1964), pp. 58-63.

SOME HISTORICAL PRESUPPOSITIONS OF HEGEL'S SYSTEM

by

Dieter Henrich

Hegel's philosophy has been the object of historical study since Rosenkranz published his biography in 1843.[1] Dilthey's monumental work [2] on Hegel's life, which gave new impetus to the interest in Hegel as Neo-Kantianism was waning, began a long series of studies concerning the history of Hegel's development.[3] All of these works set themselves the task of discovering through an understanding of textual origin the "Secret of Hegel," which systematic interpretation of the texts had been unable to solve. We are indebted to this research, which soon will be controllable only by specialists, for the great progress which it has made toward its goal. However, we still have a long way to go.

In contrast to archival research, philosophical study of the history of development seeks to provide unique evidence and criteria for critical understanding of a philosophy which has assumed historical status. It hopes to reconstruct the considerations and motives that have induced a philosopher to develop his theory. It seeks to prepare us for viewing a philosopher's thought not only as a completed system of statements that requires analysis, but rather as a response to certain ways of putting the question in a usually very complex constellation of problems. In the most important classical cases, as of Plato, Aristotle and Kant, it has been demonstrated that only in this way could the unique meaning of their most important teachings be determined with certainty and brought to discussion without involving controversy about interpretation.

Such a procedure could only be successful if the basic concepts and positions of an author are not taken as given but arrived at once again as discoveries shared with him. Most studies of the history of development, for instance those concerning Kant, miss their goal because they start implicitly from that which they seek to elucidate and therefore move in circles and tautologies. It is more difficult than it seems to avoid this error. It is a general law of memory that we can only recall what is past in connection with its later consequences. The study of the history of development in such cases must free itself from this, above all in those instances where the consequences have been most important.

In the case of Hegel's development there are additional and special difficulties. His thought is not the result of quiet, academic labor, which – as in the case of Kant – was achieved after many decades of solitary effort. Its origin cannot be observed in isolation, because it grew in daily contact with important friends. We cannot adequately understand Hegel's direction without knowing clearly the directions in which they were moving. In addition they all belonged to an era of revolutionary events: in politics and society as well as in consciousness and thought. And they regarded themselves as seismographs for this general upheaval and their work as contributions toward its success. Knowledge of the historical constellation of events and problems is therefore significant to a greater extent and degree for their history than it would be in Kant's case – comparable to that knowledge that actually would be required for understanding Plato, if the information were available.

The *Critique of Pure Reason* appeared in 1781. When Hegel entered the university, the discussion of the new critical philosophy had almost reached its height. Fichte's *Doctrine of Knowledge* was published in 1794. Only a few months later Schelling brought out a work in which he sought to go beyond Fichte's position. And in 1797 Hegel wrote texts which charged that the theories of freedom of both Kant and Fichte were tentative and inadequate. It has not been sufficiently noted how it was possible for this group of young friends to set out to command the whole attention of a philosophical school which Kant had founded only fifteen years before – at a time when many of Kant's important works still had not yet appeared. This requires an explanation, and it can only come from the motives behind these texts and from the circumstances in which they originated. It is true that the ideas in the texts could show why they were written, but not how they came to be written so quickly and with such self-confidence and with the certainty of being inevitably in accordance with the principles laid down by Kant.

In what follows I wish to consider several relationships which are essential to such an understanding of the account of the origination of

Hegel's thought. When Hegel attached himself to Kantianism along with his friends, it occurred under peculiar circumstances pertaining to their studies in Tübingen and the discussions of their older colleagues in the Tübingen Stift. The situation in theology in their time and at their university determined to a considerable degree how they began. The original direction and the initial changes in Hegel's critical theory of religion, which we come to know in the early writings (*HtJ*), as well as the degree of originality in his analyses, can only be judged in these contexts.

Understandably, these will only be briefly sketched out here. Detailed exposition must be left to more extensive studies, where the sources which form the basis of this sketch will be presented. The most important of these, hitherto unknown, are the following: 1. the manuscripts and letters of Immanuel Diez, Tutor at the Tübingen Seminary from 1789-92; 2. unpublished theological and philosophical writings by the early Schelling (1792/93); 3. the manuscript for a systematic essay by Sinclair, a friend of Hölderlin and Hegel (1795/96).

1. Rousseau and the moral theology of Kant

Jean Jacques Rousseau's theory of religion was of great importance in the philosophical development of Kant, as well as of Hegel. Kant developed his moral theology, which became the instrument of a sweeping critique of theology, under the impact of Rousseau. And the manner in which Hegel appropriated this moral theology was also directly influenced by Rousseau. Hegel revered Rousseau's work as much as that of his philosophical mentor Kant himself. Besides Kant, Rousseau is by far the most significant influence on Hegel's early texts.

Rousseau had directed the Cartesian criterion of evidence into the subjective realm: Everything must be considered as immediately convincing, to which we in "the sincerity of the heart" cannot deny our assent. Thus religious certainty too can only be obtained by assuring ourselves of what is given by ourselves in, and is inseparable from, our consciousness. Religion based on external evidence is as groundless as the Encyclopedists' criticism of religion which attacks only such outward proofs, as if that were enough to undermine the convictions of the heart ("conscience").

Part of our self-experience is that we feel guilt and remorse over unjust actions. These feelings include the conviction that we are free beings and faced with commands which we are able to fulfill. Self-certainty and the consciousness of freedom are in this sense inseparable.[4]

Objections arise, however, to our certainty of the reality of this freedom, objections which are based on observations and considerations which must occur to the common sense of every man. One objection is: in the self-certainty of conscience and freedom there is not only a demand for ethical action, but a promise as well: "be just and you will be happy." Rousseau heard this in himself with the same clarity as the reproaches of conscience for ill deeds. But if one considers the present state of things, nothing will be found that fulfills this promise. The good man must reckon not with reward, but with sacrifices. This observation leads one to doubt whether that promise is perhaps illusory. If that is the case, however, then one also must assume that the Ideal of virtue, with which the promise is connected, is also a false idea. Another objection is: the experience of the good in one's conscience is in conflict with the principles of reason, which directs our action in the world according to rules of cleverness. Our reason teaches us how we can best perceive our own interests. Outside of the individual conscience there is no evidence for the existence of an order for which "the general interest" is final purpose. The order of Reason taken in itself always leads back to the single individual.

Rousseau counters both causes of doubt with a principle of evidence which sees self-certainty as the highest source of all certainty: since I am definitely aware of myself as a free being, I can also be sure that everything is real that undermines the grounds for doubting, when doubt arises from rational cleverness and calculation. If the promise of happiness is not fulfilled in this life, then there must be another life in which what was promised will be fulfilled. And if reason knows only that order in which each follows his own interest, still through conscience one can believe in the guarantor of another order, in which the general interest is the highest purpose. This order is guaranteed by a being that has been called "God" from time immemorial. To doubt the Deity would make a reasonable conviction of the existence of the Good impossible. If Deity is real, on the other hand, then reason and conscience are in harmony. Therefore we cannot doubt God's existence, any more than we can question our own existence as free beings. In this way self-certainty answers the doubt of wordly wisdom and calculating reason with assertions that permit the assumption that ethical ideals are not illusions. Self-certainty is at the same time the source of certainty of the truth of these assertions.

Kant was deeply impressed by this theory. Several times he quoted Rousseau's dictum: "If God does not exist, then only the evil man has his rights by reason, the good man is insane." [5] Rousseau convinced him of the possibility of establishing a philosophical theology on the basis of ethics alone.

The structure itself he could not borrow from Rousseau. Where Rousseau relies on the evidence of conscience, the theorist of practical reason must make explicit the consequences which go to make up such evidence, namely that the good man deserves happiness and that only God can guarantee the reality of an ethical order.

Kant's moral theology has the appearance of a consistent and unified theory. This is particularly how those contemporaries saw it, who were inclined to use it as a weapon of criticism against the inherited theology. In truth it must itself be seen historically – as a long line of attempts, in the end unsuccessful, to give Rousseau's teachings a secure theoretical foundation and consistent expression.

As Kant's students began to apply his moral theology in their criticism, Kant himself was still unsure of many aspects. In the works he had already published, at least two completely different forms were to be found. In 1793 he offered a new version in his *Religion within the Limits of Reason Alone*, this time accompanied by a casual admission of uncertainty.[6] At first this situation in no way held back the reception of his moral theology. Just as Rousseau had previously convinced Kant with his general idea, the implications of which had still to be unfolded, so Kant won conviction more through his idea of subordinating all religion totally to freedom than through the arguments with which he derived the principles of rational religion from the consciousness of freedom. However, such lack of clarity contained the possibilities for future criticism of the theory and for future applications that contradicted the intentions of both Rousseau and Kant. To their surprise the young Kantians in Tübingen found themselves confronted with these possibilities.

Rousseau had derived the certainty of God and immortality simply from the necessity of defending the certainty of the reality of ethical ideals against the causes of doubt. The strength of the conviction that the good should be accomplished is great enough to effect even the conviction concerning the existence of those assumptions which must be present if the ethical good is not an illusion.

Kant's early moral theology was unable to hold to precisely this thought of Rousseau. Kant's moral theology was based on the following consideration: It is not a feeling, but a general rule of reason which is the foundation of our ethical consciousness. It is this rule which brings into our sensuously motivated striving an order which could never inhere in it. For our inclinations orient us toward the most heterogeneous goals, which could never be achieved together or coordinated in a convincing order of priority. They are only combined externally under the contradictory ideal of happiness. Each man at each moment sees his happiness in something else. If reason is the ordering power for the pursuit of happiness, then it must bear some relation to happiness. It is, in fact, the condition for a meaningful concept of happiness. As such it should also be able to promise future happiness, in the event that its condition is fulfilled. With this thought the foundation of ethics leads into moral theology.

At first Kant was of the opinion that only in this way may we understand how we are able with our reason to offer resistance to all our sensuous motivations. Although initially restricting our quest of happiness, it offers simultaneously the sole well-founded hope of true happiness. And without this hope the moral law might be applauded and admired, but it would never become the basis of real action.[7]

The weaknesses of this theory, which can still be found in the *Critique of Pure Reason,* are easy to demonstrate: it in no way allows for the pathos of a pure autonomy which is characteristic of moral theology. For reason, if it is to be effective, must be dependent on a man's hope for personal happiness. Moreover, this hope cannot be derived completely from the relation of the moral law to the demand for happiness to which it gives order. The fulfillment of a precondition, which in this is obviously not a sufficient one, is neither a promise nor even a reason for the certainty of the fulfillment of such a promise. Therefore practical reason, in search of sufficient motivational power for its law, must have recourse to strategies of persuasion. The vague prospect of happiness, to come after the fulfillment of its rational preconditions, should move one to submit to the precondition. Whoever sees through this connection would do well to renounce rationally ordered happiness. He would also escape thereby the unpleasant ethical demand and could continue consistently to struggle for earthly fragments of enjoyment and the good life. Kant himself later admitted that his early theory entangled itself in contradictions and compromised the autonomy of reason with techniques of self-persuasion.[8]

Kant's mature theory, which can be found in the *Critique of Practical Reason* and the *Critique of Judgement,* has a more convincing form: the moral law commands us to help our fellow men in accordance with their merit and to contribute to the establishment of a condition in the world in which the good man would no longer suffer while vicious men harvest the fruits of happiness. We cannot pretend, however, to be able to achieve such a state on our own resources. If the course of the world were such that the laws of nature worked to the benefit of evil, the efforts of our ethical wills would be in vain. The goal which we are commanded to follow would be imaginary. And the assumption that things are really in such a state can be supported by observations. No one, of course, can consistently continue a course of action aimed at a goal which he believes imaginary. This manner of action must itself seem illusory. We are bound, however, by the strength of our reason, always to follow the demands of morality. The consciousness of obeying thereby a necessary law of our own rational nature includes therefore the certainty that our goal of action is not imaginary. The necessary presupposition for a rational concept of the reality of this goal is, however, the assumption of the existence of God and a future life.

With this theory Kant obviously goes beyond his own first thoughts and reaches back to Rousseau's doctrine. It is protected against the objections and the misuse to which his first theory gave rise. On the other hand it relates morality and happiness in a far more external way. Whereas in the first theory the moral law was the form of any possible happiness, here happiness, insofar as it agrees with morality, is merely an element in the ultimate purpose which we strive after in all ethical action. At first Kant did not thoroughly examine why we should need such a final purpose, why it should be impossible to do what is good without conceiving its particular end in terms of the final goal. In 1793 he admitted that no necessary relation existed between the two. In that case, however, moral theology becomes finally a dispensable appendage to an ethics of autonomy.

What is implied as the dilemma of Kant's moral theology, disguised by Kant himself in the conflict between the two versions, came to public expression in the conflict of the young Kantians at the University in Tübingen and their theology teachers who had to defend orthodoxy from the attack of Kantianism. While the theologians attempted to demonstrate above all the compatibility of moral theology and orthodoxy with the help of Kant's first version, Schelling and Hegel, acting in the name of autonomy, soon dispensed altogether with the form of a theory of ethical belief in God which Kant had given to it. The theologians wished to show by means of Kant's earlier doctrine that the autonomy of the will was too weak to determine the will without the hope of happiness – that is, that morality is *nothing* without religion. The young Kantian opposed them with the thesis that autonomy was complete without introducing any of the traditional concepts of God or immortality – that is, that morality is *everything* when freed of this kind of religion.

2. *Kantianism and biblical criticism*

Since 1760 theology too had entered into a process of transformation. Above all Jacob Salomo Semler had developed the historical tool of biblical criticism. In keeping with the principle of protestantism to start solely from the meaning of the text, Semler investigated philologically various key texts for orthodox dogma. He believed he was able to show that in several cases these passages had been distorted in the process of transmission. He could often reconstruct even the circumstances of such distortion. Particularly the church fathers, who were greatly influenced by Greek philosophy, had repeatedly given such texts a sense quite different from the original meaning, and this was what first made the traditional dogmatics possible.

It is easy to see the consequences such biblical exegesis must have had in a period already disposed to make the insights of reason take precedence as the criteria of all possible dogmatics. It opened the possibility of depriving particularly objectionable items of dogma of their foundations in holy scripture: for instance the doctrine of the trinity and the doctrine of satisfaction. An understanding of original Christianity seemed to become possible, one which would be in agreement with the insights of philosophy. A new attempt to harmonize reason and revelation in the protestant spirit promised greater success than ever before.

The new critical theology had not only provided the philological tools for examining a text, it also had demonstrated the need to understand a passage in its original sense as well as the possibilities of corruption through historical circumstances. A dogmatic analysis of word-meanings of the texts must lead to insoluble controversies. The sense of a text can be made clear only from the situation in which it was written. Thereby the spirit of the times and of the oriental peoples must also be taken into consideration. Thus, through the new theology philological criticism, the knowledge of oriental languages, and historical-psychological acumen all became equally the preconditions for scientific work which was to reclaim the true meaning of the teachings of Christ, freed of all subsequent distortions. Studies such as Schelling's "On Myths, Historical Legends and Philosophical Themes of Earliest Antiquity" [9] and Hegel's on the "Spirit of Christianity" were only possible in such a context.

But the degree to which Semler's method led to a dissolution of the tradition did not depend on philological mastery alone and on the actual state of the texts. It was also determined by the theologian's interest in knowledge and his philosophical convictions. Beside Semler's own position that was indebted to traditional church doctrine, many varieties of revision of dogmatics appeared – from an outright defense of orthodoxy to the thesis that biblical doctrine coincides with the religion of reason.

This last position was approached by Eberhard Gottlob Paulus, a professor at Jena who had been a student in Tübingen. In the preface to his periodical "Memorabilia" he gave a pregnant summation of the program of such an historically enlightened theologian.[10] And the young Kantians in Tübingen were eager to publish in his journal. Schelling's writing on myths appeared there in 1793.

Paulus himself had achieved his viewpoint even before Kant became so influential. He did not equate enlightened religion with Kantian moral theology. But this was exactly the case for the best of the critical students at Tübingen around 1790. On Christmas eve of 1794 Hegel wrote to Schelling that he had read his essay in Paulus's "Memorabilia" and found him on his old familiar path, clearing up or "enlightening important theological concepts and gradually helping to clear away the old sour dough." [11] We can see how this was to be effected from the running commentary to the Epistles to the Romans and Galatians that Schelling wrote in the winter of 1792 and the summer of 1793 – before Hegel had left for Berne. They are nothing more than an attempt to prove, with the philological means of the new critical theology, that Christ's original doctrine according to St. Paul is identical to Kant's ethics of pure reason. Where the text cannot make this identity plausible, Schelling argues with reasons drawn from the spirit of the time: Christ could only make his doctrine of a purely spiritual law clear to his audience by resorting to certain images and putting his own personality in the foreground.[12] Schelling did not neglect to explain Christ's prophecy of "the Kingdom of God" in such a way as to include a coming political revolution on earth, which would make the law of reason universally operative.[13]

These manuscripts of Schelling – his "theologische Jugendschriften" – difficult as they are to decipher, have up to now not been used, possibly because they were taken to be notes from lectures Schelling had heard. But who in Tübingen would have represented such views from the lecture podium? In the final third of the eighteenth century that university was the last bastion of a scientific orthodoxy.

Gottlob Christian Storr, who occupied the first theological chair and whose renown as a scholar was widespread, was a master of Semler's techniques. He used them, however, to defend the doctrinal system of the church against attacks from the enlightenment. This was at first confined to exegetical works, but during Hegel's years of study came to include a textbook on systematics and critical writings on the philosophy of religion.

According to Storr it is a misunderstanding of the essence of Christianity to think it should simply stimulate reason and reinforce rational insights. Rather its revelation must be a chief determinant of our judgments. This doctrine carries authority. And it requires that we trust its proclamations. Such belief presupposes, of course, that the tradition upon which one relies be worthy of belief. Only in this sense is the confirmation of reason necessary, and this is settled by textual criticism. This criticism of texts, according to Storr, does not lead to the radical reductions suggested by followers of Semler. Rejected books such as the Revelation of St. John, and rejected doctrines such as that of the trinity and the satisfaction, are to be included in doctrinal authority.

Young students in sympathy with the movement of liberation in their time had to offer passionate opposition to such theology. This resistance was also provoked by the sort of life they were forced to lead in the Tübingen Stift. It was strictly organized according to external rules and was criticised as unique in its time by Friedrich Nicolai and a Prussian academic inspector, who had been appointed to visit universities.[14] The students in the Stift felt this subjection to rules to be a suppression of the spirit of freedom and with it all of the better tendencies of their time. Storr's theology, the ordinances of the Stift, and the constitution of the state, which protected both, seemed to most of the students to justify revolution – a revolution such as that which was begun in the more liberal faith, in Kant's philosophy, and in the political life of France.

The early writings of Schelling and Hegel set themselves the goal of opposing Storr and the forces he aligned himself with. Schelling, who had gone through the cloister school system and who commanded general respect, despite his youth, because of his knowledge of oriental languages, made more use of the methods inherited from Semler. Hegel had come from the gymnasium in Stuttgart and was less well prepared for theology, but more advanced than Scheling in history and psychology. The differences in their earliest manuscripts can be explained from this background.

Schelling's first writings are documents of his great native talent. And one can already see some of the characteristics of Hegel's thought in his work on popular religion (*Volksreligion*). Neither can be seen, however, as the nucleus of a future system of philosophy. They rather belong to the context of a religious Enlightenment which makes use of Kantianism as the most progressive system of insight. Thus in the beginning of 1795 Schelling wrote that the only thing that interested him "up until a year ago were historical studies of the Old and New Testament and the spirit of the first Christian centuries." [15] By that he certainly means his critical writings based on Kant. Hegel also wants to contribute to this task from Berne. He admits that, in contrast to Schelling, he is not familiar with the newer speculations of theoretical philosophy. They seem to him hardly applicable in the cause of the critique of religion for the interests of humanity.

Schelling's shift to philosophical theory was evidently motivated by a shift made by the real enemy of his endeavor in 1793, i.e. by the Tübingen orthodoxy.[16] In order to understand how this came about we must know its background.

Storr was for a long time apparently of the opinion that his exegetical theology would be able to assert itself as scholarship against Kantian interpretations of the Bible. As a pious man and a competent philologist he believed that he was in possession of an unimpeachable insight. But the increasingly radical character of the attacks on the authority of revealed religion, wherever it went beyond reason, must have caused him concern. A further and more important source of anxiety arose from the activity of Immanuel Diez, a tutor at the seminary, whom a friend of Hegel once called "a Kantian enrage." [17] Until quite recently we knew nothing more about him than his appellation. Now we are in a position to say that Diez was in fact the most radical Kantian ever to have tutored at a university. He had directed a passionate polemic against the oath required of every protestant minister about to assume office, an allegiance to the credo of the established church. Later he directed his criticism against dogmatics, which seemed to him, in the light of conclusions taken from Kantian philosophy, to be a smoke-screen deception, an attempt to elicit support for absolutely senseless propositions in the service of a repressive regime. He accomplished his critique with the tools of Kant's theoretical philosophy.

Kant had shown that all our concepts that claim to go beyond experience are without reality – with the sole exception of the concept of freedom. But Dogmatics speaks of God's deeds, supernatural occurrences, and a heavenly kingdom as if these were comprehensible entities. In this sense Diez claimed it was "a foolish enterprise to plant on ground that has no foundation." [18] He who casts his eye "aimed with the Kantian telescope" on the Christian religion, will "see nothing but transcendental illusion and empty chimeras instead of objective knowledge."

Diez, who was supposed to lead young theologians in their studies, was himself consistently drawn in this way to a total rejection of Christianity. Christ and his apostles, believing they have insight into a realm of spirits, are phantasists; those who believe them, all theologians and the whole Christian flock, are lost in superstition. In this sense Diez was willing, along with a well-known polemical tract of the early 18th century, to label Christ a fraud.

This Kantian indeed knew Kant's moral theology, but his reading of it is absolutely within the confines of the theoretical philosophy: that is, the assertion of God's existence can only be made as an assumption for the sake of our ethical life, never as a descriptive assertion of God's being. Christ and his theologians, however, are interested in another sort of certainty.

The radical polemics of Diez met with resistance even from most of his friends, but had an immense effect nevertheless. His closest friend Süsskind, Storr's eventual successor in Tübingen, first turned from theology to church history under the impression of his (Diez's) doubt. Other friends determined to avoid religious service in Swabia and to seek positions in other German states. Actually Diez was a cautious person, whose radicalness came forth only after long suffering from suppression. He agitated mainly among his friends and did not speak with total candor with his students. However, he was the one who introduced the sharpness of tone into the new Tübingen criticism. And he was effective as well through his example when he resigned his position as tutor, gave up a secure and comfortable future as a minister, and took up the study of medicine. In 1796 he was infected while caring for Typhus patients and died at the age of thirty. His decision for ethical practice and finally his death in the service of others were the realization of his critique of theology and his completely practical Kantianism.

Even if Storr had not been able to discern the radicalisation of his students from the many indications, Süsskind's reports would have been sufficient. This young theologian was not only a friend of Diez, but also Storr's close relative. So Storr decided to counter the radical versions of Kantian philosophy and to attempt to demonstrate the compatibility of orthodoxy and Kant's doctrine. Süsskind aided him in this, apparently providing him with important arguments. And he contributed an appendix to Storr's book, *Remarks on Kant's Philosophical Doctrine of Religion*, directed against Fichte's *Critique of all Revelation*, which had just appeared.[19]

Storr made use of just those elements in Kant's moral theology through which it differed, to its own disadvantage, from Rousseau's conception.

In its earlier form it began with the idea that moral law would not have sufficient motives for action without belief in God and immortality. If this is the case, if we cannot consistently do good without religion, then it is our *first* duty to provide foundation and encouragement for religious convictions. The historical aspect of the Christian religion contributes, however, a great deal to the substantiation, support, and revival of moral belief. Therefore it is a postulate of practical reason to lend credence to moral belief insofar as it is credible. Such credibility is demonstrated by the historical criticism of texts. And thus orthodoxy has inadvertently become the only means of giving rational morality a firm foundation. The theory of autonomy has become a means for defense of the theology of authority.

Schelling and Hegel could only see an inversion of the actual sense of Kant's doctrine in Storr's argumentation. But, although it contradicted completely its spirit, it could still rely on Kant's texts. Therefore it became necessary to protect Kant against the weaknesses of his own presentation. This could certainly have been effected by scrupulous interpretation. But it did not fit with Kant's role as the apostle of freedom to defend him with philological techniques. Moreover, his best disciples, Reinhold and Fichte, had just demonstrated that Kant's path should be pursued beyond his own position to grasp fully his spirit. And so Schelling gave up historical criticism of the Bible and soon wrote a book, which in connection with Fichte, showed that Storr's comprehension of Kant was not simply a departure from his actual meaning, but rather the exact opposite of the true critical philosophy of freedom.[20]

Hegel initially did not have such means at his disposal. He had to hold fast to Kant himself, but opposed Storr by calling into doubt those principles of Kantian moral theology which Storr followed: the intrusion of orthodoxy was only possible if one connected the consciousness of ethical freedom with hope of personal happiness. This connection has absolutely no foundation. Only where the sense of servility was dominant could one have said that he who dies for a good cause was worthy of a better fate.[21]

3. Hölderlin's design of a system and Hegel's earliest problems

The moment that Hegel dispensed with Kant's moral theology while retaining the Kantian basis of his thought, he became, strictly speaking, a simple critic of every traditional sense of religion. For he lacked the basis for introducing a rational being that could be distinguished from our own ethical consciousness – the basis for introducing a concept of God. Religion had become for him simply the way in which men, living in communities, learn to know the pure ideal of autonomy and are able to make it the sole motive of their actions. Whether as an establishment of the state or as a spontaneous product of the human sense of freedom, religion is the best means of promoting morality. This it can accomplish without speaking of a supersensible being and without promising that the desire for happiness will eventually be satisfied. Such belief is only the expression of the lack of "consciousness that reason is absolute, complete in itself – that its infinite idea must be created out of itself free from alien admixture." [22]

In this formulation Hegel is speaking a language which is not that of Kant. It contains an echo of the confession which Schelling had given him in February of 1795.[23] Hegel had learned from this that Schelling, with the help of Fichte but also reaching back to Spinoza, had developed a doctrine of freedom which was immune to Storr's strategy of argumentation. Just as the world was everything for Spinoza, so Schelling now saw his all in the ego – the ego which is not determined or limited by objects, but posited absolutely in freedom. "There is no supersensible world for us other than the absolute ego. God is nothing but the absolute ego." In the context of Fichte's *Doctrine of Knowledge*, particularly in the new form given it by Schelling, such formulations assume a completely different meaning than they do in the context of Hegel's Kantianism. For Fichte and especially for Schelling, this ego is a force of action beyond the individual and before all consciousness, from which our limited consciousness together with its moral law must be understood. It is then in no way identical with what Kant and after him Hegel called "our pure practical reason."

In this sense the object of free belief for Schelling can only be reason which is "absolute" and "complete in itself." But insofar as reason stands beyond the believer's consciousness – and reason is the ground of the believer's consciousness – the belief in reason is more than an internal relation of the finite self. It is the conscious return of finite consciousness to its origin. Only in this return can it experience itself as what it is: as the realization of an anonymous, absolute freedom.

At first Hegel was not at all prepared to follow Schelling along this path. He had up to then trusted that the theoretical tools of the *Critique of Pure Reason* would suffice for a comprehensive doctrine of freedom. He wanted to limit himself to the application of these tools. Thus he was able to use elements of Schelling's new language only in a way considerably different from Schelling's sense.

We know, however, that Hegel's thought shifted radically very soon thereafter. In the texts of the "theological writings of his youth" (*HtJ*) this shift occurs quite suddenly, despite various anticipations, almost like an incomprehensible break. While the first half of the text still discusses "morality, love and religion" on the basis of Kantian principles, a completely different theoretical orientation emerges in the second half.[24] This astounding situation is not made more comprehensible by arguing that this piece is in fact two independent texts. In any case the second can only have been written shortly after the first.

In this fragment Hegel opposes the subjective freedom of practical reason with "love", which has a completely different and higher freedom to "unite" itself with its object. This unifying capacity brings about a state were "nature is freedom, and subject and object are inseparable." [25] Hegel still calls this, in Kantian terms, an "ideal." But apparently he no longer means by it a purpose to be realized by practical reason, since precisely this ideal itself establishes insurmountable limits as to what practical freedom can will.

In this doctrine of the other freedom of love his recalling Franz Hemsterhuis is effective. Particularly his essay "On Desire," which he wrote as a follower of Plato, was read by the young seminarians, along with Heder's friendly response entitled "Love and Selfhood". This is, however, hardly sufficient explanation of Hegel's sudden departure from the Kantian foundation of his work.

It is better understood in terms of the change in Hegel's situation. From the loneliness of Berne he entered in Frankfurt a new circle of philosophizing friends, which had formed around Friederich Hölderlin. In some respects they were superior to Hegel: they had followed the most recent developments in philosophical speculation more closely than he. Some of them, as Hölderlin himself, had been in Jena, had studied under Fichte, and had participated in the discussions of his circle.

In Hegel research there has for a long time been a disagreement concerning the degree of influence which Hölderlin could have had on Hegel. Only very recently has a position been reached from which to decide this question. For documents have been found to prove that Hölderlin was in command of a philosophical conception of his own at the time of Hegel's renewed contact with him.[26] Hölderlin was really the first to criticize Fichte basically after being his student and to deny that the absolute ego can be used as a principle of philosophy. According to his view the meanings of "ego" and "subject" cannot be separated. Since "subject" can only be thought of in relation to an object and thus never as absolute, the concept of an absolute ego is nonsense. It is rather a question of seeing both subject and object in terms of their limitation. Both can be made comprehensible through a presupposition that is to be conceived neither as ego nor as object. Hölderlin calls it "Being". This Being was divided into an opposition through the act of reflection, much as Fichte has assumed for the absolute ego. Now the ultimate task of all knowledge and action is to restore this original unity. Our ethical consciousness consists in this demand for reunification. Since, as consciousness, however, only an infinite process could achieve this goal, the ideal and the certainty of this unity must be impressed upon us in another way. They are reflected in nature, which has not been completely lost to this separation, they reveal themselves in beauty, and they are grasped in love.

Because Hölderlin's strength did not lie in the analysis of concepts or the construction of consistent arguments, earlier scholars were not inclined to grant that he could have been in a position to convince Hegel, who was more capable of conceptualization. Today we can better see how he was indeed able to so do. Hölderlin's younger friend Sinclair had developed Hölderlin's ideas into an articulated design of a system. Thus, in this new circle of friends, Hegel was confronted with a philosophical system which had moved through Fichte's *System of Knowledge* and thus could present itself on the heights of the systematic development at that time. What Schelling's writings and Hegel's correspondence with him could only distantly prepare for him, the close contact with these friends quickly established as an actuality: Hegel's transition from Kantianism to a position which used Fichte's means to go beyond Fichte's principles.

That this change in Hegel's thought occurred under the influence of another thinker does not mean that he was simply appropriating an alien insight. Rather, in the thought of Hölderlin and Sinclair, Hegel found a means of explicating his own ideas and intentions, more suitable to this end than the Kantian means without sacrificing the advantages of Kantianism. Their system too was simply the result of a different attempt to find adequate theoretical expression for the common ideal of their student days.

Even in his first writings Hegel had taken up the Kantian principle of autonomy in a way peculiar to himself. For Kant, the categorical imperative was at once the principle of freedom and the basis of that constitution of law which was to bring life under strict rules. In contrast to Kant, who also held to such regimentation of life in his personal affairs, Hegel extracted from the morality of reason less the ethics of law than the appeal to freedom and spontaneity of action. He intended to secure free development for an essentially human life and to undermine the claim of all structures which placed such development under compulsion. The meaning for Hegel of this bond of friendship with Schelling and Hölderlin was "never, never to make peace with the 'system' which would rule thought and feeling." [27] In this revolt against all "chains" [28] Rousseau was his greatest source of encouragement. He drew on Rousseau where Kant could not agree with Rousseau. It is well known that Rousseau's ethics were in the tradition of the "moral-sense"-school of thought and differed from Kant in making no distinction between our consciousness of freedom and the original impulses and feelings of our heart. The young Hegel was there in complete agreement with him. And he took it upon himself to interpret Kantian autonomy as a spontaneity of our sensibility and as a joyful urbane freedom of relations in a republican state. The most repelling thing to him in the education system of the church was its asceticism — a discipline of teaching which concerns itself with the motives of belief and pious living and the way these can be made effective. In this way Hegel's interest in psychology is to be explained. For "nothing has damaged the monastic ideal of asceticism so much as the increased education of the moral sense among men and the better knowledge of the nature of the human soul" [29] A particular form of asceticism is necessarily bound up with the orthodox system, which excludes the possibility of man's acting spontaneously and out of himself. In order to safeguard the authority of Scripture and the Law, man must be led to suspect all his spontaneous motives and to press them into artificial regulations. No free relationship is to be granted him, neither to himself nor to divinity.

Thus Hegel from the beginning had interpolated elements into his Kantian theory which could not be assimilated without resistance, even though it was because of these elements that Hegel had found Kant's philosophy of spontaneity so convincing. Everything which manages to avoid the compulsions of the system seemed to him to be defended by Kant as well – not only unforced feelings, but also a sense for the beauties of nature, every desire toward unity and submission which is not commanded, the spirit of Greek festivals in a free state. For this reason, like most of his generation, Hegel saw no exclusive opposition between Spinoza's theory of rational necessity immanent in the world and Kant's morality of reason. While Kant could only explain that he had no understanding of the attempt to unite his critical philosophy with Spinoza,[30] both philosophers for the young Tübingen students were regarded equally as opponents of asceticism and the morality of regulation. Whether the absolute is thought of as being present in the world and able to unfold itself in my life or only as the inner law of my will, this is all the same in respect to orthodoxy: namely the annihilation of all its claims to an authority of a truth which must be brought upon us from outside. Thus it is understandable that Hegel, acting from his own convictions, accepted the theoretical tools which Hölderlin with Sinclair had developed out of Fichte's position. They served a common purpose: to guarantee the freedom of the feeling and beauty of life in thought. Hölderlin had agreed that for this it was also necessary to revise Fichte's philosophy of freedom, which had placed spontaneity at its center, but had not been able consistently to separate freedom from regulation.

With this shift toward Hölderlin, Hegel again came into possession of a philosophy of religion. In religion the power of free unification, which precedes all objectification, is itself raised into consciousness. That which determines our lives anterior to all opposition reveals itself in religion.

We need not dwell on this thought which is familiar from the texts. Like Schelling's doctrine of the absolute ego, it presents a step out beyond finite consciousness towards its essence and, on its own ground, a step *within* consciousness. In this sense Hegel claims to be above suspicion that he is violating the principle of autonomy.

Hegel only conceived this step beyond in connection with Hölderlin's ideas, yet in a manner quite his own. It can be shown that certain structures in Hegel's mature system of logic began to articulate themselves at a time when he still intended to stay within the limits of Kant's critical philosophy. They resulted neither from his Kantianism nor from his ethics of the comprehensive spontaneity of life. Their origin is his method of criticizing orthodoxy, which must therefore be regarded as his first really significant accomplishment. The early manuscripts from Tübingen and Berne concentrate their efforts on protecting a true sense of spontaneous life against the false asceticism of orthodoxy. But beyond that they also seek to make comprehendable *how it could come about* that the Christian teachings of freedom degenerated into the compulsive system of the church. This plan was in itself already original in the context of the contemporary opposition to orthodoxy. In order to carry it through, Hegel made use of his historical studies, the theories of state and society of his day, and particularly the pragmatic-ethical psychology which Paulus had already recommended as a means of theological enlightenment. In this medium a model slowly took form for him, the model of a process in which free self-relation comes out of itself to relate to an other which is foreign to it, in order to be subjected to this other, until finally it draws itself back to itself and liberates itself. Hegel's *Logic* later presented this process as the connection of reflection in itself and external reflection, which is the concept of the absolute itself. Hegel, abandoned by his friends, in continuing the fight against orthodoxy in the loneliness of Berne was also nurturing the seeds of the most subtle system of the coming epoch.

NOTES

1. Karl Rosenkranz, *Georg Wilhelm Friedrich Hegel's Life*, 1843, Reprint Darmstadt, 1963.
2. Wilhelm Dilthey, *Die Jugendgeschichte Hegels*, 1906, in *Gesammelte Werke*, Band IV.
3. The best outline of this literature is to be found in Carmelo Lacorte, *Il primo Hegel*, (Firenze, 1961).
4. In this sketch I refrain from naming the sources, which are primarily to be found in Emile.
5. *Kant's Works*, AA, XV, *Reflections* 4256, 4375.
6. *RiGbV*, long footnote to the preface of the first issue: "Den Schlüssel zur Auflösung dieser Aufgabe, soviel ich davon einzusehen glaube ..."
7. *CPR*, p. 841, B. See further reference in my "Der Begriff der sittlichen Einsicht und Kants Lehre vom Faktum der Vernunft" in: *Die Gegenwart der Griechen im neueren Denken* (Tübingen, 1960).
8. Reflexion 6432, *GzMdS*, AA, p. 450.
9. Friedrich Wilhelm Joseph Schelling, *Werke*, edited by Manfried Schröter (München: C. H. Beck und R. Oldenbourg, 1927), I, pp. 1-43.
10. *Memorabilien*, a philosophical-theological newspaper of history and philosophy of religions ... first issue, Jena, 1791.
11. *Letters from and to Hegel*, I, 11.
12. "Commentary on the Epistle to the Galatians" (unpublished), p. 2.
13. "Commentary on the Epistle to the Romans" (unpublished), p. 61.
14. "Friedrich Gedike und sein Bericht an Friedrich Wilhelm II," mitgeteilt von Richard Fester, I. Ergänzungsheft des Archivs für Kulturgeschichte, Berlin 1905.
15. *Letters from and to Hegel*, I, 14.
16. *Ibid.* "Wer mag sich im Staub des Altertums begraben, wenn ihn der Geist seiner Zeit alle Augenblicke wieder auf und mit sich fortreisst."
17. Compare: Henrich "Leutwein über Hegel," *Hegelstudien* III, 1965, pp. 57, 72.
18. All quotations from letters to Niethammer 1790/91 (private poss.). Compare Henrich and Johann Ludwig Doederlein, Carl Immanuel Diez, in: *Hegelstudien*, Band III, 1965, pp. 276-287.
19. Süsskinds Briefe an Diez (Handschriftenabteilung der Universitätsbibliothek Tübingen); D. Gottlob Christian Storrs Bemerkungen über Kants philosophische

Religionslehre, aus dem Lateinischen, nebst einigen Bemerkungen des Übersetzers über den aus Prinzipien der praktischen Vernunft hergeleiteten Überzeugungsgrund von der Möglichkeit und Wirklichkeit einer Offenbarung in Beziehung auf Fichtes Versuch einer Kritik aller Offenbarung (Tübingen, 1794).

20. Vom Ich als Prinzip der Philosophie, WW ed. Schröter I 75 sq. pages 120-26 are written in direct reference to the Tübingen orthodoxy.

21. *HtJ*, p. 238.

22. *Ibid.*

23. *Letters from and to Hegel*, I, 22.

24. *HtJ*, pp. 374-77. I propose to regard pages 376/77 as independent text. Compare Gisela Schüler, "Zur Chronologie von Hegels Jugendschriften," *Hegelstudien* II, 1963, p. 131.

25. *Ibid.*, p. 376.

26. All evidences to be found in Dieter Henrich *Hölderlin über Urteil und Sein*, Hölderlinjahrbuch 1965/66, pp. 73-96.

27. *Letters from and to Hegel* I, 38.

28. "Leutwein über Hegel," p. 56. Compare *HtJ*, p. 6 and others.

29. *HtJ*, p. 208.

30. Compare Kant's essay "Was heisst sich im Denken orientieren?" of the year 1786.

COMMENT ON

DIETER HENRICH

SOME HISTORICAL PRESUPPOSITIONS OF HEGEL'S SYSTEM

by

Charles E. Scott

Professor Henrich's paper is fascinating not only because it provides new information concerning the influences which helped to mold the young Hegel, but also because it employs an approach to philosophical interpretation which promises to disclose the "Secret of Hegel." This disclosure will come primarily not through textual exegesis, but through a study of what is termed textual origins and the history of Hegel's development. I want to focus on Professor Henrich's understanding of *Entwicklungsgeschichte*, first in order to understand it clearly and secondly in order to question it in relation to some of Hegel's own philosophical ideas.

A study of the history of development proposes, according to Professor Henrich, three things: 1. to provide "unique evidence and criteria" for understanding critically a particular philosophy; in this context I understand *unique* to mean "not to be found in the texts themselves"; 2. to investigate and reconstruct the historical situation out of which a system of thought arose, and this means that one focuses on those encountered, lived problems of the time which motivated the particular philosophical reflections under consideration; and 3. thereby to understand the "unique meaning" of the ideas such that one has outflanked and obviated the textual and systematic controversies. The aim of such a study is to put these controversies to rest by analyzing and discovering interpretative criteria through the historical situation which gave birth to the ideas in question.

In order to carry out this project one must imaginatively relive the historical situation and work out of it to the author's own position. One does not start with the theory he wants to understand. He rather starts with the situation to which a given theory responded and in which it developed. He rethinks that theory out of the problems, moods, and ideas of the generating situation. Hence, Professor Henrich points out, one must free himself from the enormous temptation of looking at the theory primarily in terms of the consequences which followed the theory. One must concentrate, rather, on the theory's genesis.

Specifically, in the case of Hegel, we must understand: 1. the thought of his friends in interaction with whom he developed his early ideas, 2. the revolutionary temperament of their time in order to understand their predisposition toward radically changing their tradition, 3. the speedy departure from Kant when his thought was just beginning to be felt, and 4. the theological climate at the Tübingen Stift in order to see to what Hegel was reacting in his early theological writings.

The first question I want to pose regarding this method of approach is: Does an historical interpretation always significantly negate what is interpreted? I am disposed to answer the question affirmatively, and I am concerned that Professor Henrich's understanding of the study of the history of development might take negation too lightly. First, it seems to me that my coming back to an historical situation is iself a consequence of the theory that I want to understand, and that my return occurs always at least in part because of the consequences born of the philosophy in question. Professor Henrich holds that if we begin solely with consequences we immediately underestimate the importance of the origins of the idea in question. I think that is right. I also think that he is right in placing emphasis on the idea's historical emergence. But I think that he implies in addition that by studying the development of a philosophy we can avoid what as Hegelians we might call the negation of origins through their consequences. And that is where I become uneasy. I want to suggest that we already have negated the origins by returning to them, because our return is a consequence of the origins to which we return now and which are in a thoroughly mutated form, by means of historical mediations; that when we return to the development of an idea we are necessarily abstracting from historical concreteness in order to understand what is dead in its pastness, is now abstract in its historically originating nature, and is alive only in living consequences. If my suggestion is correct, the "Secret of Hegel" is, to use a Sartrean term, secreted into the present through its consequences which are now lived in my study and appropriation of it, as well as in other living cultural forms which it has influenced. In that case my imaginative reconstruction of the development of Hegel's thought originates out of the consequences of that thought and out of much else as well. I return to it as I might return to the land of my ancestors which is now barren of them and which whispers their past presence to me out of *remembered* or *documented* events which have made my return meaningful. Professor Henrich suggests that we should free ourselves from the consequences of a philosophy so as to understand its beginning. I am suggesting that my inquiry is a consequence of the philosophy, as well as a consequence of other consequences of the philosophy, and hence that my imaginative projection into its genesis involves a necessary negation of the originative power and identity of its genesis. In order to understand our own understanding of a past philosophy, we should take with the great seriousness the consequential nature of our return to what we interpret. The history of development, I am suggesting, involves a history of the consequences which led me to return to a philosophy with interpretative interests.

Secondly, in this regard, it seems to me that interpretation of past events involves a self-critical perspective on the part of the interpreter. He sees himself in terms of a past that has weighed on him. He sees his situation in light of its heritage in order to understand himself and his world better or at least more thoroughly. The study of the history of Hegel's development is thus also an event of present self-development. Such a study is an act of mind – the interpreter's mind and, if I may be vague, the mind of the interpreter's time. He is in a process of developing, and that process, it seems to me, is intrinsic to his imaginatively reliving the interpreted development. He certainly may discover things that he did not know. He may discover that some of his interpretations are disproved or significantly modified by what he reads and understands. In that sense he finds the past over against him and wiser than he. But he makes such discoveries out of questions and problems which are unique to his development. They come as answers or irrelevancies or solutions. In that sense he obviously lives through Hegel's development as he and never as Hegel, and Hegel's time lives in the interpreter's and *not* in Hegel's time. Hegel's "development" is now conditioned by the interpreter's development and Hegel's theories are conditioned by the interpreter's theories. It would appear correct to say that although in one sense the interpreter's development has origins in Hegel's, at the interpretative level Hegel's development now originates in the interpreter's. And the "unique meaning" of Hegel's ideas are conditioned by the interpreter's ideas such that "meaning" refers to the present self-critical development of the interpreter who grasps the uniqueness of Hegel's development. The facts and events of Hegel's development and the facts and events which condition the interpreter's interests compose a dialectic in the discovered meanings. Those meanings transcend, in the sense of mutually involve, the situations of both Hegel's time and the interpreter's time such that I can say that the history of Hegel's development *as discovered* is intrinsically related to the self-development of the interpreter.

I see clearly that Professor Henrich wants to take account of history in a way that strictly textual and systematic critics did not take account of it. My question is whether Professor Henrich has been dialectical enough in his understanding of historical interpretation.

The second broad question I want to pose is: Does Professor Henrich consider his understanding of the history of development to be a thorough or only partial rejection of Hegel's understanding of *Geist*, as articulated in *The Phenomenology of Mind?* As I read and studied Professor Henrich's investigation into Hegel's early years I wondered frequently what or who was developing. Was it only Hegel and his broad company of friends? Was it in some sense of the phrase Western culture? Was it a group of individual minds or was it Mind in a more Hegelian sense? My guess is that Professor Henrich, like I, is more comfortable with a considerably finitized version of Hegel's thought than he is with Hegel's own pretensions regarding the Absolute. Otherwise he would not have identified himself so readily with a method of interpretation originating with Dilthey.

But granting scepticism about Hegel's own view of Absolute Spirit, what reality did he confront which caused him to be so dissatisfied with both Kantian thought and the theology dominating the Tübingen Stift? Presumably that reality was the freedom of consciousness, the reality of spontaneity and of creative reconciliation and negation. I thus wonder if, on Professor Henrich's terms, an investigation into Hegel's development is also an investigation into the self-realization of human freedom, and if an investigation into Hegel's departure from the theology of the time is a development that has divine as well as human significance. To put the question another way, are the unique criteria which come from a study of textual origins statements which take special account of historical events, or are they insights into human or perhaps transhuman reality which itself was developing historically? Was the interaction among Hegel, Storr, Diez, Schelling, and Sinclair an exciting situation of conflict and thought *only*, or was it a situation in which either humanity of divinity was suffering self-development through these inspiring individuals?

I am asking what "unique evidence and criteria" means when we say that the study of textual origins provides us with "unique evidence and criteria for critical understanding of a philosophy."

Finally I want to say that I appreciate thoroughly Professor Henrich's interest in understanding philosophical ideas on the basis of the lived situations out of which the written texts arose. This interest, as I have indicated, is difficult to realize hermeneutically. I want to end my remarks by asking Professor Henrich if the philosophical essay is the best model for presenting a history of development. In the early remarks of his paper he stressed the importance of rediscovering the interpreted author's ideas by encountering him in his culture and environment. Can the presentation of ideas through an essay accomplish this task adequately? What is the artistry of interpretation which presents adequately the interpreter's encounter with Hegel's encounters? Does the interpreter rely on the reader's imaginative ability to use stated ideas and relations to see what the interpreter sees, or does he present the interaction best when he moves beyond discursive presentation by means of imaginatively representing the conflicts and influences through, say, the plot, dialogue, and dramatic relationships in a novel? I believe that Professor Henrich wishes to discover the "Spirit of Hegel" by means of rational action which grasps the history of Hegel's development, by discerning and re-enacting the rational structures found in that history. I am not certain if he believes this to be a fundamentally discursive act. I believe that he rejects Hegel's concept of Absolute Spirit. Hegel's type of Phenomenology of Mind is thus not available to him. But I wonder nevertheless whether, on Professor Henrich's terms, a finite mind discerns and re-enacts past events best through discursive or nondiscursive forms of presentation.

DIETER HENRICH

SOME HISTORICAL PRESUPPOSITIONS OF HEGEL'S SYSTEM

by

Eugene Thomas Long

With the increasing availability of manuscripts relating to Hegel's formative years, scholars have turned to studies of the genesis of his thought in which they seek to document his early development with the aim of interpreting his mature philosophy on the basis of the motivations and conditions which are at its origin. Professor Henrich's paper would be a significant one if for no other reason than the fact that he contributes to this study of the genesis of Hegel's thought by making use of hitherto unknown resources to illuminate the development of Hegel's contemporaries. Hegel's relation to Kant is presented in a lucid manner and Hölderlin's thought, as systematized by Sinclair, is suggested as the key to Hegel's development beyond Kant.

I limit my comments to two, the first putting a question concerning Henrich's approach to the early so-called theological writings of Hegel and the second reflecting the contemporary relevance of Hegel's discussion with his contemporaries. Professor Henrich relates that the systematic *interpretation* of Hegel's writings has failed to produce a solution to the secret of Hegel. Therefore, he suggests that the study of the evolution of Hegel's thought is essential. This approach aims to provide a piecemeal reconstruction of the motivations and considerations which led Hegel to evolve his theory. In this way, Henrich suggests, we will come to understand his theory as an answer to specific problems to an already completed set of doctrines. However, according to Henrich, this method can be successful only if we do not accept Hegel's basic concepts and position as given, only if we begin at the beginning, so to speak, and rediscover his theory with him.

Henrich's approach to the history of philosophy is a significant one, one which Hegel's *Phenomenology of Mind* would seem to encourage.

And Henrich is, of course, quite right to suggest that we cannot pre-determine the outcome of our study without contradicting the reason for our study in the first place. However, this does not mean that Hegel's mature works are of little or no importance to our study of his early works. On the contrary, it would seem to be important as well as more Hegelian to think within the framework of a dialectic between a philosopher's earlier and later works in which each is seen to illuminate the other. Henrich certainly expects that the study of Hegel's earlier writings will illuminate his later published work. It remains unclear, however, that the significance of some principal themes and concepts within the early theological essays, even within their own context, can be understood apart from their development in Hegel's mature work. W.H. Walsh says that we cannot even assume that Hegel positively identified himself with all of the positions that are found here. Indeed, it might be that these essays could be understood as reflecting Hegel's tendency to adopt first one view and then another, carrying each through to its limits and thus leading over into other views. Adding to the confusion is the fact that while most commentators look to "The Spirit of Christianity" as the most mature of these early essays, Walter Kaufmann believes this essay to have little importance or originality. If we had no other works these early essays would probably appear to be quite arbitrary in character and we might even believe that we were dealing with the works of more than one author. We are able, it seems to me, to make sense of these theological essays only if we have in mind some tentative understanding of Hegel's later development and the main lines of thought which emerge in his published work.

Perhaps Professor Henrich would agree at this point. However, there are some places in his paper where I feel a bit uneasy and wonder what the difference would be if we were more sensitive to the experimental nature of these early essays and the emergence of themes which become important in Hegel's later works. For instance, Professor Henrich explains the difference between "The Positivity of the Christian Religion" and the last section of the fragment on "Love, Morality and Religion" as a change which takes place almost like an incomprehensible break. In contrast to the Kantian flavor of the "Positivity," Hegel is seen in the fragment on "Religion" to put Kant's subjective freedom of the practical reason in opposition with love, which possesses the freedom of unification with its object. Henrich explains this development primarily on the basis of Hegel's move to Frankfurt and his associations with Höl-

derlin and Sinclair, where Being is understood to be neither subject nor object but the presupposition of both.

There is, of course, no question about there being a change or development here. It would seem improbable that there is a change in the sense of an incomprehensible break almost as if to suggest a change of mind. This would present the problem of an increasing number of Hegels (which, of course, cannot be ruled out a priori). It also makes "The Life of Jesus," "The Positivity of the Christian Religion," and "The Spirit of Christianity" appear to be extremely arbitrary essays in which Hegel tries to impose first Kant and then the Greeks onto the teachings of Jesus.

If, on the other hand, we keep in mind the experimental and fragmentary nature of these essays as well as Hegel's tendency to adopt a point of view disclosing its limits and seeing it point beyond itself, we might see the change or turn in Hegel's thought not as an incomprehensible break but as the disclosure and development of ideas, some of which were already implicit in the early fragments on "Volksreligion," and which may supply the basis from which Hegel moves beyond Kant. Hegel's main opposition to Kant seems to derive from his (Hegel's) inclination toward unity and reconciliation, and intimations of this as well as the emerging view of love, might be found in "Volksreligion." From this point of view, the struggle witnessed in the early theological essays might be seen not so much as a struggle of allegiance to Kant as an attempt to penetrate the actual thinking of his day and in the course of doing so work out some of the implications of Hegel's view of the Greek religion and his belief in the essential unity of experience.

I want now to project my comments beyond Henrich's paper and take up Professor Christensen's suggestion that we attempt to relate Hegel's philosophy of religion to contemporary problems. Hegel can be seen in the theological essays to be struggling over against the tendency of philosophy and theology in his day to relegate God to the unknowable. The kind of agnosticism against which Hegel struggled often appeals to contemporary theologians and philosophers of religion. It is argued explicitly or implicitly that knowledge of God is not so much against reason as it is in a different dimension from reason. This posture makes it possible to maintain a kind of negative natural theology which neither contradicts nor threatens to replace the emphasis of religion on revelation and faith. But it provides no basis from which to speak of God in a significant sense.

One example of this basic problem can be found in the theology of

Rudolf Bultmann.[1] Unlike Karl Barth, Bultmann does not deny a place to natural theology nor does he intend that religious faith call for a *sacrificium intellectus*. However, the only kind of rational or natural knowledge of God that he will permit is a negative one, essentially a knowledge of man's finiteness which at best discloses man's lack of acquaintance with God. Natural knowledge of God is essentially the question of God, which finds its resolution only in the moment of faith. Demythologizing or existential interpretation provides Bultmann with a means for clarifying the meaning of human existence. But the relation to God is ultimately excluded from this analysis. And the only way that Bultmann sees to get beyond a merely negative understanding of God is by means of a yet unclarified view of analogy which seems, in the final analysis, to reduce to mere self-understanding. God remains a transcendent other except to the personal experience of faith.

Karl Jaspers is much more sensitive than Bultmann to the need for a positive relationship between faith and rational understanding but his thought also seems to suffer from the basic problem. Jaspers's searching attack on religious orthodoxy paves the way for a kind of negative knowledge of God in which reason, in the face of its limits, points us into philosopical faith. The cipher is intended to mediate between Existenz and Being. But the cipher seems ultimately to establish only a negative relation to Being, and reason seems to be abandoned to philosophical faith.

Whatever their intentions, Being or God, in the thinking of Bultmann and Jaspers, seems in the final analysis to be lost to the world. I take this general point of view to be at the heart of what we might call an uneasy truce between philosophy and theology in our time and at the heart of the contemporary problem of speaking of God in any meaningful sense. The irony of this situation is that while it has come about in part as the result of a reaction to certain tendencies in Hegel's thought, it may be that the Hegelian approach to God will be seen to supply some of the ingredients by which contemporary thought is able to respond to this problem.

Hegel can be seen in the early period to be struggling with problems very similar to those confronted by theologians and philosophers of religion today. Like Kant he does not wish to ignore the ontological difference between Being and being. But unlike Kant, being or phenomena are understood by Hegel to provide an avenue to Being. The ontological meaning of phenomena may be hidden but it is believed to be approachable by the dialectical method, a method which is itself derivable from experience. We might find here, it seems to me, an empirical anchoring for the discussion of God or Being which is perhaps more consistent with the religious claims to a disclosure of God to man than its Kantian counterparts, and which provides an avenue for moving beyond the subjectivist circle and hence to a more meaningful discussion of God.

If it is feared that this approach would mean the abandonment of the importance of revelation we are reminded that Hegel, no less than Kant, shifted the discussion of religion from an emphasis on propositional truths to the opening up of the believer to the self-disclosure of God. Hegel has no quarrel with the view of truth as disclosure but only with the tendency to mistrust the objective order in such a way as to reduce God to an unknowable. He does not reject the idea of revelation but seeks to comprehend it in a meaningful way, and to get beyond those views of revelation which on the one hand reduce it to propositional truths and on the other hand to private feelings.

To be open to Hegel at this point does not mean that we can or should simply return to Hegel and ignore the tendencies in the Hegelian approach to strip the object of thought of its transcendent character. Jaspers is always there to caution us against this danger. But it may be that we can find in Hegel's thought a beginning point and hence the germ of a philosophical approach to religion which is neither theological nor anti-theological, one which seeks from within religion to disclose its essential meaning and one which may provide a basis in experience for a more meaningful discussion of the idea of God.

NOTES

1. A more detailed analysis of what I have to say here with regard to Bultmann and Jaspers may be found in my *Jaspers and Bultmann: A Dialogue Between Philosophy and Theology in the Existentialist Tradition* (Durham, North Carolina: Duke University Press, 1968).

REPLY TO COMMENTATORS

by

Dieter Henrich

1. Before I discuss the more general and important points made by the commentators of my paper, I shall take further note of my method in this genetic study of the development of a philosopher. My intention is to avoid the disadvantages of two well-known approaches at the same time. One of these is represented by Richard Kroner, the other by Wilhelm Dilthey.

Kroner tried to show that Hegel's mature system was the fulfillment of the speculative development which began with Kant's first critique and climbed, almost like a staircase, in which every step presupposes the next, through the systems of Reinhold, Fichte and Schelling. Against this, which is Hegel's own account of his position in the history of philosophy, one can show that the historical truth is very much different from the systematical relation Hegel himself was able to see. It is more adequate to understand Fichte's, Schelling's and Hegel's systems, including their later versions (Fichte since 1801, Schelling since 1804) as parallel and independent solutions of a set of problems raised and exposed in a period of post-Kantian discussion, in which Fichte played a leading role and in which there was a common awareness of possibilities of a systematic philosophy of which Spinoza was the most promising paradigm.

This revision of the Kroner-interpretation is not only of historical interest: It is the precondition of a new understanding of the intentions and the relevance of the ideas of this epoch, which are not and cannot be adequately and finally expressed in Hegel's own words. And it is only by this interpretation that these ideas may properly be entered in the contemporary discussion and become compatible with experiences in our time.

Dilthey's method, as opposed to Kroner's, is equally untenable.

The chief point here is that the formation of Hegel's system was something in addition to the self-objectivation of a new awareness of life and history. That it was this, I would not deny. On the contrary, the longer one studies the writings and literary remains of the minor thinkers of the time, the more one becomes convinced that there was an almost irresitible tendency to bring concepts like "autonomy," "life," "spirit," and "unification" into the key-positions of philosophical analysis and that Hegel depended so far completely on the view of his generation, which Kant always thought to be simply absurd.

But, as Dilthey has it, one has to say more. The way in which this intellectual process took place was by no means a natural event like an eruption or a blossoming. It was the result of a confrontation, which was philosophical and theological at the same time. And it was brought about in a sequence of discussions which led to a continuous improvement of an understanding of the meaning and the implications of a life guided by the idea of freedom. Hence if we resign from Kroner's method of a speculative reconstruction of Hegel, which avoids the difficulties of an adequate interpretation of his mature work, we need not turn aside, as well, from a philosophical reconstruction of this work. Such a reconstruction offers the additional advantage of not starting with the result as something already given. It can on this account throw a new light on the result; apart from such a reconstruction, we cannot get beyond an immanent interpretation of the writings.

To do this, however, is not as easy as it appears. After a century of genetic studies there is still no getting to the bottom of the matter. For more than two decades we have had highly endowed specialized institutes, like the Hegelarchiv and the Hölderlinarchiv. Even so, however, much is to be gained by the effort. I could not understand anything about the true relation between Kant and Hegel before I started my own holiday-research in the archives, libraries and private collections. But now I think it is much easier than it was before to write a history of the origins of idealism which is historically true, which is also the history of a post-Kantian philosophical discussion, and not merely a broad and comparatively obscure account of the intellectual development of the period.

2. Obviously it has to be asked how one can explain the fact that the tendency of a generation, which seems to be something personal and "subjective," and the issues of a philosophical discussion can point in the same direction and lead to the same results. The answer requires much more than a few remarks I can give here. All keyconcepts of the

new generation are themselves products of a philosophical development which has deep roots in the origins of the modern age. What they found common in Kant and in Spinoza was their emphasis on the self-reference of the human being, whose essence is, like the essence of everything, not the realization of a cosmic order, established by a highest being which incorporates being and order as such. It is basically defined by its relation to itself (in Kantian terms, its autonomy). And the relation to other beings and to the world has to be understood as an implication of its self-reference, not the other way around. On this notion the spirit of the post-Kantian generation and the conceptual framework of philosophy since the Italian renaissance are at one. And because of this the young Kantians could contribute to the clarification and the elaboration of the philosophical project of an anti-Aristotelian age. The relation of time and philosophy is a bit more complicated than an alternative of the subjective-objective kind can allow. I cannot here consider how this matter is to be understood. Of course one can never forget that Hegel was the first who made available conceptual tools to deal with structures such as this.

3. After all one can already expect what my answer will be to the general hermeneutical doubt as to the possibility of genetic studies. I don't question the soundness and the importance of the remark that one should not forget the relation between the texts we are interested in and our own expectations and horizons, which always guide our interpretation. Consideration of this relation is essential if we are to understand the texts adequately. But this does not exclude an interpretaion which renders intelligible basic intentions of an author and fundamental connections between the issues he is dealing with, in such a way that the interpretation is rendered beyond any doubt. It is possible to overcome the limits of our approach to texts of high importance. These depend always on the results a philosopher came to and his strategy and rhetoric with the help of which he tried to convince his own time. It might very well be that he was not successful in preserving or communicating the evidences which made his way of arguing convincing and even necessary for himself. The situation changes when a great philosopher starts talking to his time. It may be expected that he forgets the conditions under which he developed and first justified his ideas, which, independent of their context, become subject to interpretations of all kinds, each claiming to be the true. This is no disadvantage. It is in fact the way in which progress in philosophy can take place. But if historical research is of any importance for philosophy itself, it gives us the chance for an insight into the great philosopher's own progress, which

is not fully disclosed in his final works. We can learn more from him if we see him elaborating (and not only presenting) his views and arguments. This is especially the case where there are unused potentialities in his work hidden in its systematic form and by its early reception, which might be less convincing and revealing than the thoughts he had on the route he traversed. Besides this, it is clear that we get the best possible criterion for adequacy of an interpretation of the final work if we are able to understand them as the solution, however inadequate, of problems with which we know the author was struggling. Without this criterion we lack a decisive weapon against arbitrary and simplifying interpretations and a reason for sustaining one of several proposed competing interpretations. If we don't make the point of hermeneutics carefully, we shall easily find ourselves in the position of having to accept all of these proposals as being equally justified at the same time, a situation which in my opinion is completely untenable.

With all this one does not have to deny that we have to accept certain fundamental ways of understanding and experience as something we share with the historical figure we want to understand, nor that these experiences can become changed by a philosophy and that we can never go back to the origins without knowing about this. In this sense we cannot repeat Hegel's development. But one also should not underestimate the possibilities of philosophical imagination. As human beings we can understand experiences we cannot share. And as philosphers we can follow ideas we can neither invent nor accept. And we are changing our own ideas by doing this; we are at least throwing new light on our own presuppositions and inclinations, whether we find them confirmed or not. If there is a hermeneutic circle, it should not be such a narrow one as only to exclude the most important function of historical criticism in the progress of philosophy. In our communication with the great philosophers, we cannot merely confirm and broaden our own previous insight. We can also correct this previous perspective and bring ourselves to new and unexpected points of view. A narrow circle can neither account for this nor admit it. But such a circle is refuted by the very fact of the success of genetic studies. Nevertheless, a fundamental circularity could be found between that set of concepts like "freedom" and "unity" Hegel and his friends were committed to and our own understanding of them. But this by no means excludes the genetic approach to his work.

I wish I could discuss this in greater detail. But one cannot do everything at once. Even Hegel, who had reasons to try, could not, as we all know. To sum up I can only say I accept most of the questions of Professor Scott as meaningful, and also as very nicely put. But they are too general in the context in which they are asked for discussion of them to alter either the interpretation or the conclusions we can draw from this context.

4. I conclude with some remarks on Professor Long's comments on Bultmann and his relation to Hegel's philosophy of religion. It seems to me that they have more in common than first appears. This can be explained by the relation of both to Kierkegaard. Bultmann's existential interpretation is an analysis of the structures of the human being, which according to him leads to a twofold evidence: 1. That all ways in which men try to stabilize their lives and to broaden the range of their powers are attempts to get a justification of their being in terms of itself. Hence there seems to be a basic need of such a justification. Furthermore, the way in which the justification is sought discloses a deep insight into the impossibility of finding it in this way – a situation which Kierkegaard called "despair." 2. But because of this men are unable to accept their basic situation. They have to hide it from themselves and they will never confess that they are in despair so long as no justification can be found which is different from that which they can seek under the condition of their being in this world.

From this Bultmann proceeds to two conclusions: The insight into the true situation of men must come at the same time in which the offer of a justification is made, which never can be given by men themselves, and which requires the abandoning of all self-justification (καύχησις). It is impossible to imagine that this offer is another dream of a justification made by men. For their imagination is just the means by which they try to hide from themselves their situation of despair.

One can easily see that this theology, which Bultmann has never presented unambiguously, is an ingenious reconstruction of the teaching of St. Paul, very much in accordance with the texts, and at the same time a justification of the revelation by its own content. It is also, like Kierkegaard's analysis of "existence," something like a new version of Hegel's phenomenology, in which subjectivity as the absolute fundament of philosophy and life had to be overcome in order to show that the true absolute requires the sacrifice of the finite subject and its claims to self-fulfillment and independence.

Nevertheless it is far away from Hegel's peculiar idea: it shows the limits of finitude, but it denies that these limits can be understood in terms of that finitude, which the infinite implies in its own essence, such that the despair of men is in the end a condition of God's own self-revelation. Bultmann had to eliminate all neoplatonist implications from original Christianity. And this is of course the only possible exegesis. Hence it turns out that the question as to whether we should prefer Hegel's philosophy of religion or the theology of his professor Storr, revised, refined, but also resurrected via Hegel-Kierkegaard, implies another problem, which is also originally Hegelian: does all that happens depend upon the beginning (Sinclair) or is the beginning only the preliminary form of what is going to happen and to reveal itself (Hegel)?

THE YOUNG HEGEL AND THE POSTULATES OF PRACTICAL REASON

by

H. S. Harris

Wilhelm Dilthey, who was the first student to make a serious attempt to study the genesis of Hegel's thought, claimed that "his theological work as a whole can be adequately summed up as a confrontation with (*Auseinandersetzung mit*) Kant's *Religion Within the Bounds of Reason Alone*." [1] Hearing, the only scholar who has discussed all the early manuscripts more exhaustively than Dilthey, dissents. He will not allow that Kant's influence – or for that matter anyone else's influence, – was really preponderant in Hegel's mind, and he insists that whatever truth there is in Dilthey's dictum depends on giving a definite emphasis to the word *Auseinandersetzung,* which I suspect he wants to take in some such sense as "overcoming" or "getting away from." [2]

The general consensus of learned opinion at the present time lies somewhere between these extremes. T. M. Knox roundly asserts that "With the exception of Th. L. Haering ... readers of Hegel's *Theologische Jugendschriften* have found in the papers written at Berne the dominating influence of Kant." [3] But whereas Dilthey's original generalization applied to the whole period from 1793 to 1800, Knox is speaking only of the three years 1794, 1795, 1796; and he immediately narrows the period of Kant's dominance still further by saying that "Hegel's writings in 1795-6 are inspired almost entirely by (this) essay [i.e., *Religion Within the Bounds of Reason Alone*.]"

No one of these three views is acceptable as it stands. But of the three, the oldest, Dilthey's, is the easiest to modify into a really plausible form. Haering's view flies in the face of obvious and inescapable facts. He is driven to the most curious shifts to explain not just isolated sentences and paragraphs but whole essays, including most notably the only one that has come down to us complete – the so-called "Life of Jesus." The

current view, represented by Knox, leaves us with the awkward problem
of explaining the Kantian hiatus in Hegel's development, since there is a
marked continuity between what Hegel wrote before Christmas 1794 and
what he wrote after Christmas 1795 – it is only really *one* year, not two
as Knox says, that is in question.

Dilthey's view takes the productions of this one year as the key to
everything else, and so the problem of a hiatus does not arise. Knox takes
the work of 1795 as *one* key to all that *follows* (the other one, in his
view, being the Christian doctrine of the Holy Spirit). But he ignores the
continuity of what follows with what went before. He is right, however,
about the need for a second key. Hegel's development is not explicable
simply in terms of his reaction to Kant's philosophy of religion.

Hegel's "theological" writings are concerned with *two* focal problems.
He wishes, first, to make the religion of his own people and his own time
more *alive*, more powerful, more inward and real to people and more
effectively present in their behaviour and their everyday life; and secondly,
to make it more *rational*. These two practical aims resolve in his mind
into one and the same thing, for what he means by reason, *Vernunft*, is
like the knowledge that Socrates spoke of – it exercises both moral
authority, and actual working control over men's lives and behavior.
But if we want to understand his philosophical development it is essential
to distinguish these two aims – the problem of bringing religion to *life*,
and the problem of making it more *rational* – since the theoretical inspiration behind them is distinct. The young Hegel had no interest in philosophical problems as such – indeed he sometimes evinces open contempt
for the theoretical disputes of philosophers. The reason why he eventually
became a great philosopher in spite of this is that he was always very
clear headed and very sensitive to the *practical* importance of fine theoretical distinctions. The main reason students have failed to understand his
development is because, not realizing this, they do not read him *closely*
enough. Haering, with his enormous book in which a great part of the
material is gone over sentence by sentence, is a prime example of this
fault.

Hegel's conception of *living* religion derives from Greek sources;
whereas his conception of *rational* religion comes from the French and
German enlightenment – from Rousseau, from Mendelssohn's *Jerusalem,*
and especially from Lessing's play, *Nathan the Wise.* It is probable, I
think, that the idea of a connection between these two very different
traditions first occurred to Hegel as a schoolboy when he read the *Phaedo*
of Moses Mendelssohn, along with that of Plato, at the Gymnasium. Both

from *Emile* and from *Nathan* he got the idea that there is a certain religion of reason, which all truly pious and reflective men have aspired to in all ages and all societies; and from Mendelssohn came the further idea that there are certain identifiable basic elements in this religion of reason, and hence in all "true" religion – notably the conceptions of God as a just judge, and of the immortality of the human soul.

In his last year at the theological seminary at Tübingen, he managed to get leave of absence – apparently on grounds of illness though I suspect his sickness was mainly intellectual in nature – for a large part of the summer; and it was now, as he approached his twenty-third birthday, that he made his first attempt to write down his ideas on the subject of the reform of religion. It is certain that at the seminary he had studied the KdrV with considerable care and attention. It is probable that he had read both of the other Critiques (but perhaps not with equal care and attention). When he began to work out his ideas he had by him two books – the recently published *Critique of all Revelation,* (which appeared at Easter 1792, and was acknowledged by Fichte in Autumn), and the older work of Moses Mendelssohn, *Jerusalem, or Religious Power and Judaism,* (May 1783). He must also have read Kant's *Religion* (1793) by this time, though the earliest direct evidence that he was making a close study of this work as a whole comes from the manuscripts of the next year (1794).

In his first essay Hegel lays down three canons which a satisfactory "Folk-religion" (his term for the kind of *living* religion that he is interested in) must meet. The theoretical canon, with which we are here concerned, is that "Its doctrines must be grounded in universal reason." [4] From what he says, it is apparent that "universal reason" embraces a set of practical principles which must be both very few and very simple, although he also holds that they cannot be finally and completely expressed in verbal statement and argument. There are apparently *three* rational principles that he feels sure about: the existence of God, the immortality of the soul; and the reality of divine providence. It is clear furthermore that his confidence rests on the agreement of the Judaic tradition, the Greek tradition, the Christian tradition, and the latest philosophical tradition of "rational religion."

Among the three postulates of reason, as we may as well call them, Hegel pays most attention to the postulate of Providence; and he clearly feels that only the Greeks really understood the nature and limits of Divine Providence. We may fairly summarize the history of Hegel's early theological ideas by saying that it is the story of how all the other postulates were gradually resolved into what he thought of as the *Greek* concept of Providence – though the book of *Job* may possibly have helped as much as anything else to crystallize it in his mind, or at least to crystallize for him the errors of Christian theology and of Kant. Putting it another way, we can say that Hegel's development is the story of how the Kantian *praktische Vernunft* is gradually assimilated to and absorbed into the Greek conception of reason as the self-sufficient virtue. But the young Hegel is loyal to Kant against the Greek philosophers in one respect. It is always for him *practical* reason that is autonomous, and in the end self-sufficient; it is φρόνησις, not σοφία that is the supreme virtue of the complete life.

The principles of rational religion, Hegel thought, are very few and very simple. Yet they cannot be adequately expressed in discursive form. The full story of why he believed that the postulates of reason cannot be put into words is a complicated one.[5] The fundamental practical reason for this impossibility, however, is quite simple and easy to state. The postulates, if they are postulates of *reason,* must be *innate* in the Platonic sense. That is to say, they do not depend upon any acquired knowledge. Our consciousness of them is elicited by actual moral experience. As genuine *postulates* of *reason* – as opposed to mere propositions of the understanding – they are the crown and culmination of moral virtue itself. Hence it was peculiarly appropriate from Hegel's point of view that Socrates should not have attempted to expound them verbally until he reached the last day of a long life wholly devoted to the pursuit of virtue, and that he should have expounded them not publicly (in court, for instance) but privately in a company of intimate friends devoted to the same pursuit. In a fragment of 1794 Hegel contrasts the argument of the *Phaedo* with the Christian miracle of the Resurrection in a way which already clearly indicates his commitment to the principle of the "self-sufficiency of reason in a complete life":

> before his death he [i.e. Socrates] spoke with his disciples about the immortality of the soul, as a Greek does speak, to reason and to fancy (both together) – he spoke in such a living way, he brought this hope so close, so convincingly before them in its whole essence, (and) they had been assembling the premises for this postulate in their whole lives. This hope – (for) it contradicts human nature and the capacity of our spirit, that so much should be given us as to raise it to a certainty – he enlivened even to the point — (for) so the human spirit forgetting its mortal companion [i.e. the body] can exalt itself — that even if it should come to

pass that he rose as a spirit from his grave, and brought us greeting from the Avenging Goddess – [the reference here is to Schiller's ode "Resignation," but Hegel is not sure whether he wants to use it, for he proceeds to write down several alternative continuations of his sentence] – that he should give us more to hear than the tables of Moses and the oracles of the prophets which we have in our hearts – that even if this [i.e. his doctrine?] were to have been contrary to the laws of human nature – he would not have thought it necessary to strengthen it through Resurrection – only in poor spirits who have not the premises of this hope alive in themselves — that is the ideal (*Idee*) of virtue and of the highest good – is the hope of immortality itself, also weak.[6]

Obviously no verbal argument, or theory — such as Kant's *CPracR* for example – can possibly be conclusive, if reason itself operates only on this "existential" level with "premises" of the sort here referred to. But equally obviously Hegel is not criticizing Kant or quarrelling with him: rather indeed, he is providing his own account of why Kant's distinction between theoretical knowledge (of the understanding) and practical faith (of reason) is both right and necessary.

This was the stage that his reflections about Kant's moral proof had reached when he began to correspond with Schelling at Christmas 1794. In order to understand what follows – and also to see why Hegel himself became so preoccupied about the "postulates" of practical reason – it is necessary to know just a little about the way in which Kant's philosophy was interpreted at the seminary (where Schelling was still a student). The dominant figure at the *Tübingenstift* was the theologian G. C. Storr who expounded the New Testament as a body of revealed truth whose divine origin was guaranteed; first, by the fact that its moral content was in perfect agreement with the highest ideals of our reason; and secondly, by the miraculous power displayed by Jesus, the agent through whom the revelation was made. The Kantian critique of reason was adduced in support of this view, first, by Storr's disciple, the philosopher J. F. Flatt, and later by Storr himself,[7] who was finishing his great manual of dogmatic theology just when Kant's *Religion* was published. Flatt took *KdrV* as the decisive refutation of reason's pretensions to solve the metaphysical problems, which rational men nevertheless cannot help posing and requiring an answer for; and he pointed to Storr's doctrine of revelation as the only possible source for the required answers. Storr, in 1793, was able to support this contention by underlining certain problems which the frank admission of radical evil, and the consequent unbridgeable gap between the moral will and the holy will, created for Kant's rational theology. Knowledge of the forgiveness of sins can *only* come by revelation. Yet without that knowledge how could the most resolute believer in the postulates of practical reason escape despair? In general Storr's rational justification of revelation is all contained in the claim that only through revelation can we be preserved from moral despair. The passion with which Hegel clung to the Greek ideal of reason as that which is self-sufficient is very largely explained by his indignant rejection of this argument from human weakness.[8] But, on the other hand, his own firm distinction between the simple intuitions of reason and the subtleties of the understanding (even where he believed it was correctly employed, as in the philosophy of Kant) rested partly on his recognition that Storr was justified in replying to Kant's claim that a historically based faith cannot be a requirement of reason, since much special skill and scholarly training is needed before any estimate of its rationality could be attempted, with a *tu quoque*. (Storr's retort to Kant was that the majority of believers are equally dependent on the authority of the learned with respect to the fundamental doctrines of natural or rational religion.)

Hegel, Hölderlin, Schelling, and no doubt all the other young radicals in the *Stift*, were enraged by this perversion of Kant – which Kant could do nothing about because, as he said in the preface to his second edition in 1794, "of the difficulties which age sets particularly in the way of working out abstract ideas." This indignation against their own teachers, along with their enthusiasm for the ideals of the French Revolution, were the two things which bound Hegel and Schelling together at this time. In his first letter (Christmas Eve, 1794), Hegel naturally asked Schelling for news of old friends and of how things were in general at Tübingen; and in doing so he indicated his own belief that the reaction of Storr and his school would not in the end prevent Kant's philosophy of religion from bearing more worthy fruit. This was the point in Hegel's letter that aroused Schelling's interest. Schelling's reply consists almost entirely of a violently ironic and sarcastic attack on the Tübingen Kantians, with a paean in praise of Fichte to provide a sort of descant. His irony reached its highest pitch in the following sentences: "It's a delight to see how they can tie the moral proof onto their string. Before one knows it out jumps the god from the machine – the personal, individual being who reigns above in Heaven." [9]

Anyone who has read the encomium of Socrates' discourse in the *Phaedo* quoted above, will understand how disturbed and bewildered

Hegel must have felt about this remark. For we can now see that the encomium was itself largely animated by his rejection of the Tübingen doctrine that miracles are a necessary complement of reason; and he had no desire to be associated with the hosts of the orthodox. But it had never occurred to him that the object of the "moral proof" could be anything else but a "personal individual being reigning in heaven" (i.e., in the super-sensible world). So, rather cautiously, he asked Schelling for an explanation; and, although Schelling was surprised in his turn, he duly provided it:

> For me, [wrote Schelling], the highest principle of all philosophy is the pure absolute Ego, i.e. the Ego in so far as it is simply Ego, not yet conditioned by objects, but posited through freedom. The Alpha and Omega of all philosophy is Freedom. – The absolute Ego embraces an infinite sphere of absolute being in (which) finite spheres form themselves, which arise through the limiting of the infinite sphere by an object (spheres of *existence* – theoretical philosophy). In these there is strict causal dependence (*lauter Bedingtheit*), and the unconditioned (*das Unbedingte*) leads to contradictions. – But we *ought* to break through these limits, i.e. we ought to emerge out of the finite spheres into the infinite one (*practical* philosophy). This [i.e., practical philosophy] requires therefore the destruction of finiteness and leads us thereby into the supersensible world. "What theoretical reason was incapable of, whereas it was weakened *by the object,* that practical reason achieves." But in this [i.e., practical reason?] we can find nothing but our absolute Ego, since only this [the absolute Ego] has described the infinite sphere. There is no supersensible world for us except that of the absolute Ego. – God is nothing but the absolute Ego, the Ego in as much as it has annihilated everything theoretical [i.e., all intelligible limits], is thus equal to zero in theoretical philosophy. Personality arises through the unity of consciousness. But consciousness is not possible without an object; but for God, i.e., for the absolute Ego (,) there is no object at all since thereby [i.e., if there were one] it would cease to be absolute, – hence there is no personal God and our highest striving is for the destruction of our personality, the transition to the absolute sphere of being, which however is not *possible* in all eternity; – hence (there is) only (a) practical approaching toward the Absolute, and hence – Immortality.[10]

Hegel was probably as puzzled as any present-day reader by this strange doctrine of an impersonal Absolute Ego within which our personal consciousness is contained, and which provides, so to speak, the moral horizon of our world. The idea that the moral aim of life is the destruction of our finite personality, was not at all likely to appeal to him; and for this reason Schelling's way of deducing the postulate of immortality could never satisfy him. But the resolution of the *postulate* of God into the elementary moral facts of freedom and the awareness of practical reason itself – that he *could* appreciate, and he fairly soon adopted it as his own. He even began, rather tentatively, to use the vocabulary of the "Absolute Ego" and the "finite ego," though his declared view in his answer to Schelling (April 16, 1795, *Briefe* I, 24) was that all such metaphysical theories were bound to remain the esoteric concern of a minority of technical philosophers.[11]

Hegel's adoption of Schelling's conception of God is fairly plain in the opening paragraph of the "Life of Jesus" (9 May, 1795). This passage purports to be an explication of the meaning of the opening verses of St. John's Gospel, but it is also quite transparently an exoteric version of the esoteric theory of the Absolute Ego:

> Reason, pure and incapable of any limits is the God-head itself – According to Reason therefore is the plan of the world in general ordered; Reason it is which teaches man to recognize his vocation, and the unconditional purpose of his life; often indeed it is obscured but never wholly quenched, even in the darkness he has always retained a faint glimmer of it. Among the Jews it was John who made men conscious of this their dignity – which ought not to be something foreign to them, but which is to be sought for in itself, in their true self, not in their lineage and not in the urge towards happiness. It is not to be sought in being servants of man greatly revered [scil. explicitly Moses, or implicitly Jesus himself] but in the development of the divine spark which has been allotted to them which bears witness to them, that in a sublime sense they are the children of God. – The development of Reason is the unique source of truth and peace of mind, which John certainly did not proclaim as belonging exclusively or exceptionally to him, but which on the contrary all men could open up in themselves.[12]

Just after he finished the "Life of Jesus" Hegel heard from Schelling again, – a very downcast letter accompanied by Schelling's second philosophical essay "On the Ego as the First Principle of Philosophy, or Concerning the Unconditioned Element in Human Knowledge." It is unmistakable that Hegel's main object in his reply is to cheer Schelling up; and since Schelling's unhappiness stemmed from the mistreatment of his own first essay by reviewers and from the academic clouds that had begun to hang over Fichte, Hegel certainly had good reason to make much of, and perhaps to exaggerate, what he for his part had learned from both Fichte and Schelling and especially from the latter. But what he says appears to correspond exactly with the facts as far as we can check them, so I think it is reasonable to accept all of it as true.[13] He tells Schelling that if his latest discussion of the moral proof does not make the Tübingen Kantians see the error of their ways, nothing will. Of his own debt he says:

> I once conceived the plan of making clear to myself in an essay, what it may mean, "to draw near to God," and thought therein to find satisfaction for the postulate that practical reason governs the world of appearances, and of the other postulates. Your work has clarified in a most masterly and satisfying way what floated before me vague and undeveloped.[14]

The "postulate that practical reason governs the realm of appearances" seems to be identical with what Hegel elsewhere (both earlier and later) designates as "Providence." Certainly he did not stop reflecting and revising his ideas about that. But we must take it that he thinks Schelling has settled, at least, what the Kantian postulate of the ultimate harmony between the realm of nature and the realm of ends means, and hence what the proposition "Virtue Deserves Happiness" really implies.[15]

What Schelling says about this is contained precisely in the passage which Hegel thinks has settled the hash of the Tübingen theologians once and for all. After going through Kant's table of the categories making inferences about the Absolute Ego Schelling says:

> From these deductions it is clear, that the causality of the *infinite* Ego absolutely cannot be represented as Morality, Wisdom, etc., but only as absolute Power, which fills all infinity and suffers nothing to resist it in its sphere, not even the non-Ego represented as infinite: and that the moral law itself only gains sense and meaning for its whole embodiment in the world of sense in relation to a higher law of being, which as opposed to the law of freedom can be called the natural law. Certainly some people will not be

happy with these deductions ... those who have strung such a multitude of postulates of happiness back on to the Kantian letters, and on the one and only point of their empirical system which he seemed to have left standing ... or those who can believe that Kant holds a knowledge to be possible in practical philosophy which he holds to be impossible in theoretical philosophy, so that in the practical sphere the supersensible world (God etc.,) can once more be represented as something external to the Ego ...[16]

On this view the postulated harmony between natural and moral law reduces to the claim that the *possibility* of a moral order (which it is our duty to establish in the world) presupposes the *actual existence* of a natural order. Schelling is able to eliminate all questions about "happiness" in the ordinary sense of the word because he accepts the Kantian conception of an unachievable holiness as the only source of abiding happiness or satisfaction for a rational being and postulates an eternity of asymptotic approach to this ideal.

There is no shadow of evidence that Hegel accepted this conception of the final good of man now, any more than he accepted it when Schelling first put it to him. Throughout his life he consistently rejected what we may call the ascetic approach to rational self-sufficiency. A rationally self-sufficient life meant to him one in which all the capacities of human nature are exercised and developed to the full, and all natural desires are harmonized and satisfied in accordance with reason. He always recognized that only a *rational* society could be self-sufficient in this sense, and what he learned from Schelling in the present passage was the way in which Kant's conception of practical reason could be reconciled with Aristotle's. Briefly, practical reason in Kant's sense is the reason of the Greeks as it applies to the life of the individual citizen. The ideal of "holiness" is the standard by which rational individuals measure what can, and where necessary should, be sacrificed for the sake of moral freedom. Through Schelling's interpretation of the harmony of nature and morality Hegel was finally able to justify in terms of practical reason what he had always regarded as the valid intuition of the Greeks concerning the distinction between "fate" and "providence." We are all of us subject to the might of natural forces which may frustrate our plans, and even destroy us. We have no moral right to complain about this, or to demand to be comforted or recompensed for it in our religion. This is not the realm of "providence" at all, but of "fate" which is mightier even than Father Zeus. Toward the power of fate we must cultivate an attitude of stoic resignation; above all we must preserve, as Job did, the sense of our own dignity in relation to it, the sense of the distinction between fate and providence, of the difference between the moral freedom of the spirit and the blind necessity of nature.

So when Hegel tells Schelling that his essay has clarified the postulate that "practical reason governs the realm of appearances," I think we can say that he accepts Schelling's analysis, not merely as the correct interpretation of Kant, but as the truth *simpliciter*; whereas in the matter of "drawing near to God" Hegel only accepts Schelling's view as being the truth about Kant's ethics.[17]

The first essay in which Hegel himself *uses* Schelling's doctrine of how practical reason governs the phenomenal realm is a fragment about "positive faith" written in December 1795 or January 1796. His aim in this essay was to uncover the essential presuppositions of any attempt to ground religious faith upon the acceptance of divine authority, and at the same time to show that the reasons which lead theologians – and particularly the theologians of Tübingen – to try to do this are not good reasons for doing it. He had already proved in a previous essay ("The Positivity of the Christian Religion") that there could not possibly be a sufficient moral ground for basing religious faith upon a duty of obedience to authority, because we cannot choose to believe or not to believe as we can choose to act or not to act, and hence we cannot *obediently* choose to believe or *disobediently* refuse to believe something. There is, however, as he now goes on to show, a false belief of a very special kind, which we may come to accept, and which will lead us to think of belief itself as a matter of duty. We can discover this by examining the difference between a "positive" religious faith and any ordinary belief accepted "upon authority." A piece of historical evidence accepted (or "believed") upon the testimony of some earlier historian is accepted on the basis of a prior estimate of his trustworthiness, which we are (or should be) prepared to defend if it is challenged. But acceptance of *God's* authority can only rest, in the first instance, upon recognition of his absolute power. As we advance *toward* wisdom we become aware (perhaps) of God's beneficence, and we may eventually comprehend that He is the very source of truth. But only the *fear* of the Lord can be there when we take our first steps toward wisdom.

There is no question, Hegel thinks, but that we ought to "fear the Lord" (as for instance Job did). Everyone must recognize under *some* name – whether it be "Nature," "Fate" or "Providence" – a power which has absolute mastery over the whole realm of his natural desires.

But anyone who allows this supremacy to extend to his spiritual concerns, will be compelled to accept some "positive" faith in order to satisfy the essential demands of his own reason; and if he feels compelled to accept it, he will also feel an equal compulsion to demand that everyone else should accept it likewise.

The mistake, however, lies in supposing that reason "requires" anything lying within the scope of the almighty power. How does this confusion of our sensible needs with rational requirements arise? "How does Reason, in the postulate of the harmony of happiness and virtue (*Sittlichkeit*) which is found among all peoples and has become especially famous in recent times, come to demand something which it recognizes to be independent of itself and not rationally determinable"? [18] The answer is that this is a transitional stage in moral development. Where the moral will exists in a mind dominated by sensible needs and desires, its command is bound to be interpreted as the condition of sensible happiness. Once this transitional phase is over, once reason itself attains full and proper mastery, a man may sacrifice his whole sensible existence – his "life" – for an ideal of honour or patriotism – "and only in our times," says Hegel caustically, "have men been able to say 'that man was worthy of a better fate.' " [19]

The inference at this point would seem to be that the rational individual does not *need* to save his life; and in that case the postulate of immortality can be dispensed with altogether. But in fact Hegel has not yet done with it. For there is an element of what we may call the eudaemonist fallacy present even in the patriotic self-sacrifice of the virtuous citizen in an ancient republic. In his next essay, written sometime between April and August of 1796, Hegel begins at last to face the problem of how the doctrine of the *Phaedo* is related to his social ideal. The whole context of his discussion is once more explicitly Graeco-Roman as it was in the fragmentary essays of 1793 and 1794. The "Kantian interlude" which opened with Schelling's letter of February 4, 1795, appears now to be over. But, as we have seen, that interlude is only like the exposed tip of an iceberg. Underneath it lies Hegel's lifelong commitment to the optimistic faith of the Enlightenment in the power of human reason, and in the perfectibility of man through education. What he found in the philosophy of Kant, in particular, was the first perfectly self-conscious (philosophically clear and consistent) formulation of the meaning of *human dignity*. The essential moral freedom and absolute autonomy of the individual human being were for him the absolutely primary values on which everything else must be based. All of his early "theological" writings were part of a campaign against the surrendering of man's birthright in return for comfort against the changes and chances of mortal life, through the eventual receipt of a mess of pottage in the heaven of a benevolent despot. He admired the Greeks – and the Romans, but more especially the Greeks – because they did not look for comforts or rewards of this kind, but were ready if they had to, to die for their city. He agreed with Schelling that it was only through the experience of voluntary sacrifice that one "drew near to God." We might say that whereas Kant took the experience of *temptation* as the fundamental experience in which freedom and the moral law are revealed to us, Hegel chose rather to ground moral experience in our discovery of the capacity for voluntary *self-sacrifice*. The terms "temptation" and "sacrifice" refer of course to different aspects of the same experience – both terms may be equally applicable either as descriptions or in descriptions of the same moral situation – but a great deal hangs on which of them we take to be fundamental. Thus while Kant could speak of moral evil as an obvious, ineliminable or *radical* element in our moral experience, Hegel would never find it necessary to concede to it any such status. The desires that tempt us into sin are not in themselves evil. It is not therefore evil but only natural for us to feel tempted.[20] To overcome a temptation is to *sacrifice* the desire. And, where the desire is a natural one, it deserves to be satisfied; thus the only thing that can justify a sacrifice of this sort is the recognition of some greater good that will be achieved or preserved by it. Where that good is a *universal* good (i.e. where it pertains somehow to my moral universe as a whole, and is not just the satisfaction of some other more urgent desire of mine) the sacrifice is an act of moral freedom. Such an act brings us "nearer to God" because "sacredness" is the distinctive quality of the *universal* good which we recognize to possess an absolutely overriding value. The Supreme God of an ancient patriot was the tutelary deity of his city because it was for the city that he was prepared to die. But he was only ready to die for it because it was the visible presence of his god in the world, the visible embodiment of the good life, the visible fulfillment of all the postulates of practical reason.

All the postulates? Alas, not so. For the city is not, after all, immortal. The City of Athens between the Persian War and the war with Sparta achieved the ideal condition in which every citizen was a free autonomous individual, every one was human in his own way, and all the capacities of human nature were completely and harmoniously realized. "Good men acknowledged in their own case the duty of being good, yet at the same time they respected other people's freedom not to be so, and hence they did not set up either a divine moral code, or one which they had made or abstracted themselves to be exacted from others." [21] But this divine living thing, this *Anti-Leviathan,* like its mechanical Hobbesian opposite, was only after all a mortal God. The city too, lies in the realm of fate. When Socrates was put to death Athens' moment of glory passed; and with the triumph of Imperial Rome the Πόλις perished from the earth. It was natural therefore that Cato of Utica should commit suicide when the Roman Republic gave way to the Empire since with the overthrow of the free constitution of his country, his life in this world lost all meaning for him; [22] but it was also a sign of rationality that he turned to study the *Phaedo* on the last day of his life. The destruction of what had hitherto been the highest order of things in his eyes, made plain to him the necessity for a "higher order." [23]

In view of the context in which this remark occurs one might almost be tempted to take it as ironical, for in the body of the essay Hegel explains the triumph of Christianity over paganism in terms of the disappearance of political freedom, which made men feel utterly powerless in the grip of fate so that they threw themselves upon the mercy of the unknown God, and eagerly embraced the promise of happiness in the world to come in return for blind faith in this one. But on the one side there is the stark contrast between Socrates and the resurrected Christ that Hegel set before us in 1794; and on the other side there is his reinterpretation of the Resurrection in "The Spirit of Christianity and its Fate" (1798) to assure us that Hegel is still quite serious about the independent existence of a higher spiritual order which is removed altogether from the power of fate.

Concerning the general relation of "The Spirit of Christianity," the last and greatest of Hegel's early essays (that we possess), to Kant's ethics, T. M. Knox has already written very well. To fasten upon a particular passage in which Hegel's interpretation of the immortality of the soul is clearly and unambiguously expounded does not seem to be possible. Whatever the reasons – and I believe I know them although I cannot expound them here – it is an undoubted fact that this essay, masterpiece though it certainly is, is almost as sibylline in some ways as anything which Hegel wrote later. In that respect it is unlike most of the earlier pieces which are in general difficult to interpret only because they are fragmentary.

As far as I can understand it, however, Hegel's doctrine of the "higher order" is as follows: the spiritual realm, the realm of freedom in which *Vernunft* is self-sufficient is not at all like any ordinary conception of the "other world," or of the "after life." As we should, perhaps, expect by this time, the life of the spirit is strictly a function of life in this world. It is, quite simply, the immortal aspect of life in this world, the aspect which makes human history eternally available. It would be misleading here to speak of "personal" immortality; [24] but on the other hand it is not simply a kind of impersonal reason which is immortal either (as for instance in Spinoza's conception of God). The "spirit" which is immortal is neither personal nor impersonal but rather supra-personal or, to speak more intelligibly, *inter*-personal. Thus "the Greek spirit" is immortal, and Socrates the son of Sophroniscus of the deme Alopece is immortal in it. His immortality is an essential element in the Greek spirit. The Greek spirit achieves immortality, it becomes real *as a spirit*, when I now as a living person succeed in entering into his life and thought as it was. Athena is the immortal spirit of Athens; but we do not enter into *her* life and thought, because she never did live and think as we do. Her life *is* where anyone studies with informed sympathy the funeral oration in Thucydides (for instance). The great advance of the Christian religion over Greek religion when, after more than a decade of reflection, Hegel was at last able to identify it, lies in the fact that in the Christian God this dependence of the divine life upon human life, the dependence of the immortal spirit on the finite historical individual, is made explicit. Athena was never a real woman; but Jesus was a real man. And the record of his life, as contrasted with, for instance, the myths about the deeds of Hercules, shows us a man who was deliberately and consciously trying to make clear to his fellows just what the divine or immortal aspect of humanity is. Thus his apotheosis is not, like that of Hercules, the revelation of a natural power in its immortal aspect, but the revelation of the divinity of the human spirit as such.[25]

It is worth pointing out finally, although, as far as I know, Hegel never made this point, that the immortality of the spirit remains a *postulate*, and in the nature of things it *must* remain so. The postulate of God is completely resolved into the experienced *facts* of moral freedom and the recognition of duty; and the postulate of divine justice, the postulate of happiness as the reward of virtue, is eliminated altogether; but the postulate of immortality, although it suffers radical transformation, remains just that – a postulate. This becomes evident when we reflect on the fact that Hegel's own understanding of "the Greek spirit" has been challenged. Whether the challenge is ultimately justified or not makes no difference – indeed it is precisely the impossibility of giving a definite meaning to "ultimate justification" here that reveals the difficulty. The point is that everything on the "spiritual" level is eternally subject to criticism and reformulation. Any claim to have "understood" Socrates – or Hegel for that matter – finally and definitively, would be nonsensical. Most of the traditional problems about "other minds" arise from this "postulated" character of the spirit. Hegel, who remained all his life as resolutely commonsensical as Hume about purely intellectual scepticism, cheerfully brushes all such theoretical doubt aside. When we read the *Phaedo* he would say, we *know* whether we understand it or not, even if there are some things in it that we are not very sure about. But if some one said to him, "still, there is no such thing as final or perfect understanding here," he would retort in all probability, even more brusquely, that *of course* there cannot be such a thing as "final" understanding here, since that would reduce the immortal *life* of the spirit to the dead *eternity* of natural law. To suppose that the life of the spirit could be a known fact in *that* sense would be to raise once more the awful spectre of the divine despot. Hence the spiritual life which is *primarily* a matter of fact for me – inasmuch as, for example, I really do know what Hegel and his friends thought and felt in the *Stift* at Tübingen between 1791 and 1793, when I read their letters and manuscripts – must often appear to be only a postulate in the eyes of someone else, who is not convinced by my account of the life they led. He may even be able to convince me that what I take to be reality is only a figment of my imagination. The spirit, which is neither I nor he, has its life precisely in this dialectic of fact and postulate, in the disagreement between us and in the continuous dissolution of such disagreements.

NOTES

1. *Righby, Werke*, IV, p. 61.
2. Theodor L. Haering, *Hegel: Sein Wollen und Sein Werk*, two volumes (Stuttgart: Scientia Verlag, Aalen, 1963).
3. T. M. Knox, "Hegel's Attitude to Kant's Ethics," *Kant-Studien*, 49 (1957-58), pp. 70-81.
4. *HtJ*, p. 20.
5. Hegel's view seems to have been based on a philosophy of language which he never wrote out, because he had no interest in theoretical issues as such, and which, for the same reason, he may not even have thought about in any great detail. If he had tried to develop it he would probably have found that his assumptions were too simplistic to be quite workable; but instead he adopted the *KdrV*, lock, stock, and barrel as his theoretical philosophy, supplementing it, where necessary, with one or two principles derived from his own prior reflections.
6. *HtJ*, p. 34. The reason so many alternatives are packed into the last sentence is most probably because Hegel wished to contrast Socrates and Greek philosophical

reflection with *both* Moses and Jesus, representing the positive religions of Judaism and Christianity and the positive principles of authority and miracle. He simply noted down all the contrasts in his mind without trying to make a readable sentence.

7. *Annotations quaedam theologicae ad philosophicam Kantii de religione doctrinam.* This work was immediately translated into German (*Philosophische Bemerkungen* etc.) by C. F. Susskind, a *Repetent* in the *Stift.* Susskind added to his translation an essay of his own in which he applied the general principles and methods of Storr's school to Fichte's *Critique of All Revelation.*

8. But he eventually used something very like Storr's argument against Kant's conception of practical reason (in "The Spirit of Christianity").

9. *Briefe,* I, p. 14.

10. *Briefe,* I, p. 22.

11. For Hegel's attempt to adapt the new terminology of Fichte and Schelling to his own uses see the fragment "Die transzendente Idee von Gott," *HtJ*, pp. 361f.

12. *HtJ*, p. 75.

13. Hegel seems always to have had a very Kantian attitude toward the truth – he might not say *all* he felt, but he had no truck with "white lies."

14. *Briefe,* I, p. 29.

15. The proposition "Virtue deserves happiness" is the central concern of the sheet of notes on "The Transcendental Idea of God" mentioned in note 11. I suspect, therefore, that those notes were all that Hegel ever did toward the essay "on what it means to draw near to God."

16. *Werke,* I, pp. 201f. In his essay Schelling goes through the whole table of the categories making deductions about the Absolute Ego. It is interesting therefore that Hegel in offering his only criticism chooses to query the application of the concept of substance rather than an earlier one, on the elmentary ground that the categories have no legitimate application at this noumenal level. He is worried obviously lest the new theology should at this point decay into another form of the old ontology.

17. Alternatively we can, if we wish to, say that there is a sense in which Kant's doctrine as interpreted by Schelling really is the truth about "drawing near to God"; but then we must add that "drawing near to God" is not for Hegel, as it was for Kant, Fichte and the young Schelling, the ultimate purpose of human existence. It is only one phase or "moment" in the achievement of that purpose. We shall see what this alternative means in the sequel.

18. *HtJ*, p. 237.

19. *HtJ*, p. 238.

20. This does not mean that "evil is unreal." Natural desires can be corrupted or perverted, and in that case the temptations they pose are evil, not natural. But evil is not "radical"; it has no place in the original constitution of "nature."

21. *HtJ*, p. 223; Knox trans., p. 155. Nothing reveals more clearly than this comment the gulf between the moral rigorism of Kant, Fichte and the young Schelling and the ideal of natural spontaneity which Hegel inherited from Rousseau. As I pointed out in an earlier note, we can argue if we wish that Schelling really did clarify for Hegel what "drawing near to God" meant – but this "drawing near to God" was not in itself the end of man.

22. *HtJ*, p. 362.

23. *HtJ*, p. 223; Knox trans., p. 155.

24. Hegel does have a doctrine of the "immortality of the soul" in the Greek sense of "soul." The life-lines through which the species perpetuates itself are immortal souls that are basic constituents of our world. But this doctrine is part of his *Greek* heritage (compare *HtJ*, p. 339; Knox trans., pp. 297f).

25. Hegel uses this example *against* Christianity in the "Spirit of Christianity."

(*HtJ*, p. 335; Knox trans., p. 293 – but Knox mistranslates *ungeheure Verbindung* because he cannot believe his own eyes.) The Greeks did not worship the hero in his torment; and Hegel was still not ready in 1800 to regard the crucified Jesus as a proper image of the divine life.

COMMENT ON

H. S. Harris

The Young Hegel and the Postulates of Practical Reason

by

Warren E. Steinkraus

Unlike other scholars who see in Hegel's early writings either a fore-shadowing of his mature works or a level of insight later abandoned,[1] Professor Harris treats the *Jugendschriften* as intrinsically interesting material in the intellectual biography of a great philosopher. Among his many fascinating observations, he notes that the young Hegel sought to make religion more *alive* and more *rational*. He derived his idea of living religion from the Greeks and his idea of rational religion from the Enlightenment.

Now Kant's idea of living religion – which eventually led to his postulates of the practical reason – was doubtless prompted by his pietistic home experience. Evidence does not suggest that Hegel's early home life was characterized by any sort of warm Christian feeling. Kant always had a strong sense of his connection with ordinary people and had a lively appreciation of what he owed his parents. Hegel treated religion as an object for study. His father was something of a free-thinker [2] and Hegel "does not seem to have been very close to him." [3] His mother died when he was thirteen and even as late as September 20, 1820, the anniversary of her death, he wrote his sister: *"Heute ist der Jahrestag unserer Mutter, den ich immer im Gedächtniss behalte."* [4] But there is no direct indication that Hegel's early home life had the kind of strict conscientiousness and earnest piety which Kant saw every day.[5] If anything, it was a staid formal Lutheranism. Kant always respected Pietism; Hegel spurned and criticized it.

Is there any wonder then that an alert young student should find more appeal in the Greeks than in the apparently wooden catechetical Christianity he found as a child? He became far more familiar with the ways of the Greeks and the Romans in his Gymnasium days than he ever did with Biblical thought. Caird remarks: "The elective affinity which thus drew Hegel to the pure undefiled well of Greek art lay very deep in his nature." [6] Whereas Greek thought was mediated to him in all its intrinsic charm, his knowledge of Biblical thought and experience was filtered through the strained categories of orthodoxy. "Early penetrated by the nobility and beauty of Greece," says Rosenkranz, "he never could recognize genuine Christianity in a form which excludes the earnest serenity of antique art." [7]

By a living religion, Hegel meant one that was "more inward and real to people and more effectively present in their behavior and their everyday life." Greek religion was like this and became an ideal type for Hegel. Though a serious student, he did not observe living religion in his own time which approached this Greek type, e.g. that found among the Moravians, the Mennonites, and the Quakers. He knew more about Zeus than he did about William Penn, whose American colony surely illustrated *Volksreligion*. The whole of England was changed by the Wesleys in the eighteenth century but Hegel derived his idea of living religion from the dead Greeks. Whatever one may think about the movements mentioned, they were forms of Christianity which deeply affected the total lives of their adherents and had direct influence on community practices. Indeed, they arose in part as reactions to the dead religion of official Christianity which Hegel himself had found wanting.

His idealization of Greek religion is thus due in part to overlooking certain forms of vital religious experience prevalent in his day. The *Jugendschriften* might well have been called, Caird suggests, "Studies of Jewish and Christian religion from a Greek point of view." [8] In one essay, Hegel expresses devotional praise of the Greeks referring to the "greatness of their sentiments, their statuesque virtue free from moral ambiguity ... the grand manner of their deeds and characters," etc. (Knox, 326). Even Plato did not indulge in such undiscriminating praise of his culture. One could find notable examples of moral heroism in Christian culture, though Hegel was not inclined to look at them any more than he was willing to recognize that Greek religion with its superstitious mystery cults was as much a menagerie as Christianity. Indeed, with all his awareness of Greek thought, he fails to consider its role in the actual formulation of the Christian Scriptures and church doctrines. Jerusalem and Athens were not so far apart as the young Hegel thought.

To characterize Hegel's treatment of Christianity as "vitriolic," as Walter Kaufmann does,[9] is pure hyperbole, but there is evidence of hostility in it. Some of this may be explained, as W. H. Walsh suggests, by Hegel's "regret at the passing state of affairs in which political and religious life were closely integrated." [10] There is not much reason to think that Hegel ever made any critical study of the Scriptures as literature. Harris notes that he got his idea of rational religion from the Enlightenment from such figures as Moses Mendelssohn and Lessing. The latter's *Nathan der Weise* was written in part to defend the standpoint of the early Biblical critic H. S. Reimarus whose works Lessing arranged to have published posthumously at the request of Reimarus's daughter. Reimarus's views were revolutionary and they were attacked by the orthodox. Lessing was his champion. But Hegel paid little attention to controversies of this sort. Neither did Kant, though he apparently knew about "higher criticism." [11] H. E. G. Paulus, well-known in his day as a rationalist interpreter of the life of Jesus, was at Tübingen during Hegel's first year. Later in life, Hegel was quite friendly with Paulus but there is no evidence that Hegel gained much from Paulus at the *Stift*.

In the opening paragraph of the *Positivity*, Hegel says that "everyone sets up his own system as the Christian religion and requires everyone else to envisage this and this only." [12] But then he forthwith fails to take into account such alternative renderings. He tends to overlook the inner dynamic of Christianity. As illustrative of his inadequate grasp of early Christianity I need only cite his pejorative remark that "disenchantment for military service helped the success of Christianity." [13] He not only challenges the integrity and motives of the early Christians when he adds: "they must have welcomed a religion which preached that to shed human blood was a sin," he begs the question on the nature of Christianity itself. There was nothing cowardly or impotent about sincere Christians before the time of Constantine. They took the idea of redemptive goodwill seriously. One could argue that the impotence and cowardice developed when the church and state mutually embraced later, but it would have been impossible for Hegel to grant that.

A remark by Professor Harris further indicates the young Hegel's limited grasp of Christian theology and Biblical teaching.

> All of his early "theological" writings were part of a campaign against the surrendering of man's birthright in return for comfort against the changes and chances of mortal life, through eventual receipt of a mess of pottage in the heaven of a benevolent despot.[14]

No doubt there were some indications in the popular religious mind that such a campaign was justified. But the interpretation of the after-life as a heaven managed by a benevolent despot has no warrant in major

Christian teaching, in the thought of the early church, or in the New Testament Scriptures. Hegel read the gospels and even preached once on the Sermon on the Mount (June 16, 1793).[15] If Jesus taught anything about God it was that he was a Father who loved and providentially cared for his children, not a despot who demanded slavish acquiescence. This teaching is also foreshadowed in the prophets Hosea and Second Isaiah. I submit that Hegel campaigned against a belief that no systematic Christian theologian at the time seriously defended though it might have been an implication Hegel thought he detected. But maybe Professor Harris has oversimplified the motive of Hegel's early writings. If the young Hegel did indeed engage in such a campaign, it is not hard to see why the older Hegel was willing to put the early writings in a drawer and refuse to publish them.

Hegel's views of Judaism are virtually a caricature, though one would think that if he had read Mendelssohn seriously, he would have been less inflexible. The idea of the Covenant, so basic to the Hebrew view of Providence, the young Hegel seems unaware of.[16] He had no grasp whatever of the dynamism of the eighth century prophets and their idea of Providence. He called them "cold fanatics." Could he have understood Micah 6:8? If he had read Amos 9:7, he would have discovered that God is no special guardian of the Jewish nation and he would have avoided the totally erroneous assertion of his mature years that Judaism did not recognize the activity of God among other peoples.[17] Why as a young man he could not detect simple empirical contrasts between Jewish legalism and prophetic dynamism is a puzzle. He simply did not read the Scriptures as much or as carefully as the Greek classics. Nor does he show a grasp of the evolution of moral and religious ideas in Judaism.

Much of Hegel's youthful energy was spent trying to correct his professors' views, even trying, as Harris observes, "to settle their hash."[18] It was hard for him to listen to the lectures of G.C. Storr and J.F. Flatt at the *Stift,* and he was frequently absent. Yet Storr was something of a pioneer in New Testament studies, showing an awareness of the synoptic problem by suggesting the priority of the Marcan account in his *De Fontibus Evangeliorum* (1794). Hegel's "Schemata zu einer Evangelien harmonie" (ca. May 9, 1795) prepared near the time of writing his *Life of Jesus,* may well have been suggested to him by Storr, but Hegel had no real interest in scientific biblical scholarship even though it was under way. Albert Schweitzer notes:

Hegel was personally no friend of historical criticism. It annoyed him as it annoyed Goethe, to see the historical figures of antiquity, on which their thoughts were accustomed longingly to dwell, assailed by critical doubts.[19]

Now Storr and Flatt were scholarly men and the former's Latin treatise on Kant's *Religion* of 1793 was translated the next year into German by Süsskind, a classmate of Hegel. If he heeded Storr at all, Hegel was well aware of Kant's views on religion even though, as Harris says, there is no conclusive evidence that he read the *Religion* before 1794. Kant had high respect for Storr,[20] but both Storr and Flatt were very orthodox. The editor of an early American version of their theology opines:

> These distinguished champions of the truth sustained the cause of orthodoxy for upwards of twenty years and published from time to time, the most able replies to the several systems of infidelity which sprung up in Europe.[21]

This comment helps explain the uneasiness Hegel felt and shared with Hölderlin and Schelling at the *Stift*.

Yet Storr felt compelled to argue for the validity of revelation, urging that the New Testament was "a body of revealed truth whose divine origin was guaranteed . . . by the fact that its moral content was in perfect agreement with the highest ideals of our reason." [22] Most orthodox believers are content to regard revelation as beyond reason and as self-justifying. Storr's defense is not compelling but that he gave one at all is interesting.

Flatt viewed Kant's first *Critique* as a refutation of "reason's pretensions to solve metaphysical problems." [23] But one could claim that the first third of that *Critique* really makes revelation impossible because it establishes the mind as active and constitutive in knowing. A traditional doctrine of revelation seems to require an essentially passive, weak, receptive mind. Hegel could very well have shown his professors that the *Critique* they used to undercut rational metaphysics could as well be used to destroy their view of revelation. Had he done this, he would have needled them even more than he did.

NOTES

1. Two who think Hegel turned conservative when mature are Walter Kaufmann in his *Hegel: Reinterpretation* (Garden City: Doubleday, 1965), pp. 58-80, and G. P. Adams, *The Mystical Element in Hegel's Early Theological Writings* (Berkeley: Univ. of Calif. Press, 1910), p. 75. The second book seeks to explore the "mystical" or non-Kantian elements in early Hegel and is rather an antithesis to Harris's investigation.

2. Paul Asveld, *La Pensée religieuse du jeune Hegel* (Louvain: Publ. Univ., 1953), p. 22.

3. Kaufmann, *op. cit.*, p. 65.

4. G. Mueller, *Hegel: Denkgeschichte eines Lebendigen* (München: Francke Verlag, 1959), p. 13.

5. Asveld observes: Hegel . . . a reçu, tant dans sa famille qu'au gymnase, un Christianisme fort large, où l'accent était mis sur le côte rationnel et moral de la religion et où le surnaturel et le mystère étaient laissés dans l'ombre." (*op. cit.*, p. 27).

6. Edward Caird, *Hegel* (Edinburgh: Blackwood, 1883), p. 6.

7. Quoted in *Ibid.*, p. 7.

7a. *EtW*, p. 326.

8. *Ibid.*, p. 15.

9. W. Kaufmann, *From Shakespeare to Existentialism* (Garden City: Doubleday, Anchor Book, 1960), p. 133.

10. W. H. Walsh, "A Survey of Work on Hegel 1945-1952," *Philosophical Quarterly*, 3 (1953), p. 354.

11. See for example his letter to J. C. Lavater of April 28, 1775, in Arnulf Zweig's *Kant's Philosophical Correspondence* (Chicago: Univ. Press, 1967), pp. 79-82.

12. *EtW*, p. 67.

13. *EtW*, p. 165.

14. See pp. 72ff. preceding.

15. This date and certain others are taken from Gisela Schuler's "Zur Chronologie von Hegels Jugendschriften" *Hegel-Studien*, 2 (1963), pp. 127ff.

16. Harris observes that Hegel clearly felt "that only the Greeks really understood the nature and limits of Divine Providence." See p. ... preceding.

17. In *LPR*, Vol. II, we read that "there is not the slightest trace of thought [in Judaism] that God may have done other things as well, and that he acted in an affirmative way amongst other peoples too" (p. 210). In the verse from Amos we read: "Did I not bring Israel up from the land of Egypt and the Philistines from Caphtor and the Syrians from Kir?"

18. In a letter to Schelling he wrote that he thought it would be fun "to disturb the theologians as much as possible . . . to make everything difficult for them, to whip them out of every nook and subterfuge." (In Kaufmann, *Hegel: Reinterpretation*, p. 43).

19. A. Schweitzer, *The Quest for the Historical Jesus* (New York: Macmillan, 1910), p. 114.

20. In the Preface to the second edition of the *Religion*, Kant speaks of "the renowned Dr. Storr of Tübingen who has examined my book with his accustomed sagacity and with an industry and fairness deserving the greatest thanks."

21. S .S. Schmucker (ed.) *An Elementary Course in Biblical Theology* (translated from the work of Storr and Flatt) (Andover, Mass: Gould & Newman (1826), 1836), p. iii.

22. See p. 65 preceding.

23. *Ibid.*

COMMENT ON

H. S. Harris
The Young Hegel and the Postulates of Practical Reason

by

Thomas N. Munson

Since I have found Professor Haris' historical *aperçus* informative, my purpose is not to evaluate each detail of his reconstruction of the young Hegel's philosophical development. Rather, it is to bring to a focus the issues he has raised. Hopefully, his perspective, which is still the exception in its concentration upon the "Early Theological Writings," happily signals our emancipation from polemics. Perhaps we can now sift these writings dispassionately, avoiding both the absurdity that they are definitive of Hegel's philosophy of religion and the myopia that lightly dismisses them because they are pre-dialectical ruminations on liberty and chains, positivity and reason, objective and subjective, which were destined to lose their fragmentary character when Hegel discovered the spindle of *Aufhebung.* Rightfully, I believe, Harris has emphasized that the concern of these essays is practical, although I am not sure how this evinces "no interest in philosophical problems as such." I should prefer to say – and this is the purport of my rephrasing of Hegel's concern – that these fragments, topical though they are, are fragments precisely because they lead nowhere. They show us by and large [that is, if one takes into account Gisela Schüler's "Zur Chronologie von Hegels Jugendschriften," *Hegel-Studien,* II (1963)] Hegel thinking within, and with problems created by, his inherited theoretical framework. He applies this structure to the interests of the seminarian, thereby testing its consistency and suppleness. To my way of thinking, such an application in no way argues disinterest in, or an abandonment of, theoretical for "purely practical" concerns.

We know that the inspiration of Hegel's *Volksreligion,* as of his other reflections in the seminary and during his "humanistic years," was the Greek ideal of *kalos k'agathos*: the man who lives in ethical, religious, and political harmony thanks to the beneficial environment of the *polis*. To this ideal, as well as to the Kantian moral theory that was Hegel's resource for pondering it, the trial of Socrates posed an unmistakable challenge. In the name of his personal *daimon,* Socrates pitted himself against the ethical consensus of the city. To his detriment, he appealed to "the divine," the right of the individual conscience to exist in opposition to the claims of universal law: an appeal that, to all appearances, directly contradicted that subjugation of the individual to the universal which Hegel envisaged as the essence of Kantian morality.[1] For although the case of Socrates may have suggested to Kant his verbal resolution of this conflict – So act that your individual maxim might be a universal law – still Socrates achieved his immortality, as Harris would conceive it, by *surrendering* the immediate and so entering into the "Spirit" or value world of Greece and mankind. This surrender – on the face of it, Socrates could not have been sure that his death was crowning him with "immortality" – exhibits the unmitigated conflict between particular and universal Reason, between phenomenal "duty" and noumenal "necessity." In the abstract, we might wish the maxim of conscience – Follow your *daimon* – into universal law. But in the concrete, because personal decision may clash with the ethics of the *polis* and with the truism that everyone obviously cannot choose the extreme of Socrates' *daimon,* it is clear that a universal harmony or order, if such is to be, can only be achieved through the postulate of a God who necessarily transcends "divinized Man." Evidently, the "God" discovered by obeying the injunction of the Delphic oracle died in the draft of hemlock. He is a *dieu manqué,* who succeeds only in telling us uncompromisingly that, if we are to avoid the fate of Socrates, we must reconcile the inspirational value of "the divine" and "the immortal" with the exigencies of the human and the necessary. Kant's formula, "So act *as if . . .*" is no assurance of peace. Hence Harris' remark, if it is correct, that Hegel "is not criticizing Kant or quarrelling with him: rather indeed, he is providing his own account of why Kant's distinction between theoretical knowledge and practical faith is both right and necessary" supports my contention that Hegel's fragments were destined to remain inconclusive.

Within this purview, no "moral superiority" attaches to Christianity simply in virtue of its proclamation of the essential dignity of the human person. Rather, it offers a superior challenge in the person of Jesus, in whom the irreconcilability (the *ungeheure Verbindung*) of the divine and human is considerably heightened. Unlike Socrates, Jesus never mentioned his *daimon*. He claimed, instead, to be God. The apodictic "I am the

Way, the Truth, and the Life" adds another dimension to the issue defined by "Know thyself." It asserts the apparent contradiction that this individual is both "divine" and the "universal," the synthesis ("Life") of the right of conscience ("Truth") and the necessity of Law. Notwithstanding, Jesus suffered the same fate as did Socrates. He was not an alienated God, but he achieved no harmony with the laws, Roman and Jewish, of his society. If anything, by proclaiming a kingdom not of this world and a future reward for his followers, he renounced the sole consolation that reductionism offers: namely, an immortal memory in the hearts of mankind.

We know that a major difficulty Hegel experienced with Kant's theoretical framework was that it postulated an alienated God. On the one hand, a Supreme Legislator who, by ordering the universe, guarantees the fulfillment of our strivings for happiness and then actually fails is a *deus otiosus*. On the other hand, a God tied to the hedonism implied in the "Calvinist Ethic" is, as Hegel argued against Judaism, immoral. The fragments, therefore, insofar as they touch upon Socrates and Jesus, illustrate Hegel's effort to test Kant's hypothesis against concrete cases. A moral theory, as Hegel came to see more clearly, must carry conviction in the here and now. The actual failures of Socrates and Jesus show that morality cannot rest upon an "as if." And their eventual success ("immortality" or "resurrection") is comparable to a promise of "pie in the sky." It carries no personal assurance to us.

It would appear to me, contrary to what Mr. Harris has advocated, that an attempted reduction of the postulates neither was nor is the proper answer to Hegel's difficulties. For if "the divine" is in reality "the human," if God is Man, and if "immortality" is just another expression for the dignity of the human spirit, then, as Harris himself has indicated, we have not as yet succeeded in establishing a coherent, rational system. Our reduction has done nothing to alleviate present tension. The postulate – less euphemistically, the surd – of immortality remains to plague us. For the assertion of the intrinsic worth of the human individual is nothing but a display of our values. It recalls to mind the paradoxes and disappointments that ensue, if we are to believe Sartre and Lévi-Strauss, when life begins with a choice. Moreover, in my opinion the postulate does not rid us of eschatology. Rather, it raises the further question whether everyone who sincerely follows his conscience – even Eichmann – is entitled to a place in the "spiritual life" of our race.

At the end of his paper Harris has announced some personal committals under the title of conclusions. If religion is the ethical or moral concern of these fragments, which Hegel, understandably, assumed so long as he was thinking within Kantian guidelines, I tend to agree with him. Needless to say, this assumption is excessively narrow, and certainly unwarranted if one pretends to be thinking the entirety of the religious phenomenon. Surely a genuine commitment to Spirit requires us to take into account the recitals and experiences of religious people, for "the true religious ethic," Jensen warns us,

> is not primarily concerned with interpersonal relationships. Ethical bonds of this kind are found in the earliest human societies without requiring justification of a religious kind. The primary religious-ethical postulation in primitive religion constrains man to be constantly aware of the divine origin of the world and of the human partnership in the divinity. The initiation of awareness and the vivid preservation of a special "knowledge" of the nature of reality are therefore the truest forms of the religious attitude.[2]

NOTES

1. *HtJ*, sec. 387: "Dem Gesetz setzte er Moralität entgegen? – Moralität ist nach Kant die Unterjochung des Einzelnen unter das Allgemeine, der Sieg des Allgemeinen über sein entgegengesetztes Einzelnes . . ."

2. Adolf E. Jensen, *Myth and Cult among Primitive Peoples*, tr. by Marianna Tax Choldin & Wolfgang Weissleder (Chicago: University of Chicago Press, 1963), p. 77.

DISCUSSION

ANONYMOUS: A question to Dr. Harris: It seems to me there is something troubling about the criticism of Hegel for not being familiar with the Judeo-Christian point of view. I think it might be shown by a comparison of ἀγάπη and ἔρως in the New Testament, for example, or of the concept of covenant community, or of love in Hosea – by a comparison of these with the philosophical anthropology that Hegel sets forth in the *Phenomenology* a high degree of correlation would be found. I think I would substantially agree with Dr. Findlay when he says that the Hegelian categories are in many ways Christian rather than platonic. And I think there is a good deal of difference between the platonic, philosophical anthropology and the Hegelian, philosophical anthropology – Hegel being more and more in line with Judeo-Christian, biblical anthropology. I am wondering whether the early Hegel is not familiar with this – where did his insight into the central biblical categories (if he indeed had this) come? Was it later or just when?

HARRIS: As I respond to questions, I shall also be answering my commentators.

I think there is absolutely no defending (as representative of his position) the one statement which Professor Steinkraus referred to from the mature Hegel about there being no insight in Judaic tradition anywhere. I can only assume that at this point he reverted for a moment to a standpoint he had formed as a young man. And what I must say now is also my answer to Professor Steinkraus' complaints about Hegel's extremely inadequate accounts of Judaism in the early writings. Hegel simply was not concerned with the history of Judaism after the Mosaic period. He was concerned with the spirit of Judaism. For him, Abraham was the spirit of Judaism and Moses was its fate. (This is another paper which I might have read and did not.) The Judaism he is concerned about goes from Abraham – more specifically, from Joseph and his brothers –

to Moses. What comes later is regarded as irrelevant; it doesn't contribute to world spirit. All of the values of the prophetic tradition he may be said to have taken up and given proper treatment in Christianity. He was not, after all, one to fail to distinguish between a soothsayer and a social prophet.

DARREL E. CHRISTENSEN (WOFFORD COLLEGE): I should like to direct a question to Professor Harris. You say on your concluding page that immortality, even in the special sense in which you have defined it, here remains a postulate. In the *Phenomenology* and in later works, there are numerous instances of positing and postulation which are moments in various phases of Hegel's dialectic. A condition of perception, for example, is the positing of a bare undifferentiated "this," which cannot actually be perceived apart from a "not-this" which is its necessary condition. At a more advanced stage of the dialectic, the positing of the empty abstract notion of "thing" is a necessary moment of the dialectic of the thing and its attributes. In view of this positing character of reason itself, just what does it come to when you make this affirmation that immortality, even in this special sense, is for Hegel to remain a postulate?

HARRIS: I am very glad you asked this question because this touches upon what I really wish to say to my commentators. Knowing that I was overtime, I deliberately omitted the last page of my paper, which I thought we would be discussing.

First I must reply for Hegel, and then for myself. The Hegel of 1798, or the Hegel of 1800, would not have stopped where I stopped. Professor Munson commented that the account which I have given of Hegel's investigations of religion, if taken as an account of the whole of religious experience, is extremely inadequate. This, no matter how you regard this way of going about such an account. This is quite true, as Hegel at any stage of his development would have admitted. At the stage in which we are presently interested, he has religion as his ultimate category. And religion as his ultimate category certainly isn't confined to a kind of doctrine of divinized man. What Professor Steinkraus, following G. P. Adams, calls the mystical element of Hegel's doctrine doesn't deserve to be called mystical. If Professor Henrich is correct, it wasn't mystical even in the earliest Hegel writings. What assumes prominence, rather, is a doctrine of the divine life, and the problem then is that of thinking of "pure" life, as Hegel calls it in the spirit of Christianity. This, I think, is what he addressed himself to in that lost manuscript which may have been the best of his early manuscripts. This, which we shall call "The System Fragment," probably contained a philosophy of religion in the full sense and the plan for his *Volksreligion* built upon Christian foundations.

So you should not suppose that where I stop is where Hegel stopped. Still, where I stopped is where I started with Hegel and that is with the section on evil and forgiveness in the *Phenomenology*. It is to understand the *Phenomenology* that I have set out on this long path of re-creating Hegel's development and what I say on the final page of my paper about the problem is really about the problem of this re-creation. To say that immortality even in the sense in which I think it is given in Hegel's earliest doctrine of the Spirit, to say that this remains a postulate is to say something important about the whole problem of human communication and particularly about the problem of understanding a past thinker. So, if I may, I will now read my last page.

HEGEL'S PHENOMENOLOGY OF MIND AS A DEVELOPMENT OF KANT'S BASIC ONTOLOGY

by

W. H. Werkmeister

At first glance it must seem that the topic of my paper has very little, if anything, to do with the encompassing theme of this Symposium: "Hegel and the Philosophy of Religion." Nevertheless, I submit that, as a matter of fact, it goes to the very heart of the issue; and I hope that my argument will make this clear.

In limiting my considerations to Hegel's *Phenomenology* I assume that this work is in a very real sense representative of Hegel's philosophical intention – an assumption which can be justified, I am sure, on internal as well as on extremal evidence. Such justification, however, is irrelevant to the problem now before us.

I

As I read Hegel's *Phenomenology,* its basic concern is the preservation of man's finitude within the process of unfoldment which is the self-manifestation of Absolute Spirit: and this, I submit, is a religious theme, re-echoing in existentialist thought from Kierkegaard to the present. My problem, however, is: In what sense is this theme a development of Kant's basic ontology? And how did Hegel cope with it? An answer to these questions depends on our understanding of Kant's basic ontology and its implications.

We must realize, first of all, that Kant is a "system thinker"; that his various works are but interdependent parts of an over-arching whole, and that his ultimate concern is man in his relation to God. We misunderstand Kant when we see him only as preoccupied with problems of epistemology and/or of ethics. To be sure, Kant first concentrated on epistemological problems and thereafter developed his ethics, finally dealing with "religion within the bounds of reason alone." But even the *Critique of Pure Reason* already prepared the ground for Kant's moral and religious ideas. And let us not forget his much-quoted satement: "I had to suspend (*aufheben*) *knowledge* in order to make room for *faith*." [1] The Kantian philosophy, in other words, is one all-inclusive system and can be truly understood only as such. And when it is so understood, its very heart and essence turns out to be an ontology – and it does so despite the fact that Kant himself once stated that "the proud name of an Ontology ... must ... give place to the modest title of a mere Analytic of pure understanding," [2] a remark perfectly justified in its context but not applicable to Kant's system as a whole.

The specific ontological problem with which I am concerned here, the problem which is crucial for the Kantian system but which Kant himself did not solve and for which Hegel's *Phenomenology of Mind* does provide a solution, is encountered almost at once when we examine the *Critique of Pure Reason;* for here Kant demonstrates that for reasons which he regards as good and sufficient the external world is a world of phenomena only. But what is the nature of the subject which experiences that world? Is it also a phenomenon?

To be sure, Kant emphatically states that "empirical realism is beyond question"; [3] that "even our inner experience is possible only on the assumption of outer experience;" [4] and that "the consciousness of my existence is at the same time an immediate consciousness of the existence of other things outside me." [5] Moreover, as *this* particular empirical subject I know myself only under the forms of space and time and, therefore, only as phenomenon. Kant himself insists on this point when he states that in *CPR* "the objects of experience as such, *including even our own subject* [my italics], were explained as only *appearances.*" [6]

All appearances, when "taken together" (and this must include the empirical subject), "lie, and must lie, in *one* nature"; and "there are certain laws which first make a nature possible, and these laws are *a priori.*" [7] More significantly, "nature" is "the sum of appearances in so far as they stand, in virtue of an inner principle of causality, in thorough-going interconnection." [8] The principle of causality, in other words, is constitutive of nature. But if this is so, then it is obvious that the empirical subject being itself a phenomenon and therefore a part of nature, cannot also be the transcendental ground which is constitutive of nature itself; and Kant does not say that it is. Indeed, he specifically states that "the understanding is something more than a power of formulating rules through comparison of appearances; it is itself the lawgiver of nature." [9] The understanding, in other words, is not simply the ability of the empirical subject to formulate "rules" on the basis of empirical evidence. As transcendental ground of the world of phenomena it must be transcendental to the empirical subject as well as to the object. And right here the problem with which I am concerned arises.

It is beyond dispute, I believe, that, in the *Critique of Pure Reason,* Kant takes "the object ... in a twofold sense, namely as appearance and as thing-in-itself." [10] I submit that Kant's theory of knowledge rests upon a similar distinction involving the subject; that we must distinguish, in other words, between a subject which, as part of nature, is phenomenon, and a subject-in-itself which is constitutive of nature. Kant's discussion of the "transcendental unity of apperception" [11] and of the role which that unity plays in cognition implies as much. But Kant himself has left no room for doubt in the matter; for he has stated that "we know our own self only as appearance, not as it is in itself." [12]

My problem is now obvious: How is the empirical subject related to the transcendental subject? Are we as empirical subjects simply an appearance of a subject-in-itself? If so, are we still in a real sense subjects at all – subjects of action, that is, and not merely of observation? Kant himself was aware of this problem but brushed it aside rather lightly. Here is what he said: "How the 'I' that thinks can be distinct from the 'I' that intuits itself [i.e., that knows itself as phenomenon] ... and yet, as being the same subject, can be identical with the latter; and how, therefore, I can say: 'I, as intelligence and *thinking* subject, know myself as an object that is *being thought* ... and yet know myself, like other phenomena, only as I appear to myself ...' – these are questions that raise no greater nor less difficulty than how I can be an object to myself at all ..." [13] I repeat: The problem is this: How is the empirical subject related to a transcendental subject-in-itself? How does it preserve its own integrity as an empirical subject and, more importantly, as a moral agent?

II

In our attempt to clarify the problem here involved we initially face an apparent dualism of thing-in-itself and subject-in-itself; for the confrontation of an empirical object and an empirical subject in the only knowledge relation encountered in our experience is the result of a thing-in-itself eliciting a response, and a transcendental subject-in-itself im-

posing the conditions under which alone experience is possible and phenomena exist. It remains to be seen whether or not this dualism is
final in Kant's philosophy.

We approach this problem by examining briefly what Kant had to say
about the thing-in-itself – keeping in mind, however, that he is here
struggling with an idea which, at first, was not quite clear in his own
mind.

"If the senses present to us something merely *as it appears*," Kant
tells us, "this something must also in itself be a thing." [14] But this "transcendental object," this thing as it is in itself, is "the completely indeter-
minate thought of *something* in general"; we "know nothing of what
it is in itself." [15] However, the concept of a thing-in-itself is "not in
any way contradictory." [16] Moreover, it is unavoidable; for when we
call something a "mere phenomenon," we "at the same time" form
the idea of "an *object in itself*." [17] Still, for our sense-bound experience this idea must remain "a problem." [18] "That is to say, we have
an understanding which *problematically* extends further" than our experience based on sense-intuitions;[19] and in this "problematic sense" the
concept is "indispensable" "as setting limits to sensibility." [20] It is
"a merely *limiting concept* (*ein Grenzbegriff*)" but is "no arbitrary
invention." [21]

Moreover, to a *non-sensory* intuition (one which we do not possess)
the concept would have a "positive sense." [22] In any case, "through
this concept of a noumenon" our understanding acquires "a negative
extension." [23] That is to say, in the process of setting limits to our sensibility, our understanding "does indeed think for itself an object in itself, but only as transcendental object, which is the cause of appearance
and therefore not itself appearance." [24] The phrase, "which is the cause
of appearance," adds special significance to an otherwise indefinable
concept. This fact is underscored when Kant says later that "the faculty of sensory intuition is strictly only a receptivity," and that "the *nonsensible cause*" of the phenomena "cannot be intuited by us as object"
and remains "completely unknown to us." [25] Although its nature remains unknown, the transcendental "object" must be its "cause" also.
Do thing-in-itself and subject-in-itself begin to fuse into one and the
same reality?

Let us consider the problem from another point of view. Is it possible
that essential characteristics of the empirical subject indicate something
about the nature of the transcendental subject?

To begin with, Kant tells us that "the assertion, '*I exist thinking*,' is no mere logical function, but determines the subject (which is then at the same time object) in respect of existence"; [26] and "in the consciousness of our existence there is contained a something *a priori*, which can serve to determine our existence ... as being related, in respect of a certain inner faculty, to a nonsensible intelligible world" [27] – and this in strict conformity with the basic "postulate of reason" that "if the conditioned is given, a regress in the series of all its conditions is *set* us *as a task*." [28] The "existence of appearance," therefore, which is "never self-grounded but always conditioned," requires that we look for an object "in which this contingency may terminate." [29] This means that we must look for a thing that is "completely determined in and through itself." [30] "The concept of such a being is the concept of God." [31] Although we can *prove* neither the existence nor the non-existence of God, "the supposition which reason makes of a supreme being, as the highest cause," [32] gives at least unity to the world of phenomena – including the existence of our own empirical selves.

But there is still another side to the argument – one based upon the facts of our moral existence.

Kant is quite explicit in his statement that it is "one and the same reason which judges a priori by principles, whether for theoretical or for practical purposes." [33] The realms of nature and of morality, though constituted differently, are therefore but manifestations of the same ultimate reality – reason. Good and evil, Kant tells us, do not refer "originally" to objects (as do the "categories of the theoretically employed reason") but are "without exception modes of a single category, that of causality, so far as its determining ground consists in reason's idea of a law of causality which, as the law of freedom, reason gives itself." [34] The transcendental subject is, thus, not only the constitutive ground of the world of phenomena, it is the moral lawgiver as well; and it is a lawgiver in supreme freedom. Its freedom is "the keystone of the whole architecture of the system of pure reason and of speculative reason as well." [35] To be sure, "we do not understand" this freedom, "but we know it as the condition of the moral law which we do know." [36] It is freedom in a transcendental, not in an empirical sense.

In the Dialectic of pure speculative reason, Kant now reminds us, we discovered that "the same act, which as belonging to the world of sense is always ... mechanically necessary, can at the same time, as belonging to the causality of the acting being in so far as it belongs to the intelligible world, have a sensuously unconditioned causality as its foundation"; [37] that is, it is free. This freedom, however, lies entirely in the realm of noumena, i.e., in the realm of the thing-in-itself.

It is important at this point to note that, for Kant, the "theoretical employment" of reason is subordinate to its "practical employment"; that, indeed, even "the ultimate intention of nature in her wise provision for us has, in the constitution of our reason, been directed to moral interests alone." [38] This passage, I submit, assumes the essential fusion of thing-in-itself and subject-in-itself. What initially appeared to be a transcendental dualism has now given way to the monism of a subject-in-itself. Corroborative passages can be found readily in Kant's writings.

<h1 style="text-align:center">III</h1>

My question now is: How can we further characterize the nature of the subject-in-itself?

In the *Critique of Pure Reason* Kant has shown that as long as cognition depends for its subject-matter on sensory intuition, knowledge can not be extended beyond the world of phenomena. Although it is possible – nay, necessary – even in such a situation to refer to a thing-in-itself and a subject-in-itself, nothing can be said about their nature. However, as far as Kant is concerned, the moral law, being "absolutely inexplicable from any data of the world of sense or from the whole compass of the theoretical use of reason," defines the "pure intelligible world" "positively and enables us to know something of it" [39] – namely, that it is "nothing else than nature under the autonomy of the pure practical reason." [40]

But we know something else, too. Because pure reason in its "practical application" is a lawgiver who, in supreme freedom, gives laws to itself and, thus, is a form of causality, the "objective reality of a pure concept of the understanding [namely, causality] in the field of the supersensuous, once ushered in, gives objective reality to all the other categories." [41] Although this fact does not encourage pure theoretical reason "to run riot into the transcendent," [42] it at least makes it possible to speak intelligibly about the "intelligible world" of a subject-in-itself. The categories are now applicable to the unconditioned as well as to the conditioned, to the world of noumena as well as to the world of phenomena – but only in matters of "practical concern."

When we now ask: What is the origin and ultimate ground of duty, Kant replies that it "cannot be less than something which elevates man above himself as a part of the world of sense"; indeed, "it is nothing else than *personality*." [43] It is that aspect of a "person" which transcends the world of phenomena and therefore "belongs to the intelligible world." [44] It is that which is "holy" in man and "places before our eyes the sublimity of our own nature," "of our own supersensuous existence." [45] We now know that, as far as Kant is concerned, it makes sense to speak in terms of "personality" when we refer to a subject-in-itself.

At once, however, a difficulty arises – a difficulty which entails the problems with which I am here concerned.

The empirical subject – so we know from the *Critique of Pure Reason* – exists as phenomenon and is subject to all the laws which constitute and, thus, determine the realm of nature. But this same subject is "conscious also of his own existence as a thing-in-itself," and "to himself" is "determinable only by laws which he gives to himself through reason." [46] The difficulty which I find here lies in the fact that the empirical subject – the human being, here and now – who is "conscious of his own existence as a thing-in-itself," is a finite self, whereas "pure practical reason," being the true law-giver, is not so limited. Not only does the moral law hold for all rational beings, reason itself in its "practical application" is constitutive of the "kingdom of ends" and, more importantly yet, "God is the morally practical reason legislating for itself." [47]

I am fully aware of the fact that Kant also said: "In the order of ends, man . . . is an end-in-himself, i.e., he is never to be used merely as a means for someone (even for God) without at the same time being himself an end." [48] But this is precisely my problem. How can we reconcile the idea that man is an "end-in-himself" whose dignity as a self-legislative human being must not be violated – not even by God – with the idea that God is pure practical reason itself, legislating for all rational beings? To put it differently: How can we preserve man's freedom as a self-legislative being when God himself, as practical reason incarnate, is the universal law-giver? And this question, I submit, Kant does not answer. He speaks rather vaguely of the "inscrutable wisdom through which we exist" and which itself is "worthy of veneration." [49] But this is an evasion rather than a solution of the problem. And I should like to add that neither Kant's *Groundwork of the Metaphysic of Morals* nor his *RwLR* resolve the problem; for we must not forget that the difficulty with which we are concerned here was first encountered when we asked how the empirical cognitive subject is related to the transcendental subject-in-itself which is constitutive of the whole world of phenomena.

IV

Before turning to a more detailed consideration of Hegel's solution of the unresolved problem of Kant's ontology, let me indicate briefly Hegel's critical reaction to the Kantian position. Thus we read in *HtJ*: "According to Kant, morality is the subsuming of the individual to the universal, the victory of the universal over an opposing individual." [50] This, I submit, is but another way of pointing up the crucial problem of Kant's ontology which troubles me.

Moreover, Hegel sees in the Kantian commitment to the moral law a diremption of the human being who, living in two worlds, can exist only in inner disharmony; [51] whereas Hegel himself is interested in the re-affirmation of the "unity of man." [52]

But Hegel's criticism of Kant's philosopical position extends to epistemogical considerations as well as to the foundations of morals. What is decisive and fatal for Kant's theory of knowledge, so Hegel believes, is the separation of matter and form in cognition, which, as we have seen, entails the problem of the relation of the empirical subject to the transcendental subject-in-itself. It is Hegel's aim to eliminate this dualism, to make clear how subject and object in cognition can be one and the same reality and yet be different, both preserving their essential identity not only despite but because of their interdependence. The process of overcoming the dualism, of transcending the separation of phenomena and thing-in-itself, of appearance and true reality in cognition is, of course, the Dialectic – which, far from being a method externally applied, is a disclosure of the inner dynamics of reality itself. It is the self-revelation of the Absolute.

The problem with which we are concerned recurs in the form of the relation of the finite to the infinite, of man to his God. And here again Hegel takes issue with Kant, regarding the latter's "perpetual Ought" as the "bad infinity" which, though "it is negation of the finite," "cannot truly rid itself of finitude." [53] As Hegel sees it, "the finite is not a Determinate Being on its side, and the infinite a Determinate Being or Being-in-Itself beyond . . . that which was determined as finite." [54] Both, the finite and the infinite, "are in themselves only as mediation"; i.e., they are but moments in the Dialectic. "But with relation to reality and ideality . . . the finite is taken as real and the infinite as of ideal nature." [55] The importance to our problem of this statement will become clear in time.

One last point needs to be made before we turn to Hegel's constructive development of Kant's basic ontology and to his solution of the problem that Kant did not solve – the position and function of the empirical subject relative to the subject-in-itself. Kant's references to "pure reason" and "practical reason," emphasized in the titles of his two major works no less than in the separation of the problems discussed in those works, suggest a dualism within reason itself which could be very troublesome in a basic ontology. But it would be a radical misunderstanding of Kant were we to regard such a dualism as either intended by him or as entailed in his over-all position. To be sure, in the *Foundations of the Metaphysics of Morals* Kant said that "reason would overstep all its bounds if it undertook to explain how pure reason can be practical." [56] But in *KdpV* he speaks of "the theoretical use of reason" and "the practical use of reason" [57] and specifically states that "pure reason ... alone ... is unconditionally practical," [58] thus implying that, ultimately, reason is only one. And this one reason, as "efficient cause through ideas," posits the determining ground of the causality of man as a sensuous being," [59] More pointedly stated, practical reason is but "pure reason ... in its practical use." [60]

Other passages might be cited to the same effect; but the point is clear: Kant ultimately admits only one reason which, as reason in its practical employment, has "commanding authority as the supreme legislator" [61] – in the world of phenomena no less than in the moral realm.

Related to this reason is the will as "a faculty of choosing only that which reason, independently of inclination, recognizes as practically necessary." [62] Thus, while reason is ultimately only one, "will" is here conceived as a separate faculty. Moreover, the "divine" or "holy" will is "of itself ... necessarily in union with the law" – i.e., with the moral law; and 'ought" is here "out of place." [63] But it is otherwise with the human will, for whom the "holiness of will" is "a practical ideal" toward which all finite rational beings must strive "even though they cannot reach it." [64] A new dualism has thus been introduced into the Kantian system. One more facet has been added to the many-faceted problem of the relation of the finite empirical self to the Absolute which Hegel attempted to solve. And it is this problem which takes us right to the heart of our topic: Hegel and the Philosophy of Religion.

V

I submit that Hegel's basic orientation, his whole mode of thinking, is essentially religious. At its very core, his philosophy is but religion coming to understand itself. The world in which we find ourselves is the Absolute in its dialectic self-unfolding; and the reality of God is no other than the self-manifestation of the Absolute in and through this process. It is at the same time the object of knowledge as well as of faith. Hegel's brief interpretation of a progressive development of religious ideas [65] supports rather than disproves this fact.

But seen in this perspective of an over-all religious metaphysics, the status of the empirical self becomes once more the crucial issue – just as it was in the philosophy of Kant; for it is in our own self-consciousness that the Absolute attains knowledge and understanding of itself. It is here that it realizes itself, in both its subjective and objective manifestations, as Absolute Spirit. And it is here, in our own self-consciousness, that the Absolute discloses itself to itself.

Small wonder, then, that it has been said again and again that in Hegel's philosophy the empirical self, the human individual, is "swallowed up" in the Absolute; that he loses all significant self-identity as a person, as a self-active and morally responsible being. And if this were so, then, far from having solved the crucial problem of Kant's ontology, Hegel would have made human existence illusory and would have destroyed every meaningful basis of religious faith as well.

VI

But let us now take a close look at the most relevant passages in Hegel's *Phenomenology of Mind*. As we do so, let us keep in mind that in the dialectic of an unfolding knowledge, subject and object are both manifestations of the same reality, each finding its fulfillment and clarification in the other; that consciousness, "in the form of understanding," "looks through the intervening play of forces into the real and true background of things"; [66] and that "with self-consciousness" we have "passed into the native land of truth." [67] "Being 'in-itself' and being 'for an other' are here the same." [68] Indeed, in the form of self-consciousness "consciousness ... passes from the dark void of the transcendent and remote supersensuous, and steps into the spiritual daylight of the present." [69]

As we consider our more specific problem, our first reference must be to Hegel's interpretation of the "unhappy consciousness"; for it is in the form of the "unhappy consciousness" that our personal existence is most poignantly realized. The "particularity of consciousness" has at this stage of the dialectic not yet been "harmoniously reconciled with pure thought itself." [70] Consciousness in all its particularity has not yet discovered that "the unchangeable" is "its own self." [71] But precisely here is where the difficulty arises. Hegel himself has pointed it out: "If consciousness were, for itself, an independent consciousness," then it might regard the rest of reality as being "of no account"; but "consciousness is unable of itself to cancel that reality." [72] In fact, it realizes its own dependence upon that reality and develops "a sense of its own unity with the unchangeable." [73] But if such is the case, how can the essential independence of the empirical self be preserved?

To be sure, in the form of the "unhappy consciousness" the individual is fully aware of his own particularity; but this "torn soul," in which the particular is opposed by the universal, confined to its "narrow self" and "petty activity," is "a personality brooding over itself, as unfortunate as it is pitiably destitute." [74] Kierkegaard, realizing in "fear and trembling" his own existence, made his redeeming leap into faith. And Heidegger, finding in anxiety the most revealing aspect of human existence, took refuge in a metaphysics of poetry. But neither Kierkegaard nor Heidegger had a solution for the Kantian problem. However, it is from this point on that Hegel's solution begins to emerge.

The key idea has been succinctly stated by Hegel himself. This is what he said: "In principle action is only really action when it is the action of some particular individual"; and, "in its particularity," consciousness "is all of reality." [75] When sublated, it is "the universal"; it is "Reason" writ large. [76] And since consciousness is "all of reality," there is in Hegel's philosophy no room for a Kantian thing-in-itself.

However, "actual concrete reason" is not yet "in truth all reality." It is "driven on to raise its formal certainty into actual truth." [77] When this "level of truth" has been achieved, "reason is spirit" and is "aware of itself as its own world, and of the world as itself." [78] To be sure, we have now reached the level of man's cultural existence; but it is precisely here that our problem finds its solution.

It is at this level in the self-manifestation of the Absolute that "essential being and concrete reality" consist in the knowledge which "consciousness has of itself." [79] This knowledge reveals that "the world" is "absolutely its own will"; that it is "concretely embodied universal will," but will also as "the self-conscious essential being of each and every personality." [80] And now comes what I regard as the crucial turn in the argument: "Each individual consciousness" realizes itself only "in a work which is a work of the whole." [81] Its purpose is the universal purpose, its language universal law, its work universal achievement." [82] The "individual itself" is "universal consciousness and will." [83] This appears to mean, as critics of Hegel have maintained again and again, that the individual has been absorbed in the universal; that he is nothing but a pawn in the dialectic game of the Absolute. But this interpretation, I submit, is a complete misreading of Hegel, who specifically stated that, "for the universal to pass into a deed, it must gather itself into the single unity of individuality, and put an individual consciousness in the forefront; for universal will is an actual concrete will only in a self that is single and one." [84] Lest this statement also be misunderstood, Hegel adds almost at once that "the highest reality of all ... is the freedom and singleness of actual self-consciousness itself." [85]

But there is more to the argument.

It may be remembered that Kant regarded duty, that "stern command" which "often requires self-denial," [86] as "nothing else" than an expression of "the pure practical reason" – of a will, that is, which exists "in a sphere entirely different from the empirical." [87] This interpretation of duty Hegel repudiates as an "empty abstraction," insisting that duty "finds its reality and content solely in some definite actual existence, an actuality which is actuality of consciousness itself ... as an individual." [88] This "single simple self" is something "actual and concrete"; and duty is "no longer the universal appearing over against and opposed to the self." It is now "the law which exists for the sake of the self," [89] and is something "immediately actual" – the "moment," namely, of relating oneself to others [90] and, in this sense, being universal.[91]

In retrospect, Hegel says, it is "the utterance of individuality" that is "the absolutely real, the ultimately substantial" [92] – an individuality which, in the actuality of conscience, has for the first time attained a "certainty of itself." [93] Conscience, however, is "moral genius and originality"; it is "divine creative power" and, at the same time, it is "service of God." [94] "Its action is the contemplation of ... its own proper divinity." [95] What I would like to stress in this whole line of thinking is Hegel's contention that "with the completion of conscience" the distinction between "abstract consciousness" and "self-consciousness" has disappeared. We now know that even "abstract consciousness" is but 'this self, this individual self-existence which is certain of itself." [96] No one could stress more emphatically the reality of the individual. But Hegel adds that, "in the purpose of its action," "this particular self" is "conscious of itself as this particular individual," and is conscious of "what it is for itself and what it is for others." [97] It will not let itself be used as an "external instrument," for what can be used as an instrument is a "thing" rather than a person.[98]

Enough has been said, I believe, to point up the stress which Hegel places upon the reality and actuality of the individual. Throughout the *Phenomenology* the argument has been the concretization of Absolute Spirit in the individual who is at once particular and universal. As Hegel puts it succinctly: It is the "self" that "accomplishes the life of Absolute Spirit." [99]

VII

The unresolved problem inherent in Kant's basic ontology – so we have seen – is the relation of the empirical self to the transcendental subject-in-itself. The problem arises at the level of cognition as well as at the level of ethics and culminates in the problem of man's relation to God. Hegel's argument throughout the *Phenomenology* is designed to eliminate the whole idea of a thing or a subject in itself.[100] The process of the dialectic, from beginning to end, is but a step by step clarification of the self-manifestation of the real – a process in which "particularity" becomes "reconciled with the universal," [101] in which "the oneness of the particular consciousness with the unchangeable" is "the essential reality." [102]

I am well aware of the fact that, in the context of the "ethical world," Hegel states that "individuality" has "the significance of self-consciousness in general." But he adds at once that "ethical substance is ... Absolute Spirit realized in the plurality of distinct consciousnesses definitely existing." [103] To be sure, as far as Hegel is concerned, no individual exists by himself or for himself alone; [104] but it is the individual, nevertheless, that alone is the distinct, the definitely existing consciousness. It is as "self-existent particulars" that individuals create their world of culture [105] and, in creating that world, mold themselves into what they inherently are.[106] The process in which the individuals thus "cultivate" themselves is "the development of the actual world." [107] It is the process of making "spiritual reality" itself "actual and concrete." [108] In this process, however, the particular self "makes its own content," drawing that content "from itself as a natural individuality." [109]

What I mean to stress throughout in my interpretation of his philosophy is (1) the emphasis Hegel places upon the actual and concrete individual, and (2) the creative role which this individual plays in the concretization of Absolute Spirit. Where Kant's system found its anchorage in the idea of a transcendental subject-in-itself, Hegel's system centers around a process of unfoldment in which the concrete individual is the active agent, transforming at every stage the abstract universal into concrete reality. The diremption implied in Kant's distinction between a world of phenomena and a world of noumena has been overcome; and in this sense the problem which Kant did not solve has found its solution. Reality is now interpreted as the process of unfoldment of self-consciousness and reason, taken as a whole, but actualized only in its "stages" or "moments" as encountered in the progressive self-certainty and self-realization of concrete individuals.

It is now clear, I am sure, why and in what sense the problem which Kant did not solve, but for which Hegel provided a solution in the *Phenomenology*, goes right to the heart of religion. Briefly stated, it is this: If concrete individuals in their actuality as self-conscious beings play the crucial part in the concretization of Absolute Spirit which, in Hegel's philosophy, they do play, then what is the relation of these individuals to God or, more pointedly, what is God's relation to them?

I shall omit here any reference to Hegel's views on "natural religion" and on "religion in the form of art," [110] and shall turn at once to his discussion of the meaning and the implications of "revealed religion." This discussion proceeds from the premise, backed up by the whole argument of the *Phenomenology*, that "Absolute Spirit has taken on the shape of self-consciousness"; that it is "the belief of the world" that "spirit exists *in fact* ... as an actual human being"; and that "the believing mind sees, feels, and hears this divinity." [111] Consciousness, in other words, starting from its "immediate present existence," "recognizes God" in that existence.[112] God is not "set up as something thought" or something "imaginatively represented" – as He was for Kant (for whom He was the ultimate subject-in-itself) – but is incarnate "as a real individual human being." [113] And in this incarnation "the Divine Being" is revealed as "essentially self-consciousness." [114] Divine nature is "the same" as human nature, and is directly intuited as such.[115] And now, "existing as a concrete actual self-consciousness," Absolute Being has for the first time attained "its supreme reach of being." [116] God is revealed as He is. "He is real as Spirit." [117] But Spirit, "when self-consciousness is immediate," is *this* particular "individual self-consciousness" – a self-consciousness which is transcended in thought as being universal; but it is transcended "without losing its reality in this universality." [118] And this human being, "which Absolute Being is revealed to be," and "as an individual," [119] now undergoes the dialectic of self-clarification which we have come to know from the very beginning of our sojourn through the *Phenomenology.*

There is, however, a new perspective to the argument; for, in revealed religion, Spirit and "the moments distinguished in it," belong to the "sphere of figurative thinking." [120] This "pictorial" mode of thinking, not being the "notional thinking" required for true understanding,[121] must be "sublated." [122] The merely "imaginative idea" which the religious consciousness has of an ultimate reconciliation of "the world" and "essential Being" [123] must now be substantiated in Absolute Knowledge.

In the dialectical process of self-unfolding and self-clarification "came is the sole argument of the *Phenomenology,* self-consciousness "came before us" in the form of a "particular mode or shape of consciousness." [124] In its "pure inwardness" it was "the self-intuition of God Himself." [125] In this form, however, self-consciousness is "objectless" and "disappears into thin air." It finds realization "partly in the acts performed" and "partly in religion." [126] Indeed, what in religion was merely "a way of imagining," finds fulfillment in "the action proper of the self"; [127] and "the knowledge that the action of the self within itself is all that is essential" and is "all existence" as well.[128] It is "the last embodiment of spirit." It is *"Absolute Knowledge."* [129] This knowledge, including all "moments" as well as the whole "process" of its realization is "pure self-existence of self-consciousness." [130] The content of this knowledge is "the spirit which traverses the whole range of its own being." [131] It is the process of "transforming" the object of consciousness into an object of self-consciousness. [132] Until and unless spirit completes this process, it cannot reach its own completion as self-consciousness; it cannot truly exist or know itself as spirit. "But the process of carrying forward this form of knowledge of itself is the task which spirit accomplishes as actual History." [133] The whole process, however, is a dialectic; and in this dialectic of development the concrete human individual performs a crucial task; for it is in human self-consciousness alone that God comes to know Himself. It is only in self-consciousness that He is for Himself. And since God's reality consists of His being for Himself, it is only through the intermediacy of our human reality that God is real. He is as much our finitude as our human self in its aspirations and ultimate hope is the anticipation of the infinite.

This, I submit, is Hegel's solution of the Kantian problem that goes right to the heart of religion.

NOTES

1. *CPR*, Preface to the second edition, p. XXX, B ed.
2. *Ibid.*, p. 247, A ed.
3. *CPR*, p. 375, A ed.
4. *CPR*, p. 275, B ed.
5. *CPR*, p. 276, B ed.
6. *KdpV*, p. 6.
7. *CPR*, p. 263, B ed.
8. *CPR*, p. 446, B ed.
9. *CPR*, p. 126, A ed.
10. *CPR*, p. xxvii, B ed.
11. *CPR*, p. 107ff, A ed.
12. *CPR*, p. 156, B ed.
13. *CPR*, p. 155, B ed.
14. *CPR*, p. 249, A ed.
15. *CPR*, p. 253, A ed.
16. *CPR*, p. 310, B ed.
17. *CPR*, p. 306, B ed.
18. *CPR*, p. 344, B ed.
19. *CPR*, p. 255, A ed.
20. *CPR*, p. 256, A ed.
21. *CPR*, p. 255, A ed.
22. *CPR*, p. 307, B ed.
23. *CPR*, p. 312, B ed.
24. *CPR*, p. 344, B ed.
25. *CPR*, p. 522, B ed.
26. *CPR*, p. 429, B ed.
27. *CPR*, pp. 430-1, B ed.
28. *CPR*, p. 526, B ed.
29. *CPR*, p. 594, B ed.
30. *CPR*, p. 604, B ed.
31. *CPR*, p. 608, B ed.
32. *CPR*, p. 707, B ed.
33. *KdpV*, p. 121.
34. *KdpV*, p. 65.
35. *KdpV*, p. 3.
36. *KdpV*, p. 4.
37. *KdpV*, p. 104.
38. *CPR*, p. 829, B ed.
39. *KdpV*, p. 43.
40. *KdpV*, p. 44.
41. *KdpV*, p. 57.
42. *KdpV*, p. 57.
43. *KdpV*, p. 86.
44. *KdpV*, p. 87.
45. *KdpV*, p. 88.
46. *KdpV*, p. 97.
47. *KOP*, p. 819.
48. *KdpV*, p. 131.
49. *KdpV*, p. 150.
50. *HtJ*, p. 387.
51. *HtJ*, pp. 265-7.

52. *HtJ*, p. 303.
53. *Science of Logic*, I, p. 155.
54. *Ibid.*, p. 160.
55. *Ibid.*, p. 163.
56. *GzMdS*: IV, p. 459.
57. *KdpV*, p. 15.
58. *KdpV*, p. 16.
59. *KdpV*, p. 48.
60. *KdpV*, p. 91.
61. *GzMdS*: IV, p. 441.
62. *GzMdS*: IV, p. 412.
63. *GzMdS*: IV, p. 413.
64. *KdpV*, p. 33.
65. e.g., *Phen*, 681-785.
66. *Phen*, p. 190.
67. *Phen*, p. 219.
68. *Phen*, p. 218.
69. *Phen*, p. 227.
70. *Phen*, p. 257.
71. *Phen*, p. 257.
72. *Phen*, p. 260.
73. *Phen*, p. 261.
74. *Phen*, p. 264.
75. *Phen*, pp. 267, 274.
76. *Phen*, p. 272.
77. *Phen*, p. 283.
78. *Phen*, p. 457.
79. *Phen*, p. 600.
80. *Phen*, p. 601.
81. *Phen*, p. 601.
82. *Phen*, p. 602.
83. *Phen*, p. 602.
84. *Phen*, p. 604.
85. *Phen*, p. 604.
86. *GzMdS*: p. 407.
87. *KdpV*, pp. 33f.
88. *KdpV*, p. 648.
89. *KdpV*, p. 649.
90. *KdpV*, p. 650.
91. *KdpV*, p. 651.
92. *KdpV*, p. 651.
93. *KdpV*, p. 651.
94. *KdpV*, p. 663.
95. *KdpV*, p. 663.
96. *KdpV*, p. 664.
97. *KdpV*, p. 668.
98. *KdpV*, p. 669.
99. *KdpV*, p. 795.
100. *Phen*, See in particular, p. 280.
101. *Phen*, p. 253.
102. *Phen*, p. 255.
103. *Phen*, p. 466.
104. *Phen*, p. 504.

105. *Phen*, p. 514.
106. *Phen*, p. 515.
107. *Phen*, p. 516.
108. *Phen*, p. 517.
109. *Phen*, p. 668.
110. *Phen*, pp. 698-749.
111. *Phen*, p. 757.
112. *Phen*, p. 758.
113. *Phen*, p. 758.
114. *Phen*, p. 759.
115. *Phen*, p. 760.
116. *Phen*, p. 760.
117. *Phen*, p. 761.
118. *Phen*, p. 762.
119. *Phen*, p. 762.
120. *Phen*, p. 789.
121. *Phen*, p. 767.
122. *Phen*, p. 779.
123. *Phen*, p. 784.
124. *Phen*, p. 795.
125. *Phen*, p. 795.
126. *Phen*, p. 795.
127. *Phen*, p. 797.
128. *Phen*, p. 797.
129. *Phen*, p. 797.
130. *Phen*, p. 798.
131. *Phen*, p. 798.
132. *Phen*, p. 801.
133. *Phen*, p. 801.

COMMENT ON

W. H. WERKMEISTER
HEGEL'S PHENOMENOLOGY OF MIND AS A DEVELOPMENT OF
KANT'S BASIC ONTOLOGY

by

Murray Greene

Of the many basic and interesting questions raised in Professor Werkmeister's paper, I would like to dwell on only one: Kant's denial of the
possibility of a theoretical knowledge of the self "in itself" and Hegel's
overcoming of this denial. Werkmeister develops this issue mainly in
terms of the relation of the finite empirical self to the divine infinite
Spirit. I would like to concentrate on the specific grounds of Kant's
exclusion from theoretical knowledge of the self as spirit. It is Hegel's
overcoming of these grounds, I believe, that opens the realm of the spiritual to a philosophical knowledge that is more than a "making room
for faith."

The question of the possibility of a knowledge of the self "in itself"
needs to be seen in the context of the Cartesian formulation of the problem of knowledge during the rise of modern science. The new science
seemed to offer but two alternatives for a knowledge of the self: either
a reduction of "spirit" to matter in motion, as in Hobbes,[1] or, as in
Descartes or Leibniz, an affirmation of the reality of the self as spirit
but in a manner which Kant in his "critical" philosophy could only
reject as "dogmatic" and philosophically untenable. As Werkmeister
says, Kant remained ever concerned to preserve the realm of the spiritual
for philosophy. But, we must also note, Kant was likewise concerned to
demonstrate the basis for certainty of the new (Newtonian) science.
Kant found he could do both only by excluding the spiritual from theoretical knowledge. Hence, despite Werkmeister's proper admonition against
viewing Kant "only as preoccupied with problems of epistemology,"
we cannot overlook the fact that Kant's overriding aim of demonstrating
the possibility of a certain knowledge of the external world largely determined his stance toward the possibility of a knowledge of God, the soul,

and man's moral freedom. The Kantian solution of the problem of knowledge, directed essentially toward a knowledge of nature, rules out in
principle a knowledge of Spirit. In seeking to regain the realm of Spirit
for a philosophical knowledge that is more than a "rational faith,"
Hegel attacks the root conception of the Kantian critical enterprise, its
meaning of a "critique" of knowledge.

Kant's approach to the problem of knowledge, as Hegel notes, would
first examine our faculty of cognition as an "instrument" before we can
"take up the work for which it is employed." [2] As applied to the problem of a knowledge of the self, this approach entails that, for the knowing subject to know itself as it is "in itself" it would have to be at
once instrument and object known through the instrument. This, for
the Kantian approach to knowledge, is for various reasons impossible.
In the first place, lacking a sensible intuition of the self as such, our
understanding can only have an "empty concept" of the pure self. Further, the categories of the understanding cannot be employed in knowing
as an "object" their own very source, the self as transcendental ego;
for this would mean the knowing by the instrument of what makes it
"knowing" in the first place.[3] And finally, we cannot even know the self
as "appearance" with the same kind of apodictic certainty that we can
know the external world of phenomena. For "where we are dealing with
the corporeal realm," says Kant, "much that is a priori can be synthetically known from the mere concept of an extended body," but when
we are dealing with the self, "nothing whatsoever that is a priori can
be known synthetically from the concept of a thinking being." [4]

Thus in the Kantian critical approach to the problem of knowledge,
the victory gained for a knowledge of nature is bought at the price of
a knowledge of self. The condition for the possibility of a knowledge
of the corporeal is at the same time the condition for the impossibility
of a knowledge of the spiritual.

For Hegel, however, the victory is a specious one and the price is
falsely exacted. Hegel rejects the whole Kantian approach of viewing
cognition as an "instrument," with the concomitant "awkward" circularity to the knower's knowing himself.[5] There is indeed a circularity,
says Hegel, but one that by no means vitiates itself. On the contrary, it
is precisely in this self-relation that the ego manifests itself as notion,
"the absolute self-relation which, as separating judgment (*Ur-teil*),
makes itself its own object and is just this process of thereby becoming
a circle." But this concept of the ego as the inner self-distinguishing
of notion, says Hegel, is what Kant wishes to "ward off" in order to
hold fast to the non-self-distinguishing the, "notion-less." [6]

Kant's holding fast to the "notion-less" means here the Kantian conception of ego as but abstract self-identity which must go "outside" itself in sensory experience for all its knowledge, including knowledge of self. This going outside self, which is inherent in Kant's view of knowledge as an "instrument," is a bequeathal of the Cartesian separation of the thinking ego and nature as extension.[7] To be sure, says Hegel, self-consciousness as the mere "I am I" is but a tautology and abstract self-identity that must obtain a concrete content in experience.[8] But this need not mean that experience is limited to sensuous experience nor that sensuous experience consists in some affection by an "other" defined once and for all as an independently subsisting "thing-in-itself." Rather these are presuppositions, Hegel claims, which are implicit in any critique of knowledge that first examines cognition as an "instrument" or 'medium through which the light of truth reaches us." [9] Such a critique "presupposes a distinction of ourselves from this knowledge," sets asunder from the start what knows and what is to be known. It is through an overcoming of this sunderance that Hegel seeks to regain the realm of Spirit – and the self as spirit – for a philosophic knowledge that is more than a *Vernunftglaube*. From Hegel's critique of the Kantian approach to knowledge is born the radicalized critique of knowledge that constitutes the concept of a "phenomenology."

Hegel's phenomenological critique of knowledge is a critique of the forms of knowledge by the experiencing consciousness in the course of its own experience. The phenomenological approach does not, as the Kantian approach, define experience as limited to an affection of sensibility deriving from some encounter with an irreducible *Ding-an-sich*. The phenomenological approach lets the "other" of consciousness unfold in terms of consciousness's own characterization of "other-ness." The concept of "experience" emerges from nothing else but the nature of consciousness as "on the one hand, consciousness of the object, on the other hand consciousness of itself; consciousness of what to it is true, and consciousness of its knowledge of that truth." [10] In this concept of experience lies the possibility of an immanent critique of knowledge through consciousness's own "self-examination." The standard of criticism is not provided externally by the philosopher who evaluates cognition as an "instrument"; rather the standard emerges out of and develops coterminously with the course of the movement of experience on ascending levels of consciousness.

In this movement the "natural" consciousness, which takes its object and its truth as "outside" itself, attains self-consciousness through its own inner development, the object and truth of which is its self. But since self-consciousness has emerged precisely as the truth of consciousness, the former is no mere transcendental ego as "logical subject." Having taken up into itself the whole previous content of sense certainty, perception, and understanding, the ego has implicitly a concrete content, and precisely as self-identity is now certain of itself as the essence and truth of this content.[11]

Thus in Hegel's phenomenological reconstitution of Kant's critique of knowledge, the Kantian transcendental subject becomes a self-developing actuality that determines itself together with its "object" on ascending levels of consciousness, self-consciousness, reason, and spirit. By taking consciousness not as an "instrument" for knowing a truth outside itself but rather allowing consciousness's experience to unfold in terms of its own claims to knowledge, Hegel demonstrates that ego is the inner self-distinguishing of notion, whose "other" is in truth but its own self. In tracing the movement of experience through an unparalleled richness of forms of self-consciousness, of reason's claims to the truth of nature and man, of individual life styles, of cultural, historical, and religious realities, Hegel demonstrates that their universal permeating life is Spirit. In this way, out of Kant's concept of transcendental subject, there emerges in Hegel's *Phänomenologie des Geistes* a new dialectical principle of subjectivity that makes possible a philosophic knowing of Spirit and of the self as spirit.

NOTES

1. The words "incorporeal substance" are but sounds which can "signifie nothing at all." *Leviathan* (Oxford, 1962), p. 30.

2. *Wallace*, p. 17, and *Phen*, p. 131. Kant's own words are: "to prepare the ground beforehand by a critique of the organ," *CPR*, p. xxxvi, ed. B.

3. "We can thus say of the thinking 'I' (the soul) ... that it does *not* know *itself through the categories*, but knows the categories, and through them all objects in the absolute unity of apperception, and so *through itself*. Now it is, indeed, very evident that I cannot know as an object that which I must presuppose in order to know any object ..." *CPR*, p. 402, ed. A. (Kant's italics). "The subject of the categories cannot by thinking the categories acquire a concept of itself as an object of the categories. For in order to think them, its pure self-consciousness, which is what was to be explained, must itself be presupposed." *CPR*, p. 422, ed. B. If we may offer a crude analogy, the telescope can be trained upon any star of the heavens but cannot be turned to look upon itself.

4. *CPR*, p. 381, ed. A. "The cause," Kant says, is: "Although both are appearances, the appearance to outer sense has something fixed or abiding which supplies a substratum as the basis of its transitory determinations and therefore a synthetic concept, namely, that of space and of an appearance in space; whereas time, which

is the sole form of our inner intuition, has nothing abiding, and therefore yields knowledge only of the change of determinations, not of any object that can be thereby determined. For in what we entitle 'soul,' everything is in continual flux and there is nothing abiding except ... the 'I,' which is simple solely because its representation has no content, and therefore no manifold ..." *CPR*, p. 381, ed. A. This position, Hegel says, means in effect a return to Hume, who says "I never can catch *myself*" as a pure self. *SL*, II, p. 418.

5. *SL*, II, p. 418.

6. *SL*, p. 419.

7. "But lest we should always be uncertain as to the powers of the mind, and in order that we may not labour wrongly and at random before we set ourselves to think out things in detail, we ought once in our life to inquire diligently what the thoughts are of which the human mind is capable." (Descartes, *Rules for the Direction of the Mind*, Rule VIII) Here we see the seed of the Kantian critical approach which would examine the faculty of cognition prior to its use. On Hegel's critique of Descartes, see *Phen*, p. 136.

8. *Phen*, p. 219.

9. *Phen*, p. 131.

10. *Phen*, p. 141. Since both "object" and its "knowledge" are "for the same consciousness, it is itself their comparison," the standard for criticism and the knowledge to be criticized "are ready to hand in consciousness itself," and this provides the phenomenological definition of experience as "this dialectic process which consciousness executes on itself – on its knowledge as well as on its object – in the sense that out of it the new and true object arises." *Phen*, p. 142.

11. *Phen*, p. 220.

COMMENT ON

W. H. WERKMEISTER
HEGEL'S PHENOMENOLOGY OF MIND AS A REFLECTION OF
KANT'S BASIC ONTOLOGY

by

George Schrader

The paradox of knowledge which Kant set forth in such prominence is that with the progression of our knowledge the being inquired
about recedes further and further into the background. The more elab-
orate our knowledge, the more completely is the object itself hidden
from our scrutiny. The reason is, of course, that knowledge is the medium
through which we apprehend, categorize, conceptualize, and objectify
the reality which confronts us. In its assessment of empirical knowledge,
critical reason is forced to distinguish between being-as-known (as object
or phenomenon) and being-in-itself. The thing-in-itself is not, as many
of Kant's interpreters have assumed, a second object which stands back
of and is causally related to the object as known. It is rather the phenomenon itself considered in independence of the cognitive relationship. It
is thus a *modal* rather than a substantive distinction that is involved
here. Moreover, this distinction cannot be abrogated since it is necessarily invoked by every cognitive effort. Like Heidegger's principle of
"ontological difference," for which indeed it may have provided the
foundation, it represents a limit which in principle cannot be surpassed.
Any future metaphysics must, therefore, eschew speculation and take a
transcendental turn. If ontology is to be meaningfully pursued, it must
find a new procedure and a new access to being itself. The prophet of
the new ontology was not long in announcing himself. Hegel not only
proclaimed a new way of doing ontology but made use of the very
modal distinctions which for Kant seemed to make any scientific ontology forever impossible.

Professor Werkmeister has correctly interpreted the modal distinction
in Kant between phenomena and things-in-themselves as of pivotal significance for Kant's ontology. Moreover, he is thoroughly justified in

regarding this issue as of crucial importance for the relationship between Kant and Hegel. His emphasis upon the fundamentally important *practical* office of reason in Kant and the centrality of the finite individual subject in Hegel provides a useful corrective to the standard interpretations of both philosophers. My disagreements with Werkmeister are relatively minor. Still, it may be important that they be registered and explored lest we regard the transition to Hegel's ontology as following too easily from Kant.

First, though I would agree that the distinction between the empirical subject and the subject-in-itself is of primary ontological significance for Kant, it is no more fundamental than the object/thing-in-itself distinction which cuts across the entire critical philosophy. It is instructive in this regard to consider the development of Heidegger's ontology which began precisely with this question. In his "fundamental ontology" Heidegger made no attempt to transcend the Kantian limits with respect to the object of knowledge. Or at least not in so far as the object is other than the knower. In the famous "turn" or "Kehre" in Heidegger's thought, it is the Being of the phenomenon in the more inclusive sense which stands in the forefront of Heidegger's concern. As several of Heidegger's interpreters have observed, as Heidegger's ontology is developed and expanded it resembles Hegel's more and more. My point here is that if a new way in ontology was to be found after Kant it had not only to find a way of integrating the empirical subject with the notion of the subject-in-itself, but of making the phenomenon of experience serve as the vehicle for the disclosure of being.

As Werkmeister shows, Hegel made constructive use of the principle of ontological difference in developing his phenomenological ontology. It was Hegel's genius to see that for an entity to be objective (for-another) it must exist, also, for itself. Moreover, its being for others and for itself necessarily involves an internal relationship to its being-in-itself. The most interesting and most complex feature of Hegel's ontology is his use of mediation. No being is unmediated in the sense of being simple and self-subsistent. Conversely, no being can fully mediate itself in the sense of achieving its own self-integration. The confrontation with the object is important in posing the problem of access to the being of the object. But it is significant, also, – and this is the point which Werkmeister has stressed – in the problem it raises for the reflexivity of the self. Interestingly enough, for Hegel it is precisely those conditions which give rise to and constitute the problem which facilitate its resolution. The modal concepts are the primary categories with which we must work in following out the process of dialectical becoming.

So far as Kant's ontology is concerned, I must take issue with Werk-meister's claim that "the Kantian philosophy... is one all-inclusive sys-tem and can be truly understood only as such." In spite of Kant's refer-ences to the 'system of pure reason,' it can be persuasively argued, I believe, that Kant was in many respects a programatically *anti-systematic* philosopher. It is not the case, of course, that Kant did not have power-ful systematic interests or even that he was not genuinely metaphysical in his concerns. It is rather that Kant advanced powerful arguments to show that no all-inclusive system of pure reason is possible. Even if we take seriously, as I think we must, Kant's assertion that there is one and only one reason and that practical reason is primary, there is no apparent way in which we can unify the world-views of science and morality. To have a unified systematic view of man and nature, it is necessary to find a different answer to the antinomies of reason than the one Kant offered. In fact one of the reasons why Kant occupies such an important place in modern philosophy is that he was systema-tically ambiguous. He was a philosopher more of tension than of inte-grated unity. It is exceedingly difficult ever to remain altogether with Kant on any key issue – which means that we have to make decisions as to how we are to resolve the tensions and ambiguities in his thought. Hegel's own response to Kant represents what is surely the most brilliant and most important response to this feature of Kant's philosophy. Al-though it is easy to be persuaded that the development from Kant to Hegel is both logical and natural, this fact should not prompt us to conclude that no decisive options have been exercised. If we overstress the systematic character of Kant's philosophy we may lose sight of the fact that the idea of system is an ideal of reason rather than an estab-lished ontological principle governing all processes and activities of man and nature.

I must disagree, also, with Werkmeister's assertion that "when it is so understood, its very heart and essence turns out to be ontology..." I would not want to dispute the fact that Kant exhibited a deep and abiding ontological concern which permeated all of his investigations. He regarded the striving for the "unconditioned" to be an ineradicable concern of human reason. But Kant's ontological concern was in many respects far more *negative* than positive. Kant was not, I believe, alto-gether dismayed about the impossibility of attaining knowledge of things in themselves. He had a strong sense of the transcendence and unfathom-able mystery of being itself. Moreover, there is reason to believe that Kant took a certain pride in the conviction that he had permanently guaranteed that this mystery would never be dispelled by the human intellect. Positively viewed, Kant's transcendental philosophy was, as he characterized it, more a metaphysics of pure reason than an ontology of pure being.

It is, perhaps, for basically the same reason that I disagree with what I understand to be Werkmeister's identification in Kant of the trancendental subject with the subject-in-itself. Kant does refer to the "I am" and strongly suggests that the being of the self is at the foundation of both the empirical subject and the transcendental ego. But, so far as I know, he never identified the transcendental subject with the subject-in-itself. On the contrary, in the *Paralogisms* Kant staunchly refused any such identification. Although his terminology is inconsistent and his usage confusing on this point, neither does he identify the transcendental object with the thing in itself. The relationship between the empirical subject and the transcendental ego is, as Werkmeister points out, one of the most important and most difficult problems in Kant. And so too, is the ontological status of the transcendental ego. Kant never identified these concepts nor provided any basis for identifying them. We may speculate hypothetically about them, but can never hope to arrive at a completely warranted answer.

As I read Kant, no answer to this problem is provided by practical reason. It is, to be sure, one and only one reason which operates theoretically and practically. With this point I fully agree. But I do not see how this helps us out with the problem of the subject-in-itself. Werkmeister identifies the transcendental subject of the First Critique with the moral subject of the Second Critique, but this strikes me as a stronger conclusion than is warranted by the evidence. We know that man is a legislator and that reason is constitutive in two radically different ways with respect to nature and morality. But we have no theoretical basis for claiming that it is one and the same subject which legislates in the two spheres. The presumption is strong that they are in some sense the same or, at least, stem from a common source. But even if they are identical, it is at the transcendental rather than the ontological level of analysis.

I must admit that Kant often talks as if the moral subject were the ontologically real subject and, hence, equivalent to the subject-in-itself. The fact is, however, that when he had occasion to discuss this point systematically, he refused the identification. At most, I would argue, the identification is suggested rather than explicitly avowed in the passages cited by Werkmeister. This point is of some importance with respect to the relationship between the ontologies of Kant and Hegel – that is, if we can speak in this way of Kant's ontology. As I read Kant, even in so late a work as the *Critique of Judgment,* the notion of the radical transcendence of being remains prominently on the scene. The 'super-sensible substrate' which we are required to invoke in accounting for our aesthetic experience remains radically transcendent and beyond our attempts to conceptualize or otherwise to incorporate it within a unified and immanent world. Herein lies the basic philosophical differ-ence between Kant and Hegel. Hegel permits no thing-in-itself within his system because for him transcendence is a dimension of absolute consciousness. Kant not only permits but preserves and protects the rad-ical transcendence of being itself. Kant was, after all, a philosopher of limits. The principle of ontological difference constitutes both the provo-cation and the limitation for philosophical inquiry.

I must differ on one final point with Werkmeister's Kant interpreta-tion. He cites a passage from the *Opus postumum* to the effect that "God is the morally practical reason legislating for itself." There are in fact a number of such passages, but also statements which reflect Kant's earlier views on the matter. The character of these reflections is such that no reliable conclusions can be drawn as to Kant's positive doctrines. In his published writings Kant referred to the moral law "as if" it were the voice of God. But that is not the same as identifying it with the voice of God.

As I have indicated earlier, I am quite happy with Werkmeister's interpretation of Hegel and especially applaud his stress on the role of the finite consciousness. Hegel does offer a new ontology which takes its departure from the Kantian impasse. In my comments I have sought to stress that the transition from Kant to Hegel is more abrupt than Werkmeister suggests. Hegel's ontology cannot be developed out of Kant's without a major revision of tenets which are fundamental to the Kantian philosophy.

REPLY TO COMMENTATORS

by

W. H. Werkmeister

I

Professor Greene's commentary is, in effect, a scholarly supplement to my own paper – a supplement which not only leaves my basic thesis unaltered but tends to re-enforce it.

Professor Greene, stressing throughout the divergence of Kant's and Hegel's epistemological orientations – Kant's transcendentalism versus Hegel's phenomenological dialectic – concludes that in Hegel's "phenomenological reconstruction of Kant's critique of knowledge, the Kantian transcendental subject becomes a self-developing actuality that determines itself together with its 'object' on ascending levels of consciousness, self-consciousness, reason, and spirit." I take this to mean that, like me, Professor Greene sees Hegel's phenomenology as a development of the Kantian position, and as providing a solution for problems for which Kant had none and could have none, given his epistemological orientation.

Where, then, is the difference between Professor Greene's thesis and mine? – for a difference there is, and an important one. Stated succinctly, it is this: Professor Greene stresses throughout epistemological issues; I, on the other hand, was interested in metaphysical problems, believing them to be particularly germane to our overall topic. That the two sets of problems are interrelated is, of course, true. But a difference in selective emphasis remains; and this is crucial here.

My thesis is that Kant, making the transcendental subject the constitutive ground of the realm of nature, left unanswered, the question of the relationship between empirical and transcendental subjects. After all, the empirical subject, being itself phenomenon, cannot be the same as the transcendental subject. The problem becomes still more complicated in the realm of ethics because, as empirical subject, man is under the dominance of causal determinations; as self-legislative moral agent, however, he must be free. There thus arises in a new form the problem of the relationship of the empirical self to a self that is trans-phenomenal. Kant never solved this problem; and given his epistemological orientation, he could not solve it, for the problem arises because of that orientation.

In Hegel's phenomenology the problem arises in the form of the relationship of the finite self to the Absolute. But since the dialectic in all the richness of forms of self-consciousness, of cultural and historical realities, is but the self-manifestation of Spirit, and since man is the active agent in this process, the concrete human individual performs a crucial task; for it is in human self-consciousness that Spirit comes to know itself. It is only through the intermediacy of our human reality that Spirit – read God – is real. What in religion was merely "a way of imagining," finds fulfillment in "the action proper of the self." It is only in man's self-consciousness that God is for Himself. As I said it in my paper: He is as much our finitude as our human self in its aspirations and ultimate hope is the anticipation of the Infinite. And this, I again submit, is Hegel's solution of the bothersome Kantian Problem that goes to the very heart of religion.

II

I completely agree with Professor Schrader's concluding statement that "Hegel's ontology cannot be developed out of Kant's without a major revision of tenets which are fundamental to the Kantian philosophy – for which Kant himself found no solution and, as Professor Schrader seems willing to concede, Hegel did.

The problem is that of the preservation of man in his empirical reality and his finitude within the Hegelian conception of the self-manifestation of Absolute Spirit; and my argument is that this problem arises within the framework of Kant's basic ontology in the form of the interrelation of the empirical and the transcendental selves, of the phenomenal self and the self-in-itself.

Professor Schrader agrees that here is a problem, and that a "new way in ontology" had to be found in order to find "a way of integrating the empirical subject with the notion of the subject in itself." The theme of my paper is that Hegel's *Phenomenology of Mind* provides such a "new way." On the crucial issue, therefore, Professor Schrader and I are in essential agreement.

However, Professor Schrader apparently feels that I have "overstressed the systematic character of Kant's philosophy," and that I have assumed identities which Kant himself did not assert. It is true, of course, that Kant did not write a book conveniently entitled *My System*. And it is true also that he did recast his thoughts on crucial issues and did not eliminate all ambiguities inherent in his position. But this does not contradict my statement that Kant's various works are but interdependent parts of an over-arching whole, or that Kant was essentially a "system thinker." We understand neither his epistemology and its implications, nor his ethics, nor his aesthetics, nor his "religion within the bounds of pure reason alone" if we don't see the unifying point of view behind them all.

Is this point of view an ontology or a "metaphysics of pure reason?" This may be a purely verbal issue. I have become accustomed to using the term "metaphysics" to designate what is essentially *speculative* metaphysics – the development of a speculative hypothesis concerning the ultimate nature of reality; and Kant is obviously not a metaphysician in this sense. I have never really understood what an "ontology of pure being" might be because I do not know what *pure* being is. As far as I am concerned, ontology is primarily an analysis of the "givens" in our human situation – precisely the sort of thing that ultimately concerned Kant.

Professor Schrader objects to an identification of the transcendental subject with the subject-in-itself. Admittedly Kant never asserted this identification in so many words but "strongly suggested" it (to quote Professor Schrader); and I shall let it go at that. There is, however, this further consideration: We find in Kant references to the empirical or "phenomenal" self, the transcendental self, the self-in-itself, the phenomenal object, and the thing-in-itself – and, for good measure, the transcendental object and the transcendental unity of apperception. And then we have passages, such as the following from Kant's discussion of *Paralogisms*: "Though the 'I', as represented through inner sense in time, and objects in space outside me, are specifically quite distinct appearances, they are not for that reason thought as being different things. Neither the trancendental object which underlies outer appearances nor that which underlies inner intuition, is in itself either matter or a thinking being, but a ground (to us unknown) of the appearances." Object-in-itself and subject-in-itself here are merged into *a* ground of the appearances; and the problem which Kant did not solve (but Hegel did) is the relation of the empirical self to that "underlying ground" – the ground underlying both, phenomenal object and phenomenal self.

HEGEL'S "UNHAPPY CONSCIOUSNESS" AND NIETZSCHE'S "SLAVE MORALITY"

by

Murray Greene

"The master becomes the slave of the slave, and the slave the master of the master." [1] In some such fashion, oversimplified to be sure, we may perhaps characterize Hegel's genesis of the Judeo-Christian consciousness in *Phen*.[2] With this overall view of the triumph of the Christian "slave morality" Nietzsche would quite likely agree.[3] But for the two thinkers the meaning and consequences of this "reversal" could hardly be more different. For Nietzsche it meant a revaluation (*Umwertung*) of the life-affirming "good-bad" values of the master to the life-negating "good-evil" morality of the slave.[4] It meant the injection into Western man of that slow-spreading poison which, two millenia later, would bring to the door nihilism, the "uncanniest of guests." For Hegel too the transformation meant initially a despair of life and a self-negating by the Unhappy Consciousness (*unglückliche Bewusstsein*).[5] But implicit in this self-negating is the representation of reason (*Vorstellung der Vernunft*), the certainty of consciousness that it is "all reality." [6] From this moment forward, consciousness discovers the world "as its own new and real world" [7] in which it goes forth to plant its flag "on the heights and in the depths." [8]

How are we to understand this chasm between the two great thinkers? How and where can we begin to bring Hegel and Nietzsche into some one perspective, some relation with one another, even a relation of opposition? [9] For both thinkers the concept of "negativity" is central. Yet any relating on the basis of this difficult concept is fraught with complex problems. I can only touch upon a few aspects of a relating and hope my treatment opens up other possibilities. I shall focus on the meaning of negativity as developed by the two thinkers in their respective accounts of the Judeo-Christian consciousness as a "self-negating" consciousness.

Despite the differences between a philosophy of spirit (*Geistesphilo-sophie*) and a life philosophy *(Lebensphilosophie)*, a phenomenological genesis and a psychological "genealogy," the respective approaches to the Judeo-Christian consciousness by the two thinkers have certain things in common. In neither case does the philosopher here deal with God as he is "in himself." God and whatever is said of God in the two treatments is to be understood as bracketed, as an "appearance" to consciousness. This lies in the concept of Hegel's phenomenological enter-prise at this stage, in which the divine predicates derive precisely from consciousness's own antithetical relation to itself.[10] That in Nietzsche the divinity is "appearance" for consciousness and not an "in itself" hard-ly needs to be stressed.

In both accounts then we can say we are dealing with an appearance to consciousness. But we can go somewhat further in establishing a common ground. In both accounts that which "appears" does so in the guise of an "other" that is in essential ways the antithesis of conscious-ness as it is "for itself." [11]

Again, in both accounts, this comes to mean that the "other" is like-wise a consciousness and is so for the first.[12] Hence we are dealing with a "divided" consciousness which has in itself the "other" also. These considerations afford not only the possibility of a comparison of the two accounts but also perhaps some criteria whereby each may be judged in accordance with its claims. We may ask, for example, how is it that the one consciousness can have within itself the "other" also? What is the nature of this "internalization" (*Verinnerlichung*) that must needs be also a "duplication" or "self-sunderance" (*Verdopplung*)? And how are both "internalization" and "self-sunderance" related to the 'self-negation" that is central to both conceptions of the Christian consci-ousness?

That Hegel conceives the Unhappy Consciousness as a *Bewusstsein* is decisive for his phenomenological genesis. Internalization, duplication, and self-negation must accompany self-consciousness in every form of its concrete life on the pathway of its actualization as Spirit.[13] The move-ment of self-consciousness is therefore a "highway of despair," at whose every stage consciousness must experience "the ruin and overthrow" of itself in whatever its form of "immediate being-there." [14] As a stage on this "highway of despair" the Unhappy Consciousness contains the moments of *Verdopplung, Verinnerlichung,* and negative self-relation in the sense that every consciousness contains these moments as reflected-ness of self in "other."

In Nietzsche the self-dividedness and negative self-relation that marks the Christian morality is not conceived within the framework of the inherent self-reflectedness of consciousness as in Hegel. Nietzsche has taken himself out of the problematic of subjectivity and the subject-object relation as this had developed from Descartes through Hegel.[15] Strictly speaking, the Christian morality for Nietzsche is conceived not so much as a "consciousness" but a "life," a "nature," a "will to power." [16] In the absence, in Nietzsche's psychological genealogy, of a concept of self-reflectedness as specifically the self-reflectedness of consciousness, how will we see the Christian morality as a self-negation? How will a "life" become "life-hostile," a "nature" become "unnatural?" How will a "force" come to be "turned against itself?"

I

Nietzsche conceives the Christian morality as deriving ultimately from what he terms "bad conscience," the primordial fissure within the self that occurred with man's "forcible sundering from his animal past." [17] Bad conscience is the self's first duplication, internalization, and negative relation to itself as an instinctual life. It is the "animal soul turned against itself, taking sides against itself," when "prowling man" finally found himself "enclosed within the walls of society and peace." In bad conscience all the old instincts of "hostility, cruelty, joy in persecuting, in attacking" did not cease to make their usual demands but were transformed to new and "subterranean gratifications" (*unterirdische Befriedigungen*).

But whence does this original sunderance of man from his natural being come about? It comes in the form of a conflict between two "natures," two natural orders of men, the strong and the weak, the active and the passive, the form-giving artist nature and the form-receiving material.[18] Coming thus from two different "natures" of men, the sunderance of man from his animal past proceeds in two correspondingly different courses. In the active master nature the old savage rapacity remains turned against the outsider, and thus continues to have a natural outlet.[19] In the slave nature, however, the old instincts turn "inward" and become a "cauldron of unsatisfied hatred." The impotent vengefulness of the slave nature eventually yields the "good-evil" values of *ressentiment:* meekness, pity, self-abnegation – the foul-smelling products of the underground "workshop of ideals." [20] As a *ressentiment* this slave morality is not only a turning of weakness against strength, not only a turning

against "other" (the master), but also a turning against self, a dimi-
nution of life-force.

How are we to understand this "turning against self?" Nietzsche sees
this in terms of a blocking of instinctual energies which in the natural
life are directed "outward." Barred from discharging itself outwardly,
this flow of energies turns against the self itself. It is in this sense that
the negative self-relation has the character of an internalization. "All
instincts that do not discharge themselves outwardly turn inward – this
is what I call the internalization of man." [21]

But how does this account for the "values," the social forms that are
produced in this internalization? To speak of a blockage of a force is
not enough. Hence concurrently with the account of the internalization
of bad conscience, Nietzsche presents an account of the duplication of the
self in the social relation. This is conceived in terms of the "debtor-
creditor" relationship of "exchange."

It is in the *quid pro quo* of exchange, according to Nietzsche, that
"one person first encountered another person," that man first became
aware of himself as "man." [22] This is the originary relation of self to
"other" which eventually becomes the relation of self to God. Thus
the consciousness of "being in debt (*Schulden zu haben*) to the deity" –
which in the Christian morality will become "guilt before God" –
has its seed in "the oldest and most primitive personal relationship,
that between buyer and seller, creditor and debtor." Into the social forms
developed out of the debtor-creditor relation, the old animal instincts of
cruelty now flow and obtain socially acceptable outlets. The "turning
against self" of bad conscience can take on the forms of the debtor-creditor
relation because discharge of debt can consist in the debtor's suffering
and the creditor's making suffer.[23] This "balancing of an account" not
only sets the pattern of the relation of the self to other selves but also
that of the self to itself and to the inwardized greater "self": community,
ancestors, deity. As the tribal community grows in power and extends its
benefits, the ancestors as "creditors" become ever more powerful until
they take on the status of gods. By a logic of its own the feeling of guilty
indebtedness to the divinity grows "in the same measure as the concept
of God and the feeling of divinity" increases on earth and is carried "to
the heights." With "the advent of the Christian God, as the maximum
god attained so far," there comes "the maximum feeling of guilty
indebtedness on earth." [24]

To understand this "maximization," however, we must recall the *Umwertung* of the life-expanding "good-bad" master values to the life-

diminishing "good-evil" morality of the slave. The "maximization" of God means the "minimization" of self – "self" being understood always as a "life," a "force," a "will to power." Maximum negation of self in the slave nature means *eo ipso* maximum elevation of deity.

At this point, however, there comes a decisive turn. In the extremity of its impotent vengefulness the slave morality even bursts asunder the debtor-creditor relation. It declares the futility of all balance of indebtedness.[25] Where before the aim of the relation had been "discharge" of guilty indebtedness, now the aim is to make the feeling of guilt "eternal." Only in this way can "guilt" and "duty" be rooted in that original cleft of self, the "bad conscience." Since ancestor, community, deities have possessed the power of discharging indebtedness, the self-negation of the slave nature in its duplication is "turned back against the 'creditor' too." Now the "primal ancestor" is "burdened with a curse" (Adam, original sin); nature, "from whose womb mankind arose," is "diabolized"; existence as such is now considered "worthless." But what resolution can there be of this absolute "turning against self" in which the self negates itself in the entirely of its universal "natural" being?

Here Pauline Christianity emerges out of Judaism's slavish "no-saying" to "everything on earth." [26] God himself "makes payment to himself," "the creditor sacrifices himself for his debtor." [27] In this "stroke of genius" on the part of Christianity is born "the paradoxical and horrifying expedient that afforded temporary relief for tormented humanity."

In this way Nietzsche explains the "appearance" of God in the natural realm as the culmination of the slave nature's negation of self. The essential meaning of the "appearance" is the taking on of the form of "something existent, corporeal, real" of man's own "denial of himself, of his nature, naturalness, and actuality (*Tatsächlichkeit*)." [28] In "God" man apprehends "the ultimate antithesis of his own ineluctable (*unablöslichen*) animal instincts." This account of the "appearance," says Nietzsche, "should dispose once and for all of the question of how the 'holy God' originated." [29]

Are we obliged to accept Nietzsche's claim to have accounted for the Christian morality in general and "how the 'holy God' originated" in particular? Since that morality and "the 'holy God' " is the negation of the human self, the crucial question would seem to be whether Nietzsche's particular conception of self-negation – as a movement of a "force" turning against itself – is equal to the task demanded of it in the account. Self-negation is in Nietzsche's account a form of self-reflectedness.[30] But would not self-reflectedness here require a demonstration in terms other than those of "force"? Possibly on the biological level, as in the natural death of the organism, self-negation may be explained in terms of "forces" and "energies." But would not any "turning against self" in the form of a "morality" and a concept of "God" require demonstration in terms immanent to the mental realm as such?

Nietzsche's explanatory account is of course intentionally and explicitly a reductionism. A mental content – the Christian morality, the "appearance" of God on earth – is "reduced" to a movement of "forces." [31] To be sure, a mental account always follows along, as in the debtor-creditor relation. Since the movement of forces is taken as causally primary, however, the mental as such can never be "necessary" on its own terms; it can only be capable of fitting into the explanation in terms of force. But if, as we suggest, Nietzsche has been guilty of a mixing of categories, where in his exposition can he be faulted?

A comparison with Hegel's phenomenological account will perhaps bring to light certain difficulties in Nietzsche's exposition. The Hegelian presentation, in terms of a logos of consciousness,[32] in principle takes self-negation as a necessary moment in the self-reflectedness of consciousness. The self-negation and self-reflectedness of the Unhappy Consciousness is not in terms of a logos of force but of consciousness's "being for self" in its "otherness" as a necessary content "for" it.

II

The impetus in the phenomenological genesis of the Unhappy Consciousness is not the blocking of instinctual energies but the incommensurability (*Unangemessenheit*) between self-consciousness in its notion as "absolute negativity," and any immediate being-there (*unmittelbares Dasein*) in which self-consciousness may be "for itself" as a "limit" to its own inherent universality.[33] In its first form as desire (*Begierde*), self-consciousness seeks to verify its certainty of self in its other by destruction and consumption of the object, an independent natural life. But desire is "unable by its negative relation to the object to abolish it, because of that relation it rather produces it again, as well as the desire." [34] The truth of the desiring self-consciousness turns out to be rather that self-consciousness can attain its being-for-self only in another self-consciousness.[35] The movement toward this attainment is the life and death struggle for "recognition," a struggle which sunders self-consciousness from "its mere absorption in the expanse of life" [36] and is at the same time the emergence of the specifically human (social) realm. In this sunderance from nature through the inherent need of self-consciousness for recognition is revealed the ground of a "we" consciousness as a substantial reality.[37] Such a "we" consciousness finds no equivalent in Nietzsche.[38]

In the light of Hegel's concept of recognition we may at this point ask whether Nietzsche has offered a satisfactory account of the duplication of the self in the "exchange" relation of debtor and creditor, the relation, we recall, in which it was said that "one person first encountered another person." That man, in his most primary relation to another as a "person," is an "evaluator," a "measurer," would seem to presuppose a great deal. It would seem to require at the least a prior acceptance on the part of each that the other is an "evaluator," that each has the "right" to his evaluation, and that each has the confidence that the other, in turn, is willing to accord him this right. In a word, the exchange relation would presuppose a reciprocity and self-reflectedness that must indeed be present in the *quid pro quo* of an "exchange" but could hardly have been engendered by it. Hegel conceives the primary relation of persons in mutual recognition as a duplication, or reflectedness of self in other, through "mediation." In recognition, each self-consciousness

> is the mediating term to the other, through which each mediates and unites itself with itself; and each is to itself and to the other an immediate *für sich seiendes Wesen*, which, at the same time, is thus for itself only through the mediation.[39]

Duplication, as we saw, is crucial for Nietzsche's concept of self-negation as self-reflectedness. But mediation, whether in the Hegelian phenomenological sense or any other, is absent in Nietzsche's concept of the debtor-creditor relation. In place of the mediation conceived by Hegel phenomenologically as consciousness' being-for-self through recognition by the "other," we have only the duplication of self conceived by Nietzsche physiologically as a force turned back against itself. But where is the self-reflectedness necessary to the relationship of exchange? The self-reflectedness essential to Nietzsche's debtor-creditor relation seems of mysterious origin. If, as Nietzsche wishes us to believe, the debtor-creditor relation is the foundation of the social relationship and eventually the God relationship, we are left to wonder about the source of the self-reflectedness which will finally make possible the appearance on earth of the Christian God as "antithesis" of man's "own ineluctable animal instincts." Without an adequate account of self-reflectedness as *sine qua non* of the original relationship of exchange, Nietzsche's whole construction seems to be hanging in the air.

From the life and death struggle for recognition, in Hegel's account, emerges the master-slave relation as the first and yet one-sided form of the "we" consciousness. The slave has his being-for-self only outside himself in the form of the master. But from this being-outside-self the slave consciousness will turn back into itself, thus making possible its attainment of an independent being-for-self (*Fürsichsein*). The slave consciousness, as consciousness pressed back into itself (*in sich zurückgedrängte Bewusstsein*), however, is not seen by Hegel in terms of a force that turns against itself. The internalization of the slave is seen rather as the negative self-relation of self-consciousness in its notion as universality.

The slave consciousness' negative self-relation is its experience of the absolute fear that has shaken the slave to the depths of his being. As fear of the "sovereign master," it is the dissipation of all determinate being (*bestimmtes Sein*) from the slave's being-for-self.[40] The negativity here means that the slave consciousness does not cling to itself as caprice (*Eigensinn*) but has the possibility of a genuine universalization. This possibility, however, remains only "formal" until actualized in "labor" and "service."

That the activity of labor is an essential moment in the slave inwardization marks another important difference from Nietzsche.[41] The labor of the slave, according to Hegel, overcomes the "bad infinity" of desire. As the pressing back inward (*Insichzurückdringen*) of the slave consciousness, labor is checked desire, disappearance held off (*gehemmte Begierde, aufgehaltenes Verschwinden*). For this reason it is a formative making-stay, and in two senses. On the side of the being-in-self (*Ansichsein*), the object is "inwardized" and becomes a substantiality precisely through the in-forming activity of the being-for-self (*Fürsichsein*).[42] At the same time the slave consciousness overcomes its own absolute fluidness (*Flüssigwerden*); its labor means for its own selfhood an *aufgehaltenes Verschwinden*.[43] For this reason the products of the slave self-consciousness are not merely the products of *ressentiment*. To be sure, for both Hegel and Nietzsche the slave morality of self-denial is born out of weakness. But for Hegel this weakness (the *absolutes Flüssigwerden* of the slave self-consciousness) means the potentiality of absolute negativity and universality, a potentiality that begins to be actualized in recognition and labor. For Hegel the moral ideals of the slave consciousness – self-denial, labor, service, obedience – are not "subterranean gratifications" but rather the universal modes of man's relating himself as self-consciousness to his own natural being as being-in-self. He must first sunder himself from his natural being – as "subjectivity" he must relate himself negatively to himself as a "nature" – in order that he may wholly permeate this natural being with his subjectivity and thereby return to himself in his wholeness as Spirit.[44]

What Nietzsches terms a "stroke of genius" on the part of Christianity, namely, the "appearance" of God in the natural realm, Hegel claims to demonstrate phenomenologically through his concept of the self-reflectedness of consciousness. The stoic and sceptical self-consciousness, which have succeeded the master-slave relation, have produced a duplication in which consciousness is consciousness of self as singular, changeable, and unessential consciousness, and at the same time consciousness of its "other" as universal, unchangeable, and essential, which, however, is for it a "beyond." Unlike the sceptical consciousness from which it arises, the Unhappy Consciousness is a divided consciousness that is "for itself" a dividedness.

> It itself *is* the gazing of the one self-consciousness into another, and itself *is* both, and the unity of both is also its own essence; but *for itself* it is not yet this essence itself – it is not yet the unity of both.[45]

In its infinite pain over all existence and doing, consciousness moves to negate itself in its singularity and raise itself to the unchangeable. But in this its self-elevation (*Erhebung*) consciousness experiences precisely the emergence of the singularity in the unchangeable, and the unchangeable in the singularity. "For the truth of this process is precisely that the double consciousness is one and single." [46]

Thus the "appearance" of the unchangeable in the realm of the changeable is nothing other than the *movement* of the divided consciousness to unite itself as singular changeable consciousness with its "other" as universal unchangeable, which is in truth but its own essence. This must be understood in terms of that duplication [47] of self-consciousness which was inadequately conceived as debtor-creditor in Nietzsche but which Hegel has shown to be the essential moment of recognition.[48]

In the singular consciousness' *Erhebung* the implicit unity of the singular with the unchangeable becomes something *for* the singular consciousness. It does so in such a wise, however, that the difference (*Ver-*

schiedenheit) is still the dominant aspect. To the singular consciousness the appearing of the unchangeable as the formed unchangeable (*gestaltete Unwandelbare*) is but a happening (*Geschehen*) "just as the singular consciousness merely happens to find itself opposed to the unchangeable, and therefore has this relationship *per naturam* (*durch die Natur*)." [49]

Thus in Hegel's phenomenological demonstration of the "appearance" of God as self-reflectedness of consciousness, the appearance is the singular consciousness' own "other" qua universal taking on the figure (*Gestaltung*) of singularity. That the appearance has the aspect for consciousness of coming "durch die Natur" (the divine incarnation) derives from the fact that consciousness yet relates itself to the universal as singularity to another singularity. The appearance is not "durch die Natur" in Nietzsche's sense that what appears is but the incarnation of the slave nature's own "ineluctable animal instincts" turned "backward" against the slave nature itself.

Thus far we have seen how Hegel's phenomenological genesis, in contrast to Nietzsche's "genealogy," presents the moments of duplication, internalization, and negative self-relation in terms of a logos of consciousness rather than as a movement of force. These moments we saw expressed in the emergence of the substantial "we" consciousness of "recognition," labor as formative activity, and the "appearance" of the unchangeable as the "other" of the singular consciousness in its essential duplication. For Hegel as well as Nietzsche the "appearance" of the divinity leads to the consummation of the Christian self-negation in the ascetic ideal. But for the two thinkers this consummation has totally different meanings.

III

The Christian morality of self-negating, as expressed most acutely in the ascetic ideal, is for Nietzsche "a will to nothingness, an aversion to life." At the same time, however, it is part of nature's task "to breed an animal with the right to make promises," the "master of *free* will." To this "labor performed by man upon himself," the whole of asceticism" in a sense belongs. [50] The self-negation of the ascetic ideal, according to Nietzsche, turns into a "will to truth" which negates Christianity itself. In this negation of negation we find a certain parallel in Hegel. As developed in terms of a movement of force, however, Nietzsche's negation of negation has a different meaning and outcome than in Hegel's phenomenological development.

The paradox of the ascetic ideal, according to Nietzsche, consists in that the ascetic will to nothingness is itself a form of "will to power," a "nature," and a "force." In the "psychical cruelty" toward self of the Christian morality, the self is a "nature" whose own well-springs of self-hatred can come only from the self itself. Hence the ascetic will toward self-extirpation cannot but be a self-defeating contradiction, an attempt "to employ force to block up the wells of force." [51] As a will to power in the form of a *ressentiment* the ascetic negating of self cannot but be a reaffirming of self in inverted form.

As in Nietzsche's self-contradicting ascetic ideal, the Unhappy Consciousness's movement to annul itself as singular, unessential consciousness can only be

> the conflicting contradictory process in which opposite does not come to rest in its own opposite but produces itself therein afresh merely as an opposite. [52]

But the turning against self of the Unhappy Consciousness is not a *ressentiment,* not the negativity of a "nature" and a "force" that has turned inward in impotent vengefulness. The paradox of the Unhappy Consciousness is not that of a "nature" or a "force" but a *Fürsichsein*: the divided consciousness' incapacity of itself as singular consciousness to bring together its essential but opposing moments of singularity and universality. "Nature" to be sure is relevant, but only indirectly, only insofar as it serves, qua sensuous reality of the here and now, to reinstate the moment of singularity. For self-consciousness has already in a sense overcome its natural being. It has "risked its life" in the struggle for recognition, it has desired, consumed, labored, and in all these relations to external reality it has experienced its self-confirmation. That self-confirmation, however, has been dissolved in scepticism. As sceptical, self-consciousness's universal negating power of thought dissolves all inherent meaningfulness attached to self-consciousness' own doing and to objective reality. [53]

With the "appearance" of the unchangeable in the realm of transient singularity, all of self-consciousness' desiring, laboring, enjoying obtain the possibility of a redemption from the nihilation of scepticism but at the same time become infinitely hard to accomplish. For all of external reality now reflects the Unhappy Consciousness' own inner diremption: everything in the world must be either invested with universal meaningfulness or become a vanity of vanities.

For Nietzsche too the ascetic consciousness must put everything to the test of a universal meaningfulness:

> The ascetic ideal has a *goal* – this goal is so universal that all the other interests of human existence seem, when compared with it, petty and narrow . . .[54]

But as universal goal the self-negating becomes directed against the very morality that gave it birth. It does so by asking the question: "What is the meaning of all will to truth?' " Hereby the ascetic ideal unmasks itself as but a "metaphysical faith" deriving from *ressentiment*. The ascetic ideal thus turns into its opposite. It "finally forbids itself the lie involved in belief in God." [55]

But here we must ask Nietzsche how we are to understand the genesis of the universal goal. Does Nietzsche's conception of the paradox of the ascetic ideal adequately account for the turning of the "will to nothingness" into a "will to truth"? What has "conquered the Christian God," says Nietzsche, is "the Christian morality itself, the concept of truthfulness taken more and more strictly." But why the "more and more"? And why a "will to truth"? Does this follow in any necessary sense from the concept of the ascetic paradox as an employment of force to block up the wells of force? It seems again that Nietzsche is relying on some principle of maximization, as in the case of maximum guilty indebtedness and the advent of the "maximum God."

For Hegel too the ascetic self-negating ultimately becomes a will to truth. This derives in no sense from a maximization principle, however, but from the phenomenological elements of paradox in the Unhappy Consciousness's endeavor to rid itself of its transient singularity and be one with its own universal substantial being. Following its failure in "devotion" (*Andacht*), in labor, and enjoyment, consciousness directs itself against the very "functions of animal life." But these functions thereby become "precisely the most important consideration"; the "enemy," instead of being gotten rid of, is recreated "in its very defeat" and consciousness finds itself "constantly defiled." [56]

Yet this whole endeavor of self-negating is "mediated through the thought of the unchangeable and takes place in this relation." [57] Herein lies the implicitly positive moment in the negative. This "thought" of its own "other," which motivates consciousness' attempted self-negating, becomes the "mediator" which presents the one extreme to the other.[58] In its total surrender of itself to the "mediator," its giving up its will as a singular consciousness "is only in one aspect negative"; it is at the same time the "affirming the will as an other," specifically the "other" of itself, the universal substantial being. The universal will that now comes through the "mediator" is for consciousness the "inherent and essential will" (*an sich seiende Wille*). In consciousness' certainty of having made itself into a "thing," its own will an "objective external existence" (*gegenständliches Sein*), operated, so to speak, by the universal acting through the "mediator," there is present implicitly the unity of objective and subjective (*des Gegenständlichen und des Fürsichseins*) which lies in the notion of action. To be sure, consciousness' own action still remains for it a negative whose positive significance lies in the "beyond." But in finding its own action and being to be implicitly (*an sich*) being and action, there has arisen for consciousness the representation of reason, the certainty of consciousness that it is *alle Realität* [59] and *alle Wahrheit*.[60]

Thus for Hegel it is not the self-negation of *ressentiment* that gives birth to the rational consciousness but rather the mediated self-negation of the singular consciousness that unites it with its own universal substantial being. This, for Hegel, is in the profoundest sense a "yes-saying." [61] For Nietzsche the ascetic ideal's belief in truth is a "no-saying" and a "metaphysical faith." Linked with the belief in God, the belief in truth "turns out to be our longest lie." [62] For Hegel the rational consciousness's belief that it is in the truth does indeed rest upon the certainty (*Gewissheit*) of its unity with divinity. This, for Hegel, is the whole meaning of the movement of the Unhappy Consciousness.

IV

We cannot here follow Hegel's purported demonstration in the remainder of *Phen* that the rational consciousness' "certainty" of its being in the truth is raised to a truth in "absolute knowledge." Nor can we pursue the implications of Nietzsche's perspectivism contained in his claim that our "faith in truth" is our "longest lie." Our endeavor has been to examine the respective accounts of the Christian morality and to view them in terms of their own claims as "explanations."

We have seen in both accounts the all-important role of the concepts of internalization, duplication, and negative self-relation. In Hegel these concepts are developed according to a logos of consciousness as self-reflectedness. The movement from the desiring self-consciousness to the ascetic was a phenomenological sequence in terms of consciousness' being-for-itself through a uniting with its "object" or "other." This uniting is through a "mediation," as in the unity in opposition of self-consciousness in "recognition" and the unity of the singular with the universal in the ascetic consciousness. Negative self-relation for Hegel thus means above all "mediation."

Looked at within the scope of its own program and presuppositions, the Hegelian enterprise presents a redoubtable front to the critic. Yet Hegel's presentation may be open to challenge on grounds other than internal consistency. It is virtually a triteness to note that in the world in which we live, belief in man's unity with divinity seems never to have been at lower ebb, "self-consciousness" seems never farther from the *Gewissheit* of its being "truth" and "reality." Perhaps the all but universal scepticism and nihilism of our time is but the prelude to "another" Unhappy Consciousness.

The inner necessity and determinacy of Hegel's phenomenological seqence is lacking in Nietzsche's "genealogy." To be sure, Nietzsche claims no such necessity. In contrast to the determinate emergence of the positive from the negative in Hegel, the positive for Nietzsche comes "like fate," appears "as lightning." Like the work of the "conqueror and master race" which founds the state, the positive is an "instinctive creation and imposition of forms." The emergence of the positive is thus in no sense through a "mediation" as in Hegel. Though creation and destruction go inseparably together for Nietzsche, they do not do so in the manner of a mediation of opposites.

But that the positive appears "as lightning," should not, in our opinion, put Nietzsche beyond the pale of criticism insofar as he claims to offer his "genealogy" in the form of an explanatory account. In counterposing Hegel's phenomenology to Nietzsche's genealogy, we noted that Nietzsche's explanation of a mental content in terms of force appeared in many ways unsatisfactory. This was especially the case in the debtor-creditor duplication which forms the basis of the relation of self to deity. It appeared to be the case in the emergence of the "will to truth" as a maximized self-negation of *ressentiment*. Though Nietzsche would doubtless reject Hegel's purported demonstration of the "appearance" (to consciousness) of God in the world, Nietzsche's own explanation – "a stroke of genius on the part of Christianity" – can only be acceptable if one first acknowledges the causal primacy of the movement of force, for whose blockage the "stroke of genius" affords a "temporary relief."

In contrast to the Unhappy Consciousness, whose outcome for Hegel is a "yes-saying," Nietzsche's portrayal of modern man as a "no-sayer" seems in all too many ways compelling. Yet Nietzsche's descriptions may be right for the wrong reasons – or at least for reasons extraneous to his etiological account of the "no-sayer." For Nietzsche, modern man's "no-saying" begins with the advent of the Christian God and ends with the ascetic ideal's turning into a "will to truth." This means for Nietzsche that the Judeo-Christian morality destroys itself by coming to know itself as a *ressentiment*. But is *ressentiment* the truth of the morality? This, our examination claims to show, Nietzsche's "genealogy" has not demonstrated.

NOTES

1. We have adapted Hyppolite's statement: "le maître se révèle dans vérité comme l'esclave de l'esclave et l'esclave comme le maître du maître." Jean Hyppolite, *Genèse et Structure de la Phénoménologie de l'Esprit de Hegel*, 2 vols. (Paris, 1946), vol. I, p. 166.

2. In quoting we shall occasionally alter the Baillie translation.

3. Most of our discussion of Nietzsche will be based on *The Genealogy of Morals*, tr. W. Kaufman and R. J. Hollingdale (Vintage Books 1967), hereafter referred to as *GM*.

4. *GM, First Essay*, "Good and Evil," "Good and Bad."

5. "Consciousness of life, of its existence and action, is merely pain over this existence; for therein consciousness finds only consciousness of its opposite as its essence – and of its own nothingness." *Phen*, p. 252.

6. *Phen*, p. 267.

7. *Phen*, p. 273.

8. *Phen*, p. 280.

9. Cf. R. F. Beerling, "Hegel und Nietzsche," *Hegel-Studien*, I (Bonn, 1961), pp. 229-46.

10. *Phen*, p. 254. The word "God" does not appear in the whole treatment of the Unhappy Consciousness.

11. In Hegel the "unchangeable" is the "other" of the Unhappy Consciousness which is for itself the "changeable" or "transient" (*Wandelbare*). In Nietzsche the "creditor" is the "other" of the consciousness which is for itself "debtor."

12. The first, for example, regards itself as "guilty" before the "other."

13. In the Unhappy Consciousness we thus "have here that dualizing of self-consciousness within itself, which lies essentially in the notion of Spirit." *Phen*, p. 251.

14. *Phen*, p. 135.

15. *GM*, p. 45. Also, Walter Kaufman (tr.), *The Portable Nietzsche* (New York: Viking Press, 1954), *Twilight of the Idols*, sec. 3 of "The Four Great Errors," p. 495.

16. We shall nevertheless continue to refer occasionally to Nietzsche's conception of the "Christian consciousness" (as he sometimes does himself), particularly in contexts which virtually necessitate such usage, as in the "appearing" of God to this "consciousness."

17. *GM*, p. 85.

18. *GM*, pp. 86ff.

19. *GM*, p. 40.

20. "Bad air! Bad air! This workshop where *ideals* are *manufactured* – it seems to me it stinks of so many lies." (*GM*, p. 47)

21. *GM*, p. 84.

22. *GM*, p. 70.

23. "To what extent can suffering balance debts or guilt (*Schulden*)? To the extent that to *make* suffer was in the highest degree pleasurable..." (*GM*, p. 65.)

24. *GM*, p. 90.

25. "The aim now is to preclude pessimistically, once and for all, the prospect of final discharge; the aim now is to make the glance recoil disconsolately from an iron impossibility." (*GM*, p. 91.)

26. *The Portable Nietzsche, The Antichrist*, sections 24ff., pp. 593ff.

27. *GM*, p. 92.

28. *GM*, p. 92.

29. *GM*, p. 93.

30. Man "ergreift in 'Gott' die letzten Gegensätze, die er zu seinen eigentlichen und unablöslichen Tier-Instinkten zu finden vermag, er deutet diese Tier-Instinkte selbst um als Schuld gegen Gott..." Friedrich Nietzsche, *Sämtliche Werke* (Stuttgart: Alfred Kroner Verlag, 1964), VII, *Zur Genealogie der Moral*, II, p. 328. Here we see that the self-reflectedness inherent in Hegel's phenomenological approach is a feature also of Nietzsche's account.

31. The movement is naturally "outward" but can be turned "inward" (as "subterranean gratifications"); it can be "maximized" (in life-expanding values), "diminished" (in life-hostile morality), "balanced" and "discharged" (in the debtor-creditor relation); it determines the very consciousness of man as the "valuating animal" (*GM*, p. 70). We may note here the largely spatial and quantitative categories typical of the physical realm.

32. Hegel's account of the Unhappy Consciousness, in which the "appearance" of the unchangeable is developed purely in terms of a movement of self-consciousness, is also in a sense a reductionism, and Feuerbach and the left-Hegelians were to capitalize on this aspect of Hegel's thought. But self-consciousness for Hegel is in essence *Geist*, which manifests itself not only in the self-divided Unhappy Consciousness but as Spirit in and for itself in revealed religion (*Phen*, pp. 251, 755 ff.)

33. "Was auf ein natürliches Leben beschränkt ist, vermag durch sich selbst nicht über sein unmittelbares Dasein hinauszugehen.... Das Bewusstsein aber ist für sich selbst sein *Begriff*, dadurch unmittelbar das Hinausgehen über das Beschränkte und, da ihm dies Beschränkte angehört, über sich selbst..." *Phän*, p. 69.

34. *Phän*, p. 225. "...Da die Befriedigung nur im Einzelnen geschehen, dieses aber vorübergehend ist, so erzeugt sich in der Befriedigung wieder die Begierde." *EdpW*, 6th ed., sec. 428, p. 350.

35. "A self-consciousness has before it a self-consciousness. Only so and only then *is* it self-consciousness in actual fact; for here first of all it comes to have the unity of itself in its otherness." *Phen*, pp. 226-27.

36. *Phen*, p. 233.

37. As unity of self-consciousnesses in the freedom and independence of their opposition, self-consciousness is "diese absolute Substanz, welche... *Ich*, das *Wir*, und *Wir*, das *Ich* ist." *Phän*, p. 140.

38. "O solitude! O my home, solitude!" *Thus Spoke Zarathustra, The Portable Nietzsche*, p. 295. Neither the masterly comradeship ("all individuals are knit together by the sense of repayment") nor the collectivity of the "herd instinct" is the same as the Hegelian unity of self-consciousnesses.

39. *Phen*, p. 231.

40. "...Das absolute Flüssigwerden alles Bestehens ist aber das einfache Wesen des Selbstbewusstseins, die absolute Negativität, *das reine Fürsichsein*, das hiermit an diesem Bewusstsein ist." *Phän*, p. 148. Hegel's concept of *Fürsichsein* as absolute negativity is comparable in certain ways to the Aristotelian *nous* that must have no

particular nature of itself in order that it may be all things (*De Anima* 429a22). But *Fürsichsein* must *make* itself this universal potentiality by negating itself in every form of its *bestimmten Sein*.

41. For Nietzsche the meaning of labor is a "mechanical activity" which the dishonest morality of *ressentiment* dignifies by the title of the "blessings of work." (*GM*, p. 134)

42. The slave's *gehemmte Begierde* "passes into the form of the object, into something that is permanent and remains." *Phen*, p. 238.

43. *Phen*, p. 239.

44. That for Hegel "die Natur den absoluten Endzweck nicht in ihr selbst enthält" (*EdpW*, sec. 245) would be for Nietzsche a philosophic expression of the Christian myth of creation *ex nihilo* that leads ultimately to the spoilation of nature. *GM*, p. 113.

45. *Phen*, p. 251.

46. *Phen*, p. 253.

47. *Phen*, p. 253.

48. "The movement [of recognition] then is absolutely the double movement of both self-consciousnesses." *Phen*, p. 230.

49. *Phen*, p. 254.

50. *GM*, p. 61.

51. *GM*, p. 118.

52. *Phen*, p. 252.

53. *Phen*, p. 248.

54. *GM*, p. 146.

55. *GM*, p. 160. As in the case of a *Verinnerlichung* of force, Nietzsche sets down a law: "All great things bring about their own destruction through an act of self-overcoming: thus the law of life will have it..." *GM*, p. 161. But since we are dealing here not with a "life" in the sense of a biological organism but with "great things" such as a morality, it is not clear why there must be a "self-overcoming."

56. *Phen*, p. 264.

57. "*Die mittelbare* Beziehung macht das Wesen der negativen Bewegung aus, in welcher es sich gegen seine Einzelheit richtet, welche aber ebenso als *Beziehung an sich* positiv ist und für es selbst diese seine *Einheit* hervorbringen wird." *Phän*, p. 169. In Nietzsche, self-negation contains no such moment of mediation.

58. The "mediator" (priesthood) is "selbst ein bewusstes Wesen, denn sie ist ein das Bewusstsein als solches vermittelndes Tun." *Phän*, p. 169.

59. *Phän*, p. 171.

60. *Phän*, p. 175.

61. For the newborn rational self-consciousness it seems "as if now, for the first time, the world had come into being." *Phen*, p. 273.

62. *GM*, p. 152.

COMMENT ON

MURRAY GREENE
HEGEL'S "UNHAPPY CONSCIOUSNESS"
AND NIETZSCHE'S "SLAVE MORALITY"

by

Joseph C. Flay

PROFESSOR GREENE: Your dialectical meditation on the chasm between
Hegel and Nietzsche in respect to Christianity and Christian morality has
led us to your *decisive* conclusion that Nietzsche has not demonstrated
his claim concerning the truth of the Christian morality. But the de-
cisiveness of your conclusion is tempered by the *tentativeness* of your
beginning, a "cautious 'yes'" to the question of whether or not we can
"in truth effect a relating of a *Lebensphilosophie* and a *Geistesphilosophie,*
a psychology and a phenomenology." I understand this to mean not that
it is possible *that* we cannot think these two thinkers together, but rather
that there is a question on *how* this is to be done. In this context the
question becomes: How are we to understand Hegel and Nietzsche? How
are we to understand Hegel as Nietzsche's past and as our past? How
are we to understand Nietzsche as Hegel's future and our past?

This dialectical mood tempers your answer decisively. Your answer
reflects again the question of their relationship in many ways. Is it proper
to ask whether *in truth* we can relate *Lebensphilosophie* of Nietzsche
and *Geistesphilosophie* of Hegel when "in truth" is applicable only to the
latter? Does not Nietzsche in fact come to the same conclusions about
ressentiment and the ascetic ideal as do you when, in Part III, Section 13,
of *The Genealogy of Morals* he states:

> The kind of self-contradiction as appears to be present in the
> ascetic, "Life against Life," is nonsense, not only in psycho-
> logical terms but physiologically as well. The contradiction can
> only be apparent; it must be a kind of provisional expression, an
> interpretation, a formula, a preparation, a psychological misunder-
> standing of something whose own nature can no longer be under-
> stood, no longer be designated in itself, – an empty word, stuffed
> into an old breach in human understanding.[1]

To the contrary, Nietzsche goes on to say, life struggles "within and by means of the ascetic ideal" in a battle "with and against death." The ascetic ideal is "a device, a knack, for the preservation of Life." [2] The ascetic ideal embodies the Will to Truth and the Will to Truth is a form of the Will to Power.

But then, we must ask, why the demonstration earlier; why the first two Parts? Herein enters another question of first order: Can we ask for a demonstration by Nietzsche, when he offers us not a genealogy of morals, but a *polemic toward* a genealogy of morals? This question opens the further question: Why a polemic? and how does a polemic lead us toward a geneology? Does this lead anywhere?

But does not Hegel himself announce the death of the Will to Truth in respect to religion? Is not religion deficient in true form? And is form not inseparable from content? Does not philosophy, indeed even the history of philosophy, transcend and include within it the form of religion with its content? Is this not close to, if not identical with, Nietzsche's pronouncement that "the Will to Truth has been forced to examine itself," and that, in accordance with the law of all life, viz., "all things perish through self-transcendence," Christianity has perished by its own hand? [3] As Hegel repeats time and again, our duty is to *know* God; but to know God as philosophy knows God. What does this say for the God of religious consciousness?

The hegemony of philosophy is a radical hegemony for Hegel. I would suggest that it can lead us back to the question concerning Nietzsche's polemic and your conclusion concerning the lack of demonstration in Nietzsche. At the end of his *LPR* Hegel indicates that, in spite of the reconciliation brought about by philosophy, there remains a harsh discord between individual morality and religion itself. To be sure, the reconciliation within philosophy itself is complete.

> But this reconciliation is itself only a partial reconciliation, without external universality, and philosophy is, in this connection, a sanctuary apart, and its servants form an isolated order of priests, who must not mix with the world and who have to care for the possession of Truth. How the temporal, empirical present finds its way out of this discord and schism, how it will form itself, is to be left to it and is not the immediate practical affair and concern of philosophy.[4]

This delineation of the relationship between Truth and the particularity of finite Spirit follows inexorably from the nature of Truth as this nature is critically unfolded in *SL*. *Truth is incommensurate with individual finite thought and activity*. "Philosophy is not to be a narrative of that which happens, but rather a cognition of that which is true in happenings; and further it is to comprehend from the True that which appears in the narrative as a simple happening." [5]

Hegel, in achieving the perennial goal of philosophy, has left the age to its own devices. We can now boldly suggest that Nietzsche, far from intending to offer a reasoned psychological genetic account of Christian morality and the Will to Truth in general, intends, *and must intend,* to offer an answer to Hegel's question of how the age will resolve the discord for itself and without unconditioned truth: *with a polemic which unveils the end of the efficacy and hegemony of the Will to Truth as Will to Power*. Truth cannot sustain life, truth cannot sustain finite consciousness: only perspectival correctness can do this.

The age responds. In Nietzsche the end of the Will to Truth, in Dewey the end of the Quest for Certainty, in Marx the End of German Ideology, in Kierkegaard the Concluding Unscientific Postscript. Irony, revolution, a finite method of intelligence derived from positive science, and again irony. All a reassertion of particularity, a rejection of concrete individuality. If concrete individuality means what it means as the absolute Idea; if the Will to Truth finally articulates this absolute Idea: can the particular consciousness continue to employ the Will to Truth as its Will to Power?

But is such a dialectic present in Hegel? Is there ever the purpose of this Will to Truth such as Nietzsche describes it? You have pointed to the emergence of consciousness from nature, and have maintained that there is a difference in the respective accounts. But is there? The master-slave analysis of the genesis of self-consciousness emerges from (1) a renunciation of life in the form of desire and (2) an assertion of the irrepressible will to life. It is from fear of death that the slave consciousness (i.e., the moment of consciousness itself) emerges. The master consciousness (i.e., the moment of self-consciousness) also emerges in this form. The immediately prior form of the analysis, where there is simply life and death struggle, leaves these two moments in an immediate unity, lacking differentiation and thus concreteness, remaining limited to immediate satisfaction and the endless repetition of desire-satisfaction.

Now you have noted that desire for recognition succeeds natural desire because the latter's object (an independent natural life) is incommensurate with *Fürsichsein* in its notion, to go out beyond every "limit" of itself. That is to say, this is the crucial step; it is the first instantiation of *Fürsichsein* which in turn is the *sine qua non* for *Anund-fürsichsein* and thus the institution of the Will to Truth. The urge of consciousness (which is always, concretely, self-consciousness) is to leave all limitation behind, to be, unconditionally, as *Aufgehobensein:* to escape the eternal return of the particularizing of desire for life. But, on the other hand, the moment in which the fight to the death is abandoned and the slave emerges is the moment in which "self-consciousness becomes aware that *Life* is as essential to it as is pure self-consciousness." [6] The life-death struggle is given up in the first place in order to preserve that most important of all conditions: *Life.* The slave consciousness is a Will to Life itself, a means of preservation.

But now we have just heard that the outcome of this sacrifice is a sanctuary apart from the particularity of life.

If Truth deserts the particularity of finitude, what are we to do but desert Truth? If, according to both Hegel and Nietzsche, the original purpose of the Will to Truth, of the impulse for certainty to become truth, is to preserve that most important moment of all, Life; and if this purpose is of necessity abandoned in the culmination of this process; then must this epoch which has been surrendered not assert its particularity against this concrete individuality, the absolute Idea? And this means at least that one must desert that discourse whose form is determined by the Will to Truth: discursive rationality. We can only move *toward* a recouping of our original position, now weakened by two thousand years, by a polemic, a life-struggle, in search of the beginnings. This particularistic return to find our way as particulars, to rediscover the Will to Power, is a task which follows from Hegel's unveiling of Truth.

The polemic is long and difficult. For where is there a clue to where "salvation" lies? What form could it be in? To retrace our way through the history of the Will to Truth, a task which Heidegger has undertaken, is perhaps impossible. Entrance into Hegel's own way, the culmination of the "way of Spirit" is itself difficult to fix. Is not the whole journey directed by fate?

Must we not agree with Hegel himself that the beginning of philosophy with the Greeks has a "foreign origin they have so to speak thanklessly forgotten, placing it in the background – perhaps burying it in the darkness of the mysteries which they have kept secret from themselves." [7] And if we turn to his account of Oriental philosophy, the most obvious reference to be sought, there is no answer to this problem of beginnings. The secret, the *Unheimlichkeit,* pervades the history of the Will to Truth. The Truth has unfolded itself, but it rests in the end upon *Moira,* who is herself beyond gods and men.

I would suggest, then, that the chasm between Hegel and Nietzsche is not a chasm, but a continuity. These reflections upon your meditation on Hegel and Nietzsche do not assert the failure of Hegel's system nor the victory of Nietzsche's polemics. On the contrary, what I have said is intended to understand your conclusion through your beginning in the following way. That both we and Nietzsche do and must accept the authenticity of the Truth of philosophy, that is, of Hegel. That what follows from this Truth is the collapse of truth in so far as wisdom, *sophia,* is concerned. That, to speak in terms of that most fruitful myth of Plato, the journey back into the cave and the salvation of man is impossible given the nature of Truth, the articulation of the absolute Idea. That to understand Hegel and Nietzsche and our world today we must accept this and proceed beyond Nietzsche, to reaffirm the Will to Power and to listen for Zarathustra.

NOTES

1. Friedrich Nietzsche, *Zur Genealogy der Moral,* in *Gesammelte Werke,* XV (München: Musarion), Part III, sec. 13, p. 399.

2. *GM.*

3. *GM,* part II, sec. 27.

4. *LPR,* III, p. 151.

5. *WdL,* II, p. 226.

6. *Phän,* p. 145. Compare *EdpW,* sections 368, 375.

7. *VdGdP, Glockner,* p. 189.

COMMENT ON

MURRAY GREENE
HEGEL'S "UNHAPPY CONSCIOUSNESS"
AND NIETZSCHE'S "SLAVE MORALITY"

by

Thomas J. J. Altizer

Mr. Greene maintains that the *Aufheben* in Nietzsche is different from
Hegel's since it shows no emergence of the *new form* as immanent in
the destruction of the old. He reaches this judgment by way of a response to Nietzsche's thesis that it was the Christian morality itself, the
concept of truthfulness taken more and more strictly, which has really
conquered the Christian God. This thesis goes hand in hand with a
Nietzschean law: "All great things bring about their own destruction
through an act of self-overcoming (*Selbstaufhebung.*)" [1] Thus the Christian
God is negated and transcended by Christianity itself, an *Aufheben*
which is surely embodied in the creditor sacrificing himself for the debtor. For Nietzsche, as Mr. Greene points out, the essential meaning of
the Christian "appearance" of God in the world is the taking on of
the form of "something existent, corporeal, real" of man's own "denial
of himself, of his nature, naturalness, and actuality." [2] If the maximization of God comes from the nihilation of self, we might observe that here
it is the self-nihilation of God which maximizes Him in the eye of
His beholder. True, God's self-nihilation occurs in man's own self-denial,
but that denial is a self-overcoming (*Selbstaufhebung*) which ultimately
issues in the death of God. Again and again, Mr. Greene asks how
the goal of the will to truth can arise logically or psychologically from
the paradoxical situation of the ascetic ideal as an attempt to employ
force to block up the well of force. Why need a maximization of ressentiment, as a particular expression of will to power, take the form
of a will to truth? May we not reply by suggesting that Nietzsche
answers this question by his conception of the Incarnation? God's sacrifice or self-nihilation finally actualizes itself in the self-negation of
ressentiment, and thereby we might understand that it is Christianity's

own self-negating which "finally forbids itself the *lie involved in belief in God*." [3]

Theologically considered, we might say that for Nietzsche, the Incarnation, or the Christian appearance of God as man, occurs solely in the Passion, even if that passion is manifest only in the self-negation of man. Yet surely this self-negation is a self-overcoming which does indeed issue in the emergence of a new form as immanent in the destruction of the old. The new form is a *new* innocence, an innocence which is not prior to guilt, but which rather has died in itself to the ultimate source of guilt by actualizing in its own self-negation of *ressentiment* a negation of its indebtedness to the other, an other, which in its maximum form, is manifest as the Christian God. To say that the creditor sacrifices himself for the debtor is also to say that the creditor as creditor disappears from the consciousness of the debtor, or does so when the creditor realizes in his own self-negation the dissolution of every alien other, and therefore the dissolution of every "No." Out of the nihilism of Christianity's perishing (*Selbstaufhebung*) will emerge "The master of *free* will." Nietzsche's vision of freedom is a vision of what the Christian commonly knows as the forgiveness of sin, but if Kierkegaard had already taught the Christian that the forgiveness of sin culminates in the loss of the memory of sin, Nietzsche can teach the Christian that the forgiveness of sin must even further culminate in the loss of the memory of God, and therefore the loss of the manifestation of God, who is finally manifest only as a free or guiltless man.

An all too significant common thesis of Hegel and Nietzsche, as Mr. Greene maintains, is that the object of the religious consciousness presents itself in the form of an "other" that is in certain essential ways the antithesis of consciousness as it is for itself. So it is that each thinker understands the genesis of the early Christian consciousness by way of understanding the religious consciousness itself as a "self-negating" consciousness. Indeed, it is precisely insofar as the religious consciousness apprehends its object as an "other" that it is impelled itself to pass through the act or movement of self-negation. This truth is clearly apparent in Hegel's understanding of the "appearance" of the Incarnation. For despite the Hegelian thesis that the Incarnation makes manifest the universality of the self's own self-consciousness, the Christian believer, as understood by Hegel, apprehends the Incarnate Son of God as the antithesis of his own singularity as a being-for-self. The Christian "offense" of the Incarnation is the appearance of the Universal Word of God in the particularity of Jesus of Nazareth, and it is only insofar as the Incarnation appears in a particular or singular form that Christ is manifest as an "other" to the believer, a manifestation which alone makes possible the unique and radical act of self-negation in the Christian expressions of faith. Moreover, it is essential to the universal movement and goal of self-consciousness that the eternal be manifest as being "other" than consciousness, for apart from the act of dividing and doubling consciousness, there is no way from the singularity to the universality of consciousness, from the manifestation of consciousness as individual and alone to the actual realization of the universality of self-consciousness.

While Mr. Greene demonstrates that both Hegel and Nietzsche conceive of the Christian consciousness as an attempt toward a negation of self, he reaches the crucial judgment that their conceptions of this self-negation yield antipodal resolutions. Thus the Unhappy Consciousness of Hegel, which exists in a divided and doubled state because it experiences its own universality in the form of a transcendent beyond, is a necessary stage in the involution and evolution of Spirit because it makes possible the self-renunciation of Spirit in the form of the singularity of consciousness. For Hegel, the "positive" always and necessarily emerges out of the "negative," and there can be no true "positive" apart from the power and the labor of the "negative." Yet, for Nietzsche, as presented by Mr. Greene, the ascetic ideal is a will to nothingness, and the "No-saying" of Christianity can in no sense issue in a true "Yes-saying," but only in the orgiastic destruction of its own source and ground. For Nietzsche, self-negation is a "nature's" ever turning against itself, while for Hegel it is a continual deepening or self-realization of the being-for-itself of consciousness. We may also surmise from Mr. Greene's presentation that Hegel may truly be understood as a Christian thinker, but Nietzsche is the prophet of nihilism, *par excellence,* the thinker who has carried anti-Christianity to its ultimate resolution.

At this point let us ask if it is possible to give a theological formulation to Hegel's understanding of the Incarnation as the movement of the divided consciousness to unite itself as a singular form or mode of consciousness with its own essence as universal self-consciousness commonly it is thought that there is no *way* of undertanding Hegel theologically – e.g., Mr. Greene says that neither Hegel nor Nietzsche deal with God as he is "in himself" – and that, indeed, Hegel has brought an end to all theological language (hence the deep hostility towards Hegel on the part of almost all theologians). At bottom, I suspect that we are here dealing with the judgment that Hegel's understanding of God, or the religious form or image or *Vorstellung* of God, as being "other" than consciousness, precludes the possibility of a positive conceptualization of God. Or, some might follow Eric Voegelin and believe that in Hegel we find yet another Gnostic rebellion against God, and it is significant that Hegel seems to join the ancient Gnostics in judging the pre-incarnate forms of God to be alien and "other." Yet it is also significant that Hegel seems to be Pauline and Lutheran in his judgment that the fully alien or "other" form of God is inseparably related to a divided and doubled state of consciousness; hence here there can be no *an sich* language about God because here there can be no objective or undivided mind or speaker. It is at this point that we must say that if Hegel has spoken theologically he has done so in such a way as to transform the given or apparent nature of theological language. Therefore if we are to give theological expression to an Hegelian theme we can do so only by speaking a new theological language.

If the Christian meaning of the Incarnation can in any genuine sense be understood as a movement from a singular to a universal form of consciousness, then obviously such a movement must entail a transformation of consciousness, and a transformation which is moreover a self-transformation. In fact, for Hegel it is this movement which makes possible the advent of a true or genuine self-consciousness. It is also noteworthy that Hegel's understanding of the Incarnation is clearly rooted in Meister Eckhart, just as his understanding of the Unhappy Consciousness has a clear parallel in St. John of the Cross's understanding of the dark night of the soul. So likewise Christian mystical thinkers, like their counterparts in Judaism and Islam, had long refused an objective or dogmatic language about God. In other words, we could say that there was a Christian warrant, at least in the higher expressions of the mystical tradition, for Hegel to attempt, if such was his intention, to arrive at an understanding of the Incarnation which would transcend (*Aufheben*) all God-language. Or, differently formulated, Hegel attempted to reach a consistently "subjective" or *für sich* understanding of the Incarnation, and this demanded a total negation and transcendence of all "objective" or *an sich* language about God (in any case, it was certainly Hegel who made possible Kierkegaard's dialectical and "subjective" understanding of the Incarnation). From this perspective, we can also sense the possibility that it is only when all God-language has been negated that the inherent and fundamental meaning of the Incarnation can come into its own. But this is also to say that it is only when consciousness has ceased to be doubled or divided, or has negated that form of itself which immediately appears as other and beyond, that it is capable of expressing the meaning of such a transformation of consciousness, or even speaking the language of an ultimate movement of self-transformation.

It was Hegel himself who associated the full advent of the Unhappy Consciousness with the bitter experience that God is dead. And, as Mr. Greene has so ably demonstrated, the Incarnation, for Hegel, or the "appearance" of the unchangeable in the realm of the changeable, only becomes fully actual and real in consciousness through the agony and despair of the Unhappy Consciousness. The Unhappy Consciousness, at least in its full form, is clearly a Christian phenomenon, and it must finally resolve itself in a radical form of self-negation or self-transformation. With that self-negation every alien other loses its inherent ground, including that other which appears in the form of the isolated and individual self, and thus the No-saying of self-negation culminates in a total Yes-saying, which is possible only on the basis of the dissolution of every form of otherness. It is precisely because the Christian God, the God who "appears" *after* the movement of the Incarnation, or after or in conjunction with the movement of total self-transformation, is the purest embodiment of an alien otherness, that His death can be known as the fruit of the Incarnation, and thus as the consequence of the self-negation or self-overcoming of a singular and divided form of consciousness. So it is that Nietzsche could understand the Christian phenomenon of guilt to be a product of "bad conscience," of the internalization of man, wherein the self takes every other "into" itself, and wrecks its vengeance by indulging in an orgy of self-hatred. Only through that orgy does otherness truly disappear as "other," and then the Christian God can truly "appear" as the deification of nothingness, the will to "nothingness" pronounced holy.

If the essential meaning of the Christian "appearance" of God in the world is the taking on of the form of "something existent, corporeal, real" of man's self-negation, then the uniquely or specifically Christian meaning of God must appear as a deification of nothingness, as the will to nothingness appearing at the heart and center of an individual and singular form of selfhood or consciousness. When that self-negation or will to nothingness becomes dominant in consciousness, then that individual selfhood will have lost its given ground, and the loss of that ground brings an end to everything which is truly or actually manifest to an individual and particular form of consciousness. Thus, it is only when God becomes actual and real in consciousness as nothingness that His Christian identity and meaning is fully manifest. When no distance separates

God and man, then both God and man will have ceased to be real when isolated and apart, and the passion of God in man will have annulled that subject of consciousness which appears as individual and distinct, thereby negating and transcending every form of otherness. The "No-saying" of self-negation will have passed into the "Yes-saying" of a total form of consciousness, as God Himself appears as that total subject who fully actualizes himself here and now.

NOTES

1. *GM*, p. 161.
2. *GM*, p. 92.
3. *GM*, p. 160.

REPLY TO COMMENTATORS

by

Murray Greene

Mr. Flay agrees with me that we need a better understanding of the relation of Hegel and Nietzsche but does not agree with me on how to go about it. Rather than counterpose the two thinkers' account of the Judeo-Christian morality, as I have done, Mr. Flay would seek an internal connection. Mr. Flay suggests that the connection consists in that Hegel's Absolute Truth failed Life, and Nietzsche's attack against the Will to Truth seeks again to nourish Life. Hence Mr. Flay would not treat Nietzsche's *Genealogy* as a "reasoned psychological genetic account of Christian morality," as I have done, but rather as a "polemic" which "unveils the end of the efficacy and hegemony of the Will to Truth."

That the *Genealogy* may be taken as a polemic, and that Nietzsche's treatment of the Judeo-Christian morality may be viewed within the compass of his wider intention to renew Life, I do not disagree. But the polemic makes a certain case. Must we not judge it on its own merits? Or are we obliged to accept it because of the polemic's wider intent? Mr. Flay tells us that, since Truth in the form of the Hegelian Absolute has deserted finitude, we in turn "must desert that discourse whose form is determined by the Will to Truth: discursive rationality." But this means, it seems to me, that Mr. Flay has already accepted the polemic without having judged the case, and he is asking us to do likewise.

I am willing to listen to the polemic. But when it comes to judging the case, then I must invoke my rationality, for it is the only means I have for judging. Nietzsche too does not give up discursive rationality completely. He employs reasons. He needs rationality to make his case, and we need it to make our judgment. The question must then become: what sort of rationality is employed in making the case and what sort in judging it? If this means that we need a rationality to judge about rationality, then the paradox is not ours alone as judges, but also Nietzsche's, who would make the case.

The question therefore remains for us: what sort of rationality must we employ in judging Nietzsche's rationality? Perhaps the answer is not yet fully available to us, Hegel to the contrary notwithstanding. Yet Nietzsche will not let us go, he demands a "yes" or "no" to his claim that life's renewal can come only with the annihilation of the Judeo-Christian morality and the unveiling of Will to Truth as Will to Power. We must make a judgment and we must do so on a rational basis. Can we mount a rational critique of Nietzsche's critique of rationality? I believe we have no option but to try.

In my paper I have made use of Hegel's phenomenological rationality to point to what I consider weaknesses in Nietzsche's rationality, mainly that it takes its life-categories ultimately from the physical realm. This does not mean that the Hegelian is the ultimately valid rationality. It need not even mean that some of Nietzsche's criticisms of Hegel are not well taken. But if by use of Hegelian phenomenology we can point to failures in Nietzsche's rationality, then we need not fear aspersions against the Will to Truth and we need not become misologists.

II

Mr. Altizer defends Nietzsche's concept of *Aufheben* against my charge that Nietzsche does not show the new form as immanent in the destruction of the old. The emergence of Nietzsche's "master of free will," according to Mr. Altizer, is precisely such an instance of *Aufheben*, and the *Aufhebung* of the Christian God in the new "free and guiltless man" follows from a certain logic implicit within Christianity itself. This logic is the Christian doctrine of forgiveness of sin as expressed in the Incarnation and Passion. Since the Christian God is but a projection of the Christian sense of sin and guilt, the disappearance of sin and guilt means the disappearance of God.

In the first place, I do not see how Mr. Altizer can interpret Nietzsche as saying a "new innocence" emerges from the Passion. The Passion, or the self-sacrifice of the creditor for the debtor, Nietzsche says, "afforded temporary relief for tormented humanity." [1] This did not mean a new innocence. On the contrary, Nietzsche says it meant the possibility for man "to erect an ideal – that of the 'holy God' – and in the face of it to feel the palpable certainty of his own absolute unworthiness." [2] The new innocence for Nietzsche emerges not with the Passion but with

Christianity's self-nihilation, which comes about largely as the result of the scientific spirit. This spirit is the product of "two thousand years training in truthfulness," which develops out of the ascetic ideal.[3] But it is precisely this alleged transformation of the ascetic ideal into a "will to truth" which I have challenged in my paper, insofar as the ascetic ideal is conceived not phenomenologically as the effort of the singular self-consciousness to attain to its implicit universality, as in Hegel, but as this ascetic ideal is conceived psycho-physically by Nietzsche as an employment of force to block up the wells of force.

Mr. Altizer sees Nietzsche's vision of freedom as "a vision of what the Christian commonly knows as forgiveness of sin." Nietzsche, says Mr. Altizer, can teach the Christian that forgiveness of sin "must even further culminate in the loss of the memory of God." In this way Mr. Altizer would establish the *Aufhebung* of Christian forgiveness of sin in the new innocence of Nietzsche's "master of free will." But I think this *Aufhebung* could only be maintained by abstracting from the Christian meaning of sin as sin before God. To be sure, from the Christian point of view, to do away with God would be to do away with sin – in the sense of making the concept of sin meaningless. But only the strangest logic, it seems to me, could maintain that the converse proposition is from any Christian point of view an *Aufhebung* of the original. The conversion is indeed possible from a point of view such as Nietzsche's, which holds that the Christian God is but man's own "denial of himself." But the point at issue is whether Nietzsche has established this in his projectionist account of "how the 'holy God' originated." In my paper I have tried to show that he has not.

In pursuing his claim that Nietzsche's "master of free will" is indeed the *Aufhebung* of Christian forgiveness of sin, Mr. Altizer says that the loss of the memory of God means, for Nietzsche, that divinity now steps forth as "a free and guiltless man." I would like to point out what is not made explicit by Mr. Altizer: "man," for Nietzsche, does not mean here "mankind." Nietzsche was not Feuerbach. The "free and guiltless man" means the *Uebermensch*. If the *Uebermensch* is an instance of Nietzsche's *Aufheben* of the Christian forgiveness of sin, then I can only say I fail to see how the new is immanent in the old.

NOTES

1. *GM*, p. 92.
2. *GM*, p. 93.
3. *GM*, p. 160.

HEGEL'S REINTERPRETATION OF THE DOCTRINE OF SPIRIT AND THE RELIGIOUS COMMUNITY

by

John E. Smith

Hegel laid great emphasis on the place of religion in human culture and on the close connection between religion and speculative philosophy. Quite apart from questions concerning the adequacy and legitimacy of his interpretation of religion in general or of Christianity in particular, the fact remains that Hegel more than once described his thought as the translation of the content of classical Christianity into the form of the speculative concept. His belief that he had actually accomplished such a translation is expressed on numerous occasions throughout his many writings. Therefore, I find quite unconvincing the claims made by those who find this fact embarrassing and who must then invent the myth that Hegel was not serious or that he did not mean what he said. What grounds other than those of dogmatic preference could be brought forth to support such a claim? One side finds the religious dimension in Hegel uncongenial and concludes that it may be dismissed: the other side finds that many of Hegel's doctrines and especially his repeatedly stated view of the relation between religion and philosophy, make it impossible for us to think of eliminating the religious element in his thought while supposedly leaving his philosophy still standing. If we consult Hegel on the matter and not our own predilections and special interests, the religious dimension is essential. In this I agree with the recent study of the topic by Emil Fackenheim.

I

The concluding pages of Hegel's *Lectures on the Philosophy of Religion* are remarkable in that they strike a discordant note and contain a candid acknowledgement on Hegel's part of the gap between the state of civilization in his time and the Hegelian program of reconciliation. Contrary to the expectation of Hegel's critics, and especially the expectations of those who have formed these expectations without reading Hegel, the work does not end with a triumphant claim that all oppositions have been overcome. On the one hand, Hegel reiterates at the close of the lectures their threefold aim – to reconcile reason and religion, to comprehend the necessity of religion's many forms, and to rediscover in religion both truth and the Idea. Moreover, he claims that "for us" philosophical knowledge has resolved the discord between the community of Spirit and the finite, isolated individual. And yet, on the other hand, Hegel goes on to confess that, in fact, the reconciliation is "only a partial one, without outward universality" [1] and that under such circumstances, philosophy can only be a sanctuary cut off from the world, and those who serve in it must appear as an isolated priesthood whose members may have no traffic with the world, being constrained instead by their duty which is to guard the estate of Truth. The final sentence, though perhaps disappointing to those who expect Hegel always to claim something grand for philosophy, shows his hard-headed realism and his respect for the actual state of affairs. "How the present world," he writes, "is to find its way out of its discord, and what form it will take, are questions which it must settle for itself; to deal with these questions is not the immediate, practical business and concern of philosophy." [2]

The exact nature of the discord Hegel cites and the sense in which it can exist side by side with his claim that philosophical knowledge has resolved the problem, are obviously topics for further discussion. They serve at this point merely to launch an inquiry into Hegel's theory of the spiritual community and the living Spirit within it which is said to express the Truth of the revealed religion. The appropiate questions are: What is the nature of the Kingdom of Spirit? What is the nature of Spirit itself? What constellation of thought and events led, in Hegel's analysis, to the situation in which the spiritual community, though eternally established, fails to realize itself historically and with complete universality? In attempting to deal with these and other questions, we must concentrate on two central concepts, the concept of *Spirit*, especially in its application to the interpretation of the religious consciousness, and the concept of the *spiritual community* as the true form of the revealed religion.

II

It is a fact well known to students of Christian theology that, despite the powerful influence exercised by the Trinitarian conception of God and the doctrine of the three Persons, the Third Person or Holy Spirit was curiously neglected throughout the long development of thought from the early Greek and Latin Fathers to the end of the Middle Ages. It is not possible here to argue the case on historical grounds, but two factors may be mentioned as major reasons for the neglect. First, in the main, Roman Catholic theology interpreted the Church as the Body of Christ and thus as an extension of the Incarnation or Second Person, without special emphasis on the idea that was later to be made so central by the Reformers, namely, that the Church is the community of believers in whom the Spirit lives and works. Hegel calls special attention to this point himself in the third division of his treatment of the revealed religion; referring to the viewpoint of Catholicism, he writes, "the Spirit is more in the church merely as hierarchy, and not in the community." [3] Secondly, the idea of the Holy Spirit represents life, creativity, and power, so that it stands in tension with, if not in direct opposition to, the fixity of structure and content thought to be necessary for the survival of the church as an institution. Hence it was to be expected that the Spirit, described especially in the Fourth Gospel as the power that is to lead into all truth (implying that the full understanding of the religious content had not already been achieved in the past), would not be accorded a central place by an ecclesiastical hierarchy dedicated to the continued existence of a church already posessing authority and final truth. It is most important to keep this background in mind when we understand that Hegel made Spirit central for his philosophy of religion. In fact that doctrine forms an indispensable key to his interpretation of Christianity. In reviving the religious doctrine of Spirit, he sought to give it a new form through the hard-won philosophical concepts of his system, notably the concept of the *Begriff* itself, and the Idea. Hegel, moreover, reformulated the concept of the church as the spiritual community which is the only proper locus of Spirit, the only form which is wholly adequate to the religious content taken to be both Truth and God. In the third part of the *Ency-clopedia* [4] Hegel speaks of the "correct principle" that "God must be apprehended as Spirit in his community." This principle forms a recurring theme in the final portion of the *Lectures* on the philosophy of religion which, for the most part, constitutes the basis for the ensuing discussion.

III

In view of the vastness of Hegel's thought, it never seems quite possible to concentrate on any part of it without feeling the acute need to bring in all the rest. That is, of course, impossible, but it is equally impossible to comprehend either the doctrine of Spirit or the belief in its present actuality in the community of faith without paying some attention to at least three considerations that determine the general shape of Hegel's philosophy. These considerations, though they find peculiar application in the philosophy of religion, are by no means derivative from that enterprise itself, since they find expression in all parts of his thought.[5] To begin with, Hegel repeatedly regarded philosophy, at the ultimate point where content and form are in complete accord with each other, as the expression in the speculative form of the *Begriff* of the truth or content which is the substance of the revealed religion. This point is made in the *Phenomenology*, in the *Encyclopedia* and many times in the *Philosophy of Religion*. Religion and philosophy are said to have the same content (*Inhalt*) and to differ only in form. The religious content in the form in which it is first received is expressed as image, popular conception, and what Hegel calls ordinary thought, sometimes expressed as *Vorstellungen*, or pictorial representations, and sometimes as *Gedanke*. The task of philosophy is to raise this content to the level of *Begriff* and thus to express it in that properly speculative form of self-comprehension that characterizes philosophy as *Wissenschaft*.

Precisely what is to be understood by thinking and "justifying" the religious content can be made clear only through the doctrine of the *Begriff* itself. This brings us to the second consideration which is the relation between the *Begriff* and the *Idee*. As we know from Hegel's account of speculative thinking throughout his writings, the concept is a system of relationships embodying both life and thought, dynamics and form, which comprehends its subject matter as a *one*, as a *many*, and as a *unity of the two*, in such wise that the moments involved are distinguishable (thus satisfying the demand of analysis) but not separable (thus satisfying the continuity required for life).[6] The logical character of the moments of the Concept is manifest in the movement from the abstract unity of immediacy to mediation in which a plurality of internal content becomes explicit – with a subsequent submerging of the immediate unity so that the content appears at first as "merely other" or a mass of particularity – and so to a final stage of recovering the starting point so that the plurality resulting from mediation is seen, not as a mere collection, but as the unity of unity and multiplicity.

The concept as the form of philosophical comprehension needs to be set in relation to the Idea. In *EdpW* 7 Hegel makes it clear that it is the function of the concept to express the principal thesis of absolute idealism, namely, that realities, taken from the standpoint of lower grades of consciousness to have independent or immediate being, are, in truth, stages of the Idea. In the course of dialectical development, however, the Idea itself comes to be the object (*Gegenstand*) of the concept and is known 8 as the realization of the concept or the unity of the concept itself and that objectivity which is absolute truth. In the lower stages of cognition, the Absolute Idea (the unity of life and cognition) was made to appear as "our object," but at the apex of the system, the Idea becomes object to itself, a form of cognition which in several places Hegel identified with the νόησις νοήσεως of Aristotle's God.9 It is important to notice that, despite the reference to Aristotle and the νόησις which properly belongs to God, Hegel does not view the Absolute Idea as identical with God from within the confines of logic. The Absolute Idea cannot be fully explicated from the standpoint of logic because its full actuality requires, in addition, expression in the succeeding forms of Nature and Spirit. The Absolute Idea finds its final expression in Spirit which as fully actual self-consciousness is the only form adequate to the self-differentiating and self-identifying content. Spirit embraces both form or thought and life or dynamics; Spirit is not identical with "mind" if this is taken to mean thought and knowledge exclusively. On the other hand, Spirit is also not identical with power taken in the sense of a *nisus* for development and growth. In the concept of Spirit, Hegel was attempting to synthesize form and power in the unity of concrete individuality 10 It is especially important to bear this synthesis in mind when we come to interpret Hegel's idea of Spirit in the religious sphere, for there we encounter a long tradition of identifying spirit with power in a sense in which it is supposed to be over against thought or form. This tendency is most manifest in the opposition between "spiritual" religion and religion rooted in doctrine or conceptual interpretation. Hegel, as we shall see, rejected that opposition; for him, Spirit embraces both knowledge and love since it is at once the unifying power of love and the Truth that is actually present in the spiritual community.

The third consideration that determined the general shape of Hegel's thought is the new and central place that he gave to history. The claim that in every sphere of reality it is not the result by itself that is to be taken into account, but the result along with the process through which it came to be, established history in a place of basic importance. The special bearing of this point on the philosophy of religion becomes manifest in Hegel's interpretation of the Trinity in historical terms. The Trinity is no longer seen merely as the *totum simul* relatedness of the Three Persons in the Godhead, but instead as an historical development made manifest in ages of the world, the age of the Father, of the Son, and of the Spirit.

IV

Let us turn now to Hegel's tracing of the dialectical development of revealed religion and its culmination in the third stage when God is properly known as Spirit and is present as the reconciling power in the spiritual community. As previously noted, Hegel had been influenced by the historical interpretation of the Trinitarian conception and, while he does not abandon the *totum simul* doctrine of the relations between the Persons, there is a clear sense in which he thinks of the Persons as correlative with the ages and stages of a development in time.[11] In the third part of his exposition of the absolute religion Hegel says, "The divine makes

> itself explicit in these three forms (i.e. universality, particularity and individuality). Spirit is the divine history, the process of self-differentiation, of diremption, and of the cancelling of that diremption; Spirit is the divine history, and this history is to be regarded in each of the three forms.[12]

This passage suggests not only an historical emphasis but it appears to make the entire history one of Spirit present from the beginning. The third form, or Spirit proper, is that of individuality and represents God as returning to himself in the spiritual community, having already been manifest as the eternal Idea in itself in the kingdom of the Father, and in the element of consciousness and ordinary thought which coincides with the Kingdom of the Son. In the first stage, God is, as it were, beyond time in the eternal idea; in the second stage, time differentiates into past and future so that God becomes manifest in time. In the third stage, which Hegel repeatedly describes as *present*,[13] Spirit establishes that present as Truth which cannot be wholly contained by either the past or the future but transcends both. The consciousness of the presence of God immediately in the community is at the same time the proper apprehension of the present. By contrast with the presence of Spirit, the appearance of God in time belongs to the past. Thus, for Hegel, there is a real "historical" Jesus who, despite the misunderstandings of critics, is no "mere idea," but, as historical, this central figure actually existed in the past and therefore must be made present in and through Spirit.

The first step in the realization of God as Spirit is the founding of the spiritual community itself. For Hegel, this crucial event follows from the recognition on the part of the original members that Jesus is Christ.[14] These members first meet the sensuous individual together with his deeds, sayings, and all the events that constitute his empirical and historical life. Unlike those, however, who have tried to make this "historical" Jesus fulfill his office solely in his historical immediacy, Hegel saw that the total life cycle, *including the atoning death*, is the essential phenomenon and that this phenomenon can be truly apprehended only from a vantage point beyond the sensuous reality in the historical present. The historical person is an essential condition for the founding of the community, but his significance passes beyond his historicity. Before the members of the community can apprehend Jesus as Christ, the sensuous immediacy of the historical present must pass and be succeeded by the Spirit in the form of the comforter who is said to lead into all Truth. The completed representation of the sensuous person would be found, says Hegel, in the person of the Second Advent, but that representation belongs to the eschatology of the community and all history, and not to the founding of the community. In the meantime, the passing of the sensuous is succeeded by the outpouring of the Spirit, and the first truth that the Spirit teaches is the significance of Jesus as Christ which, in turn, becomes the *faith* upon which the community is founded. Hegel here follows the dominant Protestant conception developed by the Reformers who were unamious in maintaining, against the doctrine of the church as the extension of the Incarnation, that the church is founded on the *confession of faith* in Jesus as Christ, acknowledged by the original members and mediated by the Spirit. "The rise of the spiritual community," Hegel writes,

> appears in the form of an outpouring of the Holy Spirit. Faith takes its rise first of all in a man, a human, material manifestation; and next comes spiritual comprehension, consciousness of the spiritual . . . . This truth, however, is sure and certain by itself, although it has an historical starting point.

And he explains further,

> This transition is the outpouring of the Spirit which could make
> its appearance only after Christ had been taken away out of the
> flesh, and the sensuous, immediate present had ceased. It is then
> the Spirit appears . . .[15]

For Hegel, the spiritual community thus formed means a togetherness
of empirically real individuals who stand first as externally related in
the form of distinct individuals *vis a vis* each other. They are not
"mere" individuals or parts of some organism as yet to be established,
nor do they lose their individuality in an undifferentiated one. Such ideas
are alien to Hegel's thought, however familiar they may be to his mis-
interpreters. The spiritual community is real when the individual members
become related to each other in a new and more intimate way as a result
of their common relation to the religious truth that defines their community. Their relation to that truth is a self-conscious moment in which
each individual renounces both his fixedness and his willfulness in ac-
knowledging the reality of Spirit and truth as having been mediated in
Jesus as Christ.[16]

The actuality of the community as a present reality is at the same time
the actuality of Spirit, a living and many-sided unity which retains identity throughout all its manifestations.[17] It is Spirit that bestows on the religious community its peculiar sort of reality. As such, this community
is more than a collection of its members and more than the fact that
they are together. For Hegel, as for Aristotle, community possesses a
distinctive type of being. It is one in which a plurality of distinct members are united in virtue of the fact that each has an individual relation
to that Spirit which lives in their midst and affects their lives. In the
religious community this relation is faith; in the social and political com-
munty as envisaged by Aristotle the Spirit takes the form of *ethos*. As
present in the community, Spirit is the tri-une God and a God of many
dimensions.[18] As living, God sustains many relations with the members.
As Spirit, God is related to the members in *faith*, in *knowledge*, in the
power of reconciliation which is the meaning of Jesus as Christ, in
truth, and in *love*. In developing the dialectic of the kingdom of Spirit,
Hegel identifies Spirit in all these forms; failure to take account of them
must result in distortion. Let us consider each in turn.

Spirit is present to the individual in its most immediate form as faith
which is also a self-consciousness of truth. Hegel had a fine sense of
the delicate dialectic of faith as, on the one hand, the power of Spirit
operative in the individual person, and, on the other, as an act (*Tun*)

of self-conscious acceptance and acknowledgment by the individual of the reality of God. For Hegel, faith can be both an effect wrought and a decisive act because of the nature of the Spirit. Spirit does not affect the individual as if he were a passive or empty container, but works through self-consciousness and freedom in a manner appropriate to a reality that is finite spirit. As such, the individual *has* the faith and is at the same time aware of the fact since faith involves self-consciousness and makes itself felt in its tension with natural existence.

Spirit is not fully realized in the form of immediate faith; in the attempt to find itself, Spirit drives towards knowledge and a truth appropriate to its own nature. That truth is not of the sensuous order involving miracles and probabilities in the determination of historical details concerning Jesus and his life. Like Luther, Hegel saw in such investigations and in the curiosity displayed in doubt based on probabilities, not conscientious faith, but unbelief. "Faith," Hegel declares, "rests on the witness of the Spirit – not on miracles, but on the absolute truth, or the eternal Idea ... miracles, if they are to attest the truth of anything, must first be attested themselves." And, he concludes, "what is supposed to be attested (*beglaubigt werden soll*) by them, is the Idea which does not need them and hence has no need to attest them." [19] Hegel returns ever and again to this point; Spirit is self-authenticating in that the test of its knowledge and truth is not to be found in the historical beginning as historical, but only in the universal truth contained in that beginning and now present through Spirit in the community. "Thus," says Hegel, "the material history is the starting point for Spirit, for faith, and these two characteristics must be distinguished from each other ... it is not the material present [i.e., the historical events as such] but the Spirit which teaches the spiritual community that Christ is the Son of God ..." [20] In the end it is philosophy and not history which justifies the true content of faith. [21]

Spirit is faith and it is truth, but it is more; it is the power of reconciliation or the overcoming of the gulf between God and man. The full outworking of this reconciliation ultimately involves the dialectic of the community itself and the secular world. Here it will suffice simply to call attention to the fact that Spirit means the act of reconciliation brought into the present. Reconciliation is essentially a change in the status of man. The capacity of the individual for evil and transgression is overcome not in the sense that man can sin no more, but in the sense that, from the divine standpoint, the sinner is accepted through his faith. He continues, to be sure, to confront evil both in the world and in himself, but, through the act of reconciliation, the evil is no longer a reality in and for itself and thus is not something which man has still to overcome by an infinite striving. Spirit, as reconciliation, has cancelled the bad infinite initiated by a struggle between good and evil in which each is conceived as standing on the same level in the confrontation. Spirit teaches the individual that there is no sin that cannot be forgiven through repentance or the giving up of individual willfulness. The one exception to this truth is the sin which is against the Spirit itself, the refusal of the individual to accept Spirit – *das Läugnen des Geistes*. This rejection Hegel sees as spiritual nihilism, since Spirit is the only power able to overcome human transgression.[22]

In addition to all previous determinations, Spirit is manifest as love. Spirit as love is, in a peculiar sense, the power that most intimately unites the members in the community. For each individual in becoming a member finds added to his being a new dimension; he has become an object of the divine love as have all the other members. The person who has become incorporated into the spiritual community discovers his true worth beyond both finitude and the infinite sorrow. "The soul," Hegel says, "the individual soul, has an infinite, an eternal quality, namely, that of being a citizen in the Kingdom of God." [23] As Hegel rightly notes, the love from which Christianity draws its life transcends every form of love that is conditioned by particularity. Although he does not mention the three classic conceptions of love in the western cultural tradition – εϱῶς, φιλία, αγάπη – Hegel makes it clear that he understands the conditional character of εϱῶς and φιλία in contrast to the Christian conception. He writes, "This love is neither human love, love of persons, the love of the sexes, nor friendship..." [24] He goes on to point out that in both friendship and conjugal love there is a condition involved – each member of the pair is dependent on the particularity of the other. Hegel does not suppose that this fact vitiates either form of love since each is essential and valuable; his point is that the love pervading the spiritual community has no condition in the sense that no human factor – race, sex, age, social status and the entire range of finite distinctions among men – forms its basis. The love of the community is, as Hegel expresses it somewhat extravagantly, the love that is "mediated by the worthlessness of all particularity." [25] Stated positively, this means that the finite determinations of the person do not count insofar as the divine love is in question; the love pervading the spiritual community is the love of God – in the form of Spirit – and this love reaches to the center of the individual without regard to the historical factors that distinguish one man from another.

Over and above the particular characteristics of Spirit that have been pointed out, there is a further determination to be found in all of its manifestations. That determination is best expressed in the proposition, "Spirit is present and actual." At sev~~~~ crucial turns in his exposition, Hegel contrasts the *present* character of Spirit with *was vergangen ist.* For example, the historical Jesus, as sensuous individual, is *past,* but the significance and truth of that individual is made *present* or is "*re-presented*" by Spirit. We must not understand "representation" here exclusively in logical terms as if it were merely a symbolic surrogate; the temporal aspect would be lost and an essential feature of Spirit would be missed. Hegel speaks of Jesus as a temporal individual who was in the past and he draws a parallel with sense experience generally and with all finite existence. In each case what we begin with, whatever starts a process of development or interpretation, must be left behind, as if it belonged to a dream-like past existing only in memory. The truth, however, or whatever becomes manifest in experience is available only for Spirit which is, as Hegel says, "above all things present." [26] The theme runs throughout his discussion of Spirit and the religious community; it even serves to establish the primacy of philosophy over history in the interpretation of religion. After claiming that it is for philosophy and not history to justify the Christian content, Hegel says,

> What the Spirit effects is not history, Spirit is concerned only with what is in and for itself, not with the past, but simply with what is present.[27]

Spirit is present in power as well as in knowledge. As actual in the spiritual community which is itself actual and not a phenomenon of the past, Spirit apprehends the truth of the past events that are at the basis of the religious content. Each member of the community is able to appropriate the truth of that content and to partake of it because Spirit is actually present in him. Spirit, therefore, places each individual in a new relation to the religious content. If a person views this content merely historically, that is, as something that originated at a time in the past through the life and death of an individual who belonged to the past, he has not yet apprehended it as something known or as truth. It is the power of Spirit that bridges the gap between past and present by laying hold of the truth of the content and making it *presently* available for each individual member. Hegel saw what some of his critics have not fully appreciated in their over-zealous concern for historical foundations. It is not merely the events of the past as they might be described by the historian which are of decisive importance for the community, but rather the *religious significance* of these events as apprehended by Spirit. That significance is what is capable of being made present and available for the individual in the present. Hegel does not make the historical foundation inessential as has sometimes been claimed; it is rather that he understood the insufficiency of this foundation when separated from the interpretation which is its religious meaning and truth. If a present member of the community is to look upon the past content as something more than an historical record and to have it as a truth that has decisive importance for present life, that truth must be apprehended as such and made present for him. On Hegel's interpretation, Spirit performs both functions by its actual presence in the community and in the members.

Having considered the nature of Spirit and its role in the religious community, we must turn to Hegel's account of the dialectic of that community in history and especially to its relations with the world and the secular reality.[28] The discussion will bring us back to the topic with which the paper began – the connection, in Hegel's view, between the reconciliation that is actualized in the kingdom of Spirit and the ultimate reconciliation of God with the world in the order of cosmic history.

The spiritual community, when founded, understands itself primarily as an *inward* reality or as possessing the form of subjectivity; the culmination of such subjectivity in the individual is the celebration of the Lord's Supper in which the form of reconciliation is made especially vivid. This celebration is, for Hegel, only a moment, however, in that it is a representation and takes place for individuals who exist in the world and whose spiritual community also has a wordly existence. Consciousness of the abstract character of the first form of reconciliation coincides with the realization that *over against* the spiritual community stands what Hegel calls *"Objektivität überhaupt"* or the word.[29] This realization is of the utmost importance because it means that the spiritual community becomes involved in secularity and does not live only within itself. Objectivity assumes three forms in Hegel's analysis; first, as external and immediate world which, from the standpoint of religious dialectic, is called the "heart" and its interests; second, as the reflection of the world in abstract understanding; and third, the most adequate form of objectivity, as the concept. A complete account would have to show how Spirit realizes itself in each of these forms or elements. For our purposes, however, it is necessary to concentrate on the first form – the "heart" – because it is there that the link between the spiritual community and both *Welt* and *Weltlichkeit* is established. The dialectic of the heart shows most clearly how Hegel sought to come to terms with secular existence and to connect religion with the state and with world history.

The point has often been made that the Lutheran tradition, in concentrating the religious relationship in the faith and justification of the individual, failed to relate that relationship itself to political reality with the result that religion became irrelevant to the affairs of the state and to the entire secular world of the believer. Whatever may be the final judgment about Lutheranism on this head, Hegel's view of the relationship is quite different. For him, the truth about the individual as known from the religious standpoint is not irrelevant to his life in the world; reconciliation, though realized in the religious community, is not meant to be limited to that community. The task is, as Hegel says, "to see that this reconciliation takes place in the worldly sphere *(Weltlichkeit)* itself." [30]

The truth of the immediate religion in the heart is that the individual enjoys the real, though abstract, sense of the divine presence. The abstractness stems from the fact that the self harbors a worldly element within itself in the form of needs, impulses, interests, talents, etc. and these must also participate in the reconciliation of human and divine. Reconciliation, therefore, must pass beyond the immediacy of the heart. There is, however, an important truth in that immediacy; as an object of the divine grace through the spiritual community, the individual receives a destiny, or "vocation" *(Bestimmung)*, as Hegel calls it, in the form of an infinite worth which is at the same time the infinite certainty of Spirit itself. The destiny of the individual person for infinity is his *freedom*, something which Hegel understands in this context as the person's being related to the world and to actuality as *subjectivity at home with itself*. The substantial truth of the heart is that the individual is reconciled and established as infinite in the midst of the world; this freedom gained through religion must underlie the process by which man becomes further related to the worldly sphere. The task, then, of relating religion to the secular is the task of relating freedom to all cultural and historical forms.

The development of the substantial truth that the individual is free in accordance with his religious destiny manifests itself in three forms; each is aimed at relating reconciliation to the world that exists beyond the spiritual community. First, there is the immediate relationship in which the spiritual stands aloof from the world, thus establishing a negative relationship – asceticism – as if the truth of reconciled life were to remain in itself and undeveloped. Here we have the renunciation of the concrete element in the self and evidence of the belief that over against the spiritual, social life along with art and science have no value. Hegel rejects this form as unsatisfactory not only because it would exclude nature and set it in opposition to Spirit, but also because, as he expresses it, "It is the very nature of Spirit, to develop and differentiate itself until it reaches the worldly sphere." [31]

The second form in which reconciliation is to be related to the world involves the mutual separation of the religious and the secular. Hegel distinguishes this form from the preceding; asceticism means a negative relationship and a rejection of the world as if it counted for nothing. The situation in which the religious and the secular exist side by side in external relation implies that each has some value and that the two are supposed to have some positive relation to each other. Hegel points out that the religious side, in the form of the organized church, sought to determine the relationship by claiming its sovereignty over the secular world, while the latter remained unreconciled in its secularity. In passages that are of considerable importance for present-day discussions of sacred and secular, Hegel traces the consequences which followed from the effort of the church to dominate secular existence. The worldly element in its unreconciled or unspiritual form was absorbed into the church and the price of sovereignty was the development of a form of life in which man is no longer at home with himself, that is, is no longer free. The final outcome is the absolute contradiction of Spirit itself made actual in the corruption of the church. In seeking to dominate the secular as unreconciled existence, the church ends by becoming secularized through unreconciled secularity. Man becomes involved in worldly interests and the sacred is set aside.[32]

The third form of this dialectic involves a surprising turn which seems more dependent on Hegel's reading of modern, western history than on his speculative philosophy of religion. Spirit in the previous stage was left in contradiction with itself and therefore without a reconciliation of its truth with the world. The contradiction, Hegel declares, in what surely must be one of the most rapid transitions in his entire system; cancels itself in ethical life (*Sittlichkeit*). The argument is as follows. The principle of freedom, which he continues to regard as the *sole* truth of reconciliation,[33] is said to have forced its way into secular life with the result that secular life is brought into conformity with the concept and thus represents the concrete freedom of rational will. "It is in the organization of the state," Hegel writes, "that the divine has broken into actuality

(*Wirklichkeit*); the latter is penetrated by the former and now the secular is justified in and for itself because its foundation is the divine will." [34] The relations and institutions of ethical life in the state represent the true reconciliation of religion with secular life.

Two observations are in order at this point. First, Hegel was right in his belief that the Judeo-Christian tradition does not reject and cannot, in principle, reject, secular life as worthless or merely as an "unholy other." The high valuation placed by that tradition on the world, on the individual, on time, and on history means that secular life must be regarded as a valid expression of the potentialities inherent in the creation. Second, despite his clear sense of the need for relating the religious reconciliation to the world, Hegel failed to take into account the full force of the problem. He made the task easier for himself by reducing the content of reconciliation or the substantial truth of the revealed religion to the freedom of reason so that the problem is solved as soon as we have passed from the abstract form of this freedom to its concrete realization in ethical life which, as an expression of Spirit in accord with the concept, is the secular counterpart of the religious community. The underlying issue far transcends our present purposes, but it is too important to ignore. In defining the content of reconciliation as freedom, Hegel leaves out much in that content which makes for tension in the relation between religion and secular life. Grace, to be sure, means freedom, but it also means that man is the being who is capable of misusing his freedom and of sinning against the divine law which is precisely why he comes to stand in need of the power of forgiveness in the first place. This, too, belongs to reconciliation. Hegel does not stress the negative point and thus he fails to see that when freedom in its positive truth alone is made the basis of the secular, there inevitably develops that pride and self-certainty of both freedom and reason which tempt man to deny that he needs the reconciliation which it is the office of the spiritual community to provide. Since, however, Hegel views the dialectic of religious and secular solely in terms of the freedom of reason, we cannot pursue this line of thought further, but must return instead to his own outworking of the destiny of the spiritual community in the course of world history.

We may profitably foreshorten Hegel's account and pass over the details of his brilliant interpretation of Pietism and Enlightenment modes of thought, concentrating entirely on the manner in which the two views, though outwardly antithetical, actually come to a meeting of extremes. According to Hegel, the rationalism of the Enlightenment thinkers, no less than the stress on feeling basic to the Pietists, ends in agnosticism and in the denial that the religious content can be made intelligible. Pietism is interpreted as a retreat to individual feeling with a consequent refusal to engage in development of the doctrine in the conceptual mode Hegel deemed essential. Enlightenment, on the other hand, abjures feeling and seeks to grasp the religious content from the standpoint of abstract understanding. Both fail to advance to the truth of the concept, and both fail to appreciate the truth of Spirit as present in the community. The principal error shared by both forms is that of atomic individualism which not only makes community impossible, but works against the acceptance of the religious content at the foundation of the community. Pietism *refuses* to develop the content rationally, and Enlightenment *cannot* develop the content rationally. For the former, religion is enclosed in individual feeling, and for the latter, religion comes to be identified with morality which, at this point, Hegel identifies with abstract subjectivity or individual arbitrariness (*Willkür*).

True to his principle of finding and preserving the element of truth in every inadequate intellectual or spiritual form, Hegel maintains that Pietism was right in giving a place to feeling and in refusing to countenance the dissolution of religion into abstract dogma. Enlightenment, though it holds fast to a conception of reason which is, from Hegel's point of view, inadequate, and therefore is unable to find truth in the religious content, nevertheless holds fast to the principle of freedom and sees that the religious content must be developed in relation to reason in some form. It is important to notice that the main force of Hegel's attack on these positions has to do with their inability to sustain the spiriual community. In failing to show the rationality of the religious content, each strikes a blow at the community; for, as Hegel has been maintaining, the community is based on doctrine. When doctrine is either abandoned or deprived of truth, the community has lost the living bond which unites the members in one body. What is needed, Hegel believed, is a form of thought that is adequate to showing the rationality of the content and in such a way as to reunite the members in a community that is the locus of actual Spirit. It is precisely at this point in the analysis that Hegel begins to speak in earnest about the function of philosophy, understood in his sense of the development of the concept. Philosophy must show the truth of Spirit, and resolve the contradiction brought forth in the opposition between Pietism as the negation of freedom and Enlightenment as the expression of a freedom that is merely abstract. The standpoint of Spirit is alone adequate for expressing both the truth of the content and that concrete subjectivity which exists in the spiritual community. In claiming that concrete subjectivity has the task of showing the rationality of faith, Hegel writes,

> "That is the standpoint of philosophy, that the content [of faith] takes refuge in the concept and through thought (*Denken*) is restored and justified." [35]

And, several pages later, in his attack on the Enlightenment for its holding to the belief that there is no truth in the religious content, Hegel states his claim in behalf of philosophy even more forcefully, as the following two passages demonstrate. "Philosophy," he declares, "has the aim of knowing the truth, of knowing God, because his is the absolute truth." [36] And again, "In philosophy, which is theology, there is but one task to be accomplished, to show the rationality of religion." [37]

It seems clear that Hegel regarded his own philosophy of the concept as capable of restating the doctrine of God, already present in the immediate feeling content for faith, in a form adequate both for religion and for the sustaining of the community. He claims for his philosophical reconciliation the power to overcome the opposition between immediate feeling and abstract understanding, and to provide a new form for the religious truth that will not only restore the community but save it from the threat of individualism at the same time. I shall not follow Hegel either in the development of his position or in his defense of philosophy against those who say that it denies feeling, or against the charge that philosophy sets itself above religion as a final judge. His discussion at this point, however, should be taken seriously by those critics who say that he ignored the content of faith in favor of his own speculative metaphysics. If anything, Hegel was more in danger of accepting the content from the past as if it were something fixed that had been handed down intact in his own time. More important, however, than these issues, is to take note of the problem with which we began – the gap between the realization of Spirit in the religious community and the destiny of that community *vis à vis* the outward universality of all reality. The fact is, as Hegel notes, religious knowledge through the concept is not by its nature universal, and, furthermore, it is knowledge only *within* the community. The problem now concerns the community itself; on the one hand, it appears to be involved in such inner disruption that when it does become actual, it also begins to disappear. On the other hand, it is difficult to speak of its destruction because the kingdom of God is said to be founded eternally, and the Spirit is to live forever in its community.

"To speak of the spiritual community passing away," Hegel writes, "is to end with a discordant note." [38] Hegel continues, expressing his characteristic respect for the historical situation, "Only how can it be helped? This discordant note is in the reality before us." [39]

Hegel was in fact ending his lectures by raising a problem that is far more complex than he could easily have understood, the problem, namely, whether and in what sense there can be a Judeo-Christian civilization or indeed any "religious" civilization. The events of the past several decades have taught us to appreciate both the severity and the urgency of this problem. That there can be a *religious* community existing as one among many communities within a civilization is clear, but whether that community is capable of extending both its Spirit and its truth to civilization generally and to what might be called the community of all mankind, is at the very least doubtful. Hegel appraises the problem quite candidly and realistically; he sees that his solution is only partial. He believes that, through his philosophical reinterpretation, he has provided a valid basis for the spiritual community above and beyond divisive forces. "For us," [40] he claims, "philosophical knowledge has overcome the discord, and the aim of these lectures has been just to reconcile reason and religion, and to know religion in its manifold forms as necessary, and to rediscover in revealed religion the truth and the Idea." [41] "But," he continues, "this reconciliation is itself merely a partial one without outward university." [42] The truth is, as Hegel saw and acknowledged, philosophy may be capable of giving an intelligible interpretation of religion and thus of providing a basis for the religious community, but philosophy alone cannot resolve the problem of bringing that truth to bear on a civilization in such a way that the gap between sacred and secular is closed. The reason why this is so is clear; the problem cannot be resolved by thought alone, even by so rich and profound a type of thought as Hegel's.

NOTES

1. *VPR*, II, p. 365 (I shall be using the 1959 printing). In future notes I shall cite a passage in the original and follow with the corresponding English translation in *LPR*. In all cases I have made my own translations, but in some cases I find the above translation adequate. I have cited the English for purposes of convenience and comparison.

2. *VPR*, II, p. 356; *LPR*, III, p. 151.

3. *VPR*, II, p. 311; *LPR*, III, p. 103.

4. *EdpW*, Glockner, X, sec. 554, pp. 446f; *Wallace*, pp. 167f.

5. If, on the other hand, we follow Hegel's own statements about the identity of God and the Idea, and the ultimate identity of philosophy and theology, the philosophy of religion must no longer be seen as one part or branch among others

of the total system, but rather as its culmination. In my view, there always remains an ambiguity, at least in Hegel's form of expression, on this head. He describes the *Idee* as that which presents itself in existence and comprehends itself in all reality; his identification of the *Idee* with absolute Truth and reality demands at once that it be identified with God as well. And yet Hegel can speak of the "divine Idea" as if the expression were not redundant, thus suggesting that God is the *Idee* insofar as it is expressed in the sphere of religion. On the other hand, the account given of the Absolute Idea in the final section of the *Science of Logic* (5.327ff.) combines several possibilities. After characterizing the Idea as the identity of the theoretical and practical Idea, he goes on to say, "The Absolute Idea is the only object and content of philosophy" (the passage is found in *WdL*, Glockner, V, p. 328 and in *SL*, II, p. 466) but that it has different modes of existence – Nature and Spirit – and different modes in which it comprehends itself – art and religion. Hegel again makes the point that the content of philosophy is the same as that of religion and art, but that philosophy represents the higher form of comprehension because it works through the concept. The question is the extent to which the Idea in religion is making its appearance in a special or limited perspective and is thus the "divine" Idea rather than the Idea "itself." It is, of course, open to Hegel to say that the fully adequate realization of the Absolute Idea, *qua content*, is found in the Truth of religion, even if it remains for speculative thought to express that Truth in the form of the concept.

6. In making such a characterization one must bear in mind that the sorts of relation that obtain between the items of reality grasped by the concept undergo change as the process of self-comprehension goes forward. Thus ,for example, in logical development – the movement from Being to Essence and finally to concept – the categories come to be related to each other in an increasingly internal way. The categories of Being are like monads which confront each other externally and pass into each other reciprocally, those of Essence have a diadic or conjunctive character which Hegel describes as "pairs of correlatives," while in the sphere of the Concept, the categories of "moments" are irreducibly triadic since they must express the complete development of Being through universality, particularity and individuality.

7. *EdpW*, Glockner, sec. 160.

8. *EdpW*, Glockner, sec. 162, pp. 356f; *Wallace*, p. 291.

9. *EdpW*, Glockner, sec. 236, p. 446; *Wallace*, p. 374.

10. The problem of determining the meaning of Spirit is focused by the fact that we have difficulty translating the very title of *Phenomenology*. The term "mind" expresses only the intellectual or cognitive aspect of *Geist* and leaves out power and life. On the other hand, the term "spirit" is not entirely satisfactory because it is vague, connoting feeling or the immaterial in a general sense and not at all conveying Hegel's meaning of self-determining life and thought involved in concrete individuality.

11. The thinker chiefly responsible for this historical line of interpretation was Joachim di Fiore, a medieval thinker, who not only correlated the reign of the Persons with historical ages, but held that the age of the Spirit would begin in 1260 and that in this period a new creativity would appear breaking through the fixed forms of both religious dogma and institutions.

12. *VPR*, II, p. 219; *LPR*, III, p. 2.

13. The "limited" but not absolutely "universal" present.

14. *VPR*, II, p. 315; *LPR*, III, p. 107.

15. *VPR*, II, pp. 317f; *LPR*, III, p. 110.

16. In his doctrine of the community, expressed in terms of the theory of interpretation and triadic relations, Royce gave a more explicit formulation of the central idea involved. The members as individuals become related to the truth that founds

and defines the community and thereby become related to each other in a new way. The relation between member and member, however, is not the same as that between each member and the community itself which, for both Hegel and Royce, is not merely a collection of members, but the truth or the power which united the members.

17. Throughout the discussion of the spiritual community, Hegel uses the term *Geist* to mean God as understood, first, through the Trinitarian religious symbol, and second, through his own speculative reconstruction of Spirit as the concrete in-and-for-itself actualization of God or the eternal Idea found only in the kingdom of Spirit. There are some passages when Hegel uses the expression "der heilige Geist" to refer to the historical situation of the founding of the community. I see no ground for doubting that he identified the religious doctrine of God as Holy Spirit with his own conception of Spirit. If it be asked whether he was entirely justified in so doing, the answer would have to be long and involved. One thing is clear: Spirit, for Hegel, contained a greater emphasis on self-consciousness and knowledge than would have been characteristic of the interpretation of many theologians, especially those in the evangelical traditions where discussions of the Holy Spirit were invariably bound up with the problem of conversion and the "sincerity" of the true believer.

18. *VPR*, II, p. 318. ". . . Gott als Geist der Dreinige ist."

19. *VPR*, II, p. 326; *LPR*, III, p. 119.

20. *VPR*, II, p. 328; *LPR*, III, p. 121.

21. Hegel saw, as many over-zealous questers for the "historical Jesus" have not, that however important historical research may be for the correct determination of the religious content, such research does not bring us closer to providing whatever justification that content is to receive. Hegel's point is that when the content was present in historical form, that form, *even then*, did not provide the justification since the truth of faith was and is bound up with the significance of the starting point and that significance is available only for Spirit, i.e., for experience and thought.

22. *VPR*, II, p. 336; *LPR*, III, p. 108.

23. *VPR*, II, p. 313; *LPR*, III, p. 105.

24. *VPR*, II, p. 314; *LPR*, III, p. 106.

25. *VPR*, II, p. 314; *LPR*, III, p. 106.

26. *VPR*, II, p. 327; *LPR*, III, p. 121. *"der sich schlechthin gegenwärtig ist"*; cf. *VPR*, II, p. 340.

27. *VPR*, II, p. 328; *LPR*, III, p. 122.

28. *VPR*, II, pp. 340ff.; *LPR*, III, pp. 134ff.

29. For Hegel's doctrine of Objectivity, it is necessary to turn to the *Science of Logic*, Eng. trans., vol. 2, 343ff. This doctrine forms the second section of the theory of the concept. Objectivity embraces the domain of objects as understood through the forms of mechanism, chemism and teleology. As far as the philosophy of religion is concerned, "objectivity" means the *world* and points to the involvement of both the individual members of the community and the community itself in the worlds of natural and cultural objects.

30. *VPR*, II, p. 342; *LPR*, III, p. 136.

31. *VPR*, II, p. 342; *LPR*, III, p. 137.

32. It is interesting to note that Hegel, speaking historically, refers to the church (*Kirche*) as corrupted, but not to the Spiritual as such (*der Geistige*). The latter is said to be in "absolute contradiction" but presumably, in not being identical with any historical church, the Spiritual can escape corruption and go on to the finding of a more satisfactory way of relating itself to the world. A topic which I have not considered and which would be essential for a more complete study, is the distinc-

tion and precise relation between the "spiritual community," the "church," the "Spiritual," the "kingdom of Spirit," and the "kingdom of God." There is clearly much overlap in denotation among the terms, but determining the divergences is essential for clarity.

33. "It is the *freedom of reason* which has been won in religion which now knows itself in Spirit as existing for itself." *VPR*, II, p. 344; *LPR*, III, p. 139.

34. *VPR*, II, pp. 343f; *LPR*, III, p. 138.

35. *VPR*, II, p. 350; *LPR*, III, p. 145.

36. *VPR*, II, p. 352; *LPR*, II, p. 148.

37 *LPR*, II, p. 353; *LPR*, III, p. 148. There is a possible ambiguity in this passage; Hegel says, *"In der Philosophie, welche Theologie ist..."* which could be taken to mean either that philosophy, as such, and theology are identical, or that there is a type, a form, a task, of philosophy which is theology. I do not attempt to resolve this problem; I am inclined to think that Hegel means to refer to philosophy as such. And yet there is one further passage that must be reckoned with. Hegel writes: "This reconciliation [of thought with the concrete] is philosophy; philosophy is theology insofar as it sets forth the reconciliation of God with himself and with nature." 16.354; Eng. 4.148. Much depends on the limitation implied in "insofar."

38. *VPR*, II, p. 354; *LPR*, III, p. 150.

39. *VPR*, II, p. 354; *LPR*, III, p. 150.

40. The proper denotation of the "for us" here parallels that of the "we" in other of Hegel's writings.

41. *VPR*, II, p. 355; *LPR*, III, p .151.

42. *VPR*, II, p. 365; *LPR*, III, p. 151.

JOHN E. SMITH

HEGEL'S REINTERPRETATION OF THE DOCTRINE OF SPIRIT
AND THE RELIGIOUS COMMUNITY

by

P. Christopher Smith

Any attempt to comprehend Hegel's interpretation of Spirit must, as John E. Smith correctly assumes, deal seriously with Hegel's philosophy of religion; for indeed, it is in the religious tradition that Hegel finds the traces of philosophic truth, which 200 years of Enlightenment cynicism and skepticism had come close to obliterating. Nevertheless, though Luther, in Hegel's eyes, might be nearer to the truth than Voltaire or Holbach, he is not as near to it as Anaxagoras, Plato and Aristotle. Higher than Lutheranism stands Greek philosophy in Hegel's mind, and *Geist* as Holy Spirit in the community of worshipers proves ultimately for him to be *nous*. "Through philosophy," states Hegel, "religion receives its justification from the point of view of thinking consciousness." [1] This too John Smith has clearly recognized. He sees that Hegel interprets religion in terms of "hard-won" philosophical concepts: *Begriff* and *Idee*. We ask, however, if an interpretation of religion based on *Begriff* and *Idee* can be adequate. Ingenious as Hegel's attempt to philosophically justify religion might be, it would seem to us to preclude at least one traditional understanding of Spirit and religious community precisely because of its philosophical point of view. We wish to show how this limitation occurs and to indicate what the consequences of it are. It will be our contention that Hegel's reinterpretation of Spirit is perhaps a very old misinterpretation of it.

In order to establish our point, we must first recall briefly where religion stands on Hegel's ladder of education, the course of *Bildung*, which he describes for us elaborately in the *Phänomenologie des Geistes*. In what grade, we ask, is religious consciousness developed or undeveloped, cultivated or uncultivated? Like Plato, Hegel treats consciousness which is tied to sense perceptions as inadequate. For Plato's *doxa*,

Hegel substitutes *Meinen*. The intent, however, remains the same: consciousness here is aware of the transient "fact that . . ." but not the grounds "why." Only science, *episteme* or *Wissenschaft*, knows the clear and certain grounds for the phenomenal appearance, and such science, having these as its intentional object, has transcended the physical sensation and entered the metaphysical domain of pure reason. Clearly, then, intellect will remain inadequate as long as the thing it knows is a "given" particular. On the other hand, when thought thinks a universal thought-thing, it becomes adequate. Thought here is identical with its object and the discrepancy which engendered the dialectic between the I and the other has been eliminated – *Ich = Ich*. Generally speaking, religion fits into this scheme as the next to the last step. It is not quite thought thinking thought-things, but almost.

Religion can never claim to have completely eliminated *doxa*. Even if religion is spiritual and not physical, there remains in it a discrepancy between the knower and what is known. *Glauben* or faith remains *Vorstellen*, i.e., a way of relating to the object which presupposes the otherness of the object, its difference from the mind which conceives of it. In other words, there persists here a measure of inadequacy. To be sure, the *Vorstellungen* or ideas of religious consciousness are no longer tied to sense data. On the contrary, they are of the universal. Thus we are concerned here more with an idea in the Platonic sense of *idea* or *eidos* than in the Humean sense of "dull copy." Nevertheless, the religious idea continues to be envisioned in a particular, figurative instantiation. Thought here does not yet think concepts, but rather images: Father, Son, Mother.

Significant for us is that Hegel clearly presses religion into the framework of his Platonic, post-Kantian epistemology: for him religion is a matter of the relationship between *Anschauung* and *Begriff*. Religion as *Vorstellen* knows inadequately, which is to say that it is not yet purely conceptual, but rather, to some degree perceptual. It is not yet *nous*.

John Smith points out correctly that in a certain sense *nous* as mind or thought cannot be equated with Hegel's *Geist*; for *Geist* is not only by itself apart from the world, as is mind, rather it is the synthesis of *Logos* and natural life, thought and the world. Our point is, however, that, although Hegel's Spirit cannot be itself without "previous" externalization in natural form, its truth is ultimately the sublation of its natural existence, its return to itself. Once this truth has been discovered, we are back where we started: at thought that thinks thought-things, thought by itself unencumbered by *Anschauung, noésis noéseos*. Not only the beginning, but also the end of Hegel's encyclopedia of sciences is Aristotelian *nous*.

These points must have been brought out into the open, we think, if we are to get to the bottom of Hegel's understanding of Spirit and possibly get beyond it. For it seems to us that Hegel's synthesis is not a balanced one. Indeed, something is forgotten in it. In Hegel, we wish to argue, the philosophic has eclipsed the religious. Here, then, we differ from John Smith, who, as we understand him, feels that Hegel has achieved a true synthesis, on the one hand, of Spirit taken as power "over against thought or form" and, on the other, of religion "rooted in doctrine or conceptual interpretation."

We shall base our argument initially upon a distinction between *Geist* as *nous* and *Geist* as *pneuma,* made by Gerhard Ebeling, who writes in *Das Wesen des christlichen Glaubens,* "The pictorial image of the first (*nous*) is the unchanging clarity of light in which things are held still for the vision of an observer. The pictorial image of the second (*pneuma*) is the wind's blowing, which carries away in its motion him who is struck by it. In one case we are dealing with a timeless truth, in the other, with living power in temporal existence." [2] Ebeling goes on to argue that even *pneuma,* which the Greeks conceived of as affecting the sub-rational region of drives and passions, does not fit fully the meaning of *Geist.* For the Holy Spirit, Biblically understood, is that which penetrates the most inward center of personal being. It makes a person new precisely in that it creates in him a new heart of "flesh" where formerly there was one of "stone" (*idem*). Now, John Smith has made clear that some element of life exists in Hegel's Spirit. We question, however, whether life as Hegel means it, i.e., as externalization, could make his conception of Spirit adequate for Biblical Spirit, which like the wind, "blows where it wants."

Let us take, for instance, the presence of *Geist* as Hegel conceives of it and attempt to work out, in contrast, an understanding of Biblical presence. As John Smith discerns, *Geist* for Hegel, far from being dead historical past, is fully present to the individual. It remains, however, to clarify what kind of presence this is. In Hegel the outpouring of Spirit is precisely not an event which befalls us as the wind might sweep over us, only then to pass on. The wind comes and goes, is present and withdraws; its presence is temporal. For Hegel, on the other hand, the presence of Spirit means a breaking through that which fluctuates in time and a rising into eternal, metaphysical truth. In his Spiritual Religion we are dealing, in more or less adequate form, with the steady presence (Heidegger: *stete*

Anwesenheit) of the *Logos*. Truth for Hegel is speculative, which means that it can be envisioned. We have here a presence which is "the unchanging clarity of light in which things are held still for the vision of an observer."

We have seen that Hegel forces the religious encounter with Spirit into the framework of Platonic *paideia* leading to the envisioning of the Ideas, which Hegel calls *Wissenschaft*. The consequences of this interpretation become particularly evident when it comes to Hegel's understanding of the presence of Spirit. Spirit as something temporarily present is unthinkable for Hegel because, as such, it would not be accessible for *Wissenschaft*. On the contrary, it could only be the object of uncultivated belief (*doxa, Meinung*). It would be present to us on the level of mere *Sinnlichkeit,* as a "fact that" without a concept or reason "why." The presence of *Geist* can be experienced, says Hegel, only when the particular instantiation, Christ as a person – who for Hegel is there only as a *sinnliche Gegebenheit* – is transcended.

We might ask, however, if Spirit's presence would have to be purged of temporality in another interpretation of it which did not construe it in terms of Platonic theory of knowledge. There is, perhaps, temporal presence, the temporality of which is in no sense a defect since that which is present is in no sense there for *epistémé* or even for its inadequate form, *doxa*. And it could be that *Glauben* is not *Meinung,* i.e., inadequate knowledge of an unmediated object, but rather *fides* or *emunah,* the "truth" of my response to another personal being.

A second limitation of Hegel's conception of Spirit becomes clear if one examines what the content of Spirit is, as he understands it. The bond which unites the religious community, Hegel emphasizes, is once again a Platonic one. Love, which one might assume to be the bond among the faithful, is redirected in the spiritual event, i.e., redirected like the "mind's eye" away from particular loved people to the very idea, which transcends any particularity: "In short an objective content is the bond, not affection as such, like that of a man for a woman as this particular personality." [3]

It now becomes evident why Hegel stresses the doctrines of any religion: Spirit is present as doctrinal content. What kinds of truth does the Christian religion convey? Basically speaking those of the *Logos*. We learn of Spirit at first undifferentiated from itself, the Father, then of Spirit in natural instantiation, the Son, and ultimately, of the union of the one and the many, the universal and the particular, Holy Spirit. To be sure, the Church, with its myths and sacraments, makes these truths available to the individual on the basis of perception, not conception. Still the content is the "true" one, *das Spekulative*.

But is not a very different understanding of Spirit suppressed here? What has happened to Spirit which descends upon us like birth pains sweeping over a pregnant woman? In the envisioning of the ideal, thought thinks itself. It is self-consciousness which, having risen to *Unendlichkeit,* views before it nothing other than itself. But surely this has nothing to do with the outpouring of Spirit which comes over the finite individual and "carries him away in its motion." In the latter case it is impossible to speak of any ideal content which the individual could speculate upon. He finds himself buffeted by the *alogon* and inwardly transformed by it.

Admittedly, an explanation of what Spirit brings us, assuming that the content is not, as Hegel sees it, *objektive Wahrheit,* is called for at this point. We can only offer some suggestions here. Perhaps the most in-structive place to begin looking for an alternative to Hegel would be Emil Brunner's *Wahrheit als Begegnung.* "Where it is a matter of real, primary faith," writes Brunner,

> where God reveals himself to me in his word, the concern is not
> with a "something." ... [That] opposite me is no longer as in
> thought a something, a thing thought or talked about, which I
> bring to light through the energy of my thought. Rather, it is a
> person who speaks himself and reveals himself, who, accordingly,
> has the initiative and leadership and, we might say, assumes the
> role which in thinking I have myself. There is a transition and
> exchange here which is completely without analogy in the realm of
> thought. The only analogy to it is the encounter (*Begegnung*)
> between men, that of one person with another .... At the moment
> where he becomes a you to me, he ceases to be an object of my
> thought and the subject-object relationship is transformed into a
> relationship of personal correspondence. We have community
> with each other.[4]

We are dealing here with a temporal presence which has nothing to do with self-consciousness or speculative truth. It seems to us that Hegel, precisely because he seeks a philosophical justification of religion, cannot recognize the kind of event that Brunner describes. The immediacy of that which is present to us in the second person as a "thou art" must, of necessity, be interpreted by him as an inferior cognitive object for in-adequate, sensuous *Meinen,* as an "it is" on the level of *Sinnlichkeit.*

NOTES

1. *VPR, Lasson*, 63, p. 228.
2. Gerhard Ebeling, *Das Wesen des christlichen Glaubens* (Hamburg, Siebenstern, 1965), p. 95.
3. *VPR, Lasson*, 63, p. 179.
4. Emil Brunner, *Wahrheit als Begegnung* (Zürich, Zwingli, 1938), pp. 62-63.

REPLY TO P. CHRISTOPHER SMITH

by

John E. Smith

Professor Smith has raised some quite difficult questions and I very much appreciate them, not least because I understand what they are. I suppose that the first problem to be faced is that knowledge for Hegel is always God's knowledge in the end. Kant had a somewhat less ambitious project and he saw knowledge as man's knowledge. By contrast, Hegel always appears to be speaking from the vantage point of the divine. For, after all, the total identity of thought and being so much stressed by Hegel is never apprehended by us as such. Therefore, in Hegel we have to contend with the rather peculiar phenomenon of a finite being explicating the mind of the true Infinite. As a consequence, it will always be difficult to defend Hegel against the charge that he has overemphasized knowledge and claimed too much for man's powers. Moreover, Hegel seems open to the Kierkegaardian existential criticism of his rationalism as well as to the criticism of theologians like Brunner and others who want to make a sharp antithesis between thought and all forms of immediacy; for such critics, Spirit is not a form of reason but rather the opposite, a disorienting force, a confrontation or encounter, an occasion for an either-or decision that stands beyond all dialectical mediation. I accept the criticism as having some force against Hegel's position; Hegel overemphasized both reason and knowledge. I do not believe, however, that criticisms of Hegel's rationalism based on a conception of reason which he would have called mere understanding are valid. Hegel's reason has power in it as well as form; it is objective structure, and life, both of which take us beyond reason as "reasoning." In the end it does not help us to continue to drive the unreconcilable opposition between the immediate and rational mediation. Why? Because you are not functioning as either philosopher or theologian unless you are engaged in some form of rational mediation.

The task of the thinker is not the celebration of the immediate nor is he the guardian of its pristine character. Kierkegaard, for all of his criticism of Hegel, did not confine himself to merely pointing to immediate experience; on the contrary, he developed the most subtle and involved dialectic based on no less than a double reflection. Therefore, I raise the question whether the Kierkegaards and the Brunners, in their attempt to avoid identifying the object of faith with something merely thought or contemplated, can have the last word. They, too, must begin to interpret and say what faith means. And when you have to interpret, you are in the position, so well described by Berdyaev, of *having* to break through the mystery of God with profane and human reason – there is no other way to be a theologian. I have heard of an old Egyptian remedy for getting rid of a headache – run three times around a barn *without* thinking of a fox! It seems to me that *not* reflecting is something like not thinking of a fox. The choice is not between bare immediacy and reflection; reflection is inevitable for a rational being and the only problem is how to carry it out most effectively. Therefore, I begin by trying, as I believe Hegel was trying, to recognize the truth in pietism and the forms of immediacy, but to do so by seeing that that truth must be developed in conceptual ways. Hegel, after all, went out of his way to express the truth of immediacy whereas his critics often give the impression that he ignored it. On the contrary, he sought to find a form of reflection which would do justice to immediacy, but he is often met with the objection that his project was a mistaken one. He should not have tried to find a form of concrete, speculative reason. What, then, should he have done? Should he have been content with celebrating the immediacy of existence? That is, of course, not enough. The moment in which you try to condense yourself into bare existence, you find yourself raising the question of what it means to exist. And then you are once again forced to deal with all the hard questions; there is no way of keeping them from arising. There is no point in contrasting the vivid urgencies of existence with the supposed dead wood of mediation and reflection because nobody escapes reflection; if it is dead wood that is because we have failed to keep our mediation in touch with life. Thought can be creative, as Hegel's was.

HEGEL AND THE MARXIST-LENINIST CRITIQUE OF RELIGION

by

George L. Kline

I

A key question in any discussion of Hegel's treatment of religion concerns the relation of religion to speculative philosophy. Aspects of it are
admirably dealt with in Father Lauer's paper; it has pervaded much of
our discussion at this Symposium. The question is by no means settled.
The standard categoreal polarities are easy enough to rehearse: religion
is to speculative philosophy as *Vorstellung* is to *Begriff*; as *aufgehobenes
Moment* is to *aufhebendes Moment*; as the less "concrete" is to the more
"concrete," in Hegel's special sense of that much abused term.[1]

But to list such polarities, or to repeat Hegel's claim that religion and
philosophy have the same "content" or "object," is to raise, not to
answer, the main questions. We still need to clarify what it means to say
that religion is the *Vorstellung* of that of which speculative philosophy
is the *Begriff*; or that religion and speculative philosophy are successive
and ascending *Momente* in a dialectical *Aufhebung*; or that philosophical
speculation is more concrete$_H$ (though, of course, *less* concrete$_E$) than is
religious experience. Finally, and perhaps most difficult, would be clarification of what it means to say that religion and speculative philosophy
have the same content or object, but apprehend it in different forms or
under different modes.

Since this topic is important both for an understanding of Hegel and
for an understanding of the simplifying vulgarizations of Hegel's view of
religion by Marx, Plekhanov, and Lenin, I shall begin by making a few
preliminary remarks about it.

First, there is the question of the "identity" of the content or object
of religion and speculative philosophy. Hegel himself declares:

> Philosophy has been reproached with setting itself above religion;
> this . . . is false . . . , for it possesses this content only and no other,
> although it presents it in the *form* of thought; it sets itself merely
> above the *form* of faith, the content is the *same* in both cases.[2]

Hegel makes a similar point in the *Lectures on the History of Philosophy,* asserting that religion and philosophy have a common object – the
"supreme object," that which is true *an und für sich* – namely, God *an
und für sich,* and man in his relation to God. In the same work he identifies this common object as "absolute substance" or "universal reason
which is *an und für sich,*" adding that the difference is one of mode of
appropriation. The religious mode of appropriation of absolute substance
is "receptivity and worship," a mode of feeling; the philosophical mode
is conceptualization, a mode of thought.

In *LPR* Hegel asserted: "The content of religion and philosophy cannot
be distinct, since absolute Spirit does not have two self-consciousnesses
of itself." [3] Hegel's own lecture notes (as contrasted with those of his
students, which make up the bulk of the text of *LPR*) contain an explicit
and rather lyrical statement of the identity of the content of religion and
speculative philosophy:

> Thus God is the one and only object of philosophy. [It is the task
> of philosophy] to busy itself with Him, to know all things in Him,
> to refer everything back to Him, as well as to derive all specificity
> from Him and to justify everything only insofar as it has its source
> in Him, . . . living by His radiance.[4]

And Hegel adds: "Thus philosophy is theology, and concern with it [i.e.,
theology] or rather in it, is in itself worship." [5] Making the same point
negatively, he asserts that philosophy "is not a knowledge of the secular,
not worldly wisdom." [6]

It would have been helpful if Hegel had told us more explicitly what
he meant by "content" (*Inhalt*) and how, if at all, it differs from "object"
(*Gegenstand*). On the one hand he says, rather unhelpfully, that the content is truth (*die Wahrheit*), but he does not call the *object* of religion
and philosophy truth; on the other hand he declares that "determinateness
is content." [7] This puzzling statement is not significantly clarified by his
claim that in "absolute religion" (i.e., Protestant Christianity) "religion
is brought to complete determinateness" or "becomes completely determinate." [8] "The determinate" or "determined" (*das Bestimmte*) might
plausibly be identified with content; but determinate*ness* would seem to

be a *characteristic* of a content or an object – hence more like its form.

A further puzzle is generated by Hegel's apparent identification of thought (*Gedanke*) with content (*Inhalt*). In this context he seems to contrast *Vorstellung*, which is "representational," with thought as "non-representational." Thus he finds it difficult "to separate, in a content, what is *content as such, thought*, from what belongs to representation as such." [9] One would think that, on Hegel's view, content, *Vorstellung*, and thought would *all* be determinate, though perhaps not in equal measure (thought presumably would be more determinate – certainly more concrete$_H$ – than *Vorstellung*); *Vorstellung* would be more abstract$_H$ than thought because less adequately mediated.

To contrast thought to *Vorstellung* by identifying thought with content misleadingly suggests that thought is more directly or "immediately" related to a given content or object than is *Vorstellung*. A very un-Hegelian suggestion! Perhaps the text is corrupt (it is drawn from student lecture notes); perhaps Hegel meant to say "content as such, *conceived by* thought" or "... *grasped* by thought" or "... *transparent to* thought." Such qualifiers would at least make Hegelian sense of the passage in question.

In the *Phenomenology* Hegel contrasted religious content as a "form of representation of an other" (*Form des Vorstellens eines andern*) with philosophical content as "the action proper of the self" (*eignes Tun des Selbsts*), adding: "The concept establishes the content as the action proper of the self." [10] This is related of course to the famous *Selbstbewegung* of the concept.

We come now to the second point: the relationship of *Vorstellung* to concept. For Hegel, as we have seen, "philosophy is the activity of transforming what exists in representational form into conceptual form." [11] But exactly what is changed – what is added, what eliminated – in this transformation? Hegel's statements on this score are varied and sometimes conflicting.

He says that speculative philosophy grasps its object "as idea," i.e., as "the truth in thought," in contrast to the (religious) grasp of the object "in der blossen Anschauung als Vorstellung." [12] This last phrase is untranslatable; it may be roughly paraphrased as "in sheer perceptual beholding as [sense-] presentation." This suggests that *Vorstellung* is confined to the level of unsystematized sense-experience. But that would seem to equate it with (sense) image (*Bild*), which in fact Hegel sometimes opposes to it:

An image, he says, is "sensuous through and through, is myth; *Vor-*

stellung [is] image raised to generality; it is thought, it is permeated with thought, it is form of thought as well." [13] He goes on to give as examples the *Vorstellungen* of "right, morality, virtue, courage, the world, evil"; these, he says are spiritual or intellectual (*geistige*) *Vorstellungen*, which have an essential and genetic relation to thought,[14] and in which the general is asserted while the merely pictorial and sensuous (*Bildliche und Sinnliche*) is eliminated.

Still, *Vorstellungen* lack the necessity of concepts and in them "the general is separated from the specific." A *Vorstellung* always has a "more or less sensuous form, standing between immediate sense perception and genuine thought." The *Vorgestellte* is "marked by spatiality and temporality," although it is "objective," while the sensuous and pictorial is "subjective." [15]

Hegel exemplifies the difference between a truth as *vorgestellt* and the same truth as conceptualized in the relation of Father and Son in the Trinity. For religious *Vorstellung* it is "a begetting of the Son in eternity"; reformulated in philosophical concepts it becomes: "an other that is posited by a first, and *aufgehoben* as other [by that first], is [thus] one with it." [16]

The cognitive content of *Vorstellungen* is brought out in Hegel's claim that "insofar as religion essentially presents its content in the form of *Vorstellungen*, it has a *doctrine* and indeed a *truth*." [17] This is reminiscent of the schematic division (in the *Encyclopedia*) of art as *Vorstellung*, religion as *vorgestellter Begriff*, and speculative philosophy as pure *Begriff*. In *LPR* Hegel adds that the idea (i. e., "truth in thought") of speculative philosophy is the "conceived nature of God. To that extent what we call 'the Absolute' is equivalent to the term 'God'." [18]

A further complication is introduced by Hegel's insistence that "conceptual knowledge must be distinguished from abstract understanding," [19] and his characterization of understanding (*Verstand*) as "thought . . . in the form of *Vorstellung*." [20] This would seem to place understanding between *Vorstellung* and pure thought or conceptualization. We would thus have a four-term progression:

Sense Perception	*Vorstellung*	Understanding	Concept

to which correspond:

Art	Religion	*Verstandes-metaphysik*	Speculative Philosophy

Third, we ask in what sense religion, the level of *Vorstellung,* is *preserved,* as well as superseded and raised to a higher level, in speculative philosophy. On this point, for example, Hegel declares that religion "always remains akin to thought, even in its form and movement; and philosophy, as wholly active thought, thought which unifies what is opposed, has approached closely to religion." [21] It is not the place of speculative philosophy, Hegel adds, to deny that the content of religion is "truth for itself."

> Rather, it is precisely religion which is the true content, but in the form of *Vorstellung*. Philosophy does not have to supply [its] substantial truth, nor have men had to wait for philosophy in order to receive the ... knowledge of this truth.[22]

I take this to mean that religion supplies the "substantial truth" or "truth of the substance" of its own content, and that what philosophy adds is "formal truth," or "truth of the form," i. e., substantial truth raised to the level of concepts. According to Hegel, philosophy

> wholly shares its content, its need, and its interest with religion; its object is the eternal truth, nothing but God and the explication [or "making explicit"] of God. Philosophy explicates [or "makes explicit"] only itself when it explicates religion [or "makes religion explicit"]; and when it explicates itself [or "makes itself explicit"] it explicates religion [or "makes religion explicit"] ... Thus philosophy and religion coincide. Philosophy itself in fact is worship.[23]

Father Lauer notes that although it is "precisely the same *truth*" that is present to religion as to speculative thought, the truth present in religion is "a *given* which cannot be verified in religion itself, whereas the truth in [speculative] thought is verified in the very process of thought." [24]

Religion, according to Father Lauer,

> can ultimately know what it is knowing only in and through philosophy, which is to say that in religion man *believes* in God, but only in philosophy can he *know* what God (in whom he believes) is. [Philosophy must grasp] the ultimate totality of reality which religion presents. On the other hand, religion will be dealing in little more than empty words or symbols if philosophy does not make known to it the meaning of its own content.[25]

Fackenheim concisely sums up the main points:

> It is a central Hegelian doctrine that the true religion already is the

true "content," lacking merely the true "form" of speculative thought; that philosophy could not reach truth unless its true content pre-existed in religion; that philosophical thought therefore requires religion as its basis in life, and that the true philosophy in giving the true religious content its true form of thought, both transfigures religion and produces itself.[26]

Thus it seems clear that for the mature Hegel "complete philosophical thought does not leave behind but somehow includes and absorbs the non-philosophical [including religious] thought and life above which it rises . . . ." [27]

The widely held view that for Hegel religion is "philosophy for the masses," an "exoteric picture-thinking simply swept aside by philosophical thinking," [28] must be rejected. Hegel himself had repudiated the "prejudice" (*Vorurteil*) that "the religious, insofar as it is conceptualized, ceases to be religious." [29] He had declared that "nothing is further from the aim of philosophy than to overthrow religion." [30] And he had attacked the view that philosophy "has a corrupting, destructive, and desecrating effect upon the content of religion." [31]

II

All this is true, and yet Hegel did introduce into the history of Western philosophy the view of religion as a transition-form in the historical development of the human spirit. That this view was secularized, simplified, and vulgarized by Marx and the Russian Marxists does not mean that the view was not held by Hegel. In fact, Hegel was the first major European thinker – although Herder partially anticipated this view – to see religions as historical phenomena, phenomena that arise, flourish, and are superseded at specific times and in specific places. According to Hegel, each religion, "in its place and order, translates the discovery that humanity makes, or which God makes in man, of what God is and what man is. To retrace the stages of this discovery is to do the philosopher's work." [32]

Hegel's view, we may note, is entirely antithetical to that of the French *philosophes,* who conceived religious beliefs as essentially a mist of error and superstition which would evaporate without a trace under the morning sun of advancing "reason" and "science." The "Enlighteners" saw most of past history, and especially the Middle Ages, as a "dark age" – intellectually void, a total historical loss.

For Hegel, in contrast, nothing human is wasted or lost. He refuses to dismiss any religion as pure superstition or error: "It is human beings who have hit upon such religions, therefore there must be reason in them. . . . What is human, rational in them is *our own too,* although it exists in our higher consciousness as a dialectical phase only." [33] Each historical epoch has its function and value; each is a partial and inadequate expression of a larger and more adequate truth. The "truth of the whole" is forged out of the conflicting untruths and half-truths of the subordinate historical *Momente.*

The pre-Christian forms of religion – in particular, the religions of nature, artifact, and culture (roughly speaking: Persian, Egyptian, and Greek) – are clearly transition-forms. This does not mean that they are totally obliterated or negated; something of each of the lower forms remains in the higher, and specifically, in the highest form of historical religion, or the highest historical form of religion, Christianity. This "absolute religion," – this religion of revelation, of symbolic disclosure of the truth about Absolute Being – is a dialectical completion and transcendence of all the lower forms.

But for Hegel, as we have seen, even Christianity is not the most adequate mode of grasping the object of all religions, namely, God or the "Absolute." As Kierkegaard was to put it – perhaps a bit unfairly – Hegel viewed Christianity as the tentative and defective first edition of a book of which Hegelian speculative philosophy was the revised and authoritative second edition!

The Left Hegelians, including Marx, saw Hegel as asserting, and attempting to give a rational account of, the defective and transitional character of *all* historical religions, Christianity included. Religion for Hegel, they claimed, was a spiritual bridge – a bridge which leads to the absolute knowledge of speculative philosophy. And speculative philosophy burns its spiritual bridges behind it, leaving only the ashes of its *aufgehobene Momente* – the inferior dialectical phases which philosophy, as "absolute knowledge," has canceled, preserved, and raised to a higher level. In fact, this account is *trop nuancé* to fit the case of Marx himself (it is closer to the position of some of the other Left Hegelians). For Marx *Aufhebung,* as applied to religion, is sheer negation; he neglects or ignores its positive aspects – the aspects of "preserving and raising to a higher level." Thus, on Marx's view, religion is only "negatively present" in speculative philosophy, which means in effect that it is not present at all, that it has been (or will be) wholly excluded in the course of man's historical development.

There is not much point in charging Marx (or Plekhanov or Lenin) with infidelity to Hegel. From the beginning Marx was a "revisionist Hegelian," not the least bit interested in faithful interpretation of Hegel (or anyone else), but passionately interested in adapting and applying Hegel's (and everybody else's) ideas – using them as weapons in the historical struggle of socio-economic classes. This tendency was carried a step further by Plekhanov, and several steps further by Lenin. But both of the Russian Marxists may, with respect to their views on religion, be considered "revisionist Hegelians."

III

Up to a point Marx was a fairly faithful disciple of Hegel. At least his reading of Hegel was (a) plausible, if not altogether convincing, and (b) widely shared, even by interpreters of Hegel who were not concerned to use Hegel's ideas as weapons. I refer to the view that religion is a historically conditioned and transitional phenomenon. But beyond this point, Marx's position diverged sharply from Hegel's. Whereas for Hegel (on the Left Hegelian reading), religion points to a total truth above and beyond its own defective or partial truth, for Marx religion, as total untruth, is fated to give way to a total, and totally unreligious, truth.

Of course, the young Marx mouthed certain Feuerbachian slogans, e. g., that "man is the truth of God," and that "anthropology is the truth of theology." But such slogans belong to the *psychology,* not the philosophy, of religion. Here Feuerbach stunningly vulgarized Hegel. As Sidney Hook (a not unsympathetic expositor of Feuerbach) points out: "In Feuerbach 'the necessary self-alienation of the Idea' is naturalized and becomes the self-alienation of man, the unconscious projection of human nature in objects of worship." [34]

According to Feuerbach, what Christians call God (and Hegel calls the Absolute) is "nothing but" collective mankind in its ideal historical development. Hence, "the contradiction between the divine and the human" is "nothing more than the contradiction ... between humanity and the individual." [35]

I do not believe that Marx took this sort of thing very seriously, at least for very long. Rather, he saw a twofold "truth beyond religion." (1) On the one hand, religious *doctrine* is to be superseded by "science" – not in the broad and inclusive sense of Hegel's *Wissenschaft* ("systematic knowledge") but in the narrower sense of the empirical sciences – and perhaps of "scientific" philosophy. (Marx himself is ambiguous on this last point; but Engels often preached a positivistic dissolution of philosophy into the special sciences. Like Plekhanov later, Engels had a much more robust faith than Marx in the automatic supersession of religion by advancing science.)

(2) On the other hand, religious *attitudes* and *values* are to be superseded by secular attitudes and socialist values. The new attitudes and values, in the pre-revolutionary period, support the proletariat in its historical class struggle. In the post-revolutionary period, when the class struggle has been won, the new attitudes and values will support the Promethean struggle of a liberated mankind against the hostile forces of non-human nature.

In both cases – with respect to doctrine and also with respect to attitudes and values – religion is viewed by Marx (and the Russian Marxists) as a historically transient phenomenon, inextricably bound up with the socio-economic system of capitalist (and pre-capitalist) exploitation, and doomed to "wither away" with the approach to a non-exploitative, classless socio-economic system.

Marx's conception, expressed in the term *absterben,* though superficially reminiscent of Hegel's conception, expressed in the term *aufheben,* differs significantly on at least two counts. (a) In Hegel religion *wird aufgehoben;* it is not the case that it *hebt sich auf.* It *is* negated, preserved, and raised to a higher level in and by its succeeding *Moment* or *Momente.* It does not negate *itself,* preserve *itself,* or raise *itself* to a higher level. In Marx religion *stirbt ab,* dies out, or withers away; it negates itself, although the "self-elimination" of religion may be interpreted as an "elimination by the objective movement of history." To say that religion (or law, or morality, or the institution of the family) will wither away is to say not that it will be absorbed in the succeeding historical stage, but that it will be wiped out through the dynamic progression of human history.

(b) Hegel's conception of *Aufhebung* is dialectical and in Hegel's broad sense, "logical"; Marx's conception of *Absterben* is metaphorical, based on a biological analogy. It presupposes the conceptual model of society as a plant-like organism having leaves as well as roots. The "root" of the social plant is the network of forces and relations of economic production; the "foliage" is the system of ideologies – law, morality, art, religion. When the social revolution cuts the exploitative root of capitalist society, the ideological foliage of that society, specifically including religious beliefs and attitudes, will automatically wither and die.[36]

Religious consciousness, according to Marx, is an inverted or perverted consciousness – a product of the inverted or perverted social world of feudalism and capitalism.

"The struggle against religion," Marx asserted, "is ... indirectly [or "by mediation" – *mittelbar*] the struggle against that [socio-economic] world whose spiritual aroma is religion." [37] In a word, anti-religion is a part of the general class-struggle – a point which Lenin in due season was to emphasize.

It is philosophy's task, according to Marx, to follow up the "unmasking" of religious "sanctifications" of socio-economic alienation with the more fundamental unmasking of the "unholy" self-alienation of man in exploitative society. "The criticism of heaven turns into the criticism of the earth, the criticism of religion into the criticism of law [*Recht*] and the criticism of theology into the criticism of politics." [38]

I would sum up the respects in which Marx's critique of religion was *un*-Hegelian under three heads:

(1) *Absterbenstheorie*. The theory of the withering away of religion, although it bears a remote analogy to the Hegelian theory of *Aufhebung*, is a simplifying vulgarization, based on what to Hegel would have been an unacceptable – because both causal and biological – model of social interaction in terms of an economic *Unterbau* and an "ideological" *Überbau*.

(2) *Future-orientedness*. Marx looked to and worked for a future stage of human history, when all religion will have withered away. For Hegel the philosopher's task is to exhibit the rational structure of *past* history, not to trouble himself about the future.

(3) *Prometheanism*. Marx heartily endorsed the boastful assertion of the Prometheus of Aeschylus, "I am the enemy of all the gods," adding that "philosophy" shared the Promethean hatred of "all heavenly and earthly gods which do not recognize human self-consciousness [this is Hegelian terminology but not Hegelian doctrine!] as the supreme deity." [39] The Promethean task of placing a human stamp upon non-human nature, of subduing natural forces to man's will through social *praxis,* is clearly un-Hegelian. Hegel, indeed, would have repudiated such Prometheanism as an expression of *hybris*.

To put the point differently, Marx rejects what for Hegel is central: reconciliation (*Versöhnung*). Marx, as revolutionary, remains "Promethean" in the sense of "unreconciled" (*unversöhnt*).

In all three of these respects Plekhanov and Lenin moved even further from Hegel than had Marx.

IV

Plekhanov emphasized Marx's critique of religion as "false consciousness" or "bad science" and tended to neglect Marx's insistence that the struggle against religion must be a part of the general class struggle.[40] Lenin reversed these emphases.

For Plekhanov, religion is "pseudo-science," which inevitably will give way to genuine – wholly secular – science. For Lenin, religion in the twentieth century is capitalist "opium," an arm of bourgeois politics, which will give way, once exploitation is abolished, to the values and attitudes of socialist collectivism. Plekhanov saw religion as a pure, almost innocent, superstition; Lenin saw religion as a superstition with a sinister social purpose.

Although Plekhanov distinguished between religious "ideas" or "views" (*predstavleniya = Vorstellungen*), i. e., myths; religious attitudes or moods (*nastroyeniya*), i. e., feelings; and religious acts (*deistviya*), i. e., worship – he tended to stress the first of these to the virtual exclusion of the others. This is nicely brought out in his response to a questionnaire published in the French journal, *Mercure de France* (1907). It includes the statement: "Quant au sentiment religieux, il disparaîtra avec la dissolution de l'idée religieuse." [41] Presumably, religious worship will promptly follow suit.

As religion withers away, men will turn to the Promethean task of creating "heaven on earth." According to Plekhanov,

> Contemporary socialism is carrying out just such a task as the Greeks ascribed to Prometheus. It is giving men the means with which they will put an end to their dependence on blind, elemental forces and will subject those forces to the dominion of reason, thus attaining an unprecedented development.[42]

In some places Plekhanov – reversing the order of Hegel's historical and dialectical sequence – suggests that religion may be transitional not to knowledge or to "science" but to art. Perhaps he would see art as transitional, in turn, to science. He sometimes implies that the main function of art, on the one hand, is to popularize scientific truths, and on the other hand, to propagate "correct" moral values and social attitudes.

Plekhanov was a late-blooming *Aufklärer;* his "enlightenment" critique of religion as "bad science" was criticized by Hegel himself. In the sections of *Phän* on *Glaube und Einsicht,* and on *Aberglaube und Auf-*

klärung, Hegel points out that religion is reduced to science, and "bad science," by the *philosophes,* for whom only science is valid; and that religion gives up the battle when it accepts its critics' terms. Religion as science sinks from *Glaube* (belief) to Aberglaube (superstition).

This, in fact, seldom happened among the religious believers in Russia whom Plekhanov wished to convert to atheism; but in the generation after his death (he died in 1918) his reductionist critique of religion proved largely effective among younger Soviet citizens with higher education. But that is another story.[43]

V

The difference in style of anti-religious utterance between Plekhanov and Lenin is striking. Plekhanov, who considered religion an intellectual error, is relatively restrained and well-mannered; Lenin, who considered religion a social and moral outrage, is furiously indignant and abusive.

Since, according to Lenin, "the oppression of mankind by religion is merely a product and reflection of economic oppression within society," the proletariat must be "enlightened" not by "books or preaching" but by "its own struggle against the dark forces of capitalism." Lenin is not satisfied with "enlightenment brochures," and he explicitly warns against "an abstract, idealistic formulation of the religious question 'by reason' apart from class struggle." [44]

Lenin's own neo-Marxist theory of religion involves two basic assumptions, one concerning the *origin,* the other the *function,* of religious beliefs and attitudes. The first assumption is that religion is generated by human insecurity and fear of unanticipated and uncontrollable socio-economic change, due in the last analysis to the fluctuations of the "free" market. The second assumption is that religion invariably functions as a tool of the exploiting classes, as an "opium" (Lenin's blunter expression was "spiritual booze") which dulls and lulls the exploited masses into resigned acceptance of their bondage, forestalling socio-political revolt with the promise of an other-worldly reward for virtuous obedience to the secular rulers.

Lenin often referred to the religious "stupefaction" (*odureniye*) or "stultification" (*oduracheniye*) of the proletariat and peasantry. These terms, and the ideas behind them, though Marxist, are highly un-Hegelian.[45] Both in the *Phenomenology* and in the *Lectures on the History of Philosophy* Hegel made clear his impatience with the charge (e. g., that of Voltaire and the Encyclopedists) that religion was invented by scheming priests to deceive a credulous public. Human beings, he insisted, cannot be deceived about anything as ultimate or as decisive for their lives as religion.

But Lenin, like Marx and Plekhanov, was deaf to this Hegelian wisdom. Lenin labeled religious belief a "delirium" that was "rapidly being thrown into the rubbish-barrel by the very course of economic development," that is, by the "logic" of Marxist history.[46] However, the language of such passages, which suggests an automatic elimination of religion, is not typical for Lenin. To do away with religion, he characteristically insisted, one must take active steps to cut its socio-economic root, freeing the worker "from belief in a life beyond the grave by rallying him to a genuine struggle for a better earthly life," for the "creation of heaven on earth." [47] This last, for Lenin, is a summons not so much to the Promethean conquest of nature as to hard-headed social engineering.

VI

As is often the case, so too with our Marxist "revisionists" of Hegel – Hegel's system "includes" his critics and his vulgarizers. Marx as revolutionist fits into the stage of "absolute freedom and terror" in the *Phenomenology*. Marx's approach to religion is a "1789" and "1793" approach, in the sense of involving (a) a revolutionary end and violent means, and (b) the instrumentalizing of all values, even religious values. For Marx anti-religion is instrumental to the success of the revolutionary class-struggle of the proletariat.

Plekhanov, as we have already indicated, fits into the stage of a superficial and reductionist Enlightenment critique of religion, the stage of "belief and insight" and the succeeding stage of "superstition and enlightenment."

Lenin might be placed with Marx in the dialectical framework of 1789-1793. But, because of his revolutionary asceticism, his flamboyant rhetoric, and his heroic self-denial and, yes, self-deception, he might also be seen as a twentieth-century instance of "[Self-proclaimed] Virtue and the Course of the World" (*Die Tugend und der Weltlauf*), whose original literary model was Don Quixote. Lenin does not of course claim with Quixote to be God's strong right arm on earth, but he does make a quite parallel claim – that he is the Revolution's strong right arm in history.

That the critique of religion advanced by Marx, Plekhanov, Lenin, and their followers over the past century and a quarter (since Marx's first tentative formulations of it in 1843), has proven both barren in theory and destructive in practice would seem to suggest that there is not only greater inclusiveness but also greater philosophical depth and soundness in Hegel's own position.

NOTES

1. Several years ago I attempted to analyze Hegel's special usage of 'abstract' and 'concrete' and to show how his usage differs from both the empiricist sense and the ordinary sense of the terms. I permit myself to repeat the key paragraph of that discussion here:

> For Hegel, 'concrete' means "many-sided, adequately related, complexly mediated" (we may call this sense 'concrete$_H$'), while 'abstract' means "one-sided, inadequately related, relatively unmediated" ('abstract$_H$'). A concept or universal can quite sensibly be characterized as concrete$_H$, and at the same time, without paradox, as abstract$_E$ [the empiricist sense]. Sense particulars, or "sensuous immediacy," will necessarily be abstract$_H$, and at the same time, unparadoxically, concrete$_E$.

("Some Recent Reinterpretations of Hegel's Philosophy," *The Monist*, Vol. 48 [1964], p. 41.)

2. Because of the notorious inadequacy of translations from Hegel's German, I shall give the original text of all passages quoted. In this case the German text reads: "Die Philosophie ist der Vorwurf gemacht worden, sie stelle sich über die Religion: dies ist ... falsch, denn sie hat nur diesen und keinen anderen Inhalt, aber sie gibt ihn in der *Form* des Denkens; sie stellt sich so nur über die *Form* des Glaubens, der Inhalt ist derselbe." Hegel, *Sämtliche Werke*, ed. Glockner (Stuttgart, 1928), XVI, p. 353 (italics modified).

3. "Der Inhalt selbst der Religion und der Philosophie kann kein verschiedener sein, da es nicht zwei Selbstbewusstseine des absoluten Geistes von sich gibt ..." *VPR, Lasson*, I, p. 295.

4. To distinguish clearly between passages from *VPR, Lasson*, drawn from Hegel's own lecture notes and those drawn from student notes, the former will be designated by the letter *h* following the page number, as in the present case: "So ist Gott der eine und einzige Gegenstand der Philosophie; mit ihm sich zu beschäftigen, in ihm alles zu erkennen, auf ihn alles zurückzuführen, so wie aus ihm alles Besondere abzuleiten und alles allein [zu] rechtfertigen, insofern es aus ihm entspringt, ... von seinem Strahle lebt ... [das ist ihr Geschäft]." *VPR, Lasson*, I, p. 30*h*.

5. "Die Philosophie ist daher Theologie, und die Beschäftigung mit ihr oder vielmehr in ihr ist für sich Gottesdienst." *VPR, Lasson*, I, p. 30*h*.

6. Philosophy "ist nicht Wissen von Weltlichem, keine Weltweisheit ...." *VPR, Lasson*, I, p. 29.

7. "Bestimmtheit ist Inhalt." *VPR, Lasson*, I, p. 302*h*.

8. "... in [der] absoluten Religion ... [wo] Religion sich zu ihrer Bestimmtheit vollendet." *VPR, Lasson*, I, p. 302 *h*.

9. "Da kommt diese Schwierigkeit vor, an einem Inhalt zu trennen, was *Inhalt als solcher, der Gedanke* ist, von dem, was der Vorstellung als solcher angehört." *VPR, Lasson*, I, p. 295 (italics added).

10. " ... [D]er Begriff verbindet es, dass der Inhalt eignes Tun des Selbst ist ...." *Phän,* p. 556 (italics removed).

11. "Philosophie ist die Tätigkeit, das, was in Form der Vorstellung ist, in die Form des Begriffs zu verwandeln." *VPR, Lasson,* I, p. 295 (italics removed).

12. Cf. *VPR, Lasson,* I, p. 33.

13. "... sinnlich aus dem Sinnlichen, Mythos; Vorstellung [ist] das Bild in seine Allgemeinheit erhoben, Gedanke, gedankenvoll, Form auch für Gedanken." *VPR, Lasson,* I, p. 284h.

14. "... Recht, Sittlichkeit, Tugend, Tapferkeit, der Welt, dem Bösen: dies sind geistige [Vorstellungen], wesentlich aus dem Denken ... stammend." *VPR, Lasson,* I, pp. 284-85h.

15. "Die Vorstellung hat immer mehr oder weniger sinnliche Gestaltungsweise, sie steht zwischen der unmittelbar sinnlichen Empfindung und dem eigentlichen Gedanken.... Daher hat das Vorgestellte noch immer Räumlichkeit, Zeitlichkeit an ihm...." *VPR, Lasson,* I, p. 296; cf. also I, pp. 292h, 297, 286h, 288h.

16. "... die Erzeugung des Sohnes in der Ewigkeit." "... ein Anderes, das durch ein Erstes gesetzt und als Anderes aufgehoben, mit ihm eins ist...." *VPR, Lasson,* I, p. 297.

17. "Insofern die Religion wesentlich ihren Inhalt in Gestalt von Vorstellungen gibt, hat sie eine *Lehre* und zwar der *Wahrheit.*" *VPR, Lasson,* I, p. 285h.

18. "... [D]ie Idee der Philosophie selbst ... ist die begriffene Natur Gottes. Insofern ist das, was wir das Absolute nennen, gleichbedeutend mit dem Ausdruck Gott." *VPR, Lasson,* I, p. 30.

19. "Begriffliches Erkennen muss wohl vom *abstrakten Verstande* unterschieden werden ..." *VPR, Lasson,* I, p. 299h.

20. "... das Denken ... in Form der Vorstellung." *VPR, Lasson,* I, p. 293h.

21. Religion "bleibt ... immer dem Gedanken auch der Form und der Bewegung nach verwandt und ist ihr die Philosophie als das schlechthin tätige und den Gegensatz vereinigende Denken unmittelbar nahe gerückt." *Sämtliche Werke,* XV, p. 41.

22. "Vielmehr ist die Religion eben der wahrhafte Inhalt, nur in Form der Vorstellung, und die substanzielle Wahrheit hat nicht erst die Philosophie zu geben. Nicht erst auf Philosophie haben die Menschen zu warten gehabt, um ... die Erkenntnis der Wahrheit zu empfangen." *VPR, Lasson,* I, p. 299h (italics removed). This passage is seriously mistranslated by Spiers and Sanderson, *LPR,* I, p. 155. They make Hegel say that philosophy *does* have to supply the "substantial truth" of religion.

23. "... [D]er Inhalt der Philosophie, ihr Bedürfnis und Interesse mit der Religion ganz gemeinschaftlich ist; ihr Gegenstand ist die ewige Wahrheit, nichts als Gott und seine Explikation. Die Philosophie expliziert nur sich, indem sie die Religion expliziert, und indem sie sich expliziert, expliziert sie die Religion. So fällt Religion und Philosophie in eins zusammen. Die Philosophie ist in der Tat selbst Gottesdienst." *VPR, Lasson,* I, p. 29.

24. Quentin Lauer, S.J., "Hegel on the Identity of Content in Religion and Philosophy," this volume, p. 267.

25. See this volume, p. 275.

26. Emil L. Fackenheim, *The Religious Dimension in Hegel's Thought* (Bloomington, Ind.; Indiana University Press, 1967), p. 23.

27. *Ibid.,* p. 33.

28. *Ibid.,* p. 8.

29. "... [D]as Religiöse, in dem es begrifflich gemacht werde, aufhöre, religiös zu sein." *VPR, Lasson,* I, p. 301h.

30. "... dass es um nichts weniger zu tun [ist] als die Religion umzustossen ..." *VPR, Lasson,* I, p. 299h.

31. "... auf den Inhalt der Religion verderbend, zerstörend und entheiligend wirke." *VPR, Lasson,* I, p. 29.

32. Georges van Riet, "The Problem of God in Hegel" (trans. from the French text in *Revue Philosophique de Louvain*, Vol. 63 [1965] by Joan M. Miller), *Philosophy Today*, Vol. 11 (1967), 2/4, p. 78.

33. "Es sind Menschen, die auf solche Religionen verfallen sind; es muss also Vernunft darin... sein... [D]as Menschliche, Vernünftige in ihnen ist auch das *Unsere*, wenn auch in unserm höhern Bewusstsein nur als Moment." *Sämtliche Werke*, XV, p. 94 (italics partly removed).

34. Sidney Hook, *From Hegel to Marx* (Ann Arbor: University of Michigan Press, 1960), p. 250.

35. Ludwig Feuerbach, *The Essence of Christianity* (trans. by Marian Evans [George Eliot]) (New York: Harper Torchbooks, 1957), pp. 13f.

36. For an analysis of the Marxist conception of the withering away of ideologies and institutions, see my paper, "The Withering Away of the State: Philosophy and Practice," in *The Future of Communist Society*, ed. Walter Laqueur and Leopold Labedz (London and New York: Frederick Praeger, 1962), pp. 63-71.

37. Karl Marx, "Zur Kritik der Hegelschen Rechtsphilosophie. Einleitung," *Marx-Engels Historisch-Kritische Gesamtausgabe* (MEGA), Frankfurt, 1927. I, 1/1, p. 607; English translation: "Toward the Critique of Hegel's Philosophy of Law: Introduction," in *Writings of the Young Marx on Philosophy and Society*, ed. and trans. by Loyd D. Easton and Kurt H. Guddat (New York: Doubleday Anchor Books, 1967), p. 250.

38. *Ibid.,* p. 608; Easton and Guddat, p. 251 (italics removed).

39. Preface to doctoral dissertation (1841) in MEGA, I, 1/1, p. 10.

40. I have discussed Plekhanov's and Lenin's critique of religion in chapter 5 of my book, *Religious and Anti-Religious Thought in Russia* (Chicago: University of Chicago Press), 1968.

41. *Mercure de France*, Vol. 66 (1907), p. 619.

42. "O zadachakh sotsialistov v borbe s golodom v Rossii" ("On the Tasks of the Socialists in the Struggle against Famine in Russia"), 1892, in *Sochineniya*, Moscow-Petrograd, Vol. 3 (1923), pp. 399-400.

43. I have tried to tell it succinctly in chapter 6 of *Religious and Anti-Religious Thought in Russia*.

44. "Sotsializm i religiya" ("Socialism and Religion"), 1905, in *Sochineniya*, 5th ed., Moscow, Vol. 12 (1960), p. 146; English trans. in Lenin, *Collected Works*, Moscow, Vol. 10 (1962), p. 86.

45. These terms had also been used in the 1860's by Bakunin and in the 1880's and 1890's by Leo Tolstoy.

46. "Sotsializm i religiya," p. 146; *Collected Works*, Vol. 10, p. 87.

47. *Ibid.*, pp. 143, 146; *Collected Works*, Vol. 10, pp. 84, 87.

COMMENT ON

George L. Kline

Hegel and the Marxist-Leninist Critique of Religion

by

W. Winslow Shea

With one exception – his claim that Hegel is opposed to Promethean *hybris* – I find no disputable statements in what Professor Kline tells us. Before turning to the Promethean issue, however, I want to mention some aspects of the story which I miss in his account.

One thing I miss is the Marxist sense of historical "positivity" and of what is "concrete" in both the Hegelian and empiricist sense. As Marx says, "Philosophers do not grow out of the soil like mushrooms, they are the product of their time and people." [1] If so, are not Plekhanov's and Lenin's attacks on religion more "understandable" against the background of Czarist Russia and its Orthodox church and priesthood? Would Hegel have made more conciliatory judgments in the same situation, considering his excoriations of medieval Christianity and the Catholic church ("That infinite falsehood which rules the middle ages")? On the other hand, what about Hegel's attacks on Judaism and on the liberal Schleiermachian wing of his own Lutheranism? The old Hegel, despite the rationalizing and demythologizing tendency of *The Philosophy of Religion*, was right in claiming therein that (his) philosophy "stands infinitely nearer to positive doctrine than it seems at first sight to do." [2] Here the old conservative repudiated the Prometheanism of his youth, when he had written: "Great men have claimed that the fundamental meaning of 'Protestant' is a man or a church which has not bound itself to certain unalterable standards of faith but which protests against all authority in matters of belief." [3]

The dilemma Professors Lauer and Kline do not face in their defense of the older Hegel's claim that religion and philosophy have the same "content" is this: such an abstract identity is void of sense until the two terms and their common content are concretely specified and positively determined; but once given a definite sense, the identity seems false (or if true of Hegel's own views, unattractive). Kline may well worry, therefore, over Hegel's insistence that "determinateness is content." For Hegel not only abandons philosophy's universal critical role; he goes on from justifying a specific positive religion to that even more profane union of Church and State which turned the Feuerbachian critique of religion and theology into the Marxist critique of law and politics. "In a general sense," declares the *Philosophy of Religion*," "religion and the foundation of the state are the same: They are in their real essence identical." "Religion has no principles peculiar to itself which contradict those which prevail in the state." [5]

Here Hegel affirms that philosophy, like the religion of the (German) Protestant State, *is* "worldly wisdom." [6] Hegel rejects any "renunciation of this actual world" that would sacrifice "the entire sphere of action, of all that activity which connects itself with gain, with industries, and such . . . . Want is more rational here than such religious views." [7]

It is just this "reconciliation" of the spirit and the world, Christ and Caesar, God and Mammon, which Marx attacks as "accommodation" and "compromise" in Hegel's defense of the Protestant Ethic. For Marx the ideology of the abstract free citizen in the capitalist state constitution leaves men just as alienated from each other as does Protestant theology: Just as religion "has become the spirit of civil society, of the sphere of egoism and of the *bellum omnium contra omnes*," so "the political state, in relation to civil society, is just as spiritual as is heaven in relation to earth. It stands in the same opposition to civil society, and overcomes it in the same manner as religion overcomes the narrowness of the profane world, i.e., it has always to acknowledge it again, and allow itself to be dominated by it." [8] In the spirit of Jeremiah, or of Christ among the money changers in the temple, Marx refuses this "reconciliation" of the "real" and the "rational," this philosophical and religious sanctification of a profane society based on greed. From the standpoint of early Christianity's critique of what he called "natural society," Marx appears more "religious" than does Hegel.

Does the foregoing have any bearing on the "Prometheus" question? Well, insofar as Marx refuses Hegel's "reconciliation" and rationalization of the real in favor of revolutionary change, insofar as he rejects mere reflection on the past and sanctification of the present Christian world as "the end of our days" and "the world of perfection," in favor of faith and hope in future man, Marx is clearly more Promethean than is Hegel. But I do not think Marx is significantly more "Promethean" in the two senses given us by Kline.

The first of these senses is that of atheistic humanism, and its first commandment is the one Marx inscribed over his doctoral thesis: Thou shalt "hate all gods, heavenly and earthly, who do not acknowledge the consciousness of man as the supreme deity. There must be no god on a level with it." Kline protests that "this is Hegelian terminology, but not Hegelian doctrine!" But why not? If Hegel's terminology is not always a key to his doctrine, if he is more mystifier than mystic, can one not more plausibly say that in Hegel one finds much traditional Christian terminology but little Christian doctrine? Strauss thought him a pantheist. Bauer (and Marx, too, if he was in on it) blew *The Trumpet of The Last Judgment* against *Hegel the Atheist and Antichrist.* Feuerbach saw nothing but humanity's own alienated image in Hegel's strange new "contradiction-torn atheistic God" who has to "win his divinity." 9 And Kierkegaard felt that the philosopher of "The System" was a defender, not of the Christian faith, but of a secularized "Christendom." As Jean Hippolyte reminds us: "The philosopher who wrote that 'reading the newspapers is the morning prayer of modern man' is not so much of a theologian as one might think." 10 To use a Hegelian metaphor Croce was fond of: Hegel melted down the statues of the old gods in the crucible of his dialectical imagination and cast out a radically new one: modern bourgeois man, as enshrined in his social, economic and political institutions. If Marx is more violently Promethean in the revolutionary iconoclasm of *his* humanism, that is partly because he feels Hegel's new idols perpetuate the old religious forms of man's self-alienation and must be smashed to realize Hegel's own aim of liberating the free human spirit. Marx shares with Hegel the old Pelagian heresy that man saves and transforms himself by his own works – not by an fact of faith in some transcendent redeemer or by some act of divine grace. Hegel said:

> The essence of the Christian principle has already been shown; it is the principle of mediation. Man realizes his spiritual essence only when he conquers his natural being. This conquest is possible only on the supposition that the human and the divine nature are essentially one, and that man, so far as he is spirit, also possesses the essentiality and substantiality that belong to the idea of God.11

Hegel melts and assimilates, Marx smashes, all gods set above man.

Kline's second sense of "Prometheanism" appears in this surprising statement: "The Promethean task of placing a human stamp upon non-human nature, of subduing natural forces to man's will, is clearly un-Hegelian. Hegel, indeed, would have repudiated such Prometheanism as an expression of *hybris*." On the contrary: for Hegel (surely one of the most hybristic philosophers who ever wrote) the whole history of the human spirit, of man's self-liberation, is a series of hybristic acts, of challenging and overstepping first nature's, then his own, "given" laws and limits. Though he is as Faustian as the author of the "Prometheus Fragment," Hegel does not share Goethe's reverence for Nature. And where Kant had been filled with awe at the "starry skies above and the moral law within," Hegel viewed the former as an "ugly eczema" and the latter as merely "the private conviction of individuals, their particular will and mode of action." When Hegel celebrates the *hybris* of ancient tragic heroes and of "world-historical heroes" from Socrates to Napoleon who overstep the laws of their societies, he views them as continuing that *felix culpa* which began with man's original transgression of natural law. The first distinctively human act was the "master's" repudiation of nature's law of self-preservation – a law not just "preserved" by the slave's choice of life over recognition, for he in turn by "shaping and fashioning" transformed all nature by the cunning of his art and science. And what was the glory of Greece and its Religion of Art for Hegel if not its stamping of human forms on those of brute, dumb Nature? But for such *hybris*, men would remain in the primitive "Religion of Nature," where "The Spiritual is in this original, undisturbed unity with Nature," where men huddle in animal awe and dread.

Doubtless the older Hegel tends more to "reconcile" struggling spirit with the external world – but this is a world man has made for himself. And the struggle itself is either "interiorized" in religious and philosophical reflection, or is "incarnated" in social institutions. It is just this tragic resignation to abstract syntheses in the interior of "self-consciousness" or to a "real" made "rational," which Marx criticizes. Society must be criticized and changed so long as it remains "natural," "so long as a cleavage still exists between the particular and the common interest, so long therefore as activity is not voluntarily, but naturally divided, and man's own deed becomes an alien power opposed to him, which enslaves him instead of being controlled by him." [12] Marx felt strongly (perhaps therefore somewhat unfairly) that Hegel's "theodicy" had persuaded us too soon that man's infinite task of transforming his world and nature was done, when in fact it had hardly begun. "Man is no longer in a condition of external tension with the external substance of private property; he has become himself the tension-ridden being of private property." [13]

I do not think Marx's over-simple diagnosis and vague utopianism, any more that that of simple Christianity, is a sure cure for "alienation." But modern psychological studies, like modern politics, suggest Marx was right in regarding a healthy society as one in which men exteriorize their inner needs, tensions and demons into a public, objective world where they can co-operatively *work* on them as "natural" evils. As long as man needs an enemy, better "Nature" than himself or his neighbor. Here a creative and forward-looking Promethean philosophy of *practice* seems a necessary counterpart to Epimethean reflections and "painting grey on grey," whether as historical reflection on how far we have come, or in analytic studies, or in some "intellectual love of God." Because I think these mythic brothers ought to be reconciled I look more to the earlier Marx and the earlier Hegel (and maybe an earlier Christianity), and away from the older Hegel's reflections on a form of Christianity grown old. For I think Professor Kline has well shown how hard it is to reconcile two such philosophies as Hegelianism and Marxism once they have hardened their categories and ossified into ideologically rigid systems, into the theologies or even "religions" of Idealism and Materialism.

NOTES

1. Karl Marx and Frederich Engels, *Marx and Engels on Religion* (New York: Schocken Books, 1964 reprint of the 1957 Moscow edition), p. 30.

2. *LPR*, I, p. 32.

3. *EtW*, "On the Positivity of the Christian Religion," p. 128.

4. *Marx and Engels on Religion*, pp. 36-7.

5. *LPR*, I, pp. 247 and 249. Cf. the statement from Vol. III, p. 138, cited in John Smith's symposium paper: "It is in the organization of the state that the divine has broken into actuality; the latter is penetrated by the former and now the secular is justified in and for itself because its foundation is the divine will."

6. *LPR*, I, 250. Kline's quote that it is *"not* worldly wisdom" is in *LPR*, I, p. 19.

7. *LPR*, I, 251.

8. T. B. Bottomore (ed.), *Karl Marx: Early Writings*, "On the Jewish Question" (New York: McGraw-Hill, 1964), pp. 13 and 15.

9. *Kleine Philosophischen Schriften*, as cited by R. Tucker, *Philosophy and Myth in Karl Marx* (Cambridge University Press, 1961), p. 83.

10. Jean Hyppolite, *Études sur Marx et Hegel* (Paris: Rivière, 1955), p. 86.

11. C. J. Friedrich (ed.), *The Philosophy of Hegel* (New York: Random House, 1953), pp. 129 and 105.

12. Karl Marx, *The German Ideology* (N.Y.: International Publishers, 1947), p. 22.

13. *Early Writings,* "Economic and Philosophical MSS," p. 148.

COMMENT ON

George L. Kline

Hegel and the Marxist-Leninist Critique of Religion

by

Ignas K. Skrupskelis

If I understand Professor Kline correctly, in his view the bridge between the religious thought of Hegel on the one side and of Marx and his disciples on the other is to be sought in the thought that religion is an historical phenomenon. Both sides, which otherwise offer so sharply contrasting evaluations of religion, are said to possess this ground in common. For Hegel, religion, or at least its content, is preserved on a higher level; religion is the indispensable breeding ground of a higher form of consciousness. On the other side, for the Marxists, religion is nothing more than an element in the superstructure of bourgeois society, to be swept away with the coming of the classless social order. This is, as Professor Kline observes, a rather sharp difference. Nevertheless, these so opposed positions share the view that religion is "a transition-form in the historical development of the human spirit."

I would like to question this, to ask whether in fact, and in what sense, regardless of how he was read by Marx or any other interpreter, in Hegel's view, religion is a transition-form. I raise this only as a question, without any thesis of my own to offer. I hope to suggest certain lines of questioning, which could, if pursued further, make clearer the relation of religion to philosophy in Hegel, a relation which, as has been repeatedly emphasized during this meeting, is central to the whole of Hegel's thought.

In one way, religion is very definitely a transition-form. The religious consciousness cannot claim to be the ultimate form of consciousness; consciousness cannot rest in the religious stage, but must advance beyond it to philosophy. Of course, in some sense, religion is preserved in this advance; it is not abolished with a Marxist "good riddance." Nevertheless, an advance does take place, and religion has the character of that through which consciousness advances from art to final form. But all this leaves the status of religion rather unclear.

We can try to see some of the possibilities which are open here by asking ourselves this: on Hegelian grounds, would it make sense for a man who has followed the dialectical path from art to religion to philosophy to turn back and occupy the superseded positions? In later idealism, for example in the case of Royce, it is clear both that the physical sciences yield an inferior grade of knowledge and that it makes perfectly good sense to be a scientist. Even while maintaining the thesis that knowledge can be perfected only on the level of philosophy, Royce insists that science retains its autonomy, is in no way abolished, and need accept no interference from philosophy. Are we, in the case of Hegel's transition from religion to philosophy, dealing with an analogous instance? If the answer is yes, one could be both a Hegelian and a Christan without reservations.

The answer to the question just asked could be a negative one – I would understand Professor Kline as giving just this answer – in which case, the relations of the two would have to be viewed differently. Religion would have, in effect, transferred its functions to philosophy, and having done its service, would have retired. Of course, even here, the content of religion would be preserved, but religion as such would be abolished. Religion as such is both form and content, but on this view the form of religion would be irretrievably lost in philosophy. Its form would be exposed as a mere transition-form. Men would no longer be entitled to take the attitude of figurative thought towards the absolute, but could take only that of speculative thought.

These two appear to be the extreme interpretations of the status of religion in Hegel available to us. The second one, it should be pointed out briefly, has one undesirable consequence. Hegel at one point claims that philosophy is the consciousness of the intelligible unity of art and religion, a consciousness not only of their content, but especially of their form. "This cognition [philosophical] is thus the *recognition* of this content and its form..." [1] Or, to put it in a different way, religious life is what is comprehended by philosophy. But if religion as such is abolished – this also means that art as such is abolished – what intelligible unity is left for philosophy to be conscious of? The abolition of religion as such could mean the abolition of that life which philosophy is to comprehend. The threat of this undesirable consequence, of course, does not rule out the possibility of Hegel's holding this view.

I think it highly plausible that, for Hegel, the succession of religions does involve the result that the earlier positions can be occupied no longer, once we have risen to their successor. To this extent, I tend to agree with Professor Kline's contention that for Hegel religions are "historical phenomena, . . . that arise, flourish, decay, and are superseded at specific times and places."

It seems unlikely, for example, that a man who has risen above the very crude religion of magic could be thought of as returning to it from a higher form of religion, except, possibly, in the sense of suffering a relapse. It seems implausible for such a man deliberately to resume the lower standpoint, once he has advanced beyond it.

For Hegel, this religion of magic is something very crude. He describes it as nothing more than "the exercise of lordship over nature, . . . the sway of the magician over those who do not know." Hegel adds: "The condition of this lordship is sensuous stupor . . . ." [2] The next stage, the Chinese religion or the "religion of measure" – while still quite primitive – it even reveals traces of magic – is, nevertheless, much more sophisticated than the religion of magic. While other elements clearly are involved, quite fundamental to the difference between them is the contrast between the more and the less primitive. But on this basis, a return would seem to be impossible. When viewed from the higher position, there seems to be nothing in the earlier one to which one could return.

Hegel describes the several stages of the religion of China as "progressive efforts to grasp substance as self-determining." [3] Once again, there seems to be the suggestion that at each successive stage we are leaving the earlier ones behind. As the argument advances, we see the preceding stages as less adequate to grasp substance.

A similar interpretation can be given of the transitions between major religious types. Given his contention that it is essential to religion that it be revealed, it seems unlikely that a return to paganism could be treated by him as anything more than a relapse. Christianity is the absolute religion, and from this vantage point everything before it can be viewed as inadequate and fragmentary expressions of what Christianity embodies fully.

Can we view the transitions from art to religion to philosophy as being exactly like the transitions from the more primitive form of religion to the more advanced? It would appear that if we wanted to consider religion a mere transition form, we would have to insist upon this likeness. But how plausible is it that in both cases we should have transitions of exactly the same kind?

Even if Hegel did view the relations between art, religion, and philosophy as being in part the relations between the more primitive and the less so, as well he could have, still another element becomes prominent here. Each regards its object from a peculiar point of view. They differ not only as worse and better ways of doing the same thing, but also as ways of doing different things. Thus art regards its object in terms of sense immediacy; religion deals with it in terms of figurative thought; while philosophy – speculative thought. The standpoint of religion is no longer that of art. While the content could be preserved, the form of art as such, its peculiar way of regarding things, is not preserved. The same would appear to be true of the move from religion to philosophy. This loss of its distinctive form would suggest the possibility of returning to the superseded standpoint, precisely for the sake of that lost form.

The argument here could be a little more obvious in the case of the transition from art to religion. Presumably, if religion as such is abolished in philosophy, art as such is abolished in religion.[4] Yet, what could this abolition of art mean? It would seem odd to maintain that having understood the limitations of the standpoint of art and having risen to religion, we would then cease to paint or to write poetry. But this would seem to be the consequence of the abolition of art in religion. After all, what is lost in this case is the very standpoint of art, and how could one paint except from that standpoint? In order to paint at all, it seems, we would deliberately have to return to an attitude which we know to be inadequate, precisely because we want to depict the absolute in this inadequate, yet distinctive way. And because this standpoint does have its own distinctive form, the desire to return to it for a definite purpose seems reasonable. The return from philosophy to religion would seem reasonable in a similar way.

These conjectures are presented here only as conjectures. Of course, textual study alone can show what takes place in Hegel actually. But even as possibilities, they seem worth considering, because they help us to understand the place of religion in Hegel.

NOTES

1. *Wallace*, p. 181.
2. *LPR*, I, p. 316.
3. *LPR*, I, p. 318.
4. In the course of the discussion, Dieter Henrich suggested that Hegel, at one point, did hold the view that art will wither away, if it has not done so already. For the time when this was Hegel's view, a parallel between the two transitions cannot be drawn in the way it is done here.

REPLY TO COMMENTATORS

by

George L. Kline

I

Mr. Skrupskelis asks whether, and if so in what sense, Hegel seriously considers art and religion to be transition forms in the development of the human spirit. The clearest texts in support of the claim that he does are probably to be found in the *Vorlesungen über die Aesthetik* – a posthumous compilation of lecture notes, with the usual difficulties of *établissement de texte*. Mr. Henrich has found evidence in the notes from which the published text was drawn [1] that, until the late 1820's, Hegel spoke of art as a transition form destined to disappear, but that after 1827 (when he joined the *Berliner Kunstverein*), he began to speak of a new form of art, specific to the present age, which might continue and develop. Hegel thus appeared to break out of the confines of his own system, but only with respect to art, not with respect to religion.

Does Hegel mean to say that there is an "age of art," which is superseded by an "age of religion," which in turn is superseded by an "age of philosophy or absolute knowledge?" I share Mr. Crites' feelings about the implausibility of such a "serial" doctrine. Still, a number of texts point toward it. One is left with a puzzle.

Mr. Skrupskelis' second question is perhaps more manageable. "Would it make sense," he asks, "for a man who has followed the dialectical path from art to religion to philosophy, to turn back and occupy the superseded positions?" (p. 209.) The answer would seem to be both yes and no. In Kierkegaard's dialectic one can fall back from the ethical to the aesthetic stage, or from religiousness B to religiousness A. But Kierkegaard's is a dialectic of the existing individual, the movement of which is neither necessary nor irreversible. In Kierkegaard's view, the existing individual must keep struggling ("choosing himself") just to stay where he is. If he relaxes even for a moment he will be hurled back to a lower stage.

Hegel's dialectic, in contrast, is social, cultural, and "world-historical." Its movement is in some sense both necessary and irreversible. Cultures and societies cannot revert to lower dialectical stages, moving from the more to the less concrete $_H$, from *aufhebendes* to *aufgehobenes Moment*. But I see no reason why on Hegel's view individuals within a given society or culture could not "regress" dialectically. For example, in a culture dominated by the spirit of skepticism there might be a scattering of stoics. But they would not change the general dialectical movement; a skeptical culture could not revert to stoicism, or a Christian culture to paganism.

II

Mr. Shea has raised the issue as to whether Hegel, as well as Marx, may be called "Promethean." He has, in effect, distinguished three senses or aspects of Prometheanism: (1) rebelliousness, (2) theomachy – or, in his terms, "atheist humanism" [2] – and (3) Baconianism (the subjugation of nature by science and technology). He admits that Marx is more Promethean than Hegel in sense (1). (I would prefer to say that Marx is Promethean and Hegel non-Promethean in that sense.) And he claims that Hegel, like Marx, embraced Prometheanism in sense (2). This I deny. That Hegel – even the youngest Hegel – was no atheist seems to me (*pace* Marx, Lukács, Kojève, and Mr. Shea) to have been convincingly shown by such scholars as Grégoire, van Riet, Fackenheim, and, in the present Symposium, Father Quentin Lauer.

With respect to the third, Baconian, aspect of Prometheanism, I detect an ambiguity in Marxist talk about "putting a human stamp upon nature" and in Plekhanov's characterization of the Promethean task of socialism as a bringing of nature's "blind, elemental forces" under the "dominion of reason." Despite their essential Baconianism, such formulas suggest a fourth sense or aspect of Prometheanism, which I shall call "Aristotelian." The "dominion of reason" is here exhibited in the deep penetration of reality by *nous*. In this very special Aristotelian sense, Hegel may be called a "Promethean" and may be said to exhibit hybris, a cognitive or speculative arrogance, reminiscent of Aristotle's cognitive or speculative optimism or self-confidence. Hegel assumed, with Aristotle, that even the darkest corners of being can be lighted up by the torch of human reason, although he was more sensitive than Aristotle to the possibility that the torch might be "smoky." And yet, as Mr. Shea has pointed out, Hegel is not an optimist, but a sober pessimist. Hegelian reconciliation is not joyous but resigned and disillusioned. Mr. Shea cannot have it both ways: Prometheanism in senses (1), (2), and (3) is profoundly optimistic (and Marx was optimistic in just these respects). If Hegel is indeed a pessimist, then he cannot be a Promethean in any of these three senses.

All four of these dimensions or aspects of Prometheanism are to be found in Aeschylus' play: (1) Prometheus, the rebel against Zeus, remains stubbornly unreconciled. (2) He is – in the lines quoted by Marx in his dissertation – "the enemy of all the gods that gave me ill for good" (lines 975-76). [3] (3) He boasts that it was he who gave men fire, tools, and techniques: "I hunted out the secret spring of fire... which... became the teacher of each craft to men" (11. 110-11). Before he taught them, Prometheus declares, men "did not know of building houses...; they did not know how to work in wood" (11. 448-49). Moreover, he "first yoked beasts for them" and "discovered ships" (11. 462, 468). Prometheus concludes that he has given men "all arts that mortals have" (1. 504). (4) Finally, he gave men the gift of *logos* – reason and articulate speech. "I found them witless and gave them the use of their wits and made them masters of their minds.... I discovered to them numbering,... and the combining of letters as a means of remembering all things" (11. 442-43, 459-61).

To sum up, Hegel is a "Promethean" thinker only in sense (4). The world is "mastered" by reason only in the sense of being rendered transparent to speculative thought. Such reason is not anticipatory, not Promethean, but retrospective, Epi-methean. In clear contrast to Marx, Hegel does not regard the future of either nature or society as a realm to be conquered.

NOTES

1. Most of the manuscripts in question (student notes taken during Hegel's Berlin lectures on aesthetics) are now on deposit at the Prussian Library in West Berlin.

2. I have argued elsewhere that Marx's atheism was "humanistic" in only two senses: (1) the obvious sense of "man-centered" and (2) the weak sense of involving a future-oriented "humanism of ideals"; but that Marx was not a humanist in the stronger sense of accepting a present-oriented "humanism of principles." Even the youngest Marx was not *stricto sensu* an ethical humanist. (See my paper, "Was Marx an Ethical Humanist?" *Studies in Soviet Thought,* IX, 1969, pp. 91-103; an

earlier and briefer version of this paper was published in the Proceedings of the Fourteenth International Philosophy Congress, Vienna, 1968, Vol. 2.)

3. I have used David Grene's translation of *Prometheus Bound* in *The Complete Greek Tragedies* (ed. David Grene and Richmond Lattimore), Chicago: The University of Chicago Press, 1959, I.

"AUTHENTICITY" AND "WARRANTED BELIEF" IN HEGEL'S DIALECTIC OF RELIGION

by

Darrel E. Christensen

Three recent attempts directed toward the formalization of dialectical logic by the use of a system of symbolic notations have come to my attention.[1] Each of these involves the use of variables which may be instantiated by terms, and each, I think, is inadequate on this and another account to Hegel's Logic, the Notion.[2] In cognizance of this and of certain difficulties which seem to be in the way of the understanding and use of the dialectical method, I shall have a two-fold purpose in what follows. I shall propose a strategy for evaluating dialectic for its adherence to certain of Hegel's dialectical principles which I shall then apply to his dialectic of religion. This strategy, in brief, is to develop a two-fold test to be applied to a dialectical exposition of what is purported to be the case, one test to determine what I shall call its "authenticity," its adherence to formal properties of dialectic to be specified, and the other a material test for whether what is purported is warranted for belief. In the course of doing this, I shall hope to clarify what I see to be a central problem inherent in Hegel's criteria for Truth, and to show how the strategy proposed, in part derived from Hegel and in part at least seemingly at odds with his position, may resolve this problem, or at least make it more manageable.

A two-fold test of dialectic, though not native to Hegel's method, has in fact not infrequently been practiced where his dialectic has been subject to critical analysis. So far as I know, however, such a test has not previously been worked out systematically. I shall attempt to do this here. For reasons which will become clear, this is not to be regarded as an attempt at the formalization of Hegel's logic, at least not where formalization is taken in its more recently accepted sense in logic.

In the section immediately following, I shall set the two-fold test for dialectic defined in a preliminary way within the context of some aspects of Hegel's thought which figure in my case. I shall then give attention in turn to the test for authenticity and the test for warranty for belief.

I

By the term "Notion," Hegel refers to the whole which is the Truth.[3] At every stage of development of life and consciousness, this is to say, there is a wholeness of apprehension which, as the necessary context of what is apprehended, is Truth in the sense which that perspective admits. Hegel's dialectic is a development of successively more adequate apprehensions of the Notion, each including the essential meaning of what has preceded and been transcended, and each implying the Notion in its completeness. It is the Notion as the actuality being apprehended, moreover, which also does the apprehending. Being inclusive, this is to say, it is inclusive of subject and object as of every other discrimination within reality. In the dialectic of religion and elsewhere, successively determined concepts of the Notion are regarded as concepts of God. Thus the dialectic of religion exhibits a series of concepts of God and the development of the religious consciousness is found progressively to lead from one to another.

Two types of content are held to belong to the Notion, the one being the content of the actual world, the other the content of forms, or the system of terms, which constitutes it. The Notion may be distinguished from actuality (the former) though it is not separable from it. It is neither distinguishable nor separable from the content of forms or system of terms, but identical with it.[4]

A problem immediately follows from this understanding, which is reflected throughout Hegel's mature work.[5] Before considering this, however, two things may here be noted. In the first place, strictly speaking, the possibility of formalizing Hegel's logic by a system of symbolic notations containing variables which may be instantiated by concepts is in principle ruled out. This, because for Hegel it is the terms, dialectically derived and defined, which constitute the Notion, as I have noted, and not merely some formal properties common to operations of the mind by which these are derived.[6] What results from the attempt to formalize the Notion by the use of variables, then, must be something less or at least different from the Notion. Hegel's drive toward overcoming, and his pretention to having overcome, the character of logic as an abstract system is ignored by such an approach.

Secondly, the Notion being inclusive (not separable from any content of actuality), it seems to follow that the possibility is in principle ruled out that a correspondence test may be made between it and a dialectical account of a particular actuality, such as a phase of history. It would follow from this that, where the attempt is made to formalize Hegel's Notion with the end in view that the result should be reflected in a test of conformity of dialectical accounts with the Notion thus formalized, there is reason to suppose that it is not the formalization of the Notion that is being carried forward, but, at most, the formalization of some necessary but not sufficient conditions of the Notion.

The significance of my conclusion that the Notion is not amenable to a test for correspondence may seem to be qualified by Hegel's use of the term in various contexts in which it is "relativized." Thus, he refers to the "subjective Notion," the "objective Notion," and "Notion-form." Some *aspect* of the Notion is thus made amenable to a correspondence test with something not included within it, or not yet shown to be so included.

> The elevation of the Notion above Life means this, that its reality is the Notion-form freed so that it becomes universality. By means of this Judgment the Idea is duplicated — into the subjective Notion whose reality is itself, and into the objective Notion, which is as Life.[7]

When the context within which this duplication (by judgment) of the Idea is examined, however, it is not the Notion which is found to be duplicated, but aspects of the Notion, or spheres within which the Notion is *partially* explicit. The context is the dialectic of the Idea of Cognition. On the one hand, we are presented with the idea as the Notion of Life *not yet realized in itself* and, on the other, the Notion as merely *for itself – in so far as* it exists as abstract universality. The "not yet realized" and the "in so far as" in the above indicate that the Notion is in part merely implicit in each of the two aspects of it which are here judged to be aspects of the same. Thus the Notion conceived as "subjective Notion," "objective Notion," and "Notion-form," is not genuinely relativized at all, but merely conceived in terms of a distinguishable but not separable aspect. The case is the same as that which pertains at any level of the development of the Notion short of the Notion in its completeness, i.e. in-and-for itself.

This is further evidenced by the fact that for Hegel these three "relativized" aspects of the Notion, when regarded from a transcending perspective as fully explicit, in the last analysis are not distinguishable; each simply is the (one) Notion. Even dialectical method, as I shall have further occasion to note, is for Hegel not finally distinguishable from the Notion, and it is precisely this which constitutes the root of a basic problem respecting dialectic which it shall be my purpose in this paper to overcome. The problem in essence is this: dialectical method as Hegel conceived it is not developed in such a way as to be clearly distinguishable from the Notion, on which account it remains the Truth and the whole, and hence not amenable to a test of correspondence with a particular dialectical account of history or a phase of history.

While his use of language is sometimes equivocal at this point, as when he speaks of "conformity to the Notion," I submit that what he intends on such occasions is conformity to aspects of the Notion partially explicit in the realm being referred to (which if fully explicit would be all-inclusive). If the dialectic presents us with a problem regarding what synthesis is the high and inclusive one,[8] that there is a most high and all-inclusive one, the Notion, is regarded as settled. Thus, in the statement, "The Idea is Truth; for Truth is the correspondence of objectivity with the notion . . .", it is the *subjective* Idea and the *subjective* "Notion" which are clearly intended.[9] The "subjective Notion," along with the "objective Notion," is a member of the series of levels of the Notion's self-realization, and not the Notion in its radical completeness.

A further consideration will perhaps constitute adequate additional support for this being Hegel's understanding of the relation of the Notion to aspects of the Notion. As universality, the "Notion-form" becomes the first proposition in a syllogism, and its particularization in the world the second.[10] A difficulty here, it would seem, consists in that this universal first premise is a product of the ongoing determination of the dialectic of the actual world. In his treatment of history, as will shortly be noted,[11] Hegel indeed proposes this. The difficulty is seen to disappear, however, when it is noted that the "Notion-form" could be determined by the determination of a limited content of actuality [12] by the aid of speculation while remaining subject to further determination. That it is not essentially changed through being subject to further determination must be seen to be owing to its having the status of "Truth" in the qualified sense (only) of that term where it is applied to the "subjective Notion." If the "subjective Notion" were to be construed to be True without qualification, the account would be incoherent. Apart from assuming the position under consideration, then, Hegel's account here would be incoherent.

When the particularization of the "Notion form" in the world is re-garded as a second premise, then, this second premise reflects an aspect of the Notion only. The logic is understood to be grounded both in a dialectic of the mind – the "subjective Notion" – and the dialectic of the world – the "objective Notion" – and, most particularly, in mind and world in interaction. Here again, however, "subjective Notion" and "objective Notion," respectively, are to be understood as only aspects of the Notion, in that in each the Notion is only in part explicit.

> The Union of Universal Abstract Existence generally with the individual – the Subjective – that this alone is Truth, belongs to the department of speculation, and is treated in this general form in Logic. – But in the process of the World's History itself – as still incomplete – the abstract final aim of history is not yet made the distinct object of desire and interest.[13]

Thus, Truth is the result of the mediation of the forms of the logical Idea on the side of the subject and universal abstract existence – exis-tence, that is, which is represented as it stands independent of the sub-ject. Speculation explicates this principle in the logic as an ideal realized, on which account the form of the logical idea is to be regarded as complete. While the key to understanding history lies in finding the form of the logical idea explicit therein, this project is uncompleted because history is not completed.

From the standpoint of history viewed as a completed process, any phase of history is construed to be for notional consciousness incomplete, as has been noted, its final aim not being the object of desire and interest. From another – suppose we call it the "existentialist" – standpoint, however, Hegel holds the Notion to be exhibited in every particular in reality. Thus, while the ideal limit of the self-transcendence which can be embodied in and shaped by actuality at any given time is the Notion, the Notion as infinite and outside of time is yet fully given in each stage of the advance toward this ideal.[14] As Kosok notes, "Each subpart is in a one to one correspondence with the whole, which is the defining characteristic of an infinite totality." [15] It is this aspect of Hegel's claim for the Notion which most clearly seems to necessitate a departure from his principles in the task I am undertaking.

The Notion in its completeness and infinitude is construed from a tem-poral perspective to be given as implicit only in every particular in reality. But this all-encompassing whole is also the Truth for which one risks one's life, or which risks it for one.[16] On the one hand, the Notion given in every particular, viewed temporally, is to a degree only implicit, and, on the other, this implicitness at least approaches becoming explicit in moments of encounter and decision in "das Jetzt." The Whole that is the Truth is somehow self-authenticated in "das Jetzt." [17]

On Hegel's principles, then, is the Notion viewed as reflected in a dry and settled account of the history of an epoch? The answer may be "yes," if that history is taken up into the self in what we may appropriately refer to as an existential self-negation, but then it will no longer be dry, and having been brought to the moment of Truth, it may not be settled, at least not precisely as it was.

This, however, leaves us with a problem. There would seem to be no practically applicable criteria which may be applied to an historical account to determine whether it rightly belongs within that great and uncompleted schema, the dialectic of history. The only criterion seems to be an intuitive one, and to presuppose a god-like grasp of history as well. How, for example, may I be certain that, because I cannot come to a sense that the dialectic of light and darkness (Persian religion) is a vital part of my own religious heritage by virtue of which I come to a moment of commitment in the "now," therefore this is not an authentic theological account of the religious pilgrimage of some men? Following Hegel, since this is a part of my "subjective Notion" and ostensibly exhibited in history, I should be able to recognize it. But how am I to judge as to whether my failure to grasp this which I provisionally suppose to be my essence is due to my own want of self-awareness or to a false account? If I cannot be reasonably certain here, must not my uncertainty extend to the sphere of responsible religious commitment and action which, on Hegel's principles grow out of and are conditioned by what is construed to be the cultural heritage of the individual dialectically understood?

It may be inquired why Hegel's "lower" criteria of "Truth" are not put to use here, according to which "Truth is the correspondence of objectivity with its subjective notion..." [18] But the application of this criterion to an historical account seems equally problematical when it is noted that this "Notion-form," if it does not consist in terms, consists in nothing less than the ideas of them. In any case, moreover, this is for Hegel only a qualified sense of "Truth," seeing that the Truth that is the Notion is "the unity of the theoretical and the practical Idea, and the unity of life with the idea of cognition, the Absolute Idea come to be its own object." [19]

If Hegel's Notion, viewed in the light of man's existential encounter is not on the basis of preferred methodological principles simply to be declared meaningless, it must be acknowledged, I think, that it is not readily accommodated to the natural limitations of the investigator who wishes to ascertain whether a dialectical exposition of history, for example, is falsifiable. The criterion of what Hegel called Truth, as it pertains to dialectic, is too demanding to be adequate to the need here.

If the test of Truth is presumptuous where one is to consider judging a phase of the dialectic of nature or Absolute Spirit for its standing as dialectic, there remains no alternative, then, but to turn to criteria which might plausibly be applicable. Happily, Hegel at least recognized the problem, as is evidenced by his distinction between the Notion (the logic) and dialectical method, although, as I shall be noting, he did not maintain this distinction in a way adequate to meet the present need. Thus, the method, as opposed to the Notion, is recognized as a tool, distinct both from the "Notion" as the form of subjectivity and the "Notion" as the form of objectivity,[20] whereby the two are progressively related. "The extremes remain distinct because subject, method, and object are not posited as one identical Notion . . ." [21] The word "posited" here seems to be critical, for it is clear enough that the three are viewed as one identical Notion. What is indicated, then, is that a perspective is taken up here which *provisionally* regards them as distinct. Thus, Hegel immediately goes on to say,

> In true cognition the method is not merely a quantity of certain determinations: it is the fact that the Notion is determined in and for itself, and is the mean only because it equally has the significance of objective, so that, in conclusion, it does not merely achieve an external determination through the method, but is posited in its identity with the subjective Notion.[22]

It is clear enough from this context that the specification of dialectical method as distinct from the Notion proper which determines it is a concession to the finitude of the investigator. It is method thus conceived that can be said to be in correspondence with (and not simply identical with) its object.

> Thus the method has emerged as the Notion which knows itself and has for object itself as the Absolute, both subjective and objective, that is, as the pure correspondence between the Notion and its Reality, as an existence which the Notion itself is.[23]

It is to be noted that method is not clearly distinguished from the

Notion (or the logic) any more than are subject and object regarded as finally distinguishable from one another. If a concession is made to the finitude of the investigator (which I have shown to be necessary), the impression is left that the method as a goal as distinguished from the Notion has only a provisional status. This is to say, as subject and object regarded as distinct and separate have only a provisional status, method as pertaining to either or both has only a provisional status. The delineation of method which follows takes the form of an explanation of how the Notion determines method. The distinction thus weakened is even further weakened by a number of statements of which the following is perhaps as appropriate as any to quote out of context.

> The Notion considered by itself appeared in its immediacy; reflection, or the Notion which contemplated it, formed part of our knowledge. The method is this knowledge itself, and for this knowledge the Notion is not only as object, but as its own peculiar and subjective activity, or the instrument and means of cognitive activity, distinct from it, but as its own peculiar essentiality.[24]

Thus the method, as it turns out, is regarded by Hegel as far more than a tool; it is "an immanent and objective form" as well, and "endowed with the impulse of self development." [25] Here, as so frequently elsewhere, the account of dialectical method is so blended with the passionate rhapsody of the Notion that, if the latter remains at least in a certain sense a mystery, the former tends to partake of the mysterious. Thus, while recognizing the need for a distinction between method and Notion, Hegel failed to define his method in such a way as to maintain unambiguously such a distinction as would be required were a dialectical account to be falsifiable. In the Notion all distinctions are overcome and contained as discriminations, including the discrimination between method and the subjective and objective contents to which it pertains.

The distinction between formal and material aspects of actuality is also overcome and contained as a discrimination within the Notion. From the perspective of the infinitude of the Notion, form and content are identical.[26] Method is understood to pertain equally to formal and material aspects of the actual. This being the case, for Hegel's criteria for Truth to be two-fold would have been out of keeping with his emphasis upon the unity of the Notion, at least where the matter is viewed as from the perspective of this unified Notion.

In proposing criteria for authentic dialectic, I shall intend strictly to maintain a distinction between dialectical method and the Notion. What

I shall call authentic dialectic will be construed a necessary but not a sufficient condition of Truth in Hegel's sense. This is to be formalization of dialectical principles which, strictly speaking, falls short of adequacy to Hegel's logic by the omission of his radical principle of completeness. Seeing that the completeness of the Notion disallows that any formalization of the Notion shall be found amenable to a test of correspondence between it and something else, this principle must here be bracketed. Hegel's Notion, after all, realizes itself – becomes explicit – not by correspondence with but by opposition to, and ultimate inclusion of, precisely that of which it (at least apparently) does not correspond. From the bracketing of the principle of completeness of the Notion, it will follow that to which it (at least apparently) does not correspond. From the as realized – by inclusion – to which criteria for authenticity shall be applicable.

Along with the bracketing of the principle of completeness of the Notion, I shall bracket the subjective "Notion," which will also be to set aside the concept of the Notion as present in its completeness in the parts as in the whole. If, where the historical consciousness is making history, the latter may have plausible reference and meaning, in the case of a recorded historical account being approached critically, it seems appropriate to set it aside. This, even though it must be allowed that the "Truth" of such an account may possibly be regarded as given in what might be referred to as the existentially lived present of the reader and thus be said to reflect the infinitude and completeness which Hegel attributed to such moments.

To complement this test for authenticity, another test peculiarly appropriate to finite men is to be proposed. This is a test of whether a belief about existential reality as set forth in a dialectical account is warranted for belief.[27] Where a phase of dialectic apparently coheres well within the context of an account taken to represent a given historical epoch, it will be designated a warranted belief. This rather inadequate preliminary definition will later be supplemented.

The criteria for ascertaining that a belief is warranted, like the criteria for authenticity, are to be conceived a necessary but not sufficient condition for Truth. The test for authenticity and the test for warranted belief are thus companion pieces. Truth as pertaining to a dialectical exposition of actuality. I shall propose, is most appropriately conceived as an ideal limit to which authentic dialectic warranted for belief points. What would be required as a sufficient condition of Truth is the determination that a belief stands as warranted within an infinitely extended context of an authentic dialectical account of history.

I do not intend to imply, by the use of the double-test proposed, that the Notion as a system of concepts intuitively grasped in the "now" is philosophically meaningless.[28] I wish merely to bracket this consideration until later, as well as the consideration of whether there comes a point at which authentic dialectic warranted for belief may appropriately be affirmed to be True.

An English language statement of some formal properties which characterize Hegel's method generally is adequate to the analysis the results of which I shall present. This, principally because I find the bracketing off of superfluous presupposed meanings of terms in the interest of ascertaining formal proporties of the dialectic is more easily accomplished in this phase of Hegel's dialectic than, for example, in the dialectic of the logical idea. In my definition of terms, however, I shall introduce an element reminiscent of the most elementary part of Kosok's recursive formula,[29] and I shall indicate, as occasion arises, what modifications would need to be effected in the way he conceives his recursive formula were its use in the analysis of the dialectic of religion to produce the same results.

The following definition of dialectic finds its reflection, I would maintain, in every principal phase of Hegel's dialectic.

The highest concept of God contains the greatest increment of discrimination mediated to unity and each mediation within the dialectic is assigned its place upon the basis of this principle. At each of the several levels of the dialectic, this concept includes as discriminations within it all other actual concepts which belong to this consciousness, which concepts, in turn, may be deduced from it.[30]

This brief statement, while it is not contained in either of these works in just this form, reflects, I submit, the core of Hegel's prescription for dialectic in *VPG* and *VPR*. This, where allowance is made for the fact that is to be understood in a way commensurate with the bracketing procedure I have outlined. This is to say, no unity is regarded as finally inclusive. In addition, for this statement to be adequate to the elucidation of authenticity within the context of the dialectic of religion, it will be necessary to construe it as pertaining to a set of concepts irrespective of whether these concepts reflect a religious consciousness.[31] This, in spite of the fact that, in what follows, I must necessarily refer to aspects of the phenomenology of thought. Some definitions will perhaps lend clarity to the above statement.

Mediation (*Vermittlung*), is the process by which change is effected in a given content of thought through thought's own operation upon it, where thought is something that comes before the mind and change is said to have occurred when a given content of thought is apprehended differently than it was before. This difference is to be accounted for by a new apprehension of this content within an enlarged context and with new significance or meaning. Seeing that every given, (e), is limited, what lies beyond this limit is necessarily posited as something not (other than) that given. This something is designated negatively by its one known relation to the first given, (e); it is designated (-e). It is the as yet only negatively designated presence of a necessary, if undetermined, posit.[32] The conditioned character of the first given, (e), is taken into account as well as that of the second, (-e), in what is now given, ((e)(-e)), or (e'), a given that contains them both in their correlativity. The relation obtaining between (e) and (-e) is one of opposition (*Widerspruch*) and this opposition is contained and transcended in ((e)(-e)), or e', in turn, when viewed in repect to its limit becomes the given of a new mediation. An operation of the mind includes the realization of a want of "completeness" of a content of thought, the striving to overcome this limitation and to include the neglected element within the content of thought now altered by this inclusion. Thus every authentic dialectical development represents an opposition to a "completeness" appropriate to that which precedes, but which is no longer adequate or appropriate. Such a development implies a new "completeness" – that a more adequate synthetic concept is already a possession of the mind.[33] There is here imaged dialectical development by negation as in the Notion, even though the completeness of the Notion has been bracketed. (The quotation marks around "completeness" in the above signify that it is only a provisionally adequate completeness that is intended.) [34]

A dialectical account which cannot be characterized in these terms may not properly be considered authentic as I have herein defined the term. An exposition which may be thus characterized, though it may have no determinable relation to actuality, may be considered authentic.[35]

Before turning to the dialectic of religion, I wish to express a judgment, without attempting to justify it here, respecting Hegel's strategy in composing dialectical accounts. If justified, it may prove illuminating, and, in any case, it will contribute to the clarification of the relation between authenticity and warranted belief which I wish to propose.

Hegel attempted to arrive at the primitive meanings of terms as they arose to express discriminations in the phenomenology of consciousness and in a particular period of history. Thus, "this" and "not-this" express the apprehension of the most elementary possible and presumably

the most primitive discrimination in consciousness.[36] At a more advanced
stage of the phenomenology, and presumably later in time, the discrimination of "thing" and "its attributes" arises,[37] etc. These discriminations
cumulatively come to be formed and expressed by the use of such pairs
of correlative terms, each member of a pair referring to one side of the
total field within which the discrimination is found. In addition to containing correlatives, the dialectic consists in a hierarchy of terms (or
categories), each defined within the schema as inclusive of the one below, and each containing the essential meaning of those below.[38] (Even correlatives bound each other, and the one which arises by opposition may
be said to contain the first.) The practical consequence of this is that the
definitions assigned to terms determine their order in the dialectic. This
aside from considerations of how such definitions are arrived at – whether,
for example, by phenomenological or by historical analysis.

From this it would follow that Hegel's revision of the order of the
dialectic of Absolute Spirit, on the occasion of each reading of the course,[39]
may have been governed by an altered sense of the root meanings of
such terms as substance, good, person, beauty, utility, etc. by virtue of
which the order of inclusion was necessarily altered. It would follow,
then, that, were one to find the definitions which result from one order
of exposition to be improbable or too deviant from accepted usage, or
too deviant from the primitive root meanings of terms, in so far as these
are known, this would consitute ground for a revision of the order of a
dialectical exposition. It would also constitute ground for the introduction
or deletion of terms according to their comparative existential and/or
historical significance. In consistency with the bracketing procedure herein
specified and the stipulation that authenticity shall not imply that the
terms in a dialectical account are in conformity with actuality, the status
of terms with respect to actuality are herein to be regarded as determined
by criteria for warranted belief. These have yet to be considered.

III

I shall now present the results of an analysis of the dialectic of religion
to determine unauthenticity.[40] Because the application of the test may be
best exemplified in this way, I shall be limited in the presentation of my
analysis to unauthentic dialectic or dialectic which appears to be so
apart from considerations relating to the explicitness of definitions of
terms. It is to be construed that phases of the dialectic not considered
may be authentic and could be shown to be authentic were definitions

of terms commensurate with their authenticity presupposed as fully explicit. That terms are defined within the dialectic itself must lead one to suppose that a phase of dialectic which is not determined to be unauthentic by the stated criteria is authentic. Because definitions of terms are not uniformly complete and explicit, however, the proof of authenticity would be more tedious than the proof of unauthenticity.[41] Instances of the latter, I shall hope, will convey a sense of what constitutes authenticity adequate to the present need.

In the case of dialectic which appears to be but is not certainly unauthentic, some formal property required to constitute a case of authentic dialectic seems to be assumed rather than explicitly indicated to be present. I shall first consider some "minor" cases in which the dialectic is unauthentic or problematical.[42] Following this, I shall consider the religion of utility, the one major phase which I find to be unauthentic, at greater length.

The dialectic within the religion of sublimity,[43] as in the case with the initial triad in the dialectic of the logical idea (consisting of being, nothing and becoming) is primitive in character. Also, like the parallel phase of the logic, the opposition between opposing concepts is not strong. This is to say, the terms by virtue of their meaning do not suggest a dramatic opposition. The initial othering of God in the world is here conceived while maintaining and leaving for further development the working out of the relation or connection between God and the world. The progression within the development is almost imperceptible and seems to amount to little more than an alteration of points of view. When the implied definition of terms is assumed, however (whether historically true or existentially meaningful), and when it is kept in mind that the opposition that is a necessary condition of authenticity amounts only to this, there must be a specifiable difference in the range of inclusiveness of first, (e), and third order concepts, ((e)(-e)), the latter including the former along with the second order concept, (-e), which defines the boundary of the first, this development as a whole and its various parts may be seen to be authentic.[44]

A want of uniformity of significance of the three-fold division of the treatment accorded to each of its nine major sub-moments may be found a problematical aspect of the dialectic of religion. This three-fold division is constituted by the Notion, the historical exemplification, and worship. Hegel proposes to develop these three divisions dialectically.[45] It is not until one comes to the religion of beauty, however, that these divisions of the treatment are found to be developed in such a way as to be certainly identifiable as dialectic within the three major sub-moments of absolute religion. Hegel's failure to carry out his "architectonic" with reference to this three-fold division is evidenced in an especially clear way by the fact that the want of a dialectical relation between these divisions, where they appear in the order of exposition, does not result in unauthentic sub-moments. Had the three parts of the division been dialectically treated, the relation between the sub-moments within each of its parts would have been dialectically integral and unauthenticity in the former would necessarily have resulted in at least some inauthentic moments in the latter. This as in the case where, in the dialectic of the religion of *utility*, to be considered, the unauthenticity of the sub-moments may be seen to follow from the unauthenticity of the development of the primary triad. That Hegel's failure in most instances to develop the three-fold division dialectically is not reflected in unauthenticity in sub-moments is evidence that this aspect of his architectonic did not prove to be integral with his dialectical schematism.[46]

In order to show the unauthentic character of what Hegel proposes as the dialectic of the religion of *utility*, it will be necessary to sketch in the moments which precede it. The religion of *spiritual individuality* [47] follows the religion of *nature* and contains three principal sub-moments, the religion of *sublimity*, the religion of *beauty*, and the religion of *utility*. These three sub-moments are exemplified by Jewish, Greek, and Roman religion, respectively. Jewish religion, the religion of *sublimity,* is characterized by the idea of *power* and not yet that of *end*. The idea of God as an *end* has its first beginning here in the immediately given idea of God as *absolute person*. This *absolute person* of Jewish Religion is not yet understood to be reflected in the world as His other. This consciousness, in turn, finds reflected in nature an external conformity to an end. The essential *end* is now seen as the *moral end* which the individual must fulfill through obedience to law, now emerging in externality. Wisdom, contained in the knowledge of universals abstract and not of this world, here first finds concrete embodiment in the form of the family. God's *end* comes to be known to be the *family*. The individual as head of the family anticipates the embodiment of spirit in individual form. Self-consciousness thus, through obedience, gains for its object of worship its own nature, its universality as manifested in the Divine Powers, although this object is not recognized as its own nature.

As soon as it is seen that the finite world is put forth out of God, it follows that this world as His other is itself a part of Him. Nature is no longer viewed as the opposite of God and worthless. God is in nature, and He manifests Himself in the sensuous. This is the general concept of the religion of *beauty* (exemplified in Greek Religion). Since the sensuous is pluralistic, the one God of the Hebrews becomes the many gods of the Greeks. These gods are spiritual; this is to say they are genuine persons, and not merely personifications of particular attributes as in natural religion. They are fundamentally human, friendly, and free. Man, no longer annulled with nature, is likewise self-determined and no longer afraid. The gods have within them the very content of nobility and truth which is at the same time that of man. The individual's confidence in the gods is thus confidence in himself as well. Passing over Hegel's lengthy exposition of the religion of *beauty,* the final form of reconciliation wrought by that religion implies that the negation of the individual by himself is a crime. He expresses himself now as a free spirit. The guilty soul takes upon itself the price of compensation for guilt, thus gaining an increment of freedom. Empty and undetermined necessity remains the ruling principle of the religion of *beauty,* however, despite this series of determinations by which the attempt is made by the individual to deliver himself from the abstract necessity which he encounters as *fate.* The final issue is that the finite ends stand negated by the (from this perspective) abstract universal end which floats above the particular.

The next demand of thought is for the union of *abstract universality* with particular and individual *ends* in such a way that abstract necessity has its emptiness filled with particularity as *end.* It is proposed that the unity in the form of abstract subjectivity of the religion of *sublimity* and the moral substantiality of the empirical self-consciousness of the religion of *beauty* are mediated in the religion of *utility.* The end of the religion of *sublimity,* when it took concrete form, was the *family.* Now this end is widened to correspond with the compass of power of the Roman *State.* The unity of the One is now to represent determinateness in definite form. Thus the abstract necessity of the One is to be filled with a *concrete and particular end.*

Hegel makes it clear at the outset that, while the one-sideness of both the religion of *sublimity* and the religion of *beauty* are to be overcome, the true principles of these religions are not be taken up in this development, but only perversions of them. On the one hand, the religion of *beauty* loses the concrete individuality of the gods as well as their independent moral content and character. The gods are to be degraded to the rank of mere means. The concept of God as *sublimity,* on the other hand, is taken up minus an occupation with the supernatural.[48] This amounts to the tacit admission that this development does not conform to the dialectical principle that each concept (of God) is to contain and transcend those which have preceded it in the dialectic. Viewed in context, this religion is a regression and not a progression,[49] and is on this account unauthentic.

This digression from dialectical method (both Hegel's and that herein proposed), of which it is difficult to believe that Hegel was totally unaware, is of interest in that a mediation of the abstract universality of the religion of *sublimity* and the concrete particularity of the religion of beauty, as he develops these, is not only possible on formal grounds but a plausible historical exemplification of such a religion may be found.[50] Some further matters are to be noted from the account of the religion of *utility*.

The gods of beauty, taken over from Greek religion by the Romans, are only opposed to one another as they are independent and free to act on their own. Their character is generally such that, if they act on their own, they can be put in their place. They are mutually determined by one another and by overarching *fate*; where fate gives way to concrete determination (and hence, freedom) this determination is immediately taken into this mutual determination.

> While, accordingly, in necessity one determination depends on another and the determinate character passes away, the end is posited as identity with difference and reality in it, the unity which is determined in and for itself, and which maintains itself in its determinate character as against the determinate character of something else.[51]

The Notion thus determined, insofar as it stands free in its own nature, stands confronted by reality; it throws off its peculiar individual character to become Spirit in-and-for-itself. According to Hegel, this is not, however, achieved in the religion of *utility;* it is, rather, achieved in the first moment of *absolute religion.* Up to this point, within the dialectic of religion, and generally within the dialectic as a whole, the synthesis of one concrete universal becomes the thesis of the development which follows by a mere shift of perspective, whereby it is viewed in terms of its limit – its finitude – rather than merely in terms of what it contains. The final outcome of the deviation of the dialectic of the religion of *utility* lies in the abnormality that the succeeding thesis within absolute religion constitutes a further mediation and not merely a synthesis viewed in its finitude.

In the religion of *utility*, what is realized is a particular determination, or particular determinations, by negation (opposition) and not a totality of *ends* of the gods determined to unity. This limited determinateness of concrete reality, moreover, is given only a qualified universality, without necessity commensurate with it. Accordingly, action is in accordance with an end which lies outside the individual and which also is devoid of Spirit. It is an end which is finite and which is elevated to universality. The end of Roman religion is sovereignty as represented by Jupiter Capitolinus. Unlike Zeus, the father of gods and men, Jupiter Capitolinus carries out his role of sovereign for the Roman people, the universal family. The many gods, being brought under the sovereignty of Jupiter Capitolinus, embody finite ends raised to quasi-universality. The service of these gods is for the sake of human ends. The content being in this sense human, Hegel notes, their outward form can hardly be distinguished from the worship paid to them. The truth proposed in them is a truth which already has a realized existence. Worship is primarily merely the process whereby this content is given recognition above subjective necessity.

Thus we see evidenced a lack of cumulative import in the exposition of worship. Moreover, there is little if anything in the exposition of Roman religion not explicit in the Notion of the religion of *beauty*. The fact that no subdivisions even within the Notion of the religion of *utility* are identifiable as dialectical moments can hardly be accidental. In the nature of the case an unauthentic dialectic, where this unauthenticity is owing to a want of cumulative import (cumulative of discriminations contained within it), could hardly contain subdivisions which adhere to dialectical method. Progression cannot be gained by fractioning a lack of progression. An analysis of the other eight major subdivisions of the dialectic discloses that the religion of *utility* alone, when viewed in its entirety, proves certainly unauthentic. That by far the greater portion of the dialectic of religion is found not to be evidently unauthentic should not be surprising, seeing that the criteria used were drawn from the work itself.

Following my bracketing procedure, certain aspects of Hegel's criteria for formal adequacy of dialectic have not been included in the criteria to which I have appealed. On this account, the test here applied may be said to be Hegel's in only a qualified sense. That Hegel would have accepted the results of the foregoing analysis of his dialectic of religion may on this account be questioned. The unbracketing of the principle of completeness of the Notion and the "subjective Notion" would, however, make the conditions for authenticity more and not less stringent. That the conditions for authenticity would be more demanding suggests that the phases of the dialectic indicated to be unauthentic in the above would tend to be viewed as unauthentic by Hegel's criteria. This, despite the fact that an historical account, strictly speaking, is not falsifiable by criteria consistent with this unbracketing. Here, as in the case of the Notion in its completeness, the criteria are so demanding that a test of the sort we seek is inapplicable; self-authenticity has displaced or taken priority over any conceivable test for correspondence. The self-authenticity of Hegel's Notion, whether exhibited in God or men, unlike the case of authenticity as pertaining to dialectic, pertains to form and content and exhibits the identity of form and content. Authenticity pertains to form only.

A conclusion which seems warranted by the analysis, but which cannot be justified apart from presenting an analysis, in turn, of each of the moments of the dialectic, is that Hegel's dialectic of religion exhibits formal properties, if not necessarily all of the formal properties he attributed to dialectic. The discovery that this is the case is aided by the bracketing off of specified aspects of his dialectic which I have shown render dialectic not falsifiable.

It is possible that phases of the dialectic of religion not here proven unauthentic might be out of conformity with Hegel's Notion. Whether there are such phases which pass the formal test I have applied and yet fail this test is an existential question. I shall now propose a test to determine whether a belief is warranted.

IV

As authenticity has been herein defined, given the acceptance of the definitions successively related to one another by inclusion which are generated within it, a dialectical exposition of a set of imaginary terms might be authentic. If by excluding the consideration of whether such terms refer to anything actual (whether subjective or objective), dialectic may be found authentic, then it seems clear that authenticity of itself is an insufficient warranty of the existential meaningfulness of a dialectical account. It must also be warranted for belief. The criteria for this warranty now to be considered are proposed as a basis for determing the adequacy to history of the definitions of terms in a dialectical exposition and whether the dialectical determination of these terms by one another within the exposition adequately reflect what one may be willing, on historical grounds, to regard as causal relations and sequences of causal relations in history.

As in the case of the test for authenticity, so, for the purpose of the test of whether a belief is warranted, the speculation of Hegel that the subjective Notion conditions history as apprehended is to be bracketed and set aside. This, because the perspective appropriate to the test does not presuppose its result. Rather, this perspective views history not only without presupposing the Notion to be exhibited therein, but without presupposing dialectic (conceived apart from the principle of completeness) to be necessarily exhibited therein, but merely that it might be and with a view to discovering it where present.[52] Where discovered, moreover, it is viewed as from the bottom-up or, where it is viewed from the top-down, this is from a finite perspective not presupposing the ideal completeness of the Notion. This is in keeping with *a* perspective decribed by Hegel.[53]

It was Hegel's expectation that history would be found to exhibit the same course of development – the same dialectical progression – as he believed he had discovered to be exhibited in the phenomenology of mind (its recapitulation) and that the identity of the subjective "Notion" with the objective "Notion" might thus be established in fact as well as in speculation as the Notion.[54] Whatever may be said concerning the prospect for the execution of this grand design, it seems not improbable to suppose with Hegel that history will hardly be seen to exhibit the dialectic of terms which are not at the same time terms which are existentially meaningful to the individual who reads history. While it appears necessary that such terms must in some sense belong to the phenomenology of the contemporary consciousness of the reader of history, the proposed criteria for warranty will not require that the meanings of such terms be interrelated in such a manner as would follow their derivation through phenomenological analysis as Hegel conceived and practiced it, or that the reader is required to attribute to such terms root meanings such as a phenomenological analysis patterned upon Hegel's would discover them to have.[55]

Apart from the understanding of dialectical method, it seems improbable that unambiguously dialectical history will be written. On this account, the proposal of a test to determine whether a dialectical account is warranted for belief will necessarily reflect evolution in history more prominently than repetition or regression. Where the history is inclusive, the latter will be taken cognizance of primarily as negative elements. If a change in the account is effected upon historical grounds which render the dialectic unauthentic, the affected exposition, while it may be warranted for belief, is then implied to have a complementary status with respect to dialectical history, which is exclusively concerned with such causal relations in history as may be found commensurate with an exposition of newly and progressively actualized concepts in history or a particular phase of history.

In virtue of the fact that an authentic and warranted dialectical account implies the practical exclusion of all historical events and connections which are not a part of such an evolutionary progression, were one to presuppose less progress in history (or a phase of history) than Hegel did, a history so conceived would be less adequate for general purposes than he supposed. A strictly dialectical account of history, for example, could not contain Hegel's account of Roman religion because the latter, as has been noted, presents a regression from a dialectical advance. This is not to imply that this account is not warranted for belief as history. On the contrary, this account strikes me as a penetrating one which, though not authentic dialectic, is fairly well warranted for belief.

Should a series of short historical accounts which are authentic be connected to form a longer thread and one with more strands, it would be expected that this would result in such deletions and modifications of the causal connections construed to obtain within and between most or all of these so as to render them compatible and complementary within the larger context of coherence thus constituted. Such modifications might be affected by the presence of something in an earlier period which (if the principle of sufficient reason is assumed) must surely have left its effect upon a later period, which effect is then sought out. On the other hand, the presence of something in a later period for which a causal explanation is sought in an earlier period might determine a modification. Thus, modifications are effected from the top of the series down as well as from the bottom up. This without the abrogation of the bracketing of the principle of completeness of the Notion so long as transcendence is excluded in the interests of rendering a dialectical account falsifiable by practically applicable criteria.

Parenthetically, if this principle, along with the subjective "Notion," is unbracketed, it may be seen how a universal history could *approach* being True in Hegel's sense, as an asymptote approaches an axis of a cartesian graph. The "now" opening out to a future, pursued in self-certainty, is both informed by history as so far conceived and the latter is left in need of reformulation to explain the causal connections (as

dialectical determinants) which condition the new present. It remains unclear, however, how historical Truth, except as an ideal and a pursuit
of self-certainty, could be attained even with this unbracketing, since it
is unclear how history could be grasped as consistent and complete at
the same time, which conclusion seems to follow from dialectical principles.[56] Actuality being preeminently process for Hegel, which process
temporally understood includes a past, present and future as essential
constituents of every "now," it is perhaps not improper, nevertheless,
to regard this inclusive ideal pursuit in self-certainty as conditioned by
nothing outside of itself, and hence as Hegel's Truth. I shall now complete the statement of criteria for a belief to be warranted.

It will not be required that the series of terms be of any specified
length so long as it contains at least two terms, so long as each member
of the series is accepted as historically grounded, and so long as the determination of those later in the series by those earlier in the series reflects what are accepted as historical causal connections between historical events upon historical grounds. That there must be a minimum
of two terms amounts to the stipulation that history in the proper sense
is to be conceived as not merely the reporting of events but the report
of threads of causally related events. The sense of warranty is affected
by the evidence for having happened thus and thus. Also, the degree of
warranty for an explanation of proposed causal relation may be affected by the number of times a similar series of events has occurred and the apparent adequacy of the proposed causal connection in such cases.[57]
Where the events are well attested, moreover, the degree of warranty
will be greater the more extensive the context of coherence within which
events and connections are viewed. Such criteria as I have listed are
commensurate with an authentic dialectic of terms determined in series.

The above criteria for warranted belief as pertaining to an authentic
dialectical exposition of history are to be regarded as a necessary but
not a sufficient condition of Truth. Where the warranty for belief is strong,
owing to a high degree of certitude regarding events, causal connections
(and the parallel determinations of terms in the dialectic), and where the
defining context is inclusive of the history of the past viewed and interpreted in terms of a lived present, it points toward Truth as toward an
ideal limit. It may be construed that this ideal limit is reached in moments
of existential encounter and decision, where past, present, and future
are determined and reconstituted anew in the "now." With respect to
my present purpose, which is to show a dialectical account to be plausibly
falsifiable (inauthentic or unwarranted for belief or both) and this whether

or not one is imbued with the Notion, or even a notion of the Notion, it is not essential to hold the Truth that is the whole to be attainable. Moreover, at least in this context, it would be presumptuous to do so.

V

An adequate test to determine to what degree each of the various phases of Hegel's dialectic of Absolute Spirit is warranted for belief by the above stated criteria is a larger undertaking than I wish to attempt. Also, considerable attention has already been given, in scattered sources, to the criticism of this dialectic on historical grounds. I shall therefore be restricted to a few comments relative to the exposition of Jewish religion, perhaps the clearest example of dialectic unwarranted for belief, and of Christianity, perhaps the best warranted. The hazards of Hegel's method of attempting to select the major transition of the religious consciousness proposed to have been accomplished by each of several major religions, neglecting other happenings within the evolution of each, has been well advertised. The presentation of Jewish religion as exemplifying the religion of sublimity, for example, though dialectically authentic, presents a stilted image of that religion. The naturalism of the wisdom literature and other writings, the emphasis upon the individual found in Ezekiel and Deutero-Isaiah, the nationalism of David and the fifth century restoration movement, the overcoming of polytheism, and the emergence of the concept of God as universal, are among those developments which would dialectically transcend the account as it stands and which, had they been given recognition, would have effected at once a more complex and a less one-sided characterization of what is improperly called Jewish religion.[58] This neglect makes for an easy success in the attempt to show the superiority of Greek over Hebrew religion. That a polemical interest is at work here bears witness at least to Hegel's limitations as an historian. It is less clear what it implies respecting the worth of a dialectical account of history.

It would appear that Hegel's exposition of Christianity as the absolute religion may exemplify dialectic warranted for belief as well as and perhaps better than any other part of his dialectic of religion and history. This is owing to a richness of detail not accorded to less preferred religions as well as to a sensitivity to historical developments. This is not to say either that there is not a polemical interest reflected in this account, or that the account does not reflect his own particular sense of the march of Spirit in his own time. The latter, following his own principles, would in the nature of the case be reflected in any history worthy of the name.

I shall conclude with a further statement regarding the relation of authenticity and warranty for belief and some observations respecting how the two-fold test stands related to Hegel's treatment of dialectic.

VI

A dialectical account exhibiting the warranty for belief specified in the foregoing will also be found to be authentic. In this is reflected the commensurability of form and (here, a limited) content which for Hegel is found to be fully explicit (as an identity of the two) within the Notion. That he did not with any degree of consistency carry out the dialectic of Absolute Spirit according to the three-fold division of Notion, historical exemplification, and worship constitutes evidence. I would propose, of the difficulty he found in distinguishing the exposition of the form of the "subjective Notion" from what he found to be exhibited in history. His appropriation of what he found exhibited in history being conditioned by the form of the Notion, the same form was found to be exhibited therein so that a further overcoming of difference was rendered unnecessary.

While a dialectical account warranted for belief is authentic, an authentic dialectical exposition may not be warranted for belief. The value of the two-fold test, then, lies in that the test for authenticity may be applied apart from considerations relating to warranty for belief – apart, this is to say, from existential considerations and, it might be added, apart from the test for existential self-certainty which only may obtain as warranty for the Notion and the self-warranty of the Notion.

If a relative warranty for belief is possible, where given definitions of terms may be assumed, it is possible positively to determine authenticity. Where the formal properties of authentic dialectic are held to reflect the phenomenology of consciousness, the significance of this proof is appreciable.

The double test offers the additional advantage of rendering it unnecessary to presuppose in advance of the demonstration what Hegel held he had shown in his *Phenomenology*, the "subjective Notion." It permits us who do not yet, at least with certainty, view the process to enter into dialogue about dialectic.

There have been a sufficient number of recent expositions of Hegel's dialectical method in essential agreement on this point to render superfluous a demonstration that Hegel intended his dialectic to exhibit formal properties. It is worth noting, nevertheless, that the strategy herein pursued makes such formal properties as have been considered seem to stand out more clearly, and this without falsely equating them with what Hegel proposes to be his logic.

How is Hegel's presupposing or neglect of a material test for dialectic to be accounted for? I think this was neglect and that this neglect was owing to his preoccupation with the Notion in which Truth transcends the distinction between formal and material elements. In any case, his test for adherence of dialectic to method, by virtue of the fact that the distinction between method and Notion is blurred so that the two tend to merge, renders a dialectical account of history in principle not falsifiable. The Notion being in principle an inclusive unity of form and content, a material test of the adequacy of dialectic distinct from adherence to dialectical method seems implied to be superfluous. This matter is not, however, uniformly clear. He assumes both the from-the-top-down and from-the-bottom-up perspectives, often in rapid succession, with variations on both occasioned by the introduction of the Notion at different levels of development, thereby also occasioning much of the confusion that has followed regarding dialectical method.

Hegel nonetheless does retain the distinction between the finite bottom-up perspective upon the dialectic and the perspective of the Notion fully explicit as the form of subjective mind. The latter is often introduced by the phrase, "for we who view the process." From the bottom-up perspective, conceived as the perspective of the consciousness being considered, unless it be national consciousness, the Notion is as unknown as Kant's *noumenon* remains. It is with this perspective that the test for whether a belief is warranted accords well and even seems to be implied as a complement to the test for authenticity. The bracketing procedure I have followed has been designed to restrict me (as Hegel was not restricted) to this perspective and to make the material test for warranty for belief commensurate with this perspective.

In explicating criteria that pertain to authenticity and warranty for belief, my principal departures from Hegel are two. The first consists in the fact that the criteria proposed for authenticity are weaker than those which constitute his prescription for dialectical method by the decisive exclusion of the principle of completeness of the Notion. By this deletion, dialectic is rendered in principle falsifiable by the criteria specified. The second consists in the fact that, by diverting attention from the transcending (because partially undetermined except in speculation) Notion, I have given more concentrated attention to what is regarded as the not necessarily determined content of history and have provided criteria for judging whether it is indeed appropriately determined, and to what degree, within a dialectical exposition. The weakened criteria for formal adequacy have made the requirement of a material test apparent.

From the above it may be correctly construed that as the *content* of a dialectical exposition warranted for belief is determined to be such by virtue of having taken on the *form* of authentic dialectic, and as the form of authentic dialectic cannot be actual except it have been an actual content, the form and content of authentic dialectic warranted for belief are interdependent aspects of the same actuality. From this it follows that the concepts "authentic" and "warranted for belief" are correlatives. Like form and content, with which they are respectively concerned, one cannot be defined except by reference to the other; the name of each is the name of a relation obtaining between them viewed from one perspective. The distinction which they jointly represent is a provisional one which has no final status outside of Truth, the ideal limit to which it points. At absolute zero the poles of the discrimination merge, like every discrimination conceived dialectically. The distinction is not on this account done away with,[59] however, but contained and made fully explicit within the more inclusive concept, which represents the ideal with all its compelling power. It is methodologically essential to maintain this distinction, I propose, because man, while he envisions this absolute zero, and indeed may find it plausible to regard it as his birthplace and End, does not live there, but in a world between this limit and diffuse and disparate appearances and impressions. So long as man lives in a region in which action, passion, and method are essential, I would propose, so long as he ex-ists, and even if he ex-ists as a philosopher, it is essential. Truth being the end of a search and not the beginning, even if it conditions the beginning, it cannot be approached too hastily. The two-fold test for dialectic, accordingly, is designed as a tool to be used on the way.

Hegel, I believe, suffered a disadvantage in beginning every major exposition of dialectic following the *Phenomenology* with the Notion full-blown as his already justified starting point. I hope to have proposed a strategy which may seem plausible for reversing the order in which the Notion in its completeness comes into prominence as an aspect of dialectic. Such a reversal may point the way toward the appropriation of more of the wealth of significant insight for our time to be found in Hegel's philosophy. Rather than beginning with the Notion, it seems at least philosophically more sound to continue to point to it and to continue explicating the pointer. This preference is not greatly at odds except in point of emphasis, I suspect, with the final results in Hegel's philosophy, although it is at odds with the philosophical method he prescribed and practiced, and by which he proposed to arrive at these results. Most particularly, I should like to see it brought to the appropriation of his approach to the philosophy of religion.

NOTES

1. Yvon Gauthier, "Logique Hégélienne et Formalisation," *Dialogue*, Vol. VI, No. 2 (1967), pp. 151-65; Michael Kosok, "The Formalization of Hegel's Dialectical Logic," *International Philosophical Quarterly*, Vol. VI, No. 4 (1966), pp. 596-631; and F. G. Asenjo, "Dialectic Logic," *Logique et Analyse*, No. 4 (1965), pp. 321-6.

2. "The logic," "The dialectic of the logical Idea," and "The Notion," following Hegel, will herein have the same reference, although each will suggest a different emphasis. "The Notion" emphasizes the unity of the system of logic.

3. "Truth comes only with the Notion . . . ." *Wallace*, p .155 .

4. Für sich est die absolute Idee, weil kein Übergehen noch Voraussetzen und überhaupt keine Bestimmtheit, welche nicht flüssig und durchsichtig wäre, in ihr ist, die reine Form der Begriffs, die ihren Inhalt als sich selbst anschaut. Sie ist sich Inhalt, in sofern sie das ideelle Unterscheiben ihrer selbst von sich, und das eine der Unterschiedenen die Identität mit sich ist, in der aber die Totalität der Form als das System der Inhaltsbestimmungen enthalten ist." *EdpW*, pp. 408f. In translation,

"Seeing that there is in it no transition, or presupposition, and in general no specific character other than what is fluid and transparent, the Absolute Idea is itself the pure form of the Notion, which contemplates its content as its own self. It is its own content, insofar as it ideally distinguishes itself from itself, and the one of the two things distinguished is a self-identity in which however is contained the totality of the form as the system of terms describing its content." *Wallace*, p. 374.

It may be noted that, from the perspective of the Notion regarded as inclusive, the Notion itself is not abstract in such a sense as to admit of a formalization that would stand as adequate apart from the concrete process in which it is exhibited. It is because Hegel's logic is a logic of *concepts*, and concepts shaped by encounter with the lived world in which choices and discriminations must be made, it seems fair to say, that one can even come to have an intimation of what he means by the Notion. This logic *is* a formalization; the replacement of concepts by variables of which the concepts are then regarded as instantiations results in a further removal of the system from the ideal of the Notion beside which nothing can be set. In effect, then, Kosok's formalization does not proceed in a manner differing from mine except for this important difference. In proposing a test for authenticity, I do not propose to be formalizing Hegel's logic, but merely restating some necessary conditions of dialectic.

5. The fact that in the dialectic of Absolute Spirit the Notion as God the Father is transcendent and other to the world may be thought to be an exception. But when it is noted that God as Spirit here plays the mediating role between transcendence (God the Father) and Immanence (God the Son) which is assigned to the "Notion" conceived as dialectical method, it may be seen not to be an exception.

6. "Die inhalte der Logik, die das Denken (nicht das Bewusstsein!) zu ihrem Elemente haben, sind also Gedachtheiten, *Denk*bestimmungen, '*bestimmte* Begriffe,'

die der Begriff oder das selbstische Wissen sich aus sich selber als Inhalt vergegeben hat. Die 'reinen Bestimmtheiten' des Denkens, wie etwa Sein, Wesen, Erkennen (Wahres), Tun (Gutes), sind dieserhalb in ihrer Inhaltlichkeit und Sachlichkeit im Gegensatz zu *sinnlichen* Gegenständen des Bewusstseins immer schon mit Selbstheit und Wissen durchtränkt, andernfalls wären es weder Denkbestimmungen, noch vermochten sie sich dialektisch aus sich selber ohne Eingreifen des zuschauenden Wissens zu entwickeln." Bernhard Lakebrink, *Hegels Logik und die Tradition der Selbstbestimmung* (Leiden: E. J. Brill, 1968), p. 109.

7. "Die Erhebung des Begriffs über das Leben ist, dass seine Realität die zur Allgemeinheit befreite Begriffsform ist. Durch dieses Urtheil ist die idee verdoppelt, in den subjectiven Begriff, dessen Realität er selbst, und in den objectiven, der als Leben ist." *WdL*, II, "Die subjective Logik," p. 255. The translation is from *SL*, II, p. 416.

8. Theodor Haering, *Hegel: Sein Wollen und sein Werk*, II Band (Leipzig: Scientia Verlag Aalen, 1963), p. 120.

9. *Wallace*, p. 352.

10. *WdL*, II, p. 256.

11. See footnote No. 12 following.

12. "Es fangt deswegen in der That für die Methode keine neue Weise damit an, dass sich durch das erste ihrer Resultate ein inhalt bestimmt habe . . . ." *WdL*, II, p. 338.

13. "Die Vereinigung des Allgemeinen, an und für sich Seienden überhaupt, und des Einzelnen, des Subjektiven, dass sie allein die Wahrheit seh, diess ist speculativer Natur, und wird in dieser allgemeinen Form in der Logik abgehandelt. Aber im Gange der Weltgeschichte selbst, als noch im Fortschreiten begriffenen Gänge, ist der reine lesste Zweck der Geschichte noch nicht der inhalt des Bedürfnisses und Interesses, und indem dieses bewußtlos darüber ist, ist das Allgemeine dennoch in den besonderen Zwecken, und vollbringt sich durch dieselben." *VPG*, pp. 32f. The translation is from *LPH*, p. 25.

The most adequate explanation of Hegel's position as it pertains to this matter, I believe, is contained in the account of the trinity in the dialectic of Absolute Spirit from which the above is taken. Here the Notion, transcendent and in itself, is God the Father, the Notion realizing itself in concrete reality is God the Son, and God as Spirit is the reconciliation and mediation of these. The dialectic of Absolute Spirit is exhibited identically, to the last sub-moment, so far as I have been able to determine, in *VPG* and *VPR*, although different interests are at work in the elaboration upon the dialectic in the two works.

14. *Phen*, p. 765. Here, Spirit is held to be the content of its own consciousness in the form of pure substance. Thought is descending into existence, or individuality. The middle term between these two is their synthesis, the consciousness of passing into otherness. The third stage is self-consciousness, realized in the return from this presentation and from this otherness.

15. "The Formalization of Hegel's Dialectical Logic," p. 262.

16. Consider, for example, Hegel on "Lordship and Bondage," "Stoicism," and "The Unhappy Consciousness," and especially, in the latter, where "Dem Beußtsein kann daher nur des Grab seines Lebens zur Gegenwart kommen." *Phän*, p. 160.

17. More needs to be said here; I have intended no more than to justify a conclusion adequate to my present needs. Koyré's analysis of "das Jetzt," which has contributed to the understanding of some roots of existentialism in Hegel, will bear out the point. A. Koyré, *Études d'Histoire de la Pensée Philosophique* (Paris: Armand Colin, Cahiers des Annales, 1961), "Hegel à Jena," pp. 135-73; see especially pp. 171f. Also, see, Bernhard Lakebrink, *Hegels Logik und die Tradition der Selbstbestimmung*, "Die Existentiale Ausdeutung von Hegel's Logik,' pp. 58-70, and "Die Schranke und das Sollen," pp. 144-53.

244   *Darrel E. Christensen*

18. *EdpW*, p. 352.

19. *Ibid.*, p. 374. In the parallel but expanded account in *WdL*, Hegel notes, "Aus dieser Bestimmung des endlichen Erkennens erhellt unmittelbar, dass es ein Widerspruch ist, der sich selbst aufhebt; – der Widerspruch einer Wahrheit, die zugleich nicht Wahrheit sein soll; – eines Erkennens dessen, was ist, welches zugleich das Ding-an-sich nicht erkennt." *WdL*, II, p. 268.

20. The quotation marks indicate a use of the term "Notion" likely to be interpreted equivocally.

The Notion is for Hegel one and inclusive. "Objective Notion" then, for example, refers to this one and inclusive unity of form and content as in part explicitly and in part implicitly held to be the essential actuality of the world regarded as object and as distinct from mind, but which cannot be regarded as what it is held to be apart from the Notion. It cannot be regarded as what it is apart from its having been determined by the dialectic of the subject and the object spheres as implicitly complete and inclusive of both. The case with respect to the "subjective Notion" is similar.

"Further, besides the differences between properties, the distinction between the Notion and its actualization emerges in concrete things. In Nature and in Spirit the Notion has an external representation, where its determinateness shows itself as dependent upon the external, as transitoriness and inadequacy. Thus, although the actual something shows in itself what it ought to be, it can equally show (according to the negative Notion-judgment) that its actuality corresponds to this Notion but imperfectly, or that it is bad." *SL*, II, pp. 440f. For the original, see *WdL*, II, p. 286.

In the case of the philosopher, here also the "Notion-form" is completely explicit at the point of beginning.

21. "Die Extreme bleiben verschiedene, weil Subjekt, Methode und Objekt nicht als der eine identische Begriff gesetzt sind . . . ." *WdL*, II, p. 321. The translation is from *SL*, II, p. 469.

22. "Im wahrhaften Erkennen dagegen ist die Methode nicht nur eine Menge gewisser Bestimmungen, sondern das An- und Für-sich-Bestimmtsein des Begriffs, der die Mitte nur darum ist, weil er ebenso sehr die Bedeutung des Objektiven hat, das im Schlußatze daher nicht nur eine äussere Bestimmtheit durch die Methode erlangt, sondern in seiner Identität mit dem subjektiven Begriffe gesetzt ist." *WdL*, II, pp. 332f. The translation is from *SL*, II, p. 469.

23. "Die Methode ist daraus als der sich selbst wissende, sich als das Absolute, sowohl Subjektive als Objektive, zum Gegenstände habende Begriff, somit als das reine Entsprechen des Begriffs und seiner Realität, als eine Existenz, die er selbst ist, hervorgegangen." *WdL*, II, pp. 332f. The translation is from *SL*, II, p. 468.

24. "Wie der Begriff für sich betrachtet wurde, erschien er in seiner Unmittelbarkeit: die Reflexion oder der ihn betrachtende Begriff fiel in unser Wissen. Die Methode ist diese Wissen selbst, für das er nicht nur als Gegenstand, sondern als dessen eigenes, subjectives Thun ist, als das Instrument und Mittel der erkennenden Thätigkeit, von ihr unterschieden, aber als deren eigene Wesenheit." *WdL*, II, p. 320. The translation is from *SL*, II, p. 469.

25. *WdL*, II, p. 324. For a translation, see *SL*, II, p. 471.

26. In discussing "beginnings" of dialectical developments "like Being, Essence, and Universality," Hegel notes: "Now the determinateness which belongs to them is their immediate determinateness if they are taken for themselves, and is a determinateness as much as one which applies to any content; it therefore requires a derivation; and *it is indifferent to the method whether it is taken as determinateness of form or of content*" (Italics by the author). *SL*, Vol. II, pp. 481f. For the original, see *WdL*, II, p. 337.

As Nicolin notes, so long as form and content are distinct, the result, for Hegel, has no more than the status of formal truth, something abstract. Freedom is the condition where form and content are commensurate and indistinguishable. Friedhelm Nicolin, *Grundlinien einer Geistes wissenschaftlichen Pädogogik*, Inaugural-Dissertation zur Erlangung der Doktorwurde Genehmight von der Philosophischen Fakultät (Bonn, 1955), pp. 185f.

Were the containment within the Notion of these discriminations (consistent with Hegel's own principles) to be emphasized, however, the two-fold test I am to propose would appear less alien to Hegel's philosophy than the above suggests.

27. My choice of the term "warranted belief" for use in this context was influenced by its use in the writings and lectures of W. H. Werkmeister. W. H. Werkmeister, *The Basis and Structure of Knowledge* (New York: Harper and Brothers Co., 1948).

28. Where such a concept is held, its meaning lies precisely in that the Notion given in this moment of Truth in some sense includes all meaning, and I think it would be difficult to show such a concept meaningless.

29. "The Formalization of Hegel's Dialectical Logic," See pp. 598-605.

30. This account might with some labor have been selectively drawn from Hegel's statement of method in *SL*. It is based upon many sources, however, and most particularly by reflection on the dialectic of Absolute Spirit. While no short passage is to be found in these pages which, taken out of context, yields the sense of this account, it may, nonetheless, be drawn from *VPR*, Vol. I, "Die Eintheilung," pp. 77-100.

31. This, in keeping with the fact that this is to be a purely formal test.

32. Kosok defines dialectical opposites as "positive contraries which become negative subcontraries upon their mutual implication in a non-identity relation." I find this definition commensurate with the dialectic here considered, although Kosok's elaboration of it goes beyond what may be found exemplified here (see paragraph following), rendering this an unsuitable test case of whether it may be found exemplified in Hegel's dialectic. This definition may seem at first to be incompatible with the fact that, characteristically, the opposition between dialectical opposites is an apparent opposition only. The seeing through the apparent opposition is of course reflected in a more inclusive concept. But how, it may be asked, may an opposition which was only apparent be a logical relation of contrariety? The objection, however, fails to take account of the fact that determined identities are not being considered here, but the process by which an identity is established from something in question. That which is negatively referred to, (-e), is not a determined identity, nor is (e) in relation to (-e) a determined identity. Its indeterminacy is precisely what is under consideration. A determined identity results from the apprehension that each is a boundary condition of the other, and that either, to be thought at all, must be thought of in this way. To regard them as contraries so long as each is conceived as negatively present for the other seems intuitively correct, following Kosok, as long as the presence of an undetermined content is not reflected in the formula.

It seems to me, however, that an undetermined content would need to be (positively) reflected in the formula for the latter to be adequate to the test of authenticity I have proposed. The reconception of Kosok's "negative presence" as "a negatively designated presence of a necessary but undertermined content," however, might serve. See "The Formalization of Hegel's Dialectical Logic," pp. 608f.

33. Hegel, with his desire to justify the identity of being and thought, viewed dialectically related concepts as related by inclusion in the way that a chair is in a room, which is in a building, which is in a block, which is in a city, which is in a county, etc. The essential meaning of each of a series of dialectically related concepts is contained in the next along with (what is at least implicit in the meaning of

the next, the more inclusive, concept) the discrimination between what was encompassed in the old meaning and what is added to form the new. Observing the meanings shared between various clusters of terms (representative of concepts), and supposing that the simplest explanation of this might lie in related points of origin, he contrived to revisit the scenes of the derivations.

34. See df. of dialectic, p. 232.

35. It will be noted that in this truncated account, I have omitted mention of the hallmark of Hegelian dialectic, the dialectic of subject and object. While the subjective "Notion" has been bracketed, this is not the main reason for this omission. I have preferred to regard this as a particular dialectical exposition (even though from Hegel's perspective it is the whole of it) rather than as an aspect of method. Although it undeniably belongs to method as Hegel understands method, the bracketing procedure herein employed would be less easily maintained without compromise by regarding it as method.

Since my purpose here is not to extend dialectical logic as a "formal" system as we think of a formal system in logic today, the exposition of criteria for authenticity has been kept brief.

36. *Phen*, pp. 149-52.

37. *Ibid.*, pp. 162-5.

38. For a list of terms so related by inclusion, see the "Table of Categories" in *SL*, Vol. I, inside back cover.

39. See Charles Hegel's Vorrede to *VPH*, p. vii (*LPH*, p. xiii).

40. The analysis reported on here appears in part and in altered form, owing to a difference in intent and context, in a doctoral dissertation completed at the School of Philosophy of the University of Southern California in 1965. Darrel E. Christensen, "Some Implications for the Doctrine of God of Hegel's Concept of Thought as Mediation," (Ann Arbor, Michigan: University Microfilms, Inc., 65-9969), pp. 92-110, hereafter referred to as *Thought as Mediation*.

My analysis is based upon Philipp Marheineke's 1840 edition, sometimes referred to as the second edition, following as it does the edition hastily compiled shortly following Hegel's death and published in 1832. *VPR*, II.

In editing this work, Marheineke incorporated into it several important papers found amongst Hegel's MSS in which his ideas were developed more fully than in sketches previously used. The only English translation of the work is *LPR*.

41. In the case of terms representative of the actual world, I should suppose that, strictly speaking, it would not be possible to complete such a proof.

42. The treatment of two of these will be relegated to footnote 46.

43. Terms of the dialectic will be italicized in the foregoing accounts.

44. It may be argued that this conclusion is of trivial importance; nevertheless, this phase of Hegel's dialectic seems to present a crucial case for testing a prescription for dialectic with Hegel's actual exposition of it. His weaker sense of *Widerspruch* may be lost sight of elsewhere, with all sorts of resultant muddles. By the use of the analogy of a sailing ship tacking against the wind, McTaggart reflected this weaker sense of "opposition" which is made evident in this phase of the dialectic, and which I think is the sense which Hegel with more or less consistency intended throughout his dialectic. John McTaggart, Ellis McTaggart, *Studies in Hegelian Dialectic* (Cambridge: University Press, 1922), pp. 144f.

In any case, the weaker sense of opposition is commensurate with the proposed criteria for authenticity, which is not intended to require a dramatic sense of opposition between terms, which would necessarily be conditioned by their existential meanings.

45. *VPR*, I, pp. 75f.

46. Two other "minor" deviations which deserve mention occur within what is

clearly proposed as a dialectical development of the sacraments within *Absolute Religion. VPR*, II, pp. 388ff. One of these is constituted by the fact that it is not made explicit that the second moment is determined by the first. This (probably accidental) lack of explicitness is evident in two other instances within the dialectic being considered, both of which, like the case of the second moment of the dialectic of the Lord's Supper, are submoments several orders of subsumption removed from the primary triad of religion.

The other irregularity is in the third moment of the dialectic of *the sacraments*. According to this conception, God is present only in memory and His presence is thus merely immediate and subjective. Here, Hegel holds that the truth has been lowered to the prose of the enlightenment. The mediation of the representation of *God as outer* and of *the inwardness of faith*, which, were the form of the dialectic followed out, would constitute the third moment, is apparently conceived as taking place in the second. Curiously enough, the third moment, exemplified by the Reformed doctrine, is found inferior to the second moment, exemplified by the Lutheran doctrine. The concept of the third doctrine is not inclusive of the meaning of the second. Thus although the possibility of its being warranted for belief on historical grounds is not thereby ruled out, the account is dialectically unauthentic, since the criteria proposed for authentic dialectic do not permit what might be called regression in a dialectical account. The irregularity here is similar in type to that exhibited in the religion of untility, shortly to be considered.

The dialectic of *the sacraments* is several orders of subsumption removed from the primary triad of the dialectic of religion. If one regards triads within the dialectic which are subsumed under other triads at successively "lower" levels as belonging to successively more detailed expositions of religion, then the deletion of this phase would not materially affect the dialectic as a whole. It would be notable only to a person with a special interest in the dialectical development within which it is immediately subsumed. The case is otherwise with respect to the religion of *utility*, to which I shall give more detailed consideration. Owing to the position of this religion within the dialectic, the want of conformity here is of greater interest and its analysis more instructive.

47. *VPR*, II. For the metaphysical concept of the religion of spiritual individuality, see pp. 10-41. The third moment, the religion of utility, is presented on pp. 156-190.

48. *VPR*, II, pp. 157f.

49. It is difficult to find any reason within the dialectic for granting to Roman religion as here conceived a status other than that of a particular form of Greek religion. Hegel's reason for doing so, along with the reason for the non-dialectical development of the religion of utility, may lie in the historical prominence of the Roman state and its status for him as a model of the modern national state. Holding, as he does, that the state is the highest concrete embodiment of Spirit, and that religion is the foundation of the state, he seems to accord to Roman religion a status which he failed to justify by the dialectic.

50. *Thought as Mediation*, pp. 110-18.

51. "Während daher in der Nothwendigkeit [sic] eine Bestimmung von der andern abhängig ist und die Bestimmtheit untergeht, so ist der Zweck, als identität unterschiedener, wirklicher gesetzt, die an und für sich bestimmte Einheit, die sich gegen andere Bestimmtheit in ihrer Bestimmtheit erhält." *VPR*, II, p. 160. The translation is from *LPR*, II, p. 293.

52. This is generally in keeping with Hegel's declared intention. *LPH*, p. 9.

53. If for the Notion we substitute dialectical method, then it is the posited determination mentioned in the latter part of the following which the proposed test for warranted belief may be seen to supplement.

"In the syllogism in which now the subjective idea combines with objectivity, the first premise is that same form of immediate seizure and relation of the Notion to the Object that we saw in the End-relation. The determining activity of the Notion upon the object is an immediate communication; it spreads itself upon the Object unresisted. Here the Notion remains in its pure self-identity; but this its immediate introreflection equally has the determination of objective immediacy; that which for it is its own determination is equally a Being, for it is the first negation of the presupposition. The posited determination consequently counts equally as a presupposition which is merely found or as the taking up of something which is given, wherein the activity of the Notion itself is rather said to consist in this, that it is negative as against itself, restraining itself in face of the given and making itself passive, so that the given may be able to show itself as it is in itself and not as determined by the subject." *SL*, II, pp. 427f. See *WdL*, II, pp. 269f for the original.

Note that the posited determination here mentioned counts merely as a *presupposition* and as one *merely found* where there is an openness to *something given*. Thus we find here reflected the perspective prescribed herein by the bracketing procedure previously mentioned.

54. *Vernunft*, as herein used being understood to be the Notion, the following will pertain.

"The only thought which philosophy brings with it to the contemplation of history, is the simple conception of Reason [*Vernunft*]; that Reason is the Sovereign of the World; that the history of the world, therefore, presents us with a rational [*vernünftig*] process. This conviction and intuition is a hypothesis in the domain of history as such. In that of Philosophy it is no hypothesis." *LPH*, p. 9. For the original, see *VPG*, pp. 12f.

I do not propose to take up here to what degree Hegel's expectations respecting the underlying identity of phenomenological and historical processes (presented as realized in the Notion) was justified.

55. This is in keeping with my intention to render a dialectical account falsifiable without presupposing what Hegel held to be the result of his *Phänomenologie*, the Notion in its radical inclusiveness.

56. Kosok has gone some way in developing the relationship between Goedel's proof and the more inclusive principle within dialectical logic of which, I think, it may fairly be regarded as a particularization. "The Formalization of Hegel's Dialectical Logic," especially pp. 615-21.

I called attention to this matter in "The False Moment in Hegel's Dialectic of Religion" (unpublished), submitted to the *Journal of the History of Philosophy* in 1965.

57. Where the apprehension of a causal connection in its novelty is in question or the apprehension of causality as such, the ultimate appeal must, I suspect, be a subjective ground of which account cannot be taken here or without unbracketing the subjective "Notion" or some such notion. Important to the perspective where the brackets are retained is that correspondence tests are admitted with clear consistency.

58. Hegel allowed, it should be noted, that the various religions contain more than those traits of which he provided an historical account, noting that essential moments of the Notion show themselves (cumulatively) at every stage of the development of the religious consciousness. *VPR*, I, p. 92 or *LPR*, I, pp. 76f.

59. See my discussion of "aufgehoben" in "Nelson and Hegel on the Philosophy of History," *Journal of the History of Ideas*, Vol. XXV, No. 3 (1964), pp. 439-444. See pp. 443f.

COMMENT ON

DARREL E. CHRISTENSEN
"AUTHENTICITY" AND "WARRANTED BELIEF"
IN HEGEL'S DIALECTIC OF RELIGION

by

J. N. Findlay

Professor Christensen has written a difficult but valuable paper on Hegel, and he has also introduced me to another difficult but valuable paper on Hegel, that of Michael Kosok in the *International Philosophical Quarterly* of October 1966. Mr. Kosok and Professor Christensen share the belief that the Hegelian dialectic has a deductive pattern in terms of which it can be tested for formal validity, or, as Mr. Christensen existentially calls it, "authenticity": Mr. Kosok further thinks that the formal pattern of the Hegelian dialectic is formalizable, at least in a general way, though Professor Christensen is unwilling to go as far as this. Professor Christensen further thinks that Hegel's dialectic has a content, a material, which can at a certain level of abstraction be distinguished from its formal pattern, and that, in virtue of such a content, Hegel's dialectic can be regarded as rightly or wrongly construing some realm of fact or experience. It can, Professor Christensen says, have "warranted credibility"; for this strange, unsuitable Deweyan locution I should like to substitute "material adequacy." Now all these contentions, both of Mr. Christensen and Mr. Kosok, I should certainly have rejected out of hand before I read their two articles, for reasons very similar to those which Mr. Christensen rehearses in the first section of his paper. One reason is that it seems utterly un-Hegelian to bring the ever-living strategy of the dialectic, its essentially revisionary, (meta)-character, in virtue of which it is always criticizing its own past results and procedures from a new, outside, richer, less abstract standpoint, under a single, unvarying formula however complex: to do this would ignore its livingness, its penetrative, subversive insight, its essential creative novelty. We have with difficulty disenthralled ourselves of the Thesis-Antithesis-Synthesis pattern which had some meaning for Kant, Fichte and Schelling, but which is wholly inadequate to the dialectic of Hegel: we do not wish to enslave ourselves to a new formalism. We have, in fact, an explicit Hegelian warning against such formalism in what Hegel says of Schelling.

After reading Mr. Kosok's paper I have, however, become convinced that, provided the notion of dialectical pattern is interpreted with sufficient generality, and the notion of negation, in particular, is given the general meaning of specific otherness, so as to cover both the case of the sheerly antithetical and the case of the complementary, it is not an absurd project to formalize the general pattern of Hegel's discourse, though one then has rather an ideal exemplar that he *might* have followed than one that he did follow, and which reaches some outcomes, quite exciting, that differ quite a little from those actually reached by Hegel. Being convinced that there is *something,* however criticizable, in Mr. Kosok's paper, I am even more convinced that there is something in Mr. Christensen's notion of "authenticity." We can lay down some tests for a genuine dialectical deepening, however wide the differences of the direction in which it may lie: these tests will of course be tests derived from Hegel's own procedure, they will be immanent, not external tests. But, though immanent, they will enable us to criticize Hegel's own procedure, all of which will be in line with Hegel's own view that all genuine criticism is self-criticism, the self-revelation and self-explication of one basic *Begriff* or Idea. And once one has separated off a quasi-formal criterion or set of criteria of this sort, one also requires a criterion to take account of the other side of Hegel's treatment, its relation to content, its rich empiricism, its raising of the incredible complexities and contingencies of individual encounter into the pure ether, the quietude of thought. If Hegel's system is an ultimate, all-solvent Absolutism, then it really must dissolve at least some of the main surds of history and empirical fact, and, where its solvent action ceases, it must be plain why it ceases, why one is precisely there given over to the chequered play of contingency, which is for Hegel, as for any really sound metaphysician, an ineliminable part of the world. And here again one must be able both to elicit these criteria of warranted credibility, as Professor Christensen calls them, from Hegel's own work, and to apply them critically to his own work. We must be able to decide why Hegel's equation of the guillotine with the Categorical Imperative is really only a brilliant *jeu d'esprit,* whereas his dialectical treatment of many electrical and chemical phenomena, and of some artistic, philosophical and historical transitions, is profoundly illuminating and correct.

I return, however, to the detail of Professor Christensen's paper. Professor Christensen first rightly points out that there is no common schema, neatly stateable in terms of variables, which expresses the general pattern of Hegel's treatment, and which can be applied to all the specific notions and specific transitions in that treatment. For Hegel there is and can be no pure dialectical form which is separable from the notional contents which are its own material, its self in the form of self, and which does not vary with them and with their specific demands for completion. And, equally, we cannot abstract the pure Notion from the Notion embodied in Nature and History, and set it over against the latter, since the Notion embodied in Nature and History simply *is* the pure Notion more fully and necessarily self-specified. Even dialectic, as the pure method of Hegel, cannot be separated from the more rarefied and more concrete forms among which it operates. As Christensen rightly says, the Idea, Nature and Spirit are terms – I think he slips in calling them "propositions" – in the Absolute Syllogism, which expresses itself in their mutual interplay and inter-connection more than in any of them considered singly. Christensen then holds that there are momentary throbs of existence, cases of *das Jetzt*, in which the Notion is individualized and rendered intuitive in the fullest manner, and that it is only in such moments, and in the embracing intuition that they involve, that we can have a cogent grasp of what is because it must be, and of what must be because it is. It is very right to call attention to these existential, momentaristic aspects of Hegel, even though they are adumbrated rather than fully stated in the text. Hegel stresses *das Allgemeine* and *das Besondere* in his Notions, but *das Einzelne* is also always an understood element in them, understressed because he does not wish to give comfort to the protagonists of *Gefühl* and *Anschauung*.

Christensen then rightly observes that Hegel's method presents great difficulties to the man who wants to understand the true rationale of his thought-movements, and use it to test them, the same sort of difficulties that Descartes had with the proofs of the classical geometers, who never explain the order of discovery and construction which must have preceded the order of exposition and demonstration. A philosophical method is only valuable if it is also corrigible, if one can sort out cases where it is wrongly and unfruitfully applied from cases where the reverse is the case. A non-method like Heidegger's where practically anything can at each point be darkly and dogmatically proclaimed as the true, neglected way of regarding something, is not a method that can be applied by those not themselves subject to a periodic sibylline afflatus. Though the truth lies in a complete working out, and in it alone, there must still be pointers of some sort which tell us when our working out *is* a working out, and when it is adequate to some great territory of Nature and Spirit. There is either a deep unfrankness, or an inspired self-ignorance, or a mixture of both, in Hegel's failure to say how the dialectic came across to him, and Mr. Christensen is absolutely right in inquiring into the workings of his personal as opposed to his official dialectic. This personal dialectic is of course in essence everybody's dialectic.

Professor Christensen then sets forth a definition of dialectical progress in terms of an increment of discrimination. I should translate this into a cogent enrichment or a cogent differentiation. Every step in the dialectic, being a reflection upon the previous stage, necessarily brings into play new concepts which apply *to* the goings-on at the previous level but which are not found *among* them. This enrichment as one goes from type to type, or from language to meta-language, is a commonplace of modern formalism: we now know that, contrary to empiricism and nominalism, the realm of notions has an infinite overhangingness and top-heaviness rather than the tapering, pyramidal structure fondly believed in. It is the empirical base which is the poorest and most abstract, its notional reinterpretation etc, the richest and most astonishing. Hegel anticipated this result, but it has taken the rest of the world a century and a half to catch up with him. Mr. Christensen, following Mr. Kosok, follows a scheme in which negation is given an infinite series of reinterpretations: *e* being flanked by a negation *-e* at its own level which does not really exhaust the alternatives, which is then succeeded by a higher-level *e-e* which is a new concept, only apparently self-contradictory, which generates a new negation at its own level, and so on. The principle is of course that the sort of isolation of the *e's* from the not-*e's* which the Understanding essays, is forever unattainable, is in fact the very type of the absurd and untrue. It always brings into view some underlying unity differentiated into the mutually sundered classes which is both *e* and not-*e*, in some deeper, non-contradictory sense.

The whole notion of the dialectic here set forth is one of which I approve, though I would stress that what Professor Christensen expresses by a sign of negation could more appropriately have been expressed by a sign of complementarity or mutual requirement. Thus Appearance, *Erscheinung,* is not merely what is excluded by Essence, *Wesen,* but what completes it and makes it viable, and so for Necessity and Contingency, or End and Means, or Teleology and Mechanism and whatever. It is a well-known fact that the mutual built-inness and requirement of categories becomes so much a feature of the dialectic at higher levels that we are in the end rather dealing with a variously stressed total self-explanatoriness than with either mutual explanation or mere mutual otherness. What emerges from all these broodings and meta-broodings is in fact something which is not something, and which does not strictly speaking *emerge* from the process at all but simply *is* this process: the Spirit of Broodingness and Meta-Broodingness itself, the eternal openness and self-revision of the Idea and Spirit.

I do not, however, wish to give a lecture on Mahayana Buddhism, but to comment on Professor Christensen's paper. Mr. Christensen considers Hegel's dialectic in so far as it concerns the Jewish, the Greek and the Roman religions. Briefly, the Jewish religion places the Divine Self-explanatoriness so out of the world, and so stresses its sublime exclusion of non-self-explanatory, finite things, so limits its presence in them to the non-individual Family, as to make it just one non-self-explanatory thing among others, and so to swing over to a view where self-explanatoriness is dispersed among finite, natural realities, the classic Gods, and where its background unity becomes attenuated to the explicit abstract notion of *Ananke*. This is the Greek Religion of Beauty, the authentic dialectical development of the Jewish Religion of Sublimity. This *Ananke* now proves incapable of doing the unifying work involved, and consolidates itself in the Roman State-mechanism, presiding over individual legal atoms. Here all the gay incarnations of the Self-explanatory, the innumerable, beautiful gods, yield place to the serious Gods of Rome, each strictly confined to some wholly useful social function. What one has, Professor Christensen points out, is a mere blurring of the oppositions involved in the two previous dialectical phases, and a regression to a phase which does not really include and transcend them. Consequently he infers Roman Religion not to be an authentic phase of the dialectic, and he almost suggests that the Religion of Rome was a low and untrue existence. I am partly in sympathy with Professor Christensen, partly out of sympathy with him. In philosophy, which I do understand from within, I am certainly inclined to think that some thinkers, vastly influential, really do not count for much in the vital movement of philosophical thought. I abstain from mentioning names, but some of those I am not mentioning have been mentioned at this meeting. Perhaps the Roman religion does not count for much in the vital development of religious experience: I have always thought this of the Mohammedan religion. But one also wonders whether retreats into mediocrity after one-sided exaggeration may not sometimes be truly progressive phases, e.g. the long period of XVIIth and XVIIIth century "correctness" in poetry which took over from the XVth and XVIth century exuberance and made the Romantic revival possible.

In Section IV Mr. Christensen, using his strange Deweyan term of "warranted credibility," considers the adequacy of a dialectical account to an ordinary piece of non-philosophical history. Mr. Christensen here ignores the fact that there is a broad swath of the Hegelian system, the Philosophy of Nature, where history is not in question, since Nature only has a logical not a temporal Order. There are also considerable sections of Anthropology, Phenomenology and Psychology which are not developed by Hegel in an historical manner. These parts of Hegel are deeply true, in my view, to many aspects of external nature and the internal life of the mind, and would, I am sure, require criteria of warranted credibility as much as do the parts of Objective Spirit and Absolute Spirit which are definitely historical.

Mr. Christensen thinks that *if* History is first decanted through the procedures of causal explanation, and *if* it can then also be shown to be a progression in which the more differentiated grows continuously out of the less differentiated, it is then ripe for dialectical treatment. We can then see or fail to see forms of the Notion displaying themselves in it and evolving into higher notional forms. Professor Christensen thinks that Hegel achieved this adequacy to the given in his treatment of Christianity but not in his treatment of Judaism. I am inclined to agree. And as a person very much interested in Hegel's treatment of the ladder of natural forms which is set forth in the *Naturphilosophie*, I think that he achieved remarkable adequacy in his treatment (contrary to general belief), and that, had he had the facts of evolution to build upon, his treatment would have been even more adequate. But I confess that I do not know what the criteria of warranted credibility really are except in a very general way, and have not been helped to more clarity by the discussions of Professor Christensen. Certain dialectical treatments of Nature and History of Hegel and others seem to me profoundly illuminating, but I cannot further illuminate this illumination.

In conclusion I think Professor Christensen has raised some new and interesting questions regarding the nature and validity of Hegel's dialectical method. I myself have learnt from Hegel to *use* what I think to be a version of his method in some of my writings, but I confess to being like the poet interrogated by Socrates: I do not fully understand dialectical method, though I understand isolated instances of it. Possibly it is simply wrong to try to characterize dialectic generally: one must engage in it and live it to sample its perennial novelty.

REPLY TO PROFESSOR FINDLAY

by

Darrel E. Christensen

Before reading the article by Mr. Kosok and my own paper, Professor Findlay generously concedes that he should have rejected out of hand the suggestion that Hegel's dialectic follows a deductive pattern in terms of which it can be tested for formal validity. "One reason is that it seems utterly un-Hegelian to bring the ever-living strategy of the dialectic, its essentially revisionary, (meta)-character in virtue of which it is always criticizing its own results and procedures from a new, outside, richer, less abstract standpoint, under a single unvarying formula..." Now, he concedes that "it is not an absurd project to formalize the general pattern of Hegel's discourse," though what one then comes up with is "an ideal exemplar which Hegel *might* have followed rather than one he did follow."

I am not centrally concerned as to whether or not the strategy of a two-fold test for a dialectical account of history is Hegelian or not. Indeed, I have pointed out the sense in which this involves a marked departure from Hegel. The suggestion that it is un-Hegelian because it aims to arrive at a process form universally applicable to the type of account to which it is intended to be applicable, however, is unacceptable. Professor Findlay's contention in this regard can only be sustained, I think, by a (perhaps mistakenly apologetic) denial of the formalism in Hegel and by regarding Hegel's continuous concern throughout his major works with dialectical method as an empty and insincere pretense at formalism. The burden of evidence is very great indeed upon one who would take this position – substantially greater, I should say, than a decade ago when Professor Findlay's *Hegel – A Re-examination* appeared.

Granted that the extravagant conception Hegel had of his task was never fully complemented by execution (I have noted why, on principle, it could not be), let it not be denied that he was a formalist in the sense that he projected a very grand formal plan to be executed, and that one name for this plan was dialectical method.

My design, then, was not to out-formalize Hegel, as Professor Findlay seems mistakenly to suppose, but to take from Hegel a less pretentious formalism which might be found practically applicable to an historical account. Whether or not Hegel's account of the dialectic of religion is in conformity with the Notion, it seems to be not out of conformity with dialectic as I have here conceived it. My strategy was designed to overcome the incommensurability of Hegel's dialectical method (taken as a whole) with the necessity that a dialectical account of history be falsifiable to have practical meaning as an historical account.

Incidentally, I do not propose, as Professor Findlay asserts, that "We can hope to see or fail to see forms of the *Notion* displaying themselves" in a dialectical account of history (p. 160). Since a fair portion of my paper is directed toward the explicit denial of this, I shall only note that what we can hope to see where history is "decanted through the procedures of causal explanation," where "it can also be shown to be a progression in which the more differentiated grows continuously out of the less differentiated," and where it is "ripe for dialectical treatment," is *dialectical form* (as I have defined it) exhibited in an account warranted for belief.

"Possibly it is simply wrong to try to characterize dialectic," as Findlay concludes: one should simply do it. I am led to wonder, however, in just what sense and why it can be wrong to examine what one does, even if it turns out that the doing follows a certain pattern. Nor does this seem necessarily to do away with contingency, as Professor Findlay seems to think. In any case, Professor Findlay has given me no reason. Just possibly the sense that it is wrong to try to characterize the dialectic one does is merely a superstition. In any case, it is difficult to understand how Professor Findlay can know, or at least show, that he has done dialectic apart from being able to characterize it, as he seems to suppose that he can.

With reference to my discussion of Hegel's "inauthentic" dialectic of Roman Religion, Professor Findlay wonders whether retreats into mediocrity after one-sided exaggeration may not sometimes be truly progressive phases in history... I should like to point out that I am not here rejecting Roman Religion, but the authenticity, following my own definition of dialectic, of this dialectical account. As I noted, this account seems to me to be one of the truest in Hegel's dialectic of religion. But dialectical history only records onward marches; if one does not find reason for believing that there is progress in history, then a dialectical history is not going to seem very inclusive or very adequate, at least when it encompasses more than a particular culture or sub-culture.

As to the allegation that I have ignored the fact that there is a broad swath of the Hegelian system where history is not in question, my focus in this paper is upon dialectic as it pertains to history. Incidentally, that Hegel viewed nature as exhibiting only a logical and not a temporal order, owing to his reliance upon the pre-evolution natural scientist, introduced a strange inconsistency into his system in that it kept him from carrying through with the theme that all actuality is a mediation of (the Idea in) space and (Spirit in) time.

Professor Findlay finds that he has not been helped to greater clarity by my discussion of what he calls criteria for warranted credibility. Both for lack of space and because it would not have served the main purpose of my paper to have done so, I did not go far beyond what I think most historians will regard as common methodological assumptions here. I tried to take adequate account of the difficulties in applying the test for warranty for belief. This, even though I am claiming for the two-fold test of a dialectical account of history that it is *in principle* applicable. In essence, I suspect it has been applied for some time. I should be pleased if my attempt at a systematic exposition of it might enhance the possibility of a more adequate application.

I wish to thank Professor Findlay for including in his commentary what I trust will prove a helpful summary of what I have attempted to do in my paper.

DISCUSSION

(This discussion followed a commentary by Professor Findlay and a reply by Professor Christensen which differed considerably from those included in this volume.)

OTHO MEL ADKINS (Pasadena College): I'm not surprised that Prof. Christensen would say that the Hegelian dialectic is a non-falsifiable process. It seems to me that the very definition of falsification depends upon a complete dichotomy between A and non-A. This kind of dichotomy cannot be defined in the Hegelian dialectic.

It seems to me, however, that the attempt to understand the dialectic in terms of (e) and (-e) is again a distortion of the whole idea of the Hegelian dialectical development because it attempts to define it in Aristotelian categories which I'm afraid Hegel would consider anathema. I'm wondering whether the attempt to define dialectic in this manner is not doing a good deal to confuse us and perhaps give us the illusory hope that the Hegelian dialectic itself might be formalizable in the same manner that the Aristotelian one was. I'm wondering whether there is not a complete separation in logics here, so that we cannot "do logic," as such, in the Hegelian manner as we could "do logic" in an Aristotelian manner.

CHRISTENSEN: In indicating that I was not attempting to formalize Hegel's logic, I think I have already agreed with you more than disagreed. I think I have shown why this can't be done. As finite men, in order to falsify a dialectical account of history, we must maintain a distinction between method and Notion. Falsifiability requires that there are two things which can be compared for correspondence; all cannot be gathered up into the Notion. (Following hesitation): This doesn't reply to all that you had in mind.

Realizing the inadequacy of the above reply to the intent of Professor Adkins' question, I have taken the liberty of an editor to add the following.

If Hegel's logic is not formalizable, this is not merely because it is different in character than (traditional or modern) classical logic, but due to the particular characteristics I have noted. If you intend to suggest that no type of dialectical logic is formalizable and a dialectical account is in principle not falsifiable, I of course take issue with this. I have proposed the principal features of a dialectical logic (I prefer to call it a dialectical method) which renders a dialectical account falsifiable. Certainly I no more than Hegel am doing logic in the Aristotelian manner. That this method is different in character from a classical system of logic as we think of such today, however, does not seem to settle the question relating to whether it is internally consistent and applicable.

HEGEL ON THE IDENTITY OF CONTENT
IN RELIGION AND PHILOSOPHY

by

Quentin Lauer, S.J.

Feuerbach's judgment of Hegel's philosophy was that it was not philosophy at all but only religion in disguise. Since that time more than one effort has been made, by friends and enemies of Hegel alike, to show that Hegel's thought was not religious at all but rather the culmination of a process of secularizing philosophy which began with Bacon and Descartes. When dealing with a thought so complex – and even tortuous – as Hegel's, it would, of course, be difficult *to prove* that either side is in error, but no conscientious interpreter can gloss over the fact not only that Hegel constantly speaks of God and of religion – more, perhaps, than any modern philosopher – but also that the consciousness of the absolute which he calls religious consciousness is for him integral to the process of thought which he calls *Wissenschaft*.[1]

What can seem – and has seemed – paradoxical in this is that Hegel need yield to none in his emphasis on the secular character of thought in the sense that he sees thought as thoroughly rooted in the autonomy of human spirit. He will accept no authority outside human thought as arbiter of that thought's validity. The rationality of thought and its autonomy are identified. Nevertheless Hegel is unequivocal in his insistence that the content of philosophical thought is religious. Philosophical thought does not merely concern itself with religion as with any other phenomenon of human consciousness; thought is, for Hegel, not philosophical if it is not religious. We can to a certain extent understand this if we grasp the dialectical movement of Hegel's *Phenomenology of Spirit*, where each form of consciousness finds its "truth" not in itself but in the succeeding form which supersedes it. If each successive stage in the dialectical process is the *truth* of the preceding stage, then religion will be the truth of moral consciousness (and revealed –

Christian – religion the truth of religious consciousness as such). At the same time, however, religion will be the truth of all that precedes it. Thus, with religion the absolute as absolute is first recognized as the object of consciousness, self-consciousness, and reason. It is noteworthy that, at each stage of the dialectic, immediate certainty is overcome by a progressively more concretely universal content. Obviously this process cannot stop, until the content becomes the totality of all content, wherein reason's certainty "that it is all reality" is concretized. Thus, the "truth" of reason is in spirit, i.e. beyond mere reason, and spirit in its completeness is the content of religion – a content which, it is true, philosophy must make its own. To present Hegel's thought in this schematic way, however, is to ignore the process whereby it became the "system" it was.

We know that Hegel – like his friends Schelling and Hölderlin at Tübingen – was in his youth destined for the ministry. We know too that he – like the others – could not accept ordination in a Church whose official religion did not make sense to him; nor could he accept a far-away, authoritarian God, who did not make sense to modern man with his conviction of autonomous reason. We also know, however, from his letters during the period following his departure from Tübingen – and from the cryptic password, "Reich Gottes," which he and Hölderlin exchanged as they took leave of each other – that he left with the intention of finding a religion – and a God and a Theology – that would make sense. A glance at his *Early Theological Writings* will indicate to us that his quest took him first to Kant's moral religion and Fichte's God, who was the principle of moral order.[2]

In 1792 Fichte published anonymously his *Kritik aller Offenbarung*, which was first attributed to Kant, and in 1793 Kant published his *Religion innerhalb der Grenzen der blossen Vernunft*. Both of these works Hegel read and annotated avidly. For us to whom the concept "philosophy of religion" has become something of a commonplace it is difficult to appreciate the effect these works had on the mind of young Hegel. Here was a chance to make rational sense out of what had previously been presented simply as unquestioned divine revelation.[3] Kant in particular emphasized a principle which he had already enunciated in 1766, that religion is based on morality rather than vice versa. If religion is to be justified it must appeal to reason, and the only reason to which it can appeal is moral reason, which needs neither a superior being in order to know duty nor a superior motive in order to accomplish it.[4] Still, although an ultimate appeal to reason cannot be an appeal to God (unless they are identified), moral reason does inevitably lead to religion.

> If morality recognizes in the sacredness of its law an object of greatest reverence, then on the level of religion it sees in the form of a highest cause fulfilling that law an object of adoration and thus appears in all its majesty.[5]

Kant does not say explicitly that God is simply absolute moral will, but he does say that the only religious teaching which does count is moral teaching, which is set forth as the will of God.[6] God, then, becomes the personified idea of the good principle who can be recognized only by the good man, and religion consists in recognizing the demands of moral reason as divine commands.[8]

> *Religion* (considered subjectively) is the recognition of all our duties as divine commands. The religion in which I must know ahead of time that something is a divine command in order to recognize it as my duty is *revealed* religion . . .; on the other hand the religion in which I must first know that something is duty before I can recognize it as a divine command is *natural religion*.[9]

God is, so to speak, the universal lawgiver corresponding to universal law,[10] but He is not the one who enforces the law.[11] There is, then, a divine command, but its authority does not reside in its being divine but in the intrinsic moral value which reason finds in it. We do, however, sanctify moral duty by interpreting it as God's command,[12] and we honor God by observing the duties dictated by reason, since it is His command that we do so.[13] It is important to note that the reason here in question – as in the three *Critiques* – is individual reason universalized, i.e. recognized as authentically reason.[14]

In all this it would be going too far to say that Kant identifies morality and religion; he does, however, say that they are identical in content, even though their form is different.[15]

> The only true religion contains nothing but laws, i.e. the sort of practical principles of whose unconditonal necessity we can be conscious and which we can, therefore, recognize as revealed through pure reason (not empirically).[16]

We find much that is similar to this in *HtJ*, especially in his critique of the "positivity" of religion and religious institutions, and yet precisely in these early essays Hegel is already beginning to break with Kant in his religious thinking. It is important to note, however, right here at the outset that, although we cannot ignore these youthful efforts of Hegel – as testimony to his development and to Kant's influence on it – we must beware of seeing in them a definitive position.

The first important document to indicate the direction of Hegel's mature religious – and philosophical – thought is *Phen*. Not only does the *Phenomenology* at various stages in its description of the process of consciousness turn to forms of religious consciousness as integral to that process, but it also introduces religion in its developed form as the link between moral reason (in which spirit is present in an immediate and almost unconscious way) and the ultimate in philosophical thought, which is "absolute knowing." Gone is the emphasis on moral reason as the only possible basis of religion, and in its place stands the insistence that moral reason will find its own truth only if it moves on to the further (higher) stage of religion, where for the first time absolute spirit reveals itself as the content short of which consciousness can never become knowledge. For the first time we see emerge clearly the paradox which Fackenheims claims characterizes the whole of Hegel's mature thought, the gigantic endeavor to synthesize a faith which is essentially receptive of the divine with a rational thought which is autonomous and self-creative. Herein is presented the mystery of a human thought whose origin is both human and divine, which is no less human for being divine.[17]

What Hegel has done effectively is to dissociate himself from the rationalism of the Enlightenment and from the critical philosophy of Kant and Fichte, to insert his own thinking in the tradition of Plato and Aristotle, Plotinus and Augustine, Anselm and Spinoza, all of whom saw human thinking as somehow divine. Thought reveals itself as infinite activity (which it will do more definitely in the *Logic),* and infinite activity is seen as activity of the infinite. It could be argued, of course, that what Hegel has done is to reduce the divine to the totality of the human – and if all we had to go on were the *Phenomology*, a case might be made for that interpretation – but there are simply too many texts (even in the *Phenomenology*) which are not susceptible to that kind of reading. The result of the *Phenomenology* is to show that the ultimate *subject* of philosophical thinking, the thinking itself or thinking spirit, is at the same time the ultimate *content* of philosophical thinking. It is conceivable, of course, that one could arrive at such a conclusion without including religious consciousness in the process at all – Fichte tried it, and so did Schelling – but the fact is that Hegel considered it impossible. For him it is sheer nonsense to consider consciousness apart from its content, and the form of consciousness wherein absolute spirit first reveals itself as content – prior to that form which is thinking in the full sense – is religious consciousness. "The content of religion, therefore, expresses sooner in time than does science what Spirit is; the latter alone, however, is spirit's true knowing of itself." [18] We might note here that what motivates Hegel in his insistence that the content of religion and of science (philosophy) is identical is not his desire to rescue religion. Rather it is his desire to rescue philosophy, which would be less than universal science if the object of religion were out of its domain.

This has been long in coming. As we noted before, religious consciousness has already made its appearance in the *Phenomenology* before this, i.e., as consciousness of absolute being. What had not yet appeared was absolute being itself, i.e., spirit conscious that it is itself of which it is conscious.[19] When we get to the end of the *Phenomenology* we see that what has been happening all along is that human spirit has been progessively coming closer to a grasp of what it truly is, which is to say that spirit has been progressively manifesting itself as the truth of human spirit. Each manifestation, however, had revealed itself as inadequate, because spirit is more. In religion spirit reveals itself for what it truly is, infinite subject, self, but the manner of self-revelation is still inadequate, since the truly spiritual element in which it can reveal itself fully is thought, not emotion or representation.[20]

What has happened, then, is that the story of the absolute's appearing has slowly been unfolded before us. It takes a long time, however, before we become aware that the absolute is the ultimate content of consciousness (if it were not, knowledge would not be knowledge, because only partial). Even when we do see this we do not at first see it as the content of *knowing* consciousness. First it is imaginatively or emotionally present in consciousness, as *represented*. Only at the end is it the content of *thought*. In the overall process it is with religion that it becomes manifest that the true content of consciousness is precisely the absolute (unconditioned, infinite). It could not ultimately be the content of thought if it were not first manifested as the content of religious consciousness. This is a position which Hegel never thereafter repudiated. It is not accidental to the process of consciousness that it passes through the stages that it does, but the relationship of religion to philosophy is closer than simply that of one of the stages (or "moments") of the process to the whole of the process. The goal of the process is the grasp of what is true in all its truth, and it is only with religion's grasp of the absolute that the goal is finally in sight.

We can see, then, that although Hegel did treat explicitly of the philosophy of religion, there is a very real sense in which, for him, religion is not something *about which* one philosophizes; it is part and parcel of the process whereby philosophy becomes philosophy. Our task here will be to discover what it can mean to say that religion and philosophy are two forms of consciousness having the same content. We have already seen that for Kant religion and moral reason are two forms with one content, i.e., duty, but that is a far cry from what Hegel is saying, although it should be remarked that Hegel – even in his later years – is one with Kant in affirming the moral roots of religious consciousness.

> True religion, or religiousness, arises only for morality; it is thinking morality, i.e. a morality becoming conscious of the free universality of its concrete essence. Only from the standpoint of morality are we conscious of God as free spirit; it is vain, then, to look for true religion, or religiousness, apart from the moral spirit.[21]

The question, however, does not concern the derivation of the subjective response called religious; it concerns, rather, the object which religion and philosophy have in common. "Both [religion and philosophy] have the *truth* as their object, and that in the highest sense – in the sense that God, and God alone, is the truth." [22] It must, of course, be remembered that truth is truth in the full sense of the word only when it is thought, i.e., grasped in concept, since thought is the proper locus of truth. Philosophy, then, is the transforming of other forms of consciousness into thought,[23] while in the case of the religious consciousness, the content, i.e., *Wirklichkeit,* remains the same.

The significance of this is highlighted most strikingly, perhaps, in Hegel's introduction to VdGdP where he tries to say just what this philosophy is, of which there is a history. There we are told that philosophy is the highest form in which spirit manifests itself at any time or place – among a people.[25] To say that it is the highest form, however, is not to say that it is the only form; there are also non-philosophical ways in which the supreme idea (spirit) can be present, and these are art and religion: "The way in which the supreme idea is present for non-philosophical consciousness, for sensitive, intuitive, representative consciousness." [26] It would be a mistake, however, to look upon this non-philosophical presence as non-rational; it is not totally spiritual – since only thought is that – but it is supremely rational:

> For it [religion] is the work of self-revealing reason, its supreme, most rational work.

> Rather, this *region of the spirit is the Sanctuary in which the re-
> maining deception of the sense-world, of finite representations and
> goals, the area of opinion and arbitrariness, has been dissolved.*[27]

From the point of view of the subject, perhaps, the grasp of this supremely universal object is not purely rational activity; its presence, nevertheless, is the work of reason. "We are men, and we have reason.
Whatever is human, rational, finds an echo in us, in our feeling, emotion,
heart, in our subjectivity in general." [28] It is, in fact, the object of thought,
even though the manner of grasping it is not, properly speaking, thinking.[29] Universal reason – which, for Hegel, is not individual reason universalized – reveals itself best in human reason, but it is not limited to
that form of manifestations.[30]

It is a traditional commonplace that God reveals Himself in nature.[31]
But, says Hegel, God does not manifest Himself primarily in nature but
in the activity of man's spirit; it is man who *makes* nature the mirror
of God.[32] What is more, He reveals Himself preeminently in the symbols
of religion; [33] they do not hide God, they are means of permitting Him to
come into human consciousness.[34] What must be recognized is that, historically speaking, religion everywhere precedes philosophy. More significantly it does in two steps what philosophy does in one: in religion man first
sets God over against himself, and then through the activity of cult he
unites himself with God.[35] The point is that in religion men have set forth
the consciousness they have of the supreme being, and this, no matter
what the subjective form of setting forth, is a function of reason.[36] The
difference would seem to be that, although truth is present in religion
it is present as a *given* which cannot be verified in religion itself, whereas
the truth in thought is verified in the very process of thought.[37] Nevertheless, it is precisely the same *truth* which is common to both.[38] Ultimately, then, the God of philosophy (Spirit) is simply identical with the God of
religion – although only philosophy can see this, and only philosophy
knows God for what He is.[39]

> From this, then, we gather the relationship between Spirit and hu-
> man spirit. We must, of course, abstract from the atomic manner
> of representing individuality as fragmented and isolated. Spirit
> truly represented is simply what is aware of itself. The difference
> between individual and universal spirit, then, should be expressed
> thus: The subjective, individual spirit is the universal, divine spirit,
> to the extent that the former is aware of the latter, to the extent that
> the latter manifests itself in each subject, each man. Thus, the spirit
> which is aware of absolute spirit is subjective spirit.[40]

When the individual subject knows God, it is God who is doing the knowing, and where the grasp of God is in religious belief, the same is true; it too, is spirit's testimony to itself: [41] to be truly religious is to be aware of God.[42] At this point Hegel quotes John 16:13 – "He [the Spirit of truth] will teach you all truth," interpreting it to mean that all knowledge of truth is the presence of spirit in us.[43]

Because the individual as individual is necessarily limited, the manner in which Spirit is present in the individual is necessarily limited. In thinking this limitation is *aufgehoben*, because thinking is Spirit's consciousness of itself. In religious awareness the limitation persists, because what is present is not Spirit itself but teaching *about* Spirit, a representation (a *Vorstellung* which is *Stellvertretend*) calculated to arouse religious emotion.[44] In religion man is truly aware of Spirit, and it is truly Spirit of whom man is aware, but the awareness is not truly spiritual. "In religion spirit has a peculiar form, which can be sensible... a representation." [45] *Thought* is involved, but in a *mixed* form [46] "a form which contains more or less of the sensible." [47] This brings us back to the two-step process in religion, which in philosophy becomes one step: in religion spirit is external and is rendered *present* in representation, which is followed by identification in *worship;* in philosophy content (spirit) and form (thought) are one: "because what I think, i.e., the content of thinking, is in the form of thought, it is no longer over against me." [48]

It is unquestionably difficult to see how the content of philosophy and religion can be identical. Religion as such has never been able to see the identity. The philosophical tradition from Plato to the Middle Ages took the identity for granted. Modern rationalism (particularly of the Enlightenment) has been incapable of grasping the identity and has, therefore, been inimical to religion.[49] The point is, says Hegel, that rationalism has to be opposed to religion, but *reason* is not.[50] Reason is proper to man as man, and in order that what he do be strictly human – as opposed to what other than man can do – it must be the work of reason. Since, however, the truth of reason is not in mere reason but in spirit – where the transition from individual to universal reason has already taken place – it is only in and through spirit that what man does is truly and adequately the work of reason. If, then, it is true that in religion man relates himself to the absolute, who as absolute must be absolute truth, then religion must be the work of reason. If, moreover, true thinking is ultimately thinking of the absolute, then the absolute which thinking thinks cannot be other than the absolute to whom man is related in religion. Hegel is well on his way in his quest for a religion and a God who makes sense in a modern rational world.

What is not quite clear up to this point, however, is just what reason, or spirit, meant for Hegel. That reason is not to be separated from human reason is clear enough, but it is also clear that individual reason does not even merit the name unless it is in tune with universal reason. The problem then concerns the meaning which can be given to universal reason. It is simple enough to say that *Vernunft* designates human thinking functioning at its highest and its best (incidentally German translates the Greek νοῦς by *Vernunft*). The term is still empty if it does not say what human thinking does when it functions at the highest and best. By the same token, it is all very well to say, as does the Western tradition, that what reason thinks to be true is true, but by itself that is no more than a tautology, since a thinking which is not true simply is not reason. Thus, if it is possible to institute, as Kant seeks to do, a Critique of Reason, whereby we can determine that it is reason which is functioning, it is also possible to determine that what it asserts to be true is universally true – if not, the assertion would simply not be an assertion of reason. What reason says cannot be other than true, and to know what individual reason, as reason, says is to know what universal reason says, because reason cannot contradict reason; reason is one. So, to speak with Kant, the object of reason is universal because it is the object of reason.

For Hegel, however, the process is reversed. We do not know that a proposition is true *because* reason affirms it; we know that it is reason-functioning because what it affirms is true. The same can be said with regard to universal validity. If I *know* what is true, I also know that it must be true for all. But, says Hegel, knowing that it is true for all is the condition of knowing that it is true, not vice versa. There is no question, then, of universalizing individual reason; rather it is one of individualizing universal reason. The whole movement of the *Phenomenology* indicates just this. Consciousness, whose apex is reached in understanding (*Verstand*) is *aufgehoben* in self-consciousness, where the self can be re-recognized as a self only in a community of selves. Self-consciousness in turn is *aufgehoben* in reason (ultimately moral reason), whose dictates are not those of the individual but of the "Geist der Gemeinde." [51] Finally, reason is *aufgehoben* in spirit, because only in spirit is there consciousness of identification with the totality of spirit, which is concretely universal spirit. This is where religion comes in. There, for the first time, individual consciousness becomes aware that the object with which it seeks to be identified is universal spirit. Religion too, however, must be *aufgehoben* in absolute knowing (which is philosophy or *Wissen-*

schaft), because only there is there an awareness that the absolute can be object only if the absolute is subject. The individual subject has not been lost in the process; it has been found, because it realizes that only in the universality of subjectivity can it find the guarantee for the universality of what is objective for it.

Now, in all this one can, I suppose, argue that the absolute, or spirit, is not God in any intelligible sense of the term. One might even argue that, when Hegel says of God the same things that he says of absolute spirit he is speaking metaphorically. It is difficult to see, however, how one can argue in this way and still make sense of the mountain of texts in which the God who is the object of religion is identified with the object of philosophy.

What Hegel set out to find, as we saw before, was a religion and a God which would be compatible with modern philosophical thinking. In the beginning he may have thought that what he would find would be substitutes for Christian religion and the Christian God – perhaps the unified reason of the Enlightenment or the supreme moral principle of Kant and Fichte. What he came up with, however, was a transformed Christian religion and a transformed concept of God. As Fackenheim puts it so well, "For the early Hegel, philosophy will produce a new religion on the ruins of the old. For the mature Hegel philosophy comprehends the old religion, and this latter is not and cannot be ruined." [52] In another place he goes even further: "Hegel asserts, with unwavering insistence, that Christianity is the absolutely true content, and that his philosophy both can and must give that content its absolutely true form." [53]

It is scarcely conceivable that Hegel would have devoted so much time in his *Lectures on the Philosophy of Religion* to a justification of the "ontological proof" and then append sixteen additional lectures on the same subject, if he did not take seriously the God who is there identified with *the* concept. As early as *Glauben und Wissen* Hegel finds fault with Kant, Fichte, and Jacobi for giving up on absolute knowledge and assigning to belief the content which is absolute, i.e., God.[54] In the *Phenomenology*, as we have seen, the language may be ambiguous, but the affirmation is unequivocal: What *Wissenschaft* knows in the form of thought is the same object which religion represents symbolically.

> Thus, what in religion was *content* or form of representation by *another* is here the proper *doing* of the *self*. The concept guarantees that the *content* is the proper *doing* of the self – for, as we

see, this concept is knowledge of the self's doing in itself constituting the very essence of all reality, a knowledge of this *subject* as *substance* and of the substance as this knowledge of its own doing.[55]

The thinking knowledge with which the *Phenomenology* ends is the "presentation of God, as He is in His eternal essence before the creation of nature or of a single finite spirit" [56] with which the *Logic* begins. To know God is to know all reality, and to know all reality is to know; short of God knowledge is not fully knowledge. The thinking with which the *Logic* is concerned from beginning to end is infinite activity. But, infinite activity is the activity of an infinite subject, whose object, too, is infinite. Thought is truly thought only if it is infinite being. Thus, the *Logic* is the detailed working out of the "ontological argument," the proof of God from the infinity of thought. In this Hegel is not saying that there is no finite thought or that finite thought is not valid. What he is saying is that the finite bespeaks the infinite, and is nothing without it.

> It is the nature of the finite itself to go beyond itself, to negate its negation and become infinite. Thus the infinite does not stand *over* the finite as something complete for itself, in such a way that the finite would continue to be *under* or *outside* the infinite.[57]

It is too obvious to need mentioning that there are finite subjects as well as finite objects (the very use of the plural indicates that). By the same token there are finite thoughts and finite concepts. The point is that only in the process of passing beyond its own limitations is the finite significant at all. For it to be true it must determine itself to its truth in the totality of being: "The infinite is the finite's affirmative determination, that which it truly is." [58] There is, of course, distinction between the finite and the infinite − to deny it woulld be to affirm "the dark night in which all the cows are black" − but it is the dialectical distinction of dynamic relationship, where finite and infinite are only in the passage from one to the other.[59]

It is for this reason that it is necessary to identify the whole movement of the *Logic* with the "ontological argument"; not, however, in the sense that the *Logic* justifies the argument, but in the sense that the *Logic* depends for its justification on the validity of the argument. The "ontological argument" is not an inference from the being of the finite world to the being of its creator; it is a passage from the essential non-being of that which is *merely* finite to the essential infinity of being.

The thought which thinks infinity is infinite thought, and infinite thought is the thought of God Himself. To think truly (in reason) is to discover infinite thought, and to discover infinite thought is to discover God, i.e., to discover God thinking.

It is certainly not without significance for our present purpose that Hegel has much the same to say about the relation of finite and infinite, thought and reality, man and God, in *LPR*.

> That man knows God is in accord with the essential community (of God and man) as community of knowing, i.e., man knows God only in so far as God knows Himself in man. This knowledge is God's consciousness of self, but at the same time it is God's knowledge of man; and this knowledge of man by God is man's knowledge of God.[60]

Once more, then, we are back with the identity of content in religion and philosophy; the God of philosophy is the God of religion.

> In so far as it has achieved the universal thought is unlimited; its end is infinitely pure thought, such that any cloud of finitude has disappeared, because it thinks God, and thus religion, the thinking of God begins.[61]

Religion, then, *thinks* God, and the God whom religion thinks in one form is the God whom philosophy thinks in another – more adequate – form. God is ultimate truth, but there are not two ultimate truths, one for philosophy and another for religion, since ultimate truth is the truth of all truth.

> Truth is, of course, contained in every other sphere, but not the highest absolute truth, for this is to be found only in perfect universality of determination, and in the fact of being determined in and for itself, which is not simple determinateness having reference to another, but contains the other, the difference in its very self.[62]

Thus, whether the thought which thinks God is religious or philosophical, the God it thinks is the same God, and the thinking is God's relevation of Himself to and in the spirit of man.

> Let it suffice here merely to observe regarding the supposed opposition of the philosophy of religion and positive religion, that there cannot be *two kinds of reason* and *two kinds of spirit*: There cannot be a divine reason and a human, there cannot be a divine

spirit and a human, which would be *absolutely different.* Human reason – the consciousness of one's being – is indeed reason; it is the divine in man; and spirit, in so far as it is the spirit of God, is not a spirit beyond the stars, beyond the world. On the contrary, God is present, omnipresent, present as spirit in all spirits.[63]

It should be noted in the text just quoted that the "philosophy of religion" of which Hegel speaks is not a philosophizing about religion; it is the thinking philosophically what religion thinks religiously. It is, then, philosophy itself, the source and object of whose thinking is the divine spirit himself. Thus, Hegel's God is not one who is out there, beyond the world, but one who is present in His works, chief of which is thought as it occurs in human spirit, whether that thought be religious or philosophical.

> Religion is a product of the divine spirit; it is not a discovery of man, but a work of divine operation and creation in him. The expression that God as *reason* rules the world would be *irrational* if we did not assume that it has reference also to religion, and that the divine spirit works in the character and form proper to religion. But the development of reason as perfected in thought does not stand in opposition to this spirit, and consequently it cannot be absolutely different from the work which the divine spirit has produced in religion.[64]

With *LPR* Hegel has reached a stage of development in his thought on religion which was not clearly elaborated in the *Phenomenology.* No longer is there question merely of an identical content in both religion and philosophy; religion itself is perfected in philosophy in such a way that the two are no longer distinct; religion is now philosophical religion, because it is complete as religion in the form which is proper to philosophy. In religion at its former stage the infinite (God) is present in a thought which is itself finite; the being which was present is infinite, but the manner of its presence was finite. In philosophy – or philosophical religion – the same infinite being is present, but the manner of its presence is its own infinite self-consciousness.

> We have now reached the realized concept of religion, the perfect religion, in which it is the concept itself that is its own object. We defined religion as being in the more precise sense the self-consciousness of God. Self-consciousness in its character as conscious-

ness has an object, and it is conscious of itself in this object; this object is also consciousness, but it is consciousness as object, and is consequently finite consciousness, a consciousness which is distinct from God, from the absolute. The element of determinateness is present in this form of consciousness, and consequently finitude is present in it. God is self-consciousness. He knows Himself in a consciousness which is distinct from Him, which is in itself God's consciousness, but it is also this for itself, since it knows its identity with God, an identity which is, however, mediated by the negation of finitude. This concept constitutes the content of religion . . . . This concept is now realized, consciousness knows this content and knows that it is itself simply interwoven with this content; in the concept which is the process of God it is itself a moment . . . . This is perfect religion, the concept become objective to itself. Here it is revealed what God is: He is no longer a being above and beyond this world, an unknown, for He has let men know what He is, and this not only in external history,[65] but in consciousness.[66]

By the time we reach this over-long quotation we have no difficulty in seeing that Hegel has instituted a speculative transformation of revealed religion. What is perhaps more significant here, however, is that he has also instituted a transformation of modern philosophy. Not only may philosophy, in Hegel's eyes, not ignore God; it is, precisely as philosophy, the thought of God. Philosophical thinking is infinite activity; it is the presence of infinite spirit in the spirit of man, wherein the latter is *aufgehoben* in a thinking which must be infinite, if its object is the truth.

With this the pieces of a complex puzzle begin to fall into place. It can be doubted – and has been – that the religion Hegel speaks of is really the Christian religion, or whether the God he speaks of is truly the Christian God. Be that as it may, there can be no doubt that the God-question concerned him very deeply and that he sought to understand God in such a way that He would not only not conflict with the autonomy of philosophical thinking but would also not be an object which simply exceeded the capacity of human reason. The Christian God has always been looked on as the supreme being, infinite spirit, and absolute reality. Of Hegel's God the same can be said. Hegel's, however, is a philosophical endeavor to understand what such attributes can mean to modern man.

The other side of the same picture, the philosophical, has also become clearer. For Hegel, philosophy is a science which has absolute truth for its object and absolute knowledge as its manner of grasping this object. That knowledge is knowledge he never doubted; his problem was to describe knowledge in such a way that it would manifest itself as precisely that. When all is said and done Hegel is still working in the tradition of "transcendental" philosophy, whose task is not to *discover* – either empirically or deductively – what is the case, but to uncover the necessary conditions for what he knows to be the case and to affirm the absolute reality of those conditions. For Hegel, then, if what he has described is not true, then knowledge is not knowledge, philosophy is not philosophy.

> With regard to the *reality* of this concept, *science* does not appear in time and in *actuality* until spirit has achieved this consciousness regarding itself. As the spirit which knows what it is it does not exist sooner, never before the completion of the work of overcoming its imperfect form, of shaping its own consciousness, its essential form, and in this way identifying its *self-consciousness* with its *consciousness*. The spirit which is in and for itself and distinguished into its moments is knowing *for itself*, conceiving in general, which as such has not attained *substance*, i.e., in itself is not absolute knowing.[67]

The paradigm of all knowing is divine knowing [68] where the knowing itself is infinite and what is known is the infinite totality of the knowable.[69] If human knowing is to be truly knowing it must in some sense be divine. This it is in religion, but religion itself can ultimately know what it is knowing only in and through philosophy, which is to say that in religion man *believes* in God, but only in philosophy can he *know* what God (in whom he believes) is. Until then he knows not what he says when he says "God."

Thus, we might say that Hegel's has been a gigantic effort to rescue both Christian religion and philosophy by ultimately identifying them. It is, for him, inconceivable that philosophical knowledge should merit the designation "knowledge" if it falls short of grasping the ultimate totality of reality which religion presents. On the other hand, religion will be dealing in little more than empty words or symbols, if philosophy does not make known to it the meaning of its own content.

NOTES

1. *Wissenschaft*, which, for Hegel, is not a characteristic of philosophy but rather identical with it, is the totality of the process whereby man comes to *Wissen*. That process is described in detail in the *Phän*, whose original title was *Wissenschaft der Erfahrung des Bewußtseins*. Therein the stage of consciousness immediately preceding knowledge in the fullest sense is the stage revealed (Christian) religion, and nowhere in his writings does Hegel alter this.

2. Cf. "Volksreligion und Christentum," in *HtJ*, pp. 3-71. Here Hegel agrees pretty much with Kant that religion stands in the service of morality. Still, Theodor Häring, in his *Hegel, sein Wollen und sein Werk* (Leipzig and Berlin, 1929, 1938), makes it abundantly clear that even at this early stage Hegel did not accept fully the Kantian subordination of religion to morality (cf. I, pp. 66, 188-89).

3. Hegel did, of course, know Spinoza's *Tractatus theologico-politicus* and Lessing's efforts at biblical interpretation, but Kant and Fichte opened up to him a new world of rational religion.

4. *RiGbV*, p. 3.

5. *RiGbV*, p. 8. Cf. Kant, *Der Streit der Fakultäten*, ed. Klaus Reich (Hamburg: Meiner, 1959), p. 74: "Er fühlt sich für ein anderes Reich geschaffen als für das Reich der Sinne und des Verstandes, – nämlich für ein moralisches Reich, für ein Reich Gottes. Er erkennt nur seine Pflichten zugleich als göttliche Gebote, und es entsteht in ihm eine neue Erkenntnis, ein neues Gefühl, nämlich Religion."

6. Cf. *RiGbV*, p. 10; *Der Streit der Fakultäten*, p. 31.

7. Cf. *RiGbV*, p. 63.

8. *RiGbV*, p. 92.

9. *RiGbV*, p. 170.

10. Cf. *RiGbV*, p. 105.

11. *RiGbV*, pp. 106-107.

12. Cf. *RiGbV*, p. 111.

13. *RiGbV*, p. 114.

14. *RiGbV*, p. 143.

15. *Der Streit der Fakultäten*, p. 31.

16. *RiGbV*, p. 187.

17. Cf. Emil Fackenheim, *The Religious Dimension in Hegel's Thought* (Bloomington: Indiana University Press, 1967), p. 206.

18. *Phän*, p. 559.

19. *Phän*, p. 473.

20. Cf. *Phän*, p. 480. The term which we here translate by "representation" is *Vorstellung*. It is impossible to find on English term which will adequately translate the German term in each of its occurrences. The notion that Hegel seeks to get across in using it is that in a *Vorstellung* the object of thought is not itself present to thought but is represented by a subjective medium which stands in its place (its "representative," i.e. *Stellvertreter*). "Die Vorstellung ist als die erinnerte Anschauung die Mitte zwischen dem unmittelbaren Bestimmt-sich-finden der Intelligenz und zwischen derselben in ihrer Freiheit, dem Denken. Die Vorstellung ist das *Ihrige* der Intelligenz noch mit einseitiger Subjektivität, indem das Ihrige noch bedingt durch die Unmittelbarkeit, nicht an ihm selbst das *Sein* ist. Der Weg der Intelligenz in den Vorstellungen ist, die Unmittelbarkeit ebenso innerlich zu machen, sich in *sich selbst anschauund* zu setzen, als die Subjektivität der Innerlichkeit aufzuheben, in ihr selbst ihrer sich zu entäussern und in ihrer eigenen Äuberlichkeit in sich zu sein." *EdpW*, sec. 451.

21. *EdpW*, sec. 552.

22. *EdpW*, sec. 1.
23. *EdpW*, sec. 5.
24. *EdpW*, sec. 6.
25. Georg Wilhelm Friedrich Hegel, *Einleitung in die Geschichte der Philosophie*, the third (abreviated) ed. by Friedhelm Nicolin of the work as contained in Band 166 of the *Philosophische Bibliothek*, ed. by Hoffmeister in 1940 (Hamburg: Meiner, 1959), pp. 38f.
26. *Ibid.*, p. 42.
27. *Ibid.*, p. 43.
28. *Ibid.*, p. 46.
29. *Ibid.*, p. 48.
30. *Ibid.*, p. 52.
31. Cf. the section in *Phän* on "Beobachtende Vernunft."
32. *EdpW*, sec. 248.
33. *Einleitung in die Geschichte der Philosophie*, p. 57.
34. *Ibid.*, pp. 55-56.
35. *Ibid.*, p. 167.
36. *Ibid.*, p. 168.
37. Cf. *Ibid.*, pp. 173-74.
38. *Ibid.*, p. 175.
39. *Ibid.*
40. *Ibid.*, p. 176.
41. *Ibid.*, p. 178.
42. *Ibid.*, p. 179.
43. *Ibid.*, p. 180.
44. *Ibid.*, pp. 182-83.
45. *Ibid.*, p. 184.
46. *Ibid.*
47. *Ibid.*, p. 186.
48. *Ibid.*, p. 185. Cf. *WdL*, I, p. 30: "Das absolute Wissen ist die Wahrheit aller Weisen des Bewußtseins weil, wie jener Gang deselben es hervorbrachte, nur in dem absoluten Wissen die Trennung des *Gegenstandes* von der *Gewißheit seiner selbst* vollkommen sich aufgelöst hat und die Wahrheit, dieser Gewißheit, sowie diese Gewißheit, der Wahrheit gleich geworden ist."
49. Cf. *Phän*, pp. 187-91.
50. *Phän*, p. 191. It should be mentioned that, in Hegel's view, rationalism is also the enemy of philosophy: "Dieser Rationalismus ist der Philosophie dem Inhalte und der Form nach entgegengesetzt."
51. *Phän*, p. 391.
52. Fackenheim, *op. cit.*, p. 209.
53. *Ibid.*, p. 112.
54. Cf. *EdpW*, sec. 552, where he comes back to the same complaint. By putting the infinite out of reach of reason and handing it over to faith, Kant, Fichte, and Jacobi are simply settling for a reason which is not *reason* but *understanding*. When Hegel makes reason capable of the infinite (in fact that is what distinguishes it as reason) he is making it an infinite capacity. This it cannot be if it is merely the function of the individual (even the universalized individual).
55. *Phän*, p. 556.
56. *VdL*, I, 31.
57. *VdL*, p. 126.
58. *VdL*.
59. *VdL*, p. 125.
60. *VPR*, II, p. 496.

61. *VPR*, p. 225.
62. *VPR*, I (Glockner, vol. 15), p. 40.
63. *VPR*, p. 50.
64. *VPR*.
65. This notion of "external history" (*äusserliche Geschichte*) is familiar to us from *Phän*. It designates an *account* of the events of history, which, as the work of the historian, is external to the events themselves, which have in themselves an internal relationship constituting the historical process.
66. *VPR*, II, pp. 191-92.
67. *Phän*, p. 557.
68. This same theme we find as early as "Das Leben Jesu," *HtJ*, p. 75.
69. Cf. *WdL*, II, p. 502; also *EdpW*, sec. 213, where he says in a slightly different vein that only as Idea is the concept fully defined, because only thus is it explicitly identified with the totality of reality.

COMMENT ON

Quentin Lauer
Hegel on the Identity of Content
in Religion and Philosophy

by

James Doull

"With *LPR* Hegel has reached a stage of development in his thought on religion which was not clearly elaborated in *Phen*. No longer is there question merely of an identical content in both religion and philosophy; religion itself is perfected in philosophy in such a way that the two are no longer distinct; religion is now philosophical religion..." (p. 273). This conclusion must be altogether rejected: Hegel neither reduces religion to philosophy nor does he undertake "a speculative transformation of revealed religion" (p. 274). Rather he distinguished religion and philosophy more clearly and maintains their difference more firmly than any other philosopher. Philosophy of religion has for its purpose, in his view, not to replace religion, but to save it from confusion with other forms of spirit.

Philosophy is indeed for Hegel the highest and completest form of spirit in which even religion is comprehended. It by no means follows that religion – and one may say the same of art – is not to remain an autonomous form of spirit. Hegel's position is rather that, unless religion remains as religion, philosophy cannot be at all. Spirit can only know its absolute content in the form of the concept as it comes to this knowledge out of the immediate and reflective relations it has to the same content in art and religion. The independence of religion from philosophy is established neither empirically nor on the basis of a particular philosophy – the limits it sets to human reason – but from the nature of reason and spirit as disclosed in religion itself.[1]

That not language and imagination but thought is the ultimate vehicle of religious truth was clearly understood by the Fathers and the Medieval Doctors. This insight does not destroy religion or weaken its authority provided the believer be not misled by the finitude of the form. This is Hegel's attitude.[2]

Father Lauer's interpretation imposes itself if one suppose with him that "when all is said and done Hegel is still working in the tradition of 'transcendental' philosophy, whose task is ... to uncover the necessary conditions for what he knows to be the case and to affirm the absolute reality of those conditions." (p. 275). For then religion yields place to philosophy as knowledge of the ultimate condition, namely the absolute identity of subject and object. Into this identity religion is dissolved, and is no longer distinguished in form or content from philosophy. This is indeed the result of the *Phenomenology*, if that work be regarded as moving within the limits of the transcendental method of Fichte or Schelling. The *Phenomenology* is, however, the destruction of that method – of the externality to each other of empirical knowledge and its transcendental conditions.[3]

It does not fall within the argument of the *Phenomenology* to show how religion and philosophy are related to each other in the Hegelian philosophy. This is at once clear if one consider that the *Phenomenology* is only an introduction to philosophy. It leads to the standpoint of the Hegelian philosophy, determines nothing from that standpoint. The last insight to which it takes the reader is that the separation of Christian faith and secular freedom, their hostility or indifference to each other belongs to a subordinate standpoint. To religion is thus restored the possibility of defending its truth against secular rationalism, while to secularity is shown the possibility of making its freedom more than an unrealizable demand. The development of these possibilities no longer belongs to "phenomenology" but to "philosophy." [4]

Father Lauer considers briefly the sense of the *Logic*, with which Hegel begins the exposition of his philosophical science. He understands the *Logic* as the reduction of the finite to a "dialectical distinction of dynamic relationship, where finite and infinite are only in the passage from one to the other" (p. 271). The "whole movement of the *Logic*" he identifies with the "ontological argument," this understood as "a passage from the essential non-being of that which is *merely* finite to the essential infinity of being" (p. 271).[5]

Though he protests against it, it is hard to find in these statements anything but "the dark night in which all cows are black," the absolute identity of subject and object as set forth by Schelling. This is truly the result unless the *Logic* is also the argument from the infinite to the finite. But Father Lauer excludes this in saying that the *Logic* rather depends on than establishes the "ontological argument." What else can he mean but that the *Logic* is the reduction to identity with the infinite of a given finite content? But in that case the finite has no truth from the standpoint of the infinite, and thus we have the "dark night." [6]

Father Lauer then finds that "Hegel has much the same to say about the relation of finite and infinite, thought and reality, man and God, in *LPR* (p. 272). He at once concludes that Hegel is teaching the identity of religion and philosophy. Between the *Logic* and the *Philosophy of Religion* stands the vast argument of the *Philosophy of Nature* and the *Philosophy of Spirit*. These works oppose so abstract an interpretation of the *Philosophy of Religion*. But first it was necessary to penetrate more deeply the sense of the *Logic* – in which Hegel imparts to the concepts mentioned and others the stability of the infinite form, whereby they withstand dissolution into the "black night."

Philosophy of Religion is for Hegel neither religion nor a speculative substitute for religion. It is theology,[7] and the only theology any longer capable of saving for faith its true content undiminished by concessions to one or other form of secular rationalism. For it is the only theology that can show faith as the source and continuing foundation of secular freedom. The division between faith and the modern secular spirit, being a dividedness of the Christian spirit itself, cannot be cured without insight into the reason of faith.[8] Neither medieval theology, which rests on an extraneous philosophical reason, nor a theology which, consciously or not, adopts the standpoint of subjective reflection can attain the source of the division.[9] Nor can a supranaturalism, Barthian or some other, which would retreat beyond reason either save the implicit rationality of Christian faith or do justice to the seriousness of secular culture.[10]

It is no more necessary than in Medieval times that theology or philosophy of religion be the concern of many. As then, its practical purpose is to educate those who interpret religion to the multitude.[11] Already in Hegel's time Protestant faith was usually reduced to history, psychology or some other finite form; religion had become scientific reflection about religion, the property therefore of an enlightened minority. In philosophy of religion was the power to subordinate these forms and restore the teaching of religion, but only at such time as the need might be deeply enough felt among the people.[12]

The identity in content of religion and philosophy thus meant for Hegel no assimilation of one to the other, but for modern times such a relation of the wise to the faithful – of the thinking consideration of religion to religion itself – as was found in Patristic and Medieval times. Though all philosophy and all religion have the same content – to the extent

Quentin Lauer, S. J.

that the content of a religion is true and that a philosophy is developed and concrete – it is only in the Christian religion that the identity of content is complete and explicit. Father Lauer does not bring out this peculiar relation of the Hegelian philosophy to Christianity – to the orthodox Christianity of the Ancient Councils, and this especially in the Lutheran form. To do so it would be necessary to move from abstract concepts, such as finite and infinite, to life, truth, good, idea, nature, spirit – these in the altogether precise sense they acquire in the development of the Hegelian philosophy.[13]

NOTES

1. Philosophy is "der denkend erkannte *Begriff* der Kunst und Religion, in welchem das in dem Inhalte Verschiedene als notwendig und dies Notwendige als frei erkannt ist." *EdpW*, ed. by Nicolin and Pöggeler (Hamburg, 1959) Section 572, p. 450. Art and religion are not absorbed into philosophy in this process but rather their necessity is established: "Die Philosophie bestimmt sich hienach zu einem Erkennen von der Notwendigkeit des *Inhalts* der absoluten Vorstellung sowie von der Notwendigkeit der beiden *Formen*, einerseits der unmittelbaren Anschauung und ihrer *Poesie* und der voraussetzenden Vorstellung, der objektiven und äusserlichen Offenbarung, *anderer-seits* zuerst des subjektiven insichgehens, dann der subjektiven Hinbewegung und des Identifizierens des *Glaubens* mit der Voraussetzung."

That art and religion are necessary forms results from the primary insight of the Hegelian philosophy – that the Begriff is not immediate but mediated by Being and Reflection. The proof therefore can only be "der ganze Verlauf der Philosophie und der Logik inbesondere, welcher diesen Unterschied (sc. of speculative thought from Vorstellung and the reflective understanding) nicht nur zu erkennen gegeben, sondern auch beurteilt oder vielmehr die Natur derselben an diesen Kategorien selbst sich hat entwickeln und richten lassen" (*Ibid.*)

2. As the following from Aquinas illustrates: ". . . radius divinae revelationis non destruitur propter figuras sensibiles quibus circumvelatur . . . sed remanet in sua veritate; ut mentes quibus fit revelatio, non permittat in similitudinibus permanere, sed elevet eas ad cognitionem intelligibilium . . ." (*Summa Theologiae* 1, 1, 9 ad secundum; ed. Ottawensis, 1941).

So Hegel writes that the finite form "hindert nicht, dass der Geist seinen Inhalt, der als religios wesentlich spekulativ ist, selbst im Gebrauche sinnlichen Vorstellungen und der endlichen Kategorien des Denkens gegen dieselbe festhalte, ihnen Gewalt antue und *inkonsequent* gegen sie sei" *EdpW*, Nicholin and Pöggeler, section 573.

3. *Phän* is directed against unreflecting empiricism but more especially against the supposedly critical method of Kant. The *Einleitung* makes this clear; for example, "Der sich auf den ganzen Umfang des erscheinenden Bewußtseins richtende Skeptizismus macht dagegen den Geist erst geschicht zu prüfen, was Wahrheit ist, indem er eine Verzweiflung an den sogenannten natürlichen Vorstellungen, Gedanken und Meinungen zustande bringt, welche es gleichgültig ist, eigene oder fremde zu nennen, und mit welchen das Bewusstsein, das *geradezu* aus Prüfen geht, noch erfüllt und behaftet, dadurch aber in der Tat dessen unfähig ist, was es unternehmen will." *Phän*, p. 68.

4. The argument of *Phän* ends at the point where both the receptivity of the religious attitude and the self-certainty of the moral attitude are destroyed in their independence of each other. From the side of *Erfahrung* this is the point of complete despair; from the side of *Wissenschaft* it is the point of reconcilliation. *Phän,* pp. 554f.

It thus ends with an anticipatory sketch of the *Wissenschaft.* But its proper result is only the collapse of the standpoint of experience.

5. It seems strange that Father Lauer should say that Hegel's sixteen lectures on the proofs for the existence of God are on the ontological argument. They treat also of other, if not all, arguments, as do the two Logics.

Hegel distinguishes the ontological argument very sharply and gives it its place in the Logic at the transition from subjectivity to objectivity in *WdL.* see, "Die Objektivität," pp. 353-8. The ontological argument is not presupposed by the Logic but included within it.

6. A brief statement of the meaning of the Logic is given in *Phän,* pp. 561-2. The scepticism which *Phän* produces is overcome in that "bestimmte Begriffe" take the place of "bestimmte Gestalten des Bewußtseins."

7. "In der Philosophie, welche Theologie ist (sc. philosophy of religion), ist es einzig nur darum zu tun, die Vernunft der Religion zu zeigen.' "Hegel, *Werke,* Berlin 1840, XII, p. 353). The purpose is not to replace religious feeling and imaginative thought but to secure for them their true content: "Die Philosophie denkt, was das Subject als solcher fühlt und überlässt es demselben, sich mit seinem Gefühl darüber abzufinden. Das Gefühl ist so nicht durch die Philosophie verworfen, sondern es wird ihm durch dieselbe nur der wahrhafte Inhalt gegeben" (ibid., pp. 353f.)

8. The collision of faith and reason in modern Christendom attains the form of the "inneren Zwiespalt des Geistes und Gemüts in sich selbst"; the two sides "die in Widerspruch kommen, die Tiefe des Geistes als ihre eine und gemeinschaftliche Wurzel gewinnen, und in dieser Stelle in ihrem Widerspruche zusammengebunden, diese Stelle selbst, den Geist, in seinem Innersten zu zerüttern vermögen." *Ibid.,* p. 361.

9. *Ibid.,* pp. 363-66 and pp. 345-49.

10. On supranaturalism, see *Einleitung in die Geschichte der Philosophie,* ed. Hoffmeister, Hamburg, 1959, pp. 191-2. On what follows practically when the Church gives up its claim to knowledge, e.g., the fourth lecture *Uber die Beweise für das Dasein Gottes (Werke XII,* p. 384 seq.)

11. *Ibid.,* p. 354.

12. *Ibid.,* p. 355.

13. That Hegel's philosophical theology presents truly the profoundest in Luther's teaching is recognized by Seeberg, *Lehrbuch der Dogmengeschichte,* Darmstadt, 1959, vol. 4, pt. 1, p. 463, n. 1; p. 475, n. 1.

COMMENT ON

QUENTIN LAUER
HEGEL ON THE IDENTITY OF CONTENT
IN RELIGION AND PHILOSOPHY

by

Charles D. Barrett

The aim of this response is threefold: first, to construct an "inquiring restatement" of what seems to be Professor Lauer's basic thesis, with the hope that the interrogative inflection of the attempt will leave room for clarification and correction by Father Lauer himself; second, to open a "second front" from which to approach the Hegelian sublation of religion into philosophy; and finally, to note certain positive motifs in the Hegelian program which would seem to coincide with the interests of contemporary theology and would therefore seem to merit further investigation by theologians.

The basic question to be addressed in our *inquiring restatement* is simply "What is Lauer saying?" Is he saying only that, for Hegel, religion is the meat on which philosophy feeds, that religion supplies the object of philosophy's concern and philosophy the ultimate method of explication for religion's content? He seems to be saying *at least* this, but in identifying philosophy's content with that of religion he seems to say more: he seems to imply that philosophy sublates not only the religious object but also religious subjectivity into itself. A religious element thus enters and informs essentially not only the *content* of philosophy but also philosophical *method*. For Lauer's Hegel, it seems, philosophy shares with religion the passion of existential involvement and at the same time surpasses religion in the clarity of its awareness – an awareness which has as its object not only the religious object proper (i.e., God) but also the thinking self's involvement in, dependence on, and determination by that object proper.

If the foregoing restatement is correct, then for the Hegel of Father Lauer philosophy is not simply an academic discipline or method but also an existential vocation. It is just at this point, however, that our *second front* must be opened. It may be opened with a direct question – viz., Is the existential involvement of the Hegelian philosophy really that of the Christian individual whose faith Hegel thought he was expressing in sublimer and fuller form in his philosophy? Søren Kierkegaard, who to be sure reacted much more to the distilled and memorized Hegel of Danish "Christendom" than to Hegel himself, said No. Existentially involving though it might be, Hegel's philosophic religion could only be classed by Kierkegaard as a subtle and sublime form of Religiousness A, that religiousness which "is by no means undialectic, but ... is not paradoxically dialectic." [1] From Kierkegaard's standpoint, existential involvement in a known and universally operative dialectic is scarcely to be equated with existential involvement in a known and personally experienced diastasis whose synthetic resolution is not at all "known." The main fruit of faith in Kierkegaard's view is not confidence in a dialectical continuity and in its ability to lead one into all truth, but rather a doubt-ridden suffering whose face to the world is paradoxically that of "humor" because its meaning to the believer is that of participation in the saving paradox. In his sublation of religious knowing into philosophic, has Hegel not at the very least "domesticated" such doubt and suffering by "locating" them as moments in the dialectic? This is a question to which Lauer's paper does not speak, not did its stated scope require it to do so. His presentation does, however, raise the question of Hegel's understanding of Christianity, and it is of course just at this point that the issue is joined between Kierkegaard and Hegel. Professor Lauer could therefore render a service by going beyond his paper to speak to a question clearly raised by his paper.

Finally, I should like to note certain *points of correspondence* between the interests of contemporary theology and several motifs in the Hegelian program. One may begin, perhaps, by noting the widespread adoption by theologians of Hegel's insight into the intimate relation between selfhood, or subjectivity, and truth. For most contemporary theologians, to be sure, and particularly for those of Bultmannian stripe, this insight was appropriated by way of Kierkegaard, and they may or may not be aware of its rootage in Hegel. It not only *has* roots here, however, but has them precisely at a point where Hegel has been most condemned and castigated by existentialist theologians – the very point where Hegel sublates Christian faith into philosophy! One of Lauer's quotations from Hegel documents this:

Thus, what in religion was *content* or form of representation by *another* is here [i.e., in philosophy or *Wissenschaft*] the proper *doing* of the self. The concept [as the form of philosophical truth] guarantees that the *content* is the proper *doing* of the self – for, as we see, this concept is knowledge of the self's doing in itself constituting the very essence of all reality . . .[2]

Surely one could not find in all of Kierkegaard a clearer exposition of the tenet "Truth is subjectivity!" The Kierkegaardian departure from Hegel comes not at the point of this affirmation, therefore, but at the point of its definition. In particular Kierkegaard would not follow Hegel in his identification of individual subjectivity with universal subjectivity. This may or may not have stemmed from a failure on his part to understand the Hegelian notion of identity, a notion we shall ourselves want to question a bit later.

A second point at which one finds a striking parallel between Hegel's thought and contemporary Protestant thought lies in the efforts of both to develop more adequate models for conceiving the relation between God and the world. Professor Fackenheim, following Professor Henrich, points out that "Hegel not only *admits* contingency in addition to a necessity free from it but rather – . . . of incomparably greater consequence – insists that contingency *enters into* the necessity which in turn consist of nothing but its conquest . . . . Other speculative philosophers kept at least the divine free from chance. But it was Hegel – not Nietzsche – who first asserted that God is death." [3]

God's death is for Hegel of course a dialectical death, an incorporation into union of the principle of nonunion and an inclusion in necessity of the reality of contingency. Contemporary theologians of the Whiteheadian school also seek a dialectical understanding of their own peculiar concept of divine dependency, but the Whiteheadian model from which they set out limits them to a view which is dualistic as well as dialectical. While this enables them to skirt a problem which plagues Hegel's view of the relation between necessity and contingency – a problem to be noted momentarily – it leads them to a doctrine of divine finitude which sees God not only as dialectically related to the world but also as dualistically limited or bounded by it.[4]

A more truly Hegelian wrestling with the problem of the God-world relation may be found, perhaps, in the radical theology of Thomas Altizer. His thought is as profoundly dialectical as that of Hegel. The chief difference would appear to be that Altizer sees the contingency pole in the God-world dialectic as controlling or "conquering" the necessity pole rather than the other way about. The difficulty with this view is that the mind boggles in a morass of mystical incomprehension in trying to fathom it – a consequence which may be Altizer's way of suggesting that the relation between God and the world is supra-rational, after all.

Perhaps we may best conclude this all too sketchy treatment of the affinities between Hegel's thought and contemporary theology by noting a suggestion by Karl Barth that, in Hegel, we encounter one who might well have become a Protestant Aquinas.[5] As Professor Lauer suggests by his allusion to Hegel's championing of the ontological argument, Hegel becomes an exponent, on Protestant ground, of the analogy of being. His view of the *analogia entis* differs from the Thomist view chiefly in that he sees the relation between Being and beings as less discontinuous, more dialectical, than did St. Thomas. This means that for Hegel, as for Luther, the finite is capable of the infinite, capable not only of bearing the *likeness* of God but also of bearing his *reality*. Thus with Hegel finitude becomes the veritable expression or extension of the infinite or, as Lauer puts it, "Finite and infinite *are* only in the passage from one to the other."

Just here, however, where Hegel sees the finite as the actual bearer or expression of the infinite, a problem arises. On the face of matters, Hegel's doctrine of analogy is such that it leads one to ask whether, in at least one respect, he is not *less* Protestant than Aquinas. St. Thomas, after all, builds a kind of protestant principle into his very doctrine of analogy, holding that, while the finite may be *like* the infinite in certain respects, it can in no sense be *identified* with it. Hegel, on the other hand, with his stress on the finite's capacity to bear the infinite, definitely tends in the direction of their identification. If Fackenheim's analysis is correct, Hegel had in mind an identity of inclusion, not an identity of equation. There are points, however, if one follows Fackenheim's interpretation, where inclusion and equation tend to verge on each other. In his second chapter, for example, Fackenheim observes that, for Hegel, necessity is dialectically dependent on contingency, whose constant conquest it is.[6] How this squares with Fackenheim's later contention, made in Chapter Six,[7] that the divine love of the finite is not a love prompted by divine need, is left unclear; for, if necessity by definition must have "worlds to conquer," it clearly seems to "need" such worlds.

Neither Fackenheim nor Lauer tells us what safeguards, if any, Hegel erects against confusion of the identity of inclusion with that of equation. Such safeguards are of course present in the Lutheran tradition. Luther himself, for example, secured the discontinuity between finite and infinite by pointing to God's *freedom* – in particular, his freedom to use the finite when, where, and as he will. Does Hegel incorporate this Lutheran safeguard? If not, how does he propose to establish with clarity a discontinuity between finite and infinite? Answers to these questions from Hegel scholars of Professor Lauer's competence would surely be germane to the contemporary theological discussion, a discussion which is still disturbed by questions of natural theology to which Hegel may well speak.

NOTES

1. S. Kierkegaard, *Concluding Unscientific Postscript*, tr. by D. F. Swenson and W. Lowrie (Princeton: Princeton University Press, 1960), p. 494.

2. Cf. Karl Barth: "for Hegel ... the human subject ... stands by no means apart as if it were not concerned .... It is in his looking and only in his looking that the something seen is produced as the thing seen in the looking of the human subject. Man cannot participate more energetically (within the framework of theoretical possibility), he cannot be more forcefully transferred from the floor of the theatre on to the stage than in this theory." *Protestant Thought from Rousseau to Ritschl*, tr. by B. Cozens (New York: Harper and Brothers, 1959), p. 285.

3. E. L. Fackenheim, *The Religious Dimension in Hegel's Thought* (Bloomington: Indiana University Press, 1967), p. 19. Cf. D. Henrich, "Hegel's Theorie Uber den Zufall," *Kantstudien*, 50 (1958-9), pp. 131ff.

4. I am indebted to Professor Fackenheim for this insight. See *op. cit.*, p. 102n.

5. See *op. cit.*, p. 268.

6. *Op. cit.*, p. 19. Cf. *Ibid.*, p. 204.

7. *Ibid.*, pp. 205f.

REPLY TO COMMENTATORS

by

Quentin Lauer, S. J.

It is not mere courtesy that prompts me to express my profound gratitude to both Professor Doull and Professor Barrett for their comments on my paper. Not only have they brought up significant questions concerning my own presentation; they have also helped to make clearer to me what remains to be done, if we are to understand Hegel's contribution to the philosophy of religion and to theology itself. Although I should like to respond to each question as it was asked, that is obviously impossible. I shall attempt, then, a somewhat more general response to the whole problematic raised by the commentators.

The problem here, it seems to me, lies in Hegel's use of the term identity, or identification. What it does not mean is that religion and philosophy are one and the same or that in philosophical thought religion is swallowed up, thus losing its autonomy. The sort of dialectical identification of which Hegel speaks, wherein the absolute truth – or God, whose presence to man is man's religious response – is more adequately present in thought, whose proper object is truth, neither eliminates religion nor destroys its autonomy. What it does do – to borrow an expression from Fackenheim – is to effect a speculative transformation of Christian religion. In this, as I see it, religion becomes more truly what it really is, since God is less adequately present to man as *represented* than as *thought*. We should remember, however, that, for Hegel, to say speculative is to say far more than theoretical. As Hegel says in the Preface to the *Logic,* this is quite different from the Kantian notion of the speculative, because it contains within itself both the theoretical and the practical. This, of course, involves what we might call the Hegelian paradox, the paradox whereby he can say – as Professor Henrich said this morning – art and religion retain their autonomy even though both

art and religion are *aufgehoben* in philosophy. Religion retains its autonomy – or religion and philosophy remain distinct – precisely because
the relation of one to the other is dialectical. Religion loses neither its
autonomy nor its validity by being oriented to that grasp of absolute
truth which is philosophical thought; philosophical thought itself would
not be truly philosophical, if its content were not that of religion.

Although Hegel himself does not use the expression, I honestly think,
as I have said elsewhere ("Hegel on Proofs for God's Existence," *Kant-
studien* 55, 4, 1964), what is operative here is the Anselmian notion of
fides quaerens intellectum. The expression does not say that *fides* is in
any way abdicating as *fides* in seeking *intellectum*; rather it is constantly
following out its own vocation by tending ideally toward the *intellectum*
in which it is perfected as *fides*. Never does faith become totally knowledge, but its orientation is always toward the knowledge in which its
object is really present.

All this, of course, brings up the more important question as to whether
the religion of which Hegel speaks can in any way be identified with
religion as we try to understand it today. Professor Barrett has pointed
out that no one – including Kierkegaard – has expressed more clearly
than Hegel that "truth is subjectivity." There are, however, two differences between the Kierkegaardian – and, presumably, the contemporary
– and the Hegelian understanding of this notion. For Hegel the "subjectivity" in question is not that of the atomic individual, nor, it would
seem, does the subjectivity of truth entail for him the kind of "risk" it
does for Kierkegaard.

For Kierkegaard, as we know, religion is an existential vocation, and
philosophy – particularly Hegelian philosophy – is not. I should like to
submit that for Hegel there is one existential vocation involving both
religion and philosophy. This, of course, will not be true to one who is
convinced that the vocation of the Christian is the existential involvement
of the Kierkegaardian individual. I think, however, that one can make a
very good case – and it has been made more than once – for Hegel's
insistence on the significance of the individual, provided we remember
that for him the individual is significant only as integrated in the community, never as isolated (or abstracted) from it. For Hegel, to be a
Christian is to be in the Christian community; it is not to make some
sort of individual response to a God who seems scarcely distinguishable
from the response, it is to be in and of the community which responds.
The individual, it is true, responds both religiously and philosophically
to the God who is present in both representation and thought, but his

response binds him to the community rather than cutting him off from it.

A response such as this, it would seem, does not eliminate risk – a shared risk is still a risk – but it does eliminate the risk of isolation and, therefore, of subjective arbitrariness. It is the individual who as finite is bearer of the infinite, but this he does not by a "leap" beyond his finitude. Rather, it is through the mediation of the community in which individuality is realized that his very finitude is a passage to the infinite – or else it is abstraction. One can say, I suppose, that Hegel "with his stress on the finite's capacity to bear the infinite, definitely tends in the direction of their identification." One should bear in mind, however, that the identification is a dialectical one that does not eliminate distinction. Without the infinite the finite simply is not; to talk of it independently of the infinite is to speak abstractly. Without the finite, who is man, the infinite does not exist, for finite man is the locus of the infinite's self-manifestation. God is manifest to the community of men in art, religion, and philosophy, but the identification of finite and infinite is accomplished only in thought which is the infinite activity man shares.

DISCUSSION

MARCUS CLAYTON, JR. (Paine College): Father Lauer has said that Hegel operated within the tradition of transcendental philosophy and that his problem was to make universal reason – divine reason– concrete rather than abstract as it had been regarded. I would like to argue against this simply by calling attention to what seem to me to be some relevant considerations in the philosophy of Kant and then in the philosophy of Hegel.

Father Lauer, as I gather, reads Kant as having started with the moral law within the good will and then interprets Kant as having universalized this and presented a problem for Hegel. Although I'm sure that this could be supported by passages in Kant, it seems to me that to say this is to ignore the fact that God in the *Second Critique* was never more than a postulate of practical reason. A postulate of practical reason is more than an idea of pure reason but it is not an object of knowledge. This postulate has a certain autonomy set over against pure reason [1] and I think the two have a relation parallel to the duality of noumena and phenomenon in *CPR*. I would like, then, to look at Hegel's objection that to say that something is unknowable is to say something about it – to make a judgment. It seems to me that this was Hegel's way of resurrecting the parmenidean dictum that the same thing exists for thinking and for being. In resurrecting this dictum he made a radical break with transcendental philosophy. Here, I would call attention to Kant's own distinction between the terms transcendental and transcendent. Hegel, working from the position that what is rational is real, said a lot of things about what is real. I don't deny that he had the problem of making universal reason concrete. I do contend that this is a problem he created for himself.

Incidentally, the reason for Kant's postulate that God exists was not, as I read Kant, that God is required as a law giver and that the will which we obey, the categorical imperative, is the will of God. Indeed, the reason for the postulate is based on considerations of punishment and reward. One might move from one to the other but I don't think Kant did.

LAUER:I don't know whether I am competent to handle everything you have said. With regard to the God of Kant, it seems to me that we can look at Him from two points of view. From the point of view of *CPR,* it seems to me that God may be understood as a kind of regulative principle. When it comes to the *Second Critique,* He is a postulate of practical reason. But He is postulated in this sense – and this is what I meant by transcendental framework – that He is a necessary condition for that which Kant knows to be true in the moral order. As a necessary condition for that which he knows to be true, he knows that God is true. To know that God is true, however, is not for Kant to have God as an object of knowledge. To have God as an object, rather, is to have Him as an object of faith. And this is precisely where Hegel's criticism of Kant comes in, that Kant had made God on the level of knowledge, you might say, a regulative principle or a postulate; and on the level of objectivity he made Him to be an object of faith. Hegel wants God to be an object of both faith and of knowing or of thought, in what he considers the true speculative sense of thought.

You also called into question my contention that Hegel is in a certain sense remaining within the transcendental framework. What I mean by this is that he will not infer this God from something else which he knows, but rather sees God as the infinite presupposition of there being any kind of knowledge, life, love, or anything else.

The other question – the question about God as the lawgiver – requires going into the whole of the *Second Critique* and this might require more time than we have.

FREDERICK G. WEISS (Purdue University, Indianapolis): It seems to me that in some respects in this meeting, in an attempt to prevent the eclipse of religion by philosophy, some of us have perhaps been guilty of tending to eclipse (if we have not actually eclipsed) philosophy by our consideration of religion. The consensus, of course, is that there is to be some sort of equation of religion and philosophy and Father Lauer's paper has also tended to a certain extent to indicate this. It is hard to say just what he wants to do.

To paraphrase something Kant said, you might say that philosophy without religion is empty. But I should think we would have to add that religion without philosophy is blind. This latter deserves emphasis. There has been a good deal of talk about what religion does for philosophy and very little, if any, about what philosophy does for religion. I would like to pose this question to the abstract of Father Lauer's paper,[2] which I think brings this thing to a head. He says at the end of the first paragraph, "That which characterizes man as man is thought; but that which characterizes thought as thought is its rootedness in the divine." Now, thought as thought may be rooted in the divine, but this is not to say that thought as thought is rooted in the religious. Although there are different ways in which Hegel speaks about the divine, I don't think he means "religious" by "divine" any more than Aristotle meant "religious" when he uses the corresponding Greek term for this word. These simply are not the same. Also, he says at the end of the next paragraph that "only man can be rational" and "only man can be religious." Thus, his very religiousness is inseparable from his rationality. It seems to me it might also be said – although I don't want to appear trivial here, and I hope you will view it another way – that only man can indulge in laughter. But this, of course, means neither that laughter nor worship is essentially characteristic of the divine life. And, of course, I might again point to Aristotle who would, I think, go along with this. Now, the question is, are we to understand Hegel in the same sense as Aristotle on the life of the divine, which is thought thinking thought. And in what sense is this religious? Now, religion is made for man in a sense; it certainly isn't something made for God. And it certainly isn't something that is part of the essence of the divine life as understood in the highest sense of that term. Father Lauer seems in his paper to point to something like *credo ut intelligam*. If this is what he has in mind, I am prepared to go along. On the other hand, there has been so little talk about philosophy which one arrives at through one's beliefs and so on, and of what this does for religion. I wanted to make this point on behalf of philosophy because it would be doing Hegel a disservice not to have done so. Coming to this symposium from a study of Hegel's history of philosophy (and not the philosophy of religion) I feel obliged to make this comment.

LAUER: In a sense on the last page of my paper I am saying that philosophy without religion is empty, but religion without philosophy is blind. This, because I say that in religion, man believes in God, but only in philosophy can he know what God is in whom he believes. Until then, he knows not what he says, when he says God. I think this is precisely the kind of relationship between religion and philosophy which Hegel is setting up, in which there is a very real sense in which religion retains its autonomy, but at the same time we need philosophy if we are to know what we are talking about, this, not only when we talk *about* God, but even when we talk *to* God. And it is also for this very reason that I claim Hegel to be saying that philosophy is religious. This is not merely to say that there is a divine principle in man whereby he thinks, which divine principle does not bespeak religion. Rather, it is to say that it is religion which reveals to man that it is the divine principle in him which makes him to be what he is and through this he can then begin to try to understand what this divine principle is, which is philosophy's task.

CHARLES COURTNEY (Drew University): Many speakers have asserted the identity of content (for Hegel) of religion and philosophy during these two days; I think I am convinced of this, but one way in which Professor Lauer made this point leads me to wonder if it is such a momentous point. This, because he states that for Hegel there is an identity of content in all of the concrete forms of spirit. This means, of course, that art would be included in addition to religion and philosophy, in this grouping. The real difference, the irreducible difference, is in the mode of presence. How, if religion is re-presentation, can we say that God is present in religion?

LAUER: First of all, I think the three forms of consciousness in which the Absolute as Absolute are present for Hegel are simply, art, religion and philosophy. I mean the other forms of consciousness coming up to it in the phenomenology don't count to the same extent. In art the Absolute is present in image; in religion, in representation; and in philosophy, in thought. And I think what Hegel is saying is that image, representation and thought are all essential to the relationship which the human individual and the human spirit has to the Absolute, which is God. Now, is the presence in religion significant? Here, I think, one has to say that there is something missing from Hegel's conception of religion. Quite definitely, because the one thing that Kant does have and that Hegel is wanting is that Kant somehow or other sees the religious response as a kind of response which is unique in itself, and this independent of any kind of representation which might be involved in it. It is the response of a subject which is neither just that of moral duty nor that of cognitive union (if you want to call it that) but is a special kind of response, nearer to the moral than it is to the cognitive, but at the same time distinct from the moral also.

NOTES

1. Editor's note: Revision to eliminate ambiguity may have violated the questioner's intended meaning at this point.
2. Abstracts of this and several other papers were distributed at the Symposium.

INDEX

Information contained in the Table of Contents is not included here.